Career Creativity

Career Creativity: Explorations in the Remaking of Work

Edited by

MAURY A. PEIPERL, MICHAEL B. ARTHUR, AND N. ANAND

OXFORD
UNIVERSITY PRESS

OXFORD
UNIVERSITY PRESS

Great Clarendon Street, Oxford OX2 6DP

Oxford University Press is a department of the University of Oxford.
It furthers the University's objective of excellence in research, scholarship,
and education by publishing worldwide in

Oxford New York

Auckland Bangkok Buenos Aires Cape Town Chennai
Dar es Salaam Delhi Hong Kong Istanbul Karachi Kolkata
Kuala Lumpur Madrid Melbourne Mexico City Mumbai Nairobi
São Paulo Shanghai Singapore Taipei Tokyo Toronto

with an associated company in Berlin

Oxford is a registered trade mark of Oxford University Press
in the UK and in certain other countries

Published in the United States
by Oxford University Press Inc., New York

British Library Cataloguing in Publication Data

Data available

Library of Congress Cataloging in Publication Data

Data available

ISBN 0-19-924871-0
ISBN 0-19-924872-9 (pbk.)

10 9 8 7 6 5 4 3 2 1

Typeset by Newgen Imaging Systems (P) Ltd., Chennai, India
Printed in Great Britain
on acid-free paper by
Biddles Ltd., Guildford and King's Lynn

To all who are creatively pursuing,
or once creatively pursued, a career,
especially:

Pat Keck
Rekha Nagaraj
Jennifer Georgia
W. Scudder Georgia, Jr

PREFACE

What's the use of studying creativity? In the introductory chapter to his 1996 book Mihaly Csikszentmihalyi offers two responses to this question. One response speaks of creativity's outcomes, how they 'indirectly improve the quality of all our lives'. The other response speaks of the potential for 'enriching anyone's everyday experience'. Both responses, what we may call the productive and the personal, provide inspiration for this book.

The productive and personal arguments lead us quickly to the world of work, where we may look for creativity to occur, and to the role of time, over which we may look for creativity's effects to unfold. These lead us, in turn, to careers, simply defined as sequences of work experiences over time. The connection between the twin concepts of career and creativity seems straightforward, yet they have rarely been brought together in any systematic way. That this volume does so is the result of considerable support from a number of sources.

First we are indebted to our hosts at the London Business School in the Centre for Organisational Research, in particular Professor Rob Goffee, Deputy Dean for Executive Education and head of the Innovation Exchange, whose ideas helped shape the Career Creativity conference and this subsequent volume; Professor Nigel Nicholson, Subject Area Chair; E. C. (Lidewey) van der Sluis, formerly Research Fellow in the Careers Research Initiative at London Business School and now a member of faculty at the Free University of Amsterdam; and the many other colleagues who have given input and support to the Careers Conference Series.

This volume is the second in a series, following *Career Frontiers: New Conceptions of Working Lives* (Oxford, 2000), and like its predecessor had its beginnings in the London Business School Career Conferences. For outstanding work on the administration of the conferences and the compilation of the book we thank Barbara Bryant, Florence Chan, Graham Holloway, Jeanne-Marie Hudson, Angie Quest, Rosemary Robertson, and Anthony Senior. At Oxford University Press we are grateful for the support of Gwen Booth, Sarah Dobson, David Musson, Jacqueline Sells, and especially Hilary Walford.

For financial support of the Careers Research Initiative and the Careers Conference Series we thank Korn/Ferry International, The Economics and

Social Research Council (UK), The Executive Education group at London Business School, and the many companies who have sent representatives to the conferences. The partnership between academia and business that has been the hallmark of the conference series is largely the result of the foresight and commitment shown by these sponsoring organizations.

Our biggest thank you goes to our chapter authors, all of whom showed remarkable patience, openness, and flexibility as we collectively assembled their work into an integrated volume. We are pleased and proud to count them as colleagues in a 'virtual college' of career studies, and hope that they, and you, will continue the conversations included here. All of them welcome your comments and queries; they can be reached at the email addresses shown in the List of Contributors.

Finally, we thank our partners and families for their generous and unconditional support of us and of our work. We could not do it without them.

M. A. P.
M. B. A.
N. A.

London, 2002

CONTENTS

LIST OF FIGURES

LIST OF TABLES

LIST OF CONTRIBUTORS

José Luis Alvarez is Professor of General Management at IESE Business School (Spain). He has been Visiting Professor at the Harvard Business School and INSEAD. Professor Alvarez holds degrees in Law and Philosophy from the University of Barcelona, an MBA from IESE Business School, and an MA and a Ph.D. in Organizational Behavior from Harvard University. His research has been published in the *European Management Journal, Organization Studies, Organizations*, and *Corporate Governance*, and he has published three books. His current line of research, teaching, and consulting focuses on the development, careers, and tasks of top executives, especially on the impact of CEOs on corporate politics and governance. He can be reached at alvarez@iese.edu.

Norman Amundson is Professor of Counselling Psychology in the Faculty of Education at the University of British Columbia, Canada, and also a founding partner of Ergon Communications. He has published a number of books and articles in the career field including *Active Engagement: Enhancing the Career Counselling Process*, winner of the 2000 Best Book award by the Canadian Counselling Association. In his writings he emphasizes the importance of creativity, imagination, and action as career development strategies. He has given numerous workshops and seminars and been a frequent speaker at national and international conferences, including a keynote address at the fiftieth anniversary conference of the International Association of Educational and Vocational Guidance. He can be reached at norman.e.amundson@ubc.ca.

N. Anand is Assistant Professor of Organizational Behavior at London Business School. Anand's research interests include the following: constitution and emergence of industrial fields, organization of the commercial music industry, knowledge management in professional service firms, and behavior in financial services firms. Anand's publications have appeared in *Organization Science* and *Poetics*. He can be reached at nanand@lbs.ac.uk.

Michael B. Arthur is Professor of Management at the Sawyer School of Management, Suffolk University, Boston. He has written and researched widely on the subject of careers, including as editor of the *Handbook of Career Theory*

(1989), *The Boundaryless Career* (1996), and *Career Frontiers* (2000). He is also a co-author of *The New Careers* (1999) and of a series of articles into the application of 'intelligent career' principles in the contemporary economy. His research focuses on alternative ways to link between individual career theory and collective action. Arthur holds MBA and Ph.D. degrees from Cranfield University, UK. He can be reached at marthur@suffolk.edu.

Michelle L. Buck is Associate Director of Executive Education and Visiting Associate Professor of Management and Organizations at the Kellogg School of Management at Northwestern University. She designs customized executive education courses, focusing on leadership, and teaches MBA courses in leadership, negotiations, and organizational behavior. Her research interests span a range of topics, including alternative work arrangements, negotiations, and organizational learning. The common focus is on opportunities for transformation in the ways people go about their work, think about themselves, and interact with others. She has previously been on the faculty at McGill University in Montreal and Washington University in St Louis. She received her MA and Ph.D. in Social Psychology from Princeton University. She can be reached at m-buck@kellogg.nwu.edu.

Robert DeFillippi is Professor of Management at the Sawyer School of Management, Suffolk University, Boston. He has written widely on career theory, project-based learning and organizing, and high-technology networks. He has served as a special issue editor for *Management Learning* and is co-editor for a series of books on Research in Management Education and Development. He is also editor of the first volume in the series, *Rethinking Management Education for the 21st Century*. He is writing a book (with Michael Arthur) to be titled *Knowledge at Work: Managing Career, Community and Company Learning*. He has been a visiting professor at City University Business School (UK), and a guest speaker at many other European universities. De Fillippi holds a Ph.D. from Yale University. He may be reached at rdefilli@suffolk.edu.

Martin Evans received his bachelor's (1961) and master's (1963) degrees from the University of Manchester and an Administrative Sciences Ph.D. in 1968 from Yale. He is currently Professor of Organizational Behaviour at the Rotman School of Management, University of Toronto. He has been exploring issues in, around, and about organizations for more than thirty-five years, with a longstanding interest in methodology and causal inference. His work as a mentor of Ph.D. students was recognized by the Academy of Management when he was co-recipient of the Distinguished Educator award for 2001. His most recent work includes an examination of the structure of IQ, the implications of evolutionary psychology for management, and the impact of downsizing. Evans may be reached by way of his website at http://www.rotman.utoronto.ca/~evans/

Ellen A. Ensher is Assistant Professor in the College of Business at Loyola Marymount University in Los Angeles, California, where she teaches courses in human resource management and related topics. She has published a range of articles, book chapters, and conference proceedings related to women's career issues and mentoring in journals such as *Human Resource Development Quarterly, Journal of Vocational Behavior*, and *Journal of Career Development*. She has consulted in both the USA and overseas, implementing programs in management development, career development, and mentoring. She earned her Masters in Public Administration from the University of Southern California in 1990 and her Ph.D. in Organizational Psychology from Claremont Graduate University in 1997. She may be reached at eensher@popmail.lmu.edu.

Hugh Gunz trained as a chemist in New Zealand, and has a Ph.D. in both Chemistry and Organizational Behavior. His career started in the petrochemical industry, and he has taught on the faculties of Manchester Business School (UK) and the University of Toronto's Joseph L. Rotman School of Management, where he is Professor of Organizational Behavior. He has published papers on the careers of managers, professionals, and others, the management of technical professionals, and management education. He is the author of the book *Careers and Corporate Cultures*, published by Basil Blackwell. His research interests include the structure and mobility of managerial careers and their impact on firms' strategic management, the application of complexity science to careers, and ethical dilemmas experienced by employed professionals. He may be reached at hugh.gunz@utoronto.ca.

Douglas T. (Tim) Hall is Professor of Organizational Behavior and Director of the Executive Development Roundtable in the School of Management at Boston University. Tim is the author of *Careers in Organizations* and *Career Development*, and the co-author of *The Career is Dead: Long Live the Career, The Work Lives of Priests, The Two-Career Couple, Experiences in Management and Organizational Behavior, Turbulence in the American Workplace, Human Resource Management*, and *Career Development in Organizations*. He is co-editor of *The Handbook of Career Theory*. He is a Fellow of the Academy of Management, the Society for Industrial and Organizational Psychology, and the American Pyschological Association. He is a recipient of the American Psychological Association's James McKeen Cattell Award (now called the Ghiselli Award) for research design. He may be reached at dthall@bu.edu.

Monica C. Higgins is Associate Professor of Organizational Behavior at Harvard Business School. She earned her Ph.D. from Harvard's Graduate School of Arts and Sciences and her MBA from the Amos Tuck School of Business Administration at Dartmouth. She has worked as a consultant with Bain & Company and with Harbridge House. Her research interests are in the areas of careers, developmental relationships, and social networks. She is presently involved in a longitudinal study of the career choices of Harvard MBAs (Class of 1996), and in an examination of how the career experiences of biotechnology executives have shaped the evolution of their industry. Her work has appeared in academic journals such as the *Academy of Management Review, Journal of Organizational Behavior*, and *Journal of Applied Behavioral Science*. She may be reached at mhiggins@hbs.edu.

Kerr Inkson is Professor of Management at the Auckland campus of Massey University, New Zealand. He has held positions at the Universities of Aston (UK), Otago (where he gained his Ph.D. in 1980), and Auckland. His research interests have included organization theory, orientations to work, and careers. He was first author of *Theory K*, the best-selling management book in New Zealand's history, and co-authored *The New Careers* (1999). In 1997 he received (as first author) the Best International Paper Award of the Academy of Management. Inkson's research projects cover the psychology and career aspects of temporary work, travel as a means of career development, the development of individual 'career capital', and the application of metaphor to career theory. He may be reached at k.inkson@massey.ac.nz.

Michael Jalland is Associate Professor of strategic management at the University of Toronto. He has a Ph.D in strategic management from the University of Manchester (UK), based on studies of planning in multi-divisional organizations. His recent research has examined the relationships between organizational career streams and strategies, which has resulted in contributions to books and publications in the *Academy of Management Review, Academy of Management Executive* and *Advances in Strategic Management*. He can be reached at jalland@rotman.utoronto.ca.

Candace Jones received her Ph.D. from the University of Utah. She is an Associate Professor of Organization Studies at the Carroll School of Management at Boston College. Her research interests include inter-firm networks, project-based organizing, and careers. Her work includes careers in the film industry (*Academy of Management Executive*), how careers and the film industry co-evolved (*Organization Studies*), the emergence and governance of inter-firm networks (*Academy of Management Review*), and the dynamics of network alliances in professional services (*Organization Science*). Currently she is examining power relations among architects and engineers, and the reputation-building strategies of architectural firms. She may be reached at jonescq@bc.edu.

Mary Dean Lee is Associate Professor of Management at McGill University. Her research interests cover professional and managerial careers and alternative work arrangements. In 1999 she completed a major North American study of reduced-load work arrangements among professionals and managers in organizations, with support from the Alfred P. Sloan Foundation in New York and the Social Sciences and Humanities Research Council of Canada. She has contributed articles to such professional journals as *Academy of Management Journal, Canadian Journal of Administrative Science, Human Relations, Organizational Behavior Teaching Review*, and *Business in the Contemporary*

World. She co-authored the book *Management of Work and Personal Life* (1984). She holds a Ph.D. from Yale University, and may be reached at lee@management.mcgill.ca.

Shelley M. MacDermid is Director of the Center for Families and Co-Director of the Military Family Research Institute at Purdue University, where she is Associate Professor in the Department of Child Development and Family Studies. She earned an MBA in Management in 1988 and a Ph.D. in Human Development and Family Studies in 1990 from the Pennsylvania State University. Her research focuses on relationships between job conditions and family life, particularly in smaller workplaces. Her work has been published in academic journals including the *Journal of Marriage and the Family* and the *Academy of Management Journal*, and cited in the popular press, including the *Chicago Tribune*, the *Financial Times*, and *Working Mother*. She works extensively with corporations on family-related issues, including directing the Midwestern Work–Family Association. She may be reached at shelley@ purdue.edu.

Susan E. Murphy is Associate Professor of Psychology at Claremont McKenna College in Claremont, California, and has served as Associate Director of the Kravis Leadership Institute since 1993. She earned a Masters of Science in Psychology, a Masters in Business Administration, and a Ph.D. in Organizational Psychology, all from the University of Washington in Seattle, Washington. She has published widely on leadership and mentoring in both adult and youth populations. Her research focuses on the requirements of leadership in demanding situations. She has been a research scientist at Battelle Seattle Research Center, where she designed and delivered leadership development programs for senior managers for both domestic and international clients. She consults for organizations in the areas of management and organizational change. She may be reached at smurphy@benson.mckenna.edu.

Polly Parker is a lecturer in the Department of Management and Employment Relations in the University of Auckland. Parker's previous work as an educator, counsellor, and career consultant has informed her principal interest of career development. As a postgraduate student, she developed a card sort instrument to assess 'intelligent career' behavior. This instrument has since been refined and applied internationally, and Parker has designed and run accreditation workshops for practitioners. Her interests include leadership development, executive coaching, and a comparison of traditional and contemporary approaches to research. Her Ph.D., from the University of Auckland, is on 'Career Communities', and her research is focused on the further development of that concept. She may be reached at p.parker@auckland.ac.nz.

Maury A. Peiperl is Associate Dean and Director of the Careers Research Initiative at London Business School. He holds a BS in Engineering from

Princeton and an MBA, AM, and Ph.D. from Harvard. He has taught, written, and consulted for over fifteen years on four continents in the areas of executive careers, human resource management, performance, and change, and sits on the boards of several companies. He is a director of Learning Designs Limited (www.ldltd.com), a consulting firm specializing in performance, change, communications, and careers issues. Peiperl's publications include *Career Frontiers: New Conceptions of Working Lives* (2000), 'Getting 360 Feedback Right' (*Harvard Business Review*, 2001), 'Back to Square Zero: The Post-Corporate Career' (*Organizational Dynamics*, 1997), and *Managing Change: Cases and Concepts* (2nd edn., with Todd Jick). He can be reached at mpeiperl@london.edu.

Richard A. Peterson is Professor of Sociology at Vanderbilt University. His books include *The Industrial Order and Social Policy, Notes on Technology and the Moral Order* (with Alvin W. Gouldner), *The Production of Culture*, and *Creating Country Music: Fabricating Authenticity*. In this last work he applies the 'production of culture' perspective to the forty-year process by which country music was transformed from folk expression into a major element of the commercial music industry. His work has also focused on innovation in fine arts administration, changes in classical music, the ironies of entrepreneurship in the trucking industry, and bio-technology start-ups. He has also taught at the Universities of Wisconsin and Leeds and held visiting appointments at Harvard, Stanford, and Tilberg. He may be reached at richard.a.peterson@ vanderbilt.edu.

Gray Poehnell is a researcher, writer, counsellor, and educator in the career field. He is a founding partner in Ergon Communications, a consulting company that specializes in the research, development, delivery, and publishing of career materials and programs to international clients. This work includes the recently published *Career Crossroads: A Personal Career Positioning System*. In his commitment to develop practical creative career tools and processes, Poehnell has sought to integrate a wide range of perspectives into his work. These include perspectives on creativity itself, on the links between creativity and spirituality, on practising the craft of weaving, and on graphic design and desktop publishing. He can be reached at graypoehnell@shaw.ca.

Birgitta Södergren is Associate Professor at the Stockholm School of Economics in Sweden, working at the Center for Management and Organization. Her research focus is on organizational change and on the role of learning and knowledge formation in organizations, and she has written several books and articles in these and related areas. Her most recent work has been on new trends in the management of change, and on organizational conditions for knowledge-intensive work, a field that she will be continuing to explore further in the future. She is also engaged as a lecturer and seminar leader at the Stockholm School of Economics' Executive Education Center, and works with a network of Swedish companies to find new ways to create organizational settings that can stimulate learning processes. She can be reached at birgitta.sodergren@hhs.se.

Jeffrey A. Sonnenfeld is Associate Dean of Executive Education and Adjunct Professor of Management at Yale University. He has been a professor at Emory's Goizueta Business School and Harvard Business School, and is founder and president of the Chief Executive Leadership Institute, a non-profit educational and research institute focused on CEO leadership and corporate governance. His research has been published in academic journals such as *Administrative Science Quarterly, Academy of Management Journal, Academy of Management Review, Journal of Organizational Behavior, Social Forces, Human Relations*, and *Human Resource Management*. He has authored five books, including *The Hero's Farewell*, an award-winning study of CEO succession. He holds DBA and MBA degrees from Harvard University and an AB from Harvard College. He may be reached at sonnenfeld@mindspring.com.

Sherry E. Sullivan earned her Ph.D. from the Ohio State University, where the faculty encouraged her interest in the study of careers and retirement. Her work has been published in journals including *Journal of Applied Psychology, Journal of Management, Human Resource Management Review, Career Development Quarterly, Group and Organization Management*, and *Business Horizons*. Her current research interests include examining women's careers, academic mentoring, and the study of careers in China. Sullivan is an executive coach and consults with the John Reed Center for Careers. She can be reached via email at reedcareercenter@aol.com.

Silviya Svejenova is a Research Associate at IESE Business School, Barcelona, Spain, where she is completing her doctoral dissertation into the networking of Spanish filmmakers. She previously did graduate studies at the Economic University, Varna, Bulgaria, and completed the International Faculty Development Program at IESE Business School. She has taught courses in organizational design and change management, and delivered consulting projects and in-company training in related areas. Her collaboration with José Luis Alvarez on symbiotic careers in movie making has been extended to governance issues of creative projects, as well as to united career paths of top management tandems in an array of industries, from high technology to banking. She may be reached at ssvejenova@iese.edu.

Aimin Yan is Associate Professor of Organizational Behavior, Faculty Director of the International Management Program—China, and Research Director of the Human Resources Policy Institute of the School of Management of Boston University. He is an Advisory Professor of the Shanghai University for Science and Technology and at Dong Hua University, China. He received his Ph.D. in business administration from the Pennsylvania State University and graduated from the Bachelor of Engineering and MBA programs at the Shanghai Institute of Mechanical Engineering. Yan is co-author of *International Joint Ventures: Theory and Practice*, and a range of related articles. His study of US–China manufacturing joint ventures won him the Barry M. Richman Award for Best Dissertation of 1994 in International Management from the Academy of Management. He may be reached at aimin@bu.edu.

Guorong Zhu is a Senior Consultant at the Hay Group and doctoral candidate in organizational behavior at the School of Management, Boston University. Her dissertation study is on psychological contract alignment and repatriation success. Her research is in international human resources management, with a focus on expatriation, repatriation, and global leadership development. Zhu has published articles in *Academy of Management Review* and *Advances in Global Leadership*. She may be reached at Gurong_Zhu@haygroup.com.

1

Introducing Career Creativity

N. ANAND, MAURY A. PEIPERL, AND MICHAEL B. ARTHUR

'Today, when widespread, deep and rapid changes are taking place in the very structure of our lives, whether we desire it or not, and when still other changes seem necessary to preserve us from disaster, understanding of the creative process is particularly important because it can assist in the control of these developments.'

(Brewster Ghiselin (ed.), *The Creative Process*, 1952)

'I would like to get a dozen copies of *The Creative Process*, edited by Brewster Ghiselin, so that they may be given to our key thinking elite at NBC.'

(Sylvester L. Weaver, President, NBC, 1952)

In the aftermath of the Second World War, an edited book on creativity brought about the above exchange between the book's editor and an enthusiastic supporter. The exchange invites a question: Why was so little done over the next fifty years explicitly to connect thinking about careers to thinking about creativity? Careers, after all, must necessarily engage with 'the very structure of our lives' and especially with 'deep and rapid changes' affecting the workplace.

The exchange also invites an answer. The statement supporting the book simultaneously suggests two assumptions. The first assumption is that large institutions, like the National Broadcasting Company (NBC), were the principal intermediaries through which creativity would have its effect on society. The second assumption was that within such institutions only a few 'key thinking elite' were charged to perform creative work. If we were to subordinate our thinking about creativity to the employment systems available through the likes of NBC, we could eschew linking careers with creativity for all but an exceptional few.

We are indebted to Kerr Inkson for helpful comments on this chapter.

Times have changed, and have brought about a new urgency to view careers and creativity in a fresh way. Specifically, the urgency is to view them without relying on (but also without ignoring) traditional institutionally based ideas of 'occupational careers' or 'organizational careers'. These ideas have not become irrelevant, but they have been shown to be insufficient to assure either individual workers or host economies of a reasonably prosperous future. The contemporary challenge is better to appreciate how careers *enact*—that is, shape, as well as being shaped by—the current institutional order (Weick 1996). That challenge invites us to ask whether we can make a broader connection between careers and creativity.

LINKING CAREER AND CREATIVITY

The premise of this book is that we *can* make a broader connection. However, its making invites closer inspection of our key terms, and of the book's intentionally ambiguous title. Does the term 'career creativity' mean we are talking about the nature of careers themselves, or about the influence of careers upon the larger institutions of work and society? Our position here is that both are important, and that each brings greater relevance to the other. Careers are creative endeavors in themselves, and careers also introduce creativity into the host employment system.

Gardner (1993) supports this position in his influential view that sees creativity stemming from the interplay of people's behavior, the domain of work in which the behavior occurs, and the social arrangements through which both people and work are assessed. Gardner also provides the definition of a creative individual we use as a point of departure in this volume. It is 'a person who regularly solves problems, fashions products, or defines new questions in a domain in a way that is initially considered novel but that ultimately becomes accepted in a particular cultural setting' (Gardner 1993: 35). Gardner's definition invites comparison with a complementary definition of the career as 'the evolving sequence of a person's work experiences over time' (Arthur *et al.* 1989: 8).

Bringing the two definitions together suggests that creativity and careers demand joint consideration. Gardner's *domain* of individual creativity implicates the *work experiences* through which careers take place. His assertion that creative expression occurs *regularly* implicates the *time* over which careers unfold. The references to solving problems, fashioning products, or defining new questions link creativity with various new 'frontiers' for career studies— such as the changing assumptions about knowledge workers, or the shifting boundaries between work and non-work—that are presently being explored (Peiperl *et al.* 2000). Moreover, the study of creativity, like that of careers, spans the range of social science disciplines, and notably the disciplines of psychology (Gardner 1993), social psychology (Csikszentmihalyi 1996), sociology (White 1993), and economics (Caves 2000).

The design of this book incorporates two parts principally focused on (creative) careers themselves, and two more on the interplay between careers and the broader social and industrial contexts upon which (career) creativity is exercised. The treatment is inter-disciplinary, with an international group of authors adding a multicultural flavor to the collected chapters. The parts promote the study of career creativity from four distinct vantage points— namely (1) creative careers observed, (2) creative careers enacted, (3) careers in creative industries, and (4) careers creating industries. The range of vantage points is intended to cover the ways career creativity may be seen both to shape and to be shaped by the larger contexts in which careers unfold.

AN ILLUSTRATIVE EXAMPLE

To introduce the thinking behind the above-mentioned parts, we will next offer an introductory example. It fills the basic requirement of a widely recognized career relevant to all four parts, and illustrates some key differences across the alternative vantage points noted. It draws on the familiar world of the media. It highlights a career that links to anthropologist Marshall McLuhan's influential prediction (1994: 5) that new media—and television in particular—would shape a different world, one in which 'the globe (was) no more than a village'. The example is that of well-known media magnate Rupert Murdoch. We introduce it without intending any judgment on either Murdoch's career or its social consequences.

We recognize that the careers of elite, influential business people such as Murdoch may well provide greater opportunities for career creativity and industry-shaping behavior than do the careers of most people. However, Murdoch's career provides a useful illustration because its key features are publicly known. We also believe it provides a substantial demonstration of features present, to a more local degree, in many other careers.

Creative careers observed: models and career anchors

If careers are evolving sequences of work experiences over time, it is clear that careers are paradoxical (Martin *et al.* 1983). On the one hand, there are patterns that make some sequences of work experiences comparable to others. On the other hand, each person's career is a unique and idiosyncratic experience. There is a distinction between a person's 'work history', reflecting a publicly observable sequence of job experiences, and the subjective sense a person makes of those experiences (Nicholson and West 1989). Careers thus serve as reference points, both for shared social understanding and for personal interpretation and action.

In Murdoch's case, he was exposed in early life to some prominent models for his own career. The first was that of his father, Keith Murdoch, successively a war correspondent, an editor of the Melbourne *Herald*, an acquisitions manager, and a newspaper owner. Murdoch senior managed his group's diversification into radio broadcasting, and oversaw the introduction of new technology such as wire reports, fast presses, and radio photographic services, emphasizing their contribution to the gathering and delivering of the news (Shawcross 1997: 24). Another role model at least indirectly available to the younger Murdoch was his father's mentor Alfred Harmsworth (later Lord Northcliffe), founder of the London *Daily Mail*, whose core philosophy was to create profitable newspapers by appealing to a mass audience (Shawcross 1997: 22–3). Meanwhile, the younger Murdoch, working in England after his undergraduate studies, was impressed by the independence and autonomy displayed by another populist press baron, William Aitken (later Lord Beaverbrook), owner of the London *Daily Express* (Shawcross 1997: 39–40).

His father's early death gave Murdoch an early opportunity to respond to the role models he had witnessed. He returned to Australia at the age of 22 to take up his inheritance, the proprietorship of the Adelaide *News*. Like his father, Murdoch showed a keen desire to expand his newspaper empire, and by 1969 he also owned the Sydney *Mirror*, the Canberra *Australian*, and London's *News of the World* and *Sun*. Like Harmsworth, he used an understanding of sentiments of the mass audience to set the tone for his newspapers: bold headlines, risqué photographs, and prize-laden contests. Like Aitken, he managed a chain of newspapers of which he was owner rather than paid servant. Murdoch's own work history appeared to imitate those that he had most closely observed (Shawcross 1997: 49–88).

What, though, of Murdoch's subjective career? That is, what sense did he himself make of the work experiences he accumulated? Here, it is useful to recall Schein's concept of career anchor (1978, 1982). According to this view, people begin their careers with certain aspirations, values, and motivations, and these get selectively reinforced through early work experiences. The common result is an enduring connection between early work experiences and the person's self-concept as careers unfold (Nicholson 2000). Murdoch's early experiences as a journalist and newspaper proprietor seem to have provided him a career anchor as a 'newsman'. As Crainer (1998: 79–80) notes: 'Rupert Murdoch was brought up on a diet of newspapers.... He saw his father's newspapers in operation. He worked as a copy editor at the *Daily Express*. He has written, subbed, knows the traditional printing process inside out. These skills played an important part in the early development of his career.'

Murdoch's anchor seems to have guided his explorations into newer media, such as television and cable. After taking control of the Fox Broadcasting Network in the USA, he championed the creation of an independent news channel in the face of severe competition, stating: 'We are a news organization...to be a meaningful broadcaster, you have to have news' (Shawcross 1997: 410). The importance of this anchor seems reflected in the first significant assignment taken on by his son Lachlan—namely, to run Murdoch's Australian newspapers. Murdoch remarked: 'That's superb training, running a far-flung newspaper company in a big country like that' (Gunther 1998b).

The duality between the public and private sides of a person's career is fundamental, and underlies the questions explored in the first part of this book. Perhaps most fundamentally, what are the underlying images or metaphors that are employed in both public discourse and private reflection on careers, and in connecting between the two arenas? More particularly where creativity is involved, what knowledge exists only as tacit knowledge, and has yet to be brought into the arena of public recognition where its counterpart—namely, explicit knowledge—resides? What career systems exist or can be envisaged through which knowledge might be both generated and transferred? What, moreover, is the interface between public and private lives, and how do the latter get represented in the employment arrangements that creative people negotiate? These kinds of questions dominate the first section of this book.

Creative careers enacted: the person and the social structure

Careers, as scholars in the Chicago sociological tradition well understood, unfold through the interplay between individuals and larger social structures (Barley 1989). In this view, the boundary of a social location gets shaped by the careers it contains. The evolution of people's overlapping careers—as engineers, schoolteachers, or even hobos—gives rise to recognizable and coherent fields in which careers unfold. In turn, the fields' boundaries very much constrain the possibilities for participants' careers (Becker 1982; Gunther 1998b), as when, for example, the field of medical practice and its roles and rules bring about compliance from doctors, nurses, and technicians. The Chicago sociologists also observed that careers are relatively fluid, and that career transitions continually challenge field boundaries, so that medical practitioners and medical practice interdependently shape one another.

Murdoch's career was both influenced by and went beyond coherent fields of activity. His first significant field was that of newspapers in Australia and New Zealand. Given his role models and training, he developed an understanding of the norms and routines of this field, and his career showed the hallmarks of a transplanted British-style newspaper baron. Starting with the Adelaide *News* and *Sunday Mail* (1953), Murdoch expanded to control the Perth *Sunday News* (1956), the Sydney *Mirror* (1958), the Wellington *Dominion* (1964), and the Canberra *Australian* (1964), along with a host of smaller regional newspapers. He moved to a prominent position in Australia and New Zealand, refashioning a regionally fragmented industry along the way. He then made a geographic leap by successively adding the London-based *News of the World* (1968), and *Sun* (1969), and then turning to the USA to buy the San Antonio *Express* (1973) and the New York *Post* (1976) (Shawcross 1997: 85–93). Murdoch's career thus crossed the traditional geographic boundaries of newspaper publishing.

Murdoch did not confine his ambitions to newspapers. Like his local rivals, he was alive to the possibilities of commercial television in his native Australia, and successfully bid for a broadcasting license in Adelaide in 1957. Unlike his local rivals, Murdoch also began acquiring television businesses in the UK and the USA, and later in Asia. He teamed up with Barry Diller in 1985 and created Fox Networks, thereby altering a competitive landscape previously in the grip of an oligopoly of three major US networks (Ghemawat and Edmonds 1993). He then continued to move from one media world to another. By 1998, his company, News Corp, held controlling interests in the fields of: newspapers (exemplified above), books and magazines (HarperCollins, TV Guide), television (Fox Broadcasting, Twentieth Century Fox TV, twenty-two other stations, and several cable networks), satellite broadcasting (Star TV, BSkyB, SkyLatin America), film (Fox studio), and sports (LA Dodgers, NY Knicks, Manchester United) (Gunther 1998a).

Murdoch's career not only bridges one field (newspapers) to another (television), but also connects these fields more closely. He reportedly realized the synergy between the two media in the early 1970s, when he actively encouraged his tabloids such as the London *Sun* to cover television more extensively (Shawcross 1997). This suggestion led the tabloids, for example, to discuss and publicly speculate on the plot lines of various soap operas as well as scandals and noteworthy events in soap actors' lives; the happenings in one medium became content for another, as McLuhan (1994) had predicted. Likewise, Murdoch and his allies were able to create tighter links between his Fox film studios and his various TV broadcasting and satellite interests, between sports events and TV channels, and between his newspaper and publishing businesses.

We are not suggesting that Murdoch brought about the international realignment of the media on his own. On the contrary, Murdoch's career reflects a capacity to engage in effective collaboration with others. What we are suggesting is that the interplay between the person and the social (and political and economic) structure concerns all careers, and gives rise to a further set of questions. How, from a counseling or leadership standpoint, can we engage with and reinforce creative behavior in people's careers? What kinds of models are available from the restructuring of careers that we have witnessed? What in particular might be learned from careers that confront serious problems, and where creativity gets called to fortify career resilience, so that the person can live for a better day? How, more generally, can we think about 'meta-competencies' that provide for personal transformation despite the constraints of formal employment systems? These are the kind of questions explored in Part Two.

Careers in creative industries: commerce and creative action

Much of the writing on careers in the so-called creative industries—art, theater, filmmaking and publishing—has focused on creative producers within those industries rather than their commercial counterparts. In contrast, Murdoch's career provides an illustration of how agents of commercial interests shape the context within which creative personnel perform. A principal target of these interests is the cost of producing and releasing creative products (Turow 1992: 81).

A prominent example is now inextricably intertwined with the history of Thatcherism. Murdoch had always complained that the print unions' rules and their refusal to make the printing process more efficient had curbed productivity and profitability of the newspaper business. In 1986 his London newspapers confronted those unions by building a computerized printing plant at Wapping, East London, that made the printers' role obsolete. Taking advantage of the Conservative government's recently reformed labor laws, and of a secret alliance with the electricians' union, the newspapers weathered a landmark strike lasting almost a year without serious loss of production. When the strike had ended, the culture and economics of newspaper publishing in the UK had been profoundly transformed. The traditional ways of printing and organizing the labor force had given way to new technology and new forms of labor (Shawcross 1997: 223–37).

It would be excessive to suggest that Murdoch and his supporters acted on behalf of those creative workers—the journalists and editors—whose work had been previously constrained. Nevertheless, the example illustrates the way that intended collaborators can indulge in the 'hold-up' of potentially creative activity. As Caves (2000: 132) graphically puts it:

The curtain on Broadway goes up at 7.30. The concert is scheduled for 8 p.m. on Friday. The production cost of a motion picture is largely proportional to the number of days scheduled for filming, and most of the costs continue to be incurred when production is interrupted on short notice. Activities vulnerable to hold-up face a complex problem of contractual commitment and enforcement. Coalition partners able to stage a hold-up possess a valuable asset, because the dealmaker's high unavoidable costs define the size of the bribe that can be demanded to let activity proceed.

Murdoch's own record in managing creative personnel is reported to reflect the skillful use of social distance (Goffee and Jones 2000). He is described as taking meticulous care in appointing business leaders within his conglomerate, and in defining key political and economic parameters. He seeks to avoid antagonism with ruling political elites, and is said to be fastidious about the financial condition of his various businesses (Crainer 1998). However, he rarely interferes in the day-to-day creative decisions that his key employees make. He appears to follow implicitly the guidelines set by Amabile (1998) on managing creative personnel: setting challenging goals, granting freedom to choose the means by which to achieve goals, providing necessary resources, creating a supportive group and organization around them, and generally keeping free of too much interference.

However, the very orthodoxy of Murdoch's approach to his creative personnel raises questions. Is a distant, respectful posture the most 'creative' way to manage creativity? Or can greater value be gained from a more interactive approach? What is the range of tensions between commercial and creative activities and how do these affect or get affected by the course of people's careers? What about creativity stemming from interpersonal or small group relationships, rather than simply from individual endeavors? What kinds of signals pass from or between creative people, and how are these recognized and acted on? What support group or community attachments can people make in the service of their own creative agendas? These are the kind of questions that occupy Part Three.

Careers creating industries: legitimacy and opportunity

The emergence of new industries involves the growth of one or more dominant producer coalitions, the shaping of a regulative agenda, the management of new technologies introduced, and the preparation of customers for unprecedented products (Anand 1997). Underlying these four factors is the need to manage the socio-political climate (Aldrich and Fiol 1994) and to ensure that producers, consumers, and regulators will buy into the vision of things to come. In the autumn of his career, Murdoch was helping to shape the satellite broadcasting industry.

In the late 1980s, British Satellite Broadcasting (a consortium of British television companies) was the dominant player in the nascent industry. Murdoch's British Sky Broadcasting had been unable to join the consortium because of regulatory barriers, but he persisted in his desire to join the dominant producer coalition. His company fought a bitter and expensive battle eventually to wrest control of the consortium in a merged entity called British Sky Broadcasting (Ghemawat 1994). As the dominant firm within the industry, Murdoch's company engaged with a broad coalition of producers, striking deals with programming suppliers (such as Hollywood studios and news and sports broadcasters), equipment manufacturers (such as makers of equipment for reception of satellite broadcasting), and retailers of satellite broadcasting packages. The underlying goal was to make satellite television an attractive proposition for consumers (Shawcross 1997: 402).

Satellite broadcasting involved the introduction of a number of new technologies and new business methods, including the scrambling of broadcast movies, the leasing of commercial satellites, and the installation of satellite receiving dishes in viewers' homes. Murdoch's venture had to navigate the thorny challenges of managing the political climate that surrounded the new industry, leading to satellite television becoming a taken-for-granted technology in homes around the world (Shawcross 1997: 300–8). For millions of people, the industry spawned technology- and information-based careers that had not existed a relatively few years before.

What larger patterns can be observed in the links between careers and the creation of new industries? How flawed is the 'one-great-man' view of industry creation or transformation? How much did other people's careers coalesce with Murdoch's to create the effects witnessed in satellite broadcasting? More generally, what are the links to be observed between individually creative careers and industry-level creativity? Through what processes do creative people find and retain contact with one another to promote industry change? What are the influences of shared geographic space, or as the Web becomes more central to our lives, of shared virtual space? In what circumstances does creativity in one industry influence or relocate itself in another industry? These are the kind of questions that occupy Part Four.

A COMMUNAL INTEREST

The starting point for this book is provided by those who have previously explored the ground on which this book is placed. They include the principal writers in the social-science disciplines of psychology (Gardner 1993), social psychology (Csikszentmihalyi 1996), sociology (White 1993), and economics (Caves 2000) mentioned earlier, as well as editors and contributors to collected works that help to frame the literature (Sternberg and Davidson 1988; Runco and Pritzker 1999). Our particular slant, linking careers to creativity, takes more advantage of their efforts than we can fully acknowledge. However, we hope that, for them as well as for other readers, this particular collection adds to their insights.

The work on career creativity in this volume is linked to previous efforts to stimulate new ideas and activities in careers research (Arthur and Rousseau 1996; Peiperl et al. 2000). It is intended for a broad readership in both management and organizational studies, as well as across the root disciplines in the social sciences that have given rise to contemporary interest in both careers and creativity. It is also intended as a volume that will be both accessible and useful to a wide range of practitioners: leaders of creative or creativity-seeking endeavors, consultants on careers or creative processes, specialists in career counseling or the deployment of human resources, even individuals interested in their own 'career creativity'.

The conversation will be richer for the inclusion of all parties with a professional interest in our topic. Put another way, this book is intended to help readers do what we see contemporary careers doing—that is, building and nurturing a sense of community around shared interests. We hope this introduction has provided a useful start.

REFERENCES

Aldrich, H. E., and Fiol, C. M. (1994), 'Fools Rush in? The Institutional Context of Industry Creation', *Academy of Management Review*, 19: 645–70.

Amabile, T. M. (1998), 'How to Kill Creativity', *Harvard Business Review* (Sept.–Oct.), 77–87.

Anand, N. (1997), 'Interpretive Stance in Inchoate Industries', unpublished doctoral dissertation (Nashville, Tenn.: Vanderbilt University).

Arthur, M. B., and Rousseau, D. M. (1996) (eds.), *The Boundaryless Career: A New Employment Principle for a New Organizational Era* (Oxford: Oxford University Press).

——Hall, D. T., and Lawrence, B. S. (1989), 'Generating New Directions in Career Theory: The Case for a Transdisciplinary Approach', in M. B. Arthur, D. T. Hall, and B. S. Lawrence (eds.), *Handbook of Career Theory* (Cambridge: Cambridge University Press), 7–25.

Barley, S. R. (1989), 'Careers, Identities, and Institutions: The Legacy of the Chicago School of Sociology', in M. B. Arthur, D. T. Hall, and B. S. Lawrence (eds.), *Handbook of Career Theory* (Cambridge: Cambridge University Press), 41–65.

Becker, H. S. (1982), *Art Worlds* (Berkeley and Los Angeles: University of California Press).

Caves, R. E. (2000), *Creative Industries: Contracts between Art and Commerce* (Cambridge, Mass.: Harvard University Press).

Crainer, S. (1998), *Business the Rupert Murdoch Way* (Oxford: Capstone).

Csikszentmihalyi, M. (1996), *Creativity: Flow and the Psychology of Discovery and Invention* (New York: HarperCollins).

Gardner, H. (1993), *Creating Minds* (New York, Basic Books).

Ghemawat, P. (1994), 'British Sky Broadcasting versus Sky Television', Harvard Business School Case 9-794-031.

——and Edmonds, J. (1993), 'Fox Broadcasting', Harvard Business School Case 9-387-096.

Ghiselin, H. (1952), *The Creative Process* (New York: Signet; Berkeley and Los Angeles: University of California Press).

Goffee, R., and Jones, G. (2000), 'Why should Anyone be Led by you?', *Harvard Business Review* (Sept.–Oct.), 63–70.

Gunther, M. (1998a), 'The Rules according to Rupert', *Fortune*, 20 (26 Oct.), 62–73.

Gunther, M. (1998b), 'The Rules According to Rupert', *Fortune*, 20 (26 Oct.), 92–109.

Hall, D. T., and Associates (1996), *The Career is Dead: Long Live the Career* (San Francisco: Jossey-Bass).

Lapham, L. H. (1994), 'Introduction to the MIT Press Edition: The Eternal Now', in H. M. McLuhan, *Understanding Media: The Extension of Man* (Cambridge, Mass.: MIT Press), pp. ix–xxiii.

McLuhan, H. M. (1994), *Understanding Media: The Extensions of Man*, 2nd edn. (Cambridge: Mass.: MIT Press).

Martin, J. M., Feldman, M. S., Hatch, M. J., and Sitkin, S. B. (1983), 'The Uniqueness Paradox in Organizational Stories', *Administrative Science Quarterly*, 28: 438–53.

Mills, C. W. (1940), 'Situated Actions and Vocabularies of Motive', *American Sociological Review*, 5: 904–13.

Nicholson, N. (2000), 'Motivation–Selection–Connection: An Evolutionary Model of Career Development', in M. A. Peiperl, M. B. Arthur, R. Goffee, and T. Morris (eds.), *Career Frontiers: New Conceptions of Working Lives* (Oxford: Oxford University Press), 54–75.

——and West, M. (1989), 'Transitions, Work Histories, and Careers', in M. B. Arthur, D. T. Hall, and B. S. Lawrence (eds.), *Handbook of Career Theory* (Cambridge: Cambridge University Press), 181–201.

Peiperl, M. A., Arthur, M. B., Goffee, R. and Morris, T. (2000) (eds.), *Career Frontiers: New Conceptions of Working Lives* (Oxford: Oxford University Press).

Runco, M. A., and Pritzker, S. R. (1999), *Encyclopedia of Creativity* (New York: Academic Press).

Schein, E. H. (1978), *Career Dynamics* (Reading, Mass.: Addison-Wesley).

——(1982), 'Individuals and Careers', Technical Report 19, Office of Naval Research.

Sternberg, R., and Davidson, J. (1988) (eds.), *The Nature of Creativity* (New York: Cambridge University Press).

Shawcross, W. (1997), *Murdoch: The Making of a Media Empire* (New York: Touchstone).

Turow, J. (1992), *Media Systems in Society: Understanding Industries, Strategy, and Power* (New York: Longman).

Weaver, S. L. (1952), Jacket note on the Signet edition of Ghiselin's *The Creative Process*.

Weick, K. E. (1996), 'Enactment and the Boundaryless Career: Organizing as we Work', in M. B. Arthur and D. M. Rousseau (eds.), *The Boundaryless Career: A New Employment Principle for a New Organizational Era* (Oxford: Oxford University Press), 40–57.

White, H. C. (1993), *Careers and Creativity: Social Forces in the Arts* (Boulder, Colo.: Westview Press).

I

CREATIVE CAREERS OBSERVED

If creativity is becoming an essential element of career, then to understand creative careers we will need to use different tools from those that our traditional approaches have provided. How do you look at a career and make sense of it? Income, hierarchical status, and job satisfaction are often inadequate measures, and exit is no longer an indicator of failure. The analysis of careers is, now more than ever, a changing and divergent discipline.

Yet the observation and understanding of creative careers are themselves creative enterprises, as the first four chapters in this book illustrate, and such creative analysis may be well worth the effort. The authors, based in four different countries, focus on the observation of creative careers from four distinctive standpoints.

The first chapter in this section, by Kerr Inkson, explores the use of metaphor in career theory, particularly its capacity to foster creative thinking about careers in both theorists and career actors. Inkson advocates the use of multiple, simultaneous metaphors to extend our understanding of the multifaceted nature of careers. By uncovering the logic and definitions behind such basic and essential terms as 'career path,' Inkson brings light to the ways in which casual observers as well as researchers and career practitioners make sense of careers, often unintentionally. His purposeful approach to the use of metaphors adds depth and perspective to the understanding of creative careers, while his concluding question, 'Can metaphor express "grand theory"?', calls for more work to map and explore the explicit and implicit metaphors underlying the developing theory of careers.

Next, Birgitta Södergren considers the role of knowledge in the building of careers. Through an interview study with non-managerial knowledge workers (specialists) about their roles and careers within modern companies, Södergren shows how these contemporary employees, who are 'more and more the engines of economic growth in the information society', focus on knowledge and skills rather than career paths. But traditional managerial constructions and human-resource policies in the Swedish company settings she describes reinforce traditional hierarchical, managerial paths. The specialists work with a combination of tacit and explicit knowledge, but the managerial system focuses only on the explicit dimension. Yet tacit knowledge, for Södergren, is the basis of career growth; leadership, she says, is support for learning, rather than the creation of organizational and career structures.

Chapter 4 by Hugh Gunz, Martin Evans, and Michael Jalland goes some way toward providing new models, particularly on the topic of boundaries and creative approaches to crossing them. This chapter takes as its point of departure the assertion that creativity—finding new ways of doing things, introducing new ideas to established orders—is enhanced by the movement of people across boundaries, and is inhibited by career immobility. Yet the authors argue that unconstrained career mobility would be intolerable and unproductive; that career boundaries are still needed. The challenge is to manage mobility so that creativity can flourish. The authors show how technical and institutional factors combine to create four distinctly different kinds of career boundary around and within organizations. However, these are social artifacts rather than immutable forces and can be manipulated. The chapter presents different ways in which impermeable boundaries can be made more permeable, together with some of the costs and benefits to organizations of so doing.

Finally, in Chapter 5, Michelle Buck, Mary Dean Lee, and Shelley MacDermid look at alternative work arrangements, in particular part-time arrangements, as long-term solutions to problems of working conditions and balance. The participants in their study chose to work less and earn less in order to balance their lives. From this perspective, creativity is engendered by necessity; because their current scenario was unworkable, these people invented new ones. The chapter's findings are diverse—the authors observed people taking different paths: changing employer, going part-time in the same place, reconfiguring their job. But they found surprisingly high levels of career success, including some continued advancement, on the part of those making the shift. They describe conditions at both the individual and the institutional level that are associated with career success, and focus in particular on the win–win possibilities when these two levels work together.

By each focusing on an important aspect of career creativity, these four chapters give us a new set of tools for the observation of careers. Inkson's explication of the use of metaphor and his many new interpretations; Södergren's connecting of learning, knowledge, and career growth; Gunz, Evans, and Jalland's new metaphors for boundary spanning in the context of work organizations, and Buck, Lee, and MacDermid's re-examination of success in the light of the broader career, all infuse meaning and capability to the study of career, and provide useful tools to those engaged in the understanding of the creative, changing nature of working life.

2

Thinking Creatively about Careers: The Use of Metaphor

KERR INKSON

> Life is an incurable disease.
>
> (Abraham Cowley)
>
> 'Life is just a bowl of cherries.'
>
> (Lew Brown)

> I've looked at life from both sides now,
> From win and lose, and still somehow,
> It's life's illusions I recall,
> I really don't know life at all.
>
> (Joni Mitchell)

It is commonly agreed that metaphor—the substitution of a concept (for example, 'the manager') by another that is typically more concrete and more striking, and that carries fresh connotations (for example, 'the general', 'the politician', 'the boy scout')—is universal and inevitable. Metaphor, arguably, is not just an illustrative use of language, but also a way of cognitively appreciating and understanding the world (Ortony 1993; Grant and Oswick 1996). As I hope to show in this chapter, we do not just compose metaphors as devices of art or rhetoric: we *think* in metaphors (Mangham 1996).

In 1986 Gareth Morgan's book *Images of Organization* was published. It has been immensely influential in organization studies. Morgan's contribution was to apply a series of metaphors to organizations, and to show that new insights could be gained—by both social scientists and managers—by considering organizations from different metaphorical perspectives. Thus, the organization might be conceived of as a machine, as an organism, as a political system, as a brain, as a culture, and so on. Each image demonstrates different qualities of the organization—for example, the efficiency and rigidity of the machine, the potential for change and growth of the organism, the holistic learning capabilities of the brain. Each metaphor embodies unique truths about organizations, but none comes near expressing the whole truth. The objective is not to debate which is the most 'correct' metaphor, but to use metaphors as complements to each other, so that each new metaphor contributes to a broader, more eclectic understanding.

The metaphor approach to understanding organizations has become popular, particularly in the UK literature. Grant and Oswick (1996) note the 'liberating' force of metaphors in providing new perceptions of old phenomena, generating new social realities, and facilitating experimentation and research. Metaphors enable us to conjure up new, often more vivid images, to draw attention to special characteristics, to create new meanings. They embody creative thinking by the speaker or writer, and they encourage further creative association by the hearer or reader.

For example, consider the account by Raymond (1998) of Microsoft's software development processes, as summarized by DeFillippi and Arthur (2000). Here is the idea the authors wish to convey:

Microsoft builds its software in conditions of considerable security. The software developers are large groups of skilled professionals who are kept separate from other employees under the authority of a senior project manager...

Here is what they actually say:

Microsoft...(builds its) software like cathedrals, in that a cloistered team of software developers work...much as medieval cathedrals were built by vast armies of craftsmen under the authority of a bishop or high cleric...   (DeFillippi and Arthur 2000).

The image is thus projected, of professional expertise and secrecy, and of a closed group of 'elect' workers working to fulfill the vision of a person of high authority in the context of a quasi-religious culture. The new imagery—'cathedral', 'cloister', 'armies', 'craftsmen', 'bishop'—is more physical, more visual, and more romantic than the bald statement of reality. In essence, the writers have *created a new image* of Microsoft. They would justify this by saying that the image represents a reality that could not be adequately communicated by using straightforward descriptors. It is not hard to see why metaphor has been described as 'seductive' (Pinder and Bourgeois 1982), though of course the term 'seductive' is itself yet another metaphor!

Metaphor has been accused of being appropriate to rhetorical rather than scientific discourse, and incapable of describing physical reality (Ortony 1993). John Locke, for example, described metaphor as 'the veiling of the intellect' (Doving 1996), and railed against 'the artificial and figurative application of words...for nothing else but to insinuate wrong ideas, move passions, and thereby mislead the judgement' (Locke, in Cohen 1978: 120). Doving (1996) points out some errors that metaphors typically engender: errors of commission (when irrelevant material is forced onto the object being described), errors of omission (when key aspects of the object are left out of account), errors of inappropriateness (when the correspondences are trivial), and errors of redundancy (when a metaphor adds nothing to existing metaphors). In the positivist tradition, physical and social scientists are explicitly and implicitly encouraged to describe phenomena as empirical data show them to be, and not through the images of objects from quite different domains.

Morgan (1998) believed that 'multiple metaphor' had the potential to reveal much of the complexity in organizations: 'Using multiple metaphors to understand organization and management gives us a capacity to tap different dimensions of a situation, showing how different qualities of organization can co-exist, supporting, reinforcing or contradicting one another' (Morgan 1998: 6). The universities in which most of the contributors to this book are employed, for example, may well have characteristics of 'ivory towers', 'secret societies', 'political struggles', and 'sausage machines': each metaphor adds to the richness of the description, without invalidating any of the metaphors that have come before.

In recent work on the psychological contracts and careers of contract professionals, I found it useful to employ a series of metaphors such as 'displaced person', 'dating agency customer', 'warehouse component', 'hired gun' to emphasize different aspects of the phenomenon (Inkson *et al.* 2001). Each metaphor encapsulated a key feature of the group under investigation. It may be, similarly, that, by considering complementary metaphorical representations, career theorists, practitioners, and managers can gain insight into the general nature of careers. Perhaps, too, metaphors can provide individuals with the means to understand their own careers better.

METAPHORS FOR CAREER

Even a cursory examination of discourse about careers confirms that metaphor is a dominant influence. Most people unconsciously use metaphorical imagery to describe careers: for example, 'career path', 'fast track', 'career ladder', 'career plateau'. Do such metaphors represent deeply embedded stereotypes? Do they condition and constrain career thinking through the images they convey? Or, alternatively, do metaphors provide a means for us to think more creatively about careers, to develop new understanding of career phenomena?

Consider this generic description of careers from Schein's classic, *Career Dynamics* (1978: 22):

Each *cycle* contains *smooth, even stretches* as well as *bumpy, obstruction-filled stretches.* Usually each section is marked by *milestones* indicating where the person is and what he or she has accomplished. Finally there are *choice points* where the person must decide *which way to head*. But the *movement of life* is always forward, linked to the *biological clock* and cultural norms. One can *drift, stall,* or *stagnate,* but there is basically *no stopping* and *no turning back.* (emphasis added)

This passage of a mere seventy-seven words is replete with vivid metaphoric imagery. The basic conceptualization of the career as a *journey*—the most common of all career metaphors—is irresistible. The passage has a strong sense of movement. It asks questions of the reader. Is the journey planned? What are the smooth stretches? What are the obstructions? What are the milestones, the choice points? Is one drifting or stalling? Is it true, in these times of more varied career forms, that one can never turn back? And, in relation to issues of career creativity, is the traveler in a touring omnibus, following a well-signposted high road that many have traveled before, or on foot in unexplored terrain, creating a unique and delightful personal pathway?

In considering careers, one problem we do not face is a shortage of metaphors. Here are a few examples:

- Gunz (1990) advocated the reconceptualization of 'career ladders' as 'jungle gyms', emphasizing the possibility of diagonal, lateral, and downward career movement in complex structures.
- Hagevik (1998) used common metaphors such as 'ladder', 'lattice', 'spiral', and 'anchor' to understand the careers of health professionals.
- Rosenbaum (1989) considered much organizational career behavior as part of a 'tournament' among members seeking to compete with each other for hierarchical ascent.
- Sagaria (1989) outlined a career counseling practice for women based on a metaphor (for the client) of an artist making a quilt.
- Sonnenfeld and Peiperl's typology (1988) of company career systems into 'academies', 'fortresses', 'baseball teams', and 'clubs' has implications for the respective careers of the 'students', 'defenders', 'players', and 'club members' as well as for the companies.
- Spain and Hamel (1993) employed a 'tree' metaphor of careers for counseling practice.

Metaphors in frequent public use are implicit in much theory—for example, 'career ladders' and 'fast track' (organizational career theory), 'square pegs in square holes' (vocational fit theories), and 'going through a phase' (career stage theories). Schein's 'career anchors' (1978) present an imagery of rootedness and stability in careers, whereas Hall's metaphor (1976) of the shape-changing god Proteus stresses the flexibility and dynamism of 'protean' careers. In Levinson and Associates' *The Seasons of a Man's Life* (1978) we get a sense of career progression as 'seasonality'—inevitable, irreversible, and marked by observable transitions. The very words—'anchor', 'Proteus', 'season'—conjure up vivid and dramatic imagery that is hard to discard from our thinking in favor of more detailed, empirically supported, verbally neutral concepts. The colorfulness of metaphors, and their resonance with the thinking of ordinary people, may give them the potential to engage all of us in more creative thinking about careers than would be possible if we stuck to scientifically validated concepts and accurate, non-metaphorical language.

PHYSICAL IMAGES AS METAPHORS

The metaphor can be seen to reflect and to shape thinking particularly power-fully when it is expressed in the form of physical images. Figures 2.1 and 2.2 present two metaphors by the well-known career theorist Donald Super. The

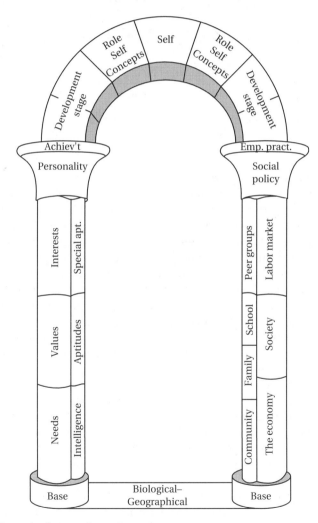

Fig. 2.1. The arch of career determinants.

Source: Super (1992: 39).

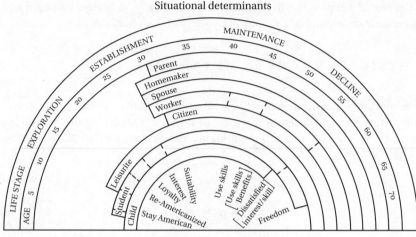

Fig. 2.2. The life-career rainbow.

Source: Super (1992: 37).

first is Super's solid, structured 'arch of career determinants', which he says was 'inspired by the Norman door of the village church at Hauxton near Cambridge' (Super 1992: 40). The second is his splendid, evocative, 'life-career rainbow', a striking visual representation of his conception of careers as a series of developing life roles (Super 1992: 36–41). In these two diagrams, Super demonstrates the utility of adopting both contrasting images of career phenomena. The first metaphor shows that a career can properly be viewed as a structure, constructed on sound architectural principles on the twin bases of individual characteristics and external opportunities; the second captures the evanescent, multiple-arena characteristics of career development.

Another well-known 'metaphor diagram' is Schein's representation (1978: 39) of career progressions as three arrow-like movements, against the structural backdrop of a cone or pyramid (Fig. 2.3).

Here, the imagery is of contained, limited movement within the boundaries of the cone. This is in marked contrast with the freewheeling, fast-traveling connotations of career conveyed in the earlier Schein quotation. The contrast marks, perhaps, the focus of Schein's work on organizations as well as on individuals: the subtitle of his book is *Matching Individual and Organizational Needs*. The 'matching' metaphor, with its imagery of profiles and templates, or square pegs being carefully measured and fitted into square holes, is also implicit in the work of Holland (1992) and other 'trait-factor' theorists (Betz *et al.* 1989). Clearly, metaphors and their associated imagery can illustrate and embody contrasting conceptualizations of careers, as well as facilitating new conceptualizations.

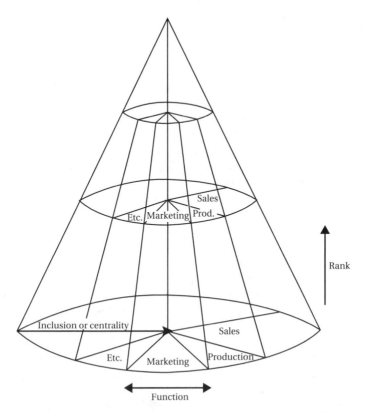

Fig. 2.3. Organizational career moves.
Source: Schein (1978: 39).

METAPHOR AND SCIENCE IN CAREER THEORY

Many behavioral scientists working in a positivist tradition are uncomfortable with the notion of metaphor. The rigorous assembling of theoretical and empirical information appears antithetical to the colorful, untestable, metaphor. Positivists seek to develop propositions in organization theory through the elucidation and empirical testing of specific hypotheses relating measurable variables rather than through 'woolly' talk about organizations being like spider plants or termites' nests (Morgan 1992). Yet even among those who seek to pursue a rigorous scientific course in their examination of social phenomena, metaphorical thinking may not only prove inevitable, but may take on a life of its own. This can be demonstrated by the examination of the work of major career theorists.

Schein

Despite the passage quoted in the section on the 'journey' metaphor, Schein, in his classic 1978 book, *Career Dynamics*, was not overly given to metaphor. Like many social scientists, he was properly concerned to provide an appropriate scientific base for his theories. Schein used metaphor in two ways. First, he encapsulated and made memorable a set of propositions that he regarded, from research evidence, as being empirically valid—as in his (1978: 124–72) concept of 'career anchors', which provided a vivid metaphor for sources of career stability. Secondly, he used metaphor in a more casual way, to share his ideas with the reader via language that he appeared to assume was common currency, as in the quotation above. For example, he talked about the 'life pattern... creating a "path" for people to follow' (1978: 81), and told us that 'the road to self-discovery is a very rocky road, with many choice points and detours to be negotiated' (1978: 172).

In these passages the journey metaphor is assumed to be common currency between writer and reader. This is part of the seductive nature of metaphor: some metaphors become so familiar that we stop seeing them as metaphors and assume they are 'real'. If metaphors are used repeatedly, few of us may question their validity (Doving 1996).

However, in association with Schein it is not the journey metaphor but the anchor metaphor that is nowadays remembered. Is this because of the rigor and persuasiveness of Schein's evidence, or because of the vividness and originality of the metaphor? If Schein had gone no further than describing the anchors, and had not named them 'anchors', but (say) 'enduring constellations of self-perceived, career-relevant, talents, motives and values' (Schein 1978: 127), would they have gained the same currency? Does the appeal of the 'career anchor' lie not in the empirical data that can be shown to support it, but in its metaphorical form, in the connotations of the term and the visual power of the symbol? Is metaphor indeed seductive? Should it be?

Hall

We observe something similar in Hall's *Careers in Organizations* (1976), which has become well known as the first reference to the 'protean career', based on the image of the Greek god Proteus, who could change shape at will—'from boar to lion to dragon to fire to flood' (Hall 1976: 201). The idea of changing the form of one's career at will is attractive, and the concept of the protean career nowadays enjoys wide popularity. Yet Hall's original (1976) work contained less than three pages on protean careers, as a summary of 'an emerging view of careers' at the conclusion of an empirically based book (Hall 1976: 200–3). The term 'protean career' was not even indexed. Once again the vividness and novelty of the metaphor apparently gave it more long-term appeal to readers than the prior 200 pages of evidence.

Every metaphor has its strengths and limitations. The strengths of the 'Proteus' metaphor are its unusual vividness, the empowerment that it provides to the heroic individual career actor, and the value in today's rapidly changing careers arena of being able to quickly improvise new ways of working. The main weakness of the metaphor, it seems to me, is the failure of the pure protean career to take account of career *history*. If the individual truly has the power to change to any form at any time, then such things as the accumulation of career skills and the nature of the job held prior to the change are irrelevant. This does not seem to be realistic. Every career is informed in some way by retrospective sense making (Weick 1996) or knowledge acquisition from that career's past (Bird 1996). No career can be more than partly protean. Proteus is, as it were, 'anchored'!

Super

Super (1957, 1992) on the whole made more use of metaphor than did Schein or Hall. There is a question whether the use of a term such as 'stage'—as in 'stages of human development'—which underpins much of Super's theory, is a metaphor or simply a descriptor. However, Super's conceptualizations of the late 'maintenance' stage of the career are striking in their use of metaphorical imagery. At this stage, according to Super, one does not attempt to 'break new ground...pioneering is done by younger men' (1957: 147). However, 'the fruits of labor can be enjoyed while the next crop is being cultivated. ...The ground he is already cultivating gives him an adequate living...' (1957: 148). Here, an agricultural imagery, with the career actor a steward of the resources accumulated in the course of the career, has taken hold.

Thirty-five years later, the same author described the same stage of the career through a much wider range of metaphors (Super 1992: 44). He noted particularly 'the competition of younger men and women' threatening those who 'would like to rest on their oars'. Many older people 'stagnate', 'mark time', 'occupy a chair' (1992: 44)—a much bleaker scenario than in his earlier work. Does the movement in Super's metaphors mark the emergence over the years of competitive forces that are inimical to the rustic career stewards that Super observed in 1957? In this, as in Super's previously mentioned metaphors of 'arch' and 'rainbow', introduced late in his own career as representative of his developing career theorizing, Super is again and again creative in his generation of new metaphors to embody new, or newly observed, phenomena.

Holland

As a last example of a major theorist using metaphor, consider Holland's *Making Vocational Choices* (1992). This book describes the outcomes of Holland's life work on 'vocational personalities', their measurement, and that of work environments. Holland's view is that long-term personality traits fit individuals to particular long-term occupational categories. It is, therefore, an embodiment of the 'square-pegs-in-square-holes' career metaphor.

Despite this, of the books I have looked at, Holland's is the most conspicuously lacking in metaphor. The obvious 'pegboard' and 'profile' metaphors are not used. *Making Vocational Choices* is erudite, rigorous, and scientific. Nothing is stated for which sound empirical evidence is not cited. Metaphors are hard to find. The language is carefully non-rhetorical. Yet, even here, Holland suddenly says, in a passage stressing the continuity of careers, 'careers tend to *snowball* over the life's course...' (Holland 1992: 54; emphasis added). Yet—a little frustratingly—Holland does not trouble to tell us what 'snowballing' is—presumably, like Schein with his 'journey', he considers the notion so obvious that no further explanation is called for. But suppose that the function of the metaphor is not to inform, but to stimulate the reader's thinking—as Morgan (1980: 612) says 'as a form of creative expression which relies on constructive falsehood as a means of liberating the imagination'. What can we do with 'snowball'?

Personally, I visualize a child creating an ever-growing snowball by rolling an initially small snowball along the ground. As far as the metaphor is concerned, I construe the snow as the experience of life that is 'picked up' and absorbed by the snowball. The snowball grows in size as one's career proceeds, absorbing each career experience into its core, always there but buried ever deeper as the snowball grows. The snowball metaphor is thus another variant of the journey metaphor, this time emphasizing the aggregation of experience as the journey continues.

But is the snowball being laboriously and deliberately assembled by its human creator, or is it speeding out of control down a hill, absorbing all the snow in its path willy-nilly? It is an extremely powerful metaphor. It engages the reader in an act of interpretation, and potentially in an act of creation. But it does not fit well in the scientific frame, and having brought it up and written half a page on it, Holland lays it aside, does not mention it again, and does not even index it. It seems that the use of metaphor is a deep-seated human response that even the most rigorous scientist cannot resist, and that slips out from time to time in all discourse.

THE 'JOURNEY' METAPHOR

'Journey' metaphors are, in my experience, very common among individuals describing their own careers. In informal seminars where I have outlined the nature of metaphor, and have asked participants to write down the metaphors that come to their minds as ways of understanding their own careers, different forms of journey are by far the most frequent. As we have seen, the notion of the career as journey is at the heart of Schein's influential *Career Dynamics* (1978). Cadin, Bailly-Bender, and Saint-Giniez (2000) describe a taxonomy of careers whose categories are defined by different types of traveler—'migrants', 'borderers', 'nomads', and so on. Taking the notion of sea journeys, Farren (1998) talks of 'sailing the good ship of career', while Hutchins (1998) parallels career to a boat that one must 'paddle like crazy'. Inkson (1997) suggests we have moved from a time of placid journeys to known destinations by ocean liner, to one in which careers are more like whitewater rafting.

The ubiquity of the journey metaphor is demonstrated by a number of the chapters in this volume. For example, in describing the careers of executive women in the entertainment industry, Ensher, Murphy, and Sullivan (Chapter 12) note that they lacked 'maps or guides telling them how to get from Point A to Point B'. However, they 'broke in', 'fast-tracked', had 'career paths' that 'diverged', 'carried new skills with them', 'broke away', and so on. According to Södergren (Chapter 3), knowledge-intensive workers 'gravitated' towards certain settings, as part of 'knowledge expeditions'. Alvarez and Svejenova (Chapter 10) describe the 'career trajectories'—a metaphor with associations of individuality and rapid ascent—of the moviemakers Pedro and Agustín Almodóvar. The breadth of the metaphor provides infinite possibilities.

CAREER PATHS AND CREATIVITY

One of the joys of metaphor is its capacity to stimulate diverse and creative patterns of thinking. This can be done not just in the generation of diverse metaphors for the same target object, but in the creative interpretation of a single metaphor, as in the 'snowball' and 'journey' examples above. This arises from the fact that most metaphors have several denotative meanings and multiple connotations, and that each metaphor stimulates unique imagery in the mind of each individual who considers it.

For example, consider that commonplace variant of the 'journey' metaphor: *career path*. What do we understand by it? A medical student may look ahead along a series of higher qualifications and work experiences that lead to the position of senior heart surgeon. A company human-resource (HR) manager may visualize logical series of promotions and interdepartment transfers for employees with high potential. Most of us, from time to time, will look back and say: 'Where have I been? What path have I followed? What sense can I make of it?' Plainly, there is no one meaning for the term 'path' as applied to careers.

Here are three dictionary definitions of 'path'.

The way or course which an animal or object follows in the air, in water, or in space.   (*Webster's Dictionary*)

In this definition, each person, animal, or object creates his, her, or its own, unique path. We all know Sinatra's cliché, 'I did it my way.' Let's call that a Type 1 path.

A way beaten or trodden by the feet of man or beast, or made hard by wheels.   (*Webster's Dictionary*)

In this definition, paths are apparently created by processes of repetition or imitation—the path is literally hammered into place by repeated, copied behavior. The precedents of early travelers literally 'pave the way' for those who come later. Let's call that a Type 2 path.

A way or track laid down for walking.   (*Concise Oxford Dictionary*)

In this last definition, it seems that someone has made a decision as to where the path should be and what it should be like, and has constructed it in advance as an aid to travelers. The path has been manufactured to a logical design. Let's call that a Type 3 path.

What types of path are career paths? Type 1, 2, or 3 paths? It seems to me that one of the features of the trend to rational organization structures that characterized much of the twentieth century, ever since Weber's description (1947, original published in German in 1924) of the internal organizational 'career system' designed to provide all the expertise a company might need from within, has been a huge drive to harness human energy by confining people to rationally designed Type 3 paths.

I have noticed this recently in work I have been doing to review the design of academic programs at the business school where I work. The professors have thought about the starting points at which students commence the journey and the destinations they may reach. The rules about the programs create a set of pathways along which students must walk if they are to obtain the credentials to which they aspire; other possible pathways are proscribed. Particular courses must be taken, but can be taken only if other, prerequisite, courses have been successfully completed. The professors assume they know better than the students what is good for them, and have constructed the path accordingly. The danger is that the autonomy, creativity, individuality, and personal learning obtainable from the personal construction of one's own, Type 1, path are lost. In large companies, the work of company HR managers and others in seeking to design hierarchical or spiral 'career paths' within organizational boundaries is similarly problematic.

Many years ago I had a friend who was a Buildings Manager at an expanding university. As new buildings went up, one of his jobs was, literally, to design and build the paths between them, and to plant grass around the paths. In the terminology above, he was expected to construct Type 3 paths: he had the power to decide where people would walk.

But that is not the way he looked at it. What he did instead was to roll all the earth between the buildings flat, plant the grass without any paths, and then wait for the buildings to be occupied. Once the buildings came into use people would begin to create their own Type 1 paths as they walked between them. As more and more people followed particular routes in the normal course of their business, Type 2 paths would emerge, 'trodden by the feet of men and women'. And, after a few months, my friend would know exactly where to put his Type 3 paths, and he would draw his plans, and move in with his paving stones. Similarly, in the already developed parts of the university, if my friend noticed muddy Type 2 paths trodden independently of the paved ones that were there, he would eventually pave them. It was a nice example of democracy, where people literally 'voted with their feet' to create the paths that suited them. But an even more empowering option might have been for him to spend the money devoted to construction and paving stones on better drainage and more hard-wearing grass, so that each person could continue to carve out his or her own, unique, Type 1 paths, without either the constraint or the distraction of manufactured paths.

At a recent academic meeting I attended a session of four papers on 'the continuing evolution of the career path'. Metaphors again! Not just 'path' but 'evolution', with its connotations of natural diversity, natural selection, development towards ever more functional forms, and of well-adapted paths that suit the environment driving out maladapted paths that do not. In the conference, some of the researchers, such as Reitman and Schneer (2000), distinguished between 'traditional' paths, within a single organization, and 'boundaryless' paths, (Arthur and Rousseau 1996) between organizations. If we focus the evolutionary metaphor, and the 'natural selection' of different 'species' of career, the implication was that *careeris boundarylessis* (Arthur and Rousseau 1996) is a more evolved species of career—or, at least, one better adapted to changing environmental conditions—which is about to render *careeris organizationis* extinct. However, some theorists, such as Gunz, Evans, and Jalland (2000), would argue vigorously against such an interpretation.

The 'boundaryless-careers' perspective would support the view that, in an increasingly dynamic and chaotic organizational world, career paths are nowadays evolving 'backwards' from Type 3 to Type 1—from logical design and efficient manufacture, to creative invention and individual trailblazing (Peiperl and Baruch 1997).

I can confirm that from everyday experience. If I tell people I am a career researcher and ask them about their career, they tend to say, 'Oh, you don't want to hear about my career, my career is strange.' It is as if they have a perception that the world is predominantly organized into Type 2 and Type 3 career paths, which everyone else is enjoying, and they have somehow been sidelined into a Type 1. The suggestion is that more career paths are Type 1— individual, self-designed, idiosyncratic, accidental, chaotic, creative—than we think.

THE 'RESOURCE' METAPHOR

One strand of career thinking embeds careers within organizations. But organizations have very different interests in careers than do the individuals who are enacting these careers. It follows that the metaphors underpinning organizational conceptions of careers are quite different from those typically employed by individuals and career theorists. Metaphors of paternalistic organizations—such as the 'happy family' (Casey 1999) and the 'football team' (Ramsay 1975)—may be used in an ideological way to serve vested interests, and to confine potentially creative career actors within the bosom of the family or the sharing of the team.

The literature on HR management and organizational career planning generates a distinctive, but influential, set of metaphors and associations. In the term 'human resource', individuals are assumed not to *have* resources under their own control but to *be* resources under the control of the organization. The career represents the individual's organizational work extended over time, and thus it becomes a long-term human resource for the organization. Through the HR terminology and thinking, the individual becomes not a person but a set of 'competencies': and metaphor thus creates a de-individualized, organizationally focused imagery of careers:

For an organization, the management of careers should be framed around the competencies it requires for competitiveness. If people are viewed as human resources, these resources need to be invested in and developed. Taken to the extreme, the shift in thinking would not only be away from jobs and towards competencies, it would be away from individual people too... (Arnold 1997: 38)

Thus, 'career planning' and 'career development systems' can be constructed at the level of the organization, such that careers are rationally developed according to a centrally determined organizational blueprint of resource requirements. In the HR metaphor, careers may be seen as a kind of mechanical componentry of the organization, albeit with some potential to change capability or functionality over time in response to company development programs. The manager of an agency for temporary workers recently told me he found it useful to conceptualize his organization as a warehouse of potentially useful component parts, each with its own specification, which he kept in a database of worker competencies (Inkson *et al.* 2001). This model is closely related to the 'machine' metaphor of organizations outlined by Morgan (1986). Managers and employees who carry it to an extreme or allow it to dominate their thinking and action are likely to adopt an orientation where power is conceded to the manager of the organization to manage its own 'resources'. In this situation the individual may lose both the sense and the reality of self-control over his or her own career.

The resource metaphor reinforces the view that careers are created by companies as an incidental by-product of their resource-developing activities. The chapters in the last part of this book focus on an obverse, and to my mind more exciting possibility: that individuals, working collaboratively to advance their careers, create and grow enterprises and industries, almost as an incidental by-product of their career-developing activities. I have argued elsewhere that it is as logical for the individual to consider the employing company to be an organizational resource for his or her career as it is for the company to consider the individual to be a human resource for its achievement of objectives (Inkson 2000).

METAPHORS FOR NEW FORMS OF CAREER

Once a basic metaphor is articulated, it can be developed to provide new perspectives on different types of career. As organizations become less structured, less planned, the scope for individuals to be creative in the construction of their own careers is enhanced. New lively metaphors are called for. Rather than organizations manufacturing careers, individuals 'craft' their careers (Poehnell and Amundson, Chapter 6). Craft involves self-customizing construction rather than production to a pre-specified blueprint. The notion of craftsmanship is nicely demonstrated and symbolized by the creative individualized work of the craft potter in contrast to the mass-produced uniformity of the modern ceramics factory (Inkson 1987). Mintzberg (1985) saw the same point when he used the metaphor of craftsmanship to describe his theories of 'emergent' business strategy, and illustrated the essay with a compelling set of images of a potter, without a plan, gradually shaping a lump of clay into an artifact.

Arthur, Inkson, and Pringle (1999) introduce metaphors of career that utilize the notion of the individual as a performer, in a musical context. They refer to notions of 'script' or 'score', arguing that traditional, occupational, and organizational careers have characteristics of scripted classical music. The contrasting image of present-day careers is jazz, already used by Hatch (1999) to good effect in the reconceptualization of organization structure. The jazz

metaphor emphasizes the improvisation, spontaneity, and self-directed the-
matic development in many contemporary careers (Arthur *et al.* 1999: 46). For
example:

Career actors may be 'furniture' (i.e. scripted) musicians, accepting career forms composed and scripted in corporations...or solo artists jamming joyfully (or anxiously) in
the ongoing composition or dissolution of their own lives. Playing corporate furniture
music may provide opportunities for virtuosity, or for collective involvement in an aesthetic activity...Improvising one's career brings greater opportunities for novel learning,
but also higher risks that one's solos will be boring and tuneless....The dissolving
architecture of great corporations challenges improvisers to blow their horns.
    But improvisation does not mean formlessness,...[nor] composing great work from
scratch....[Great jazz] improvisations [need]...basic forms... As jazz players cycle
and recycle, providing constant new experiences through the creative development of
past themes, career actors spiral their way into new industries, occupations, and
opportunities...

Another metaphor developed by Arthur, Inkson, and Pringle (1999) for the
'new careers' was that of improvisational street theater by multi-talented,
multi-roled improvisers, working not in closed troupes, but as 'roving trou-
badours'. A third metaphor, that of 'career capitalism', is based on a reversal
of the traditional model of human capital whereby organizations invest in
their people. Instead, the authors propose an obverse model where people
invest and accumulate their personal 'career capital' in the companies, occupations, industries, and other social arenas in which they work (Inkson and
Arthur 2001).
    As we can see, metaphors are fun. But they have a serious intent. Crafts-
people, jazz players, street performers, and capital investors all enact their art
spontaneously and creatively upon the world. Such artists are conscious of
goals, but they define the goals broadly defined, and change them by unconscious action as well as by rational thought. They experiment in small ways,
and build the learning from their experience into action that will develop a
better long-term result. They respond adaptively and creatively to changes in
the environment, such as unanticipated creative acts by others. A light touch
can lead to a heavyweight career.

USING METAPHOR IN PRACTICE

A related set of questions concerns career practice, for example by HR specialists, career counselors, and individuals seeking to develop their own
careers. Is metaphor potentially helpful to them? Under what circumstances

does metaphorical thinking constrain us to simplified stereotypes, or expand our vision to new and more productive ways of considering specific careers and of making choices and taking action to effect career development and change? Does metaphor assist action?

The use of metaphor to generate creative possibilities and solve applied problems is not new. In 1968 W. J. J. Gordon published a book called *Synectics*, proposing that scientific and engineering problems could be solved by teams that used metaphors creatively. Scientists and engineers were trained to think of inanimate machines and machine-parts as animals, or chemicals, or magical processes, or as self-willed human beings with problems to solve ('You *are* the system of gears; you *want* to increase the thrust. How do you do it?'). In one example, a team of engineers designing a new type of hydraulic jack and seeking to develop mechanisms that might be rigid or floppy according to changing requirements, considered the metaphors 'virus culture', 'chemical reaction', 'collapsible telescope', 'bicycle chain', and 'penis'. The metaphor that finally enabled them to solve the problem was that of 'Indian rope trick'. The process that enabled this success was that of encouraging physical scientists not only to think outside the conventional parameters of their disciplines, but to stretch their thinking flexibly through the use of metaphor to consider a range of possibilities.

In the field of organizational development, Dunford and Palmer (1993) present evidence of the high value that managers find in using different metaphors of organization to understand the companies that they work in. Morgan (1992) showed how the use of metaphors for organization (such as 'termite nest' and 'spider plant') applied by managers in the technique of 'imaginization' could assist in the development of a new 'art of creative management'. Could the metaphor principle be similarly used in personal and company-sponsored career development and in career guidance—'the art of creative career development'? Jepsen (1994) and Amundson (1998) suggest that metaphor and story, as forms of rhetoric, have great potential to bridge the gap between theory and practice in career counseling.

Presumably helping people to think creatively using metaphor, in the manner of Gordon (1968) and Morgan (1992), is a good start. Advisers may be able to use predetermined metaphors to encourage individuals to consider their own careers and career options creatively. New attitudes to career adaptation, career self-determination, and career learning may result. At the same time, 'new careers' metaphors such as jazz improvisation, self-scripted street theater, and career capital accumulation may be considered antithetical to, or at least very different from, traditional ideas of career planning, goal setting, and utilizing structured promotion systems in formal organizations. In such a context, it seems important that, again, multiple metaphors be used to provide a balanced picture.

CONCLUSION: CAN METAPHOR EXPRESS 'GRAND THEORY'?

The list of potential metaphors is apparently endless. Between them, such metaphors form a rich tapestry of alternative understandings of career phenomena. However, it is noticeable that the metaphors tend to be used in the literature piecemeal, to clarify specific views about careers, rather than in the sustained, complementary fashion employed by Morgan and others in relation to organizations.

Can we systematize, classify, and simplify the range of metaphors available to us? Can we develop (or even illustrate) grand theories of careers based on a set of metaphors or types of metaphor?

Barry (1999), for example, suggested a basic distinction into 'sense-making' metaphors such as 'anchor', and 'resource'; and 'propulsive' metaphors such as 'journey' and 'trajectory'. The passage provided earlier from Schein (1978: 22) is primarily a journey metaphor, but also mentions devices such as 'milestones' and the 'biological clock' that provide markers for sense making as the career proceeds. Is the 'journey' metaphor one of a series of meta-metaphors or master metaphors that could provide us with a template for careers similar to that Morgan provides for organizations? How are changes in career forms that simultaneously change the lexicon of career terminology (Arthur and Rousseau 1996: 370–82) also reflected in a new imagery? Are there archetypal metaphors for career—'journey', 'growth', 'component', 'match', 'performance'—that can be developed to gain a powerful new understanding of the domain? At present there seem many worthwhile utilizations of metaphor to understand and explain careers, but little sustained, integrated work. To develop such work seems well worth trying.

REFERENCES

Amundson, N. E. (1998), *Active Engagement: Enhancing the Career Counselling Process* (Richmond, BC: Ergon Communications).

Arnold, J. (1997), *Managing Careers into the Twenty-First Century* (London: Paul Chapman Publishing).

Arthur, M. B., and Rousseau, D. M. (1996) (eds.), *The Boundaryless Career: A New Employment Principle for a New Organizational Era* (Oxford: Oxford University Press).

——Inkson, K., and Pringle, J. K. (1999), *The New Careers: Individual Action and Economic Change* (London: Sage).

Barry, D. (1999), Personal communication.

Betz, N. E., Fitzgerald, L. F., and Hill, R. E. (1989), 'Trait-Factor Theories: Traditional Cornerstone of Career Theory', in M. B. Arthur, D. T. Hall, and B. S. Lawrence (eds.), *Handbook of Careers* (Cambridge: Cambridge University Press), 26–40.

Bird, A. (1996), 'Careers as Repositories of Knowledge: Considerations for Boundaryless Careers', in M. B. Arthur and D. M. Rousseau (1996) (eds.), *The Boundaryless Career: A New Employment Principle for a New Organizational Era* (Oxford: Oxford University Press), 150–68.

Cadin, L, Bailly-Bender, A.-F., and de Saint-Giniez, Veronique (2000), 'Exploring Boundaryless Careers in the French Context', in M. A Peiperl, M. B. Arthur, R. Goffee, and T. Morris (eds.), *Career Frontiers: New Conceptions of Working Lives* (Oxford: Oxford University Press), 228–55.

Casey, C. (1999), ' "Come, Join our Family": Discipline and Integration in Corporate Organizational Culture', *Human Relations*, 52/2: 155–78.

Cohen, T. (1978), 'Metaphor and the Cultivation of Intimacy', in S. Sacks (ed.), *On Metaphor* (Chicago: University of Chicago Press), 107–40.

DeFillippi, R. J., and Arthur, M. B. (2000), 'Career Creativity to Industry Influence: A Blueprint for the Knowledge Economy?', working paper for the London Business School conference on Career Creativity, 22–24 Mar.

Doving, E. (1996), 'In The Image of Man: Organizational Action, Competence, and Learning', in D. Grant and C. Oswick (eds.), *Metaphor and Organizations* (London: Sage), 185–99.

Dunford, R., and Palmer, I. (1993), 'Claims about Frames: Practitioners' Assessments of the Utility of Reframing', *Journal of Management Education*, 19/1: 96–105.

Farren, C. (1998), 'Sailing the Good Ship Career', *Training and Development* (Feb.), 42–6.

Gordon, W. J. J. (1968), *Synectics* (New York: Collier).

Grant, D. and Oswick, C. (1996) (eds.), *Metaphor and Organizations* (London: Sage).

Gunz, H. P. (1990), 'Careers and the Corporate Climbing Frame', *Leadership and Organization Development Journal*, 11/2: 17–24.

——Evans, M. G., and Jalland, R. M. (2000), 'Career Boundaries in a "Boundaryless" World', in M. A. Peiperl, M. B. Arthur, R. Goffee, and T. Morris (eds.), *Career Frontiers: New Conceptions of Working Lives* (Oxford: Oxford University Press), 24–53.

Hagevik, S. (1998), 'Career Models and Metaphors', *Journal of Environmental Health*, 61/5: 48.

Hall, D. T. (1976), *Careers in Organizations* (Glenview, Ill.: Scott, Foresman).

Hatch, M. J. (1999), 'Exploring the Empty Spaces of Organizing: How Improvisational Jazz Helps Redescribe Organizational Structure', *Organization Studies*, 20/1: 75–100.

Holland, J. L. (1992), *Making Vocational Choices: A Theory of Vocational Personalities and Work Environments*, 2nd edn. (Odessa, Fla.: Psychological Assessment Resources).

Hutchins, G. (1998), 'Paddling like Crazy', *Quality Progress*, 31/11: 144.

Inkson, K. (1987), 'The Craft Ideal and the Integration of Work', *Human Relations*, 40: 163–76.

——(1997), 'Organisation Structure and the Transformation of Careers', in T. Clark (ed.), *Advancement in Organisational Behaviour* (Aldershot: Ashgate Publishing), 165–86.

——(2000), 'Rewriting Career Development Principles for the New Millennium', in R. Weisener and B. Millett (eds.), *Management and Organizational Behaviour: Contemporary Challenges and Future Directions in Management* (Sydney: Wiley), 11–24.

——and Arthur, M. B. (2001), 'How to be a Successful Career Capitalist', *Organizational Dynamics*, 30/1: 48–61.

——Heising, A., and Rousseau, D. M. (2001), 'The Interim Manager: Prototype of the Twenty-First Century Worker?', *Human Relations*, 54/3: 259–84.

Jepsen, D. A. (1994), 'Relationships between Developmental Career Counseling Theory and Practice', in M. L. Savickas and B. W. Walsh (eds.), *Handbook of Career Counselling Theory and Practice* (Palo Alto, Calif.: Davies-Black), 135–53.

Levinson, D. J., and Associates (1978), *The Seasons of a Man's Life* (New York: Knopf).

Mangham, I. L. (1996), 'Some Consequences of Taking Gareth Morgan Seriously', in D. Grant and C. Oswick (eds.), *Metaphor and Organizations* (London: Sage), 21–36.

Mintzberg, H. (1985), 'Crafting Strategy', *Harvard Business Review*, 65/4: 66–75.

Morgan, G. (1980), 'Paradigms, Metaphors, and Puzzle Solving in Organization Theory', *Administrative Science Quarterly*, 25/4: 605–22.

Morgan, G. (1986), *Images of Organization* (Thousand Oaks, Calif.: Sage).

—— (1992), *Imaginization: The Art of Creative Management* (London: Sage).

—— (1998), *Images of Organization*, executive edn. (Thousand Oaks, Calif.: Sage).

Ortony, D. (1993), *Metaphor and Thought*, 2nd edn. (Cambridge: Cambridge University Press).

Peiperl, M. A., and Baruch, Y. (1997), 'Back to Square Zero: The Post-Corporate Career', *Organizational Dynamics*, 25/4: 7–22.

Pinder, C. C., and Bourgeois, V. W. (1982), 'Controlling Tropes in Administrative Science', *Administrative Science Quarterly*, 27/4: 641–52.

Ramsay, H. (1975), 'Firms and Football Teams', *British Journal of Industrial Relations*, 8: 396–400.

Raymond, E. S. (1998), 'The Cathedral and the Bazaar'; www.tuxedo.org/~esr/writings/cathedral-bazaar/cathedral-bazaar-1.html.

Reitman, F., and Schneer, J. S. (2000), 'Is the Traditional Career Path for Managers really Gone? Evidence from a Longitudinal Study of MBAs', paper given at the Academy of Management Meeting, Toronto, Aug.

Rosenbaum, J. E. (1989), 'Career Systems and Employee Misperceptions', in M. B. Arthur, D. T. Hall, and B. S. Lawrence (eds.), *Handbook of Careers* (Cambridge: Cambridge University Press), 329–53.

Rousseau, D. M. (1995), *Psychological Contracts in Organizations* (Thousand Oaks, Calif.: Sage).

Sagaria, M. A. (1989), 'Towards a Woman-Centred Theory of Careers: The Quilt Metaphor', *Journal of Employment Counseling*, 26/1: 11–15.

Schein, E. H. (1978), *Career Dynamics: Matching Individual and Organizational Needs* (Reading, Mass.: Addison-Wesley).

Sonnenfeld, J. A., and Peiperl, M. A. (1988), 'Staffing Policy as a Strategic Response: A Typology of Career Systems', *Academy of Management Review*, 13/4: 588–600.

Spain, A., and Hamel, S. (1993), 'The Tree Metaphor: A New Tool for Career Counselling for Women', *Canadian Journal of Counselling*, 27/3: 165–76.

Super, D. E. (1957), *The Psychology of Careers* (New York: Harper & Row).

—— (1992), 'Toward a Comprehensive Theory of Career Development', in D. H. Montross and C. J. Shinkman (eds.), *Career Development: Theory and Practice* (Springfield, Ill.: Charles C. Thomas), 35–64.

Weber, M. (1947), *The Theory of Social and Economic Organization* (New York: Free Press).

Weick, K. E. (1996), 'Enactment and the Boundaryless Career: Organizing as we Work', in M. B. Arthur and D. M. Rousseau (eds.), *The Boundaryless Career: A New Employment Principle for a New Organizational Era* (Oxford: Oxford University Press), 40–57.

3

Paths to Creativity for Knowledge-Intensive Workers

BIRGITTA SÖDERGREN

In the era of the 'knowledge society' many companies are becoming increasingly aware of the fact that their competitiveness, in terms of both customer value and shareholder value, is to an increasing extent based on knowledge. Also in society as a whole we can see that organizations play an important part in the development and spread of knowledge. Companies do not only create goods and services; they also create knowledge, for themselves, for individuals, and for society.

This also means that from the companies' perspective the 'knowledge creators'—that is, highly qualified employees—are crucial to the firm, although this is a category of employees that has not met with too much attention in earlier research or management theory. Many of these 'knowledge-intensive workers' (KIWs) (Starbuck 1992; Alvesson 1995) work as qualified specialists within the core areas of the firm.

The discussion of knowledge-intensive work is related to the creativity theme in at least three ways. First, knowledge-intensive work can be described as creative in itself—maybe not always in the artistic sense, like painters or writers, but clearly in the sense suggested by Gardner (1993). That is, important parts of KIWs' work are to define new questions, solve new problems, or create novel domains or arenas for their field of expertise. Secondly, at the personal level, KIWs are often engaged in creative careers (Anand, Peiperl, and Arthur, this volume), since their careers are knowledge based, rather than position based (Bird 1996). A knowledge-based career might be regarded as an individually and creatively designed journey, a Type 1 path, as discussed in the previous chapter, rather than following an already trodden, traditionally planned track (Inkson, Chapter 2).

Thirdly, the existence of KIWs also calls for new and more creative forms of management and human-resource management (HRM) activities.

Knowledge-intensive work and knowledge creating seem to be dependent on social processes, managerial styles, and a learning climate that differ from those supplied by many classical organizations in the rationalistic industrial society.

A good starting point to learn more about what kind of work conditions are needed in a knowledge-creating organization might be to ask the qualified specialists, KIWs themselves, how they perceive their role in the companies they work for. Is the modern, industrial company a good place to make a knowledge-based career? What about the managerial and leadership styles, control systems, and organizational structures? Is the learning climate supporting enough? What reward systems and career patterns are suitable to encourage the creation, development, and spread of knowledge?

These are questions that have been addressed in a qualitative study based on interviews with KIWs (or 'core specialists') in seven knowledge-intensive firms. The idea behind the research project has been to gain some further knowledge about the working conditions for specialists as seen from their own perspective, and about their views and thoughts about management and organization as it is presently practiced in the companies. My intention was also to get some ideas about the deeper meaning of knowledge-intensive work and knowledge-based careers.

In this chapter I will report some of the results from the study. The chapter will, however, start with a brief description about the social context—Swedish high-tech companies—in which the interviewees are working, as well as some definitions and methodological considerations.

THE EMERGENCE OF BOUNDARYLESS ORGANIZATIONS AND CAREERS

In Sweden, as elsewhere, many companies show clear signs of being under transformation, and entering the information-based society. More and more companies are becoming knowledge based, IT related, and increasingly dependent on continuous innovation.

Organizationally, large companies in Sweden are also becoming more 'boundaryless' (Arthur and Rousseau 1996a; Peiperl and Arthur 2000; Miles and Snow 1996). Companies are often organized in horizontal, process-oriented ways, the use of project organization is very frequent, and networks and virtual organizations are abundant. Increasing numbers of employees can choose to work on a consultative basis, and many employers are trying to find forms to enable the employees to work from their homes, or to apply flexible work hours.

Many business activities are also formed 'between' organizations—in networks and long-lasting relations between subcontractors and customers.

Partnerships and strategic alliances, across national as well as organizational borders, are of vital importance. There are also many small consultancy firms 'circulating' as satellites around large organizations. Accordingly, 'cellular' organizations emerge (Miles and Snow 1996).

Paradoxically, though, at the same time the number of mergers and acquisitions has increased, making large companies even larger. Many of the most successful knowledge-intensive and knowledge-creating firms operating in Sweden are large, multinational companies, some of them Swedish, others owned from abroad. And, although many firms are trying to be progressive in their efforts to develop new forms of management and organization, many of the companies are still managed as if traditional workers were dominating the workforce, and as if industrial mass production rather than knowledge creation was the main issue.

ABOUT KNOWLEDGE-INTENSIVE WORK

What is knowledge-intensive work? Above I have already used 'knowledge-intensive workers' (KIWs) as a term signifying qualified specialists. To find an expression that will give a good description of this varying and heterogeneous group of employees is not easy, but the term KIW has been used by Alvesson (1995), following Starbuck's use (1992) of 'KIF' for knowledge-intensive firms.

It is also difficult to draw a clear line between knowledge-intensive work and other forms of work. It is, for instance, sometimes argued that all kinds of work are knowledge intensive, and that it is only a matter of how we define knowledge. Some researchers have, on the other hand, claimed that professionals/specialists/KIWs are a special category of employees, not 'blue-collar' workers and not managers, but rather a 'third class' of the working world (Freidson 1986). The US National Labor Relations Board (NLRB) states in its formal definition of 'professional employees' that they are engaged in work:

- predominantly intellectual and varied in character;
- involving the consistent exercise of discretion and judgment in its performance;
- of such a character that the output produced or the result accomplished cannot be standardized in relation to a given period of time;
- requiring knowledge of an advanced type in a field of science or learning customarily acquired by a prolonged course of specialized intellectual instruction or study in an institution of higher learning (Freidson 1986).

Professionals and specialists are sometimes, though not always, authorized through some kind of a credential system—for example, occupational license, certificate, or specialized education (see also Tolbert 1996). Sometimes a professional trade evolves, characterized by common professional ethics, fraternities, and so on.

TOWARD KNOWLEDGE-BASED CAREERS?

The interview study indicated that KIWs, not surprisingly, focus on the possibilities of learning and knowledge creation more than on formal positions in
their perception of a positive development at work. Learning possibilities might
even be more important than money ('above a certain level, of course', as the
interviewees often hastily added, when this matter was brought into the
conversation).

But how deep has this shift in career perception reached? Are we seeing the
emergence of a new kind of knowledge-based careers, as suggested by Bird
(1996)—that is, careers that are concerned with the content and meaning of
work experiences, rather than with shifts in formal status? Or is the industrial,
hierarchical, 'bounded' perspective on careers still dominating the development?

Another way of putting the question is to analyze whether the ideas of
knowledge-intensive work is weakening the system as a whole. Weick (1996)
describes the occurring transformation in society towards boundaryless organizations (and, accordingly, the emerging boundaryless careers) as 'weak
situations'. A weak situation (following the ideas of Mischel 1977) is characterized by the absence of uniform expectancies concerning the desired
behavior, few established guides for actions, and unclear incentives for performance. In a weakening situation boundaries begin to dissolve, 'traditions
become less prescriptive and institutions become less structured. Traditional
career scripts may become less suitable as guides for action and interaction'
(Weick 1996: 45). Professional roles become less well defined.

Weick also notes that, in weak situations, local groups of people tend to make
sense of uncertainty by a process of collective trial and error that resembles an
evolutionary system (Weick 1996: 44). Via collective improvisation, the creation
of new images and new ways of organizing, people tend to bring order into
chaos. Such processes of self-design, Weick argues, will in the long run affect
the whole system in a bottom-up process. The whole system (society or
organization) will be affected by these micro-processes of enactment.

In this case it would mean that emerging new perceptions of work and
careers among individuals, in teams or project groups, would in the long run
bring about changes in the company as a whole. When local processes of self-
design strive for boundaryless, knowledge-based careers, the company will not
be able to stick to traditional norms about career behavior, such as planned
hierarchical advancement or promoting the most qualified specialists into
managers. Instead, organizations will have to find new ways of forming HRM
policies and career opportunities to meet the demands and expectations of the
KIWs. Since I found the idea of the weakening system intriguing, I have in this
chapter analyzed the interview data from the perspective of a weakening
organizational situation.

ABOUT THE EMPIRICAL STUDY

The research study was carried out in seven Swedish high-tech companies (most of them large, multinational, private companies, but the sample also included one smaller company and one governmental knowledge-intensive unit). Thirty-five people were interviewed, in the form of 2.5–4-hour long, personal, semi-structured interviews. The interviewees were chosen from the companies' core competence areas. The interviewees were highly qualified specialists, or 'KIWs', in high-tech professions, their age ranging from 28 to 58 years. They represent companies in the telecom industry, pharmaceutical industry, IT sector, military technology, advanced health-care equipment, radiation/nuclear technology, and the paper industry.

The work of the specialists/KIWs in the study is generally characterized by great complexity, and the expected quality or success of their output is often hard to judge in advance (and sometimes even in retrospect). More often than not they work 'on the verge of the unknown', and accordingly have vague job descriptions. Their work depends to a substantial degree on personal judgment and personal intuition. Their work is primarily immaterial, taking the form of analyses, problem solving, and so on. Not only is the output of their work physical, such as tasks performed, problems solved, projects completed, but the output itself is knowledge (Nonaka and Tekuchi 1995). They work as engineers, radio physicists, pharmaceutical experts, IT-developers, designers of health-care equipment, telecom systems, and so on.

One reason for choosing core specialists was that they are often key persons of strategic importance in knowledge-intensive firms. Another reason was that there are several studies focusing on the management of knowledge-intensive firms (e.g. Starbuck 1992; Sveiby 1994; Alvesson 1995), but relatively few studies have taken the perspective of the knowledge-intensive employees themselves (e.g. Pelz and Andrews 1966; Kunda 1992). I also had a personal interest in finding out more about this work category, since I had previously made several empirical studies with managers and traditional employees (regarding decentralization, process-based organization, and learning organization).

The interviewees were not managers (with the exception of temporary assignments as project leaders), since the idea was to discuss management with qualified people who for some reason had chosen not to make a managerial career, but had an employee's perspective. For similar reasons, the choice of interviewees did not include consultants selling their time to external clients, since the role as a free-market consultant was assumed to have its own logic, which has also been studied elsewhere (Werr 1999).

Neither is this a study of the typical dot-com employee. For some reason or another, the interviewed KIWs had chosen to stay with the larger company for some time. Thus, they were not typical 'zig-zag people', freelancers, project workers, or job-hoppers who 'pack their own parachutes' from day to day (Hirsch 1987; Baker and Aldrich 1996).

One might ask why a relatively large number of key people, with core competence and very important skills, are still around in big organizations, since there is obviously a clear option not to be a long-term employee. One answer might be that large organizations still dominate society (Perrow 1996), and therefore employees are dependent on them. Another possible answer, coming from theories on marketing and business strategy, would be that KIWs might be dependent on company brand names, which add value to their 'personal brand'. A third idea might be, as suggested by Gunz, Evans, and Jalland (2000), that many companies are characterized by intellectual differentiation and deep specialization, long project cycles and/or a strong need for commercial secrecy, which reduce mobility between firms. A fourth answer, suggested in this study, might be that the tacit and interactive nature of knowledge demands organizational settings where long relations can be built and were various kinds of knowledge can interact in complex and intricate patterns.

As always in qualitative research it is important to be aware of the context in which the research is carried out, and carefully ask whether the results can be generalized into other contexts. In this case, a clear contextual factor is the Swedish culture, since all the interviewees were working in Sweden. However, my belief is that the results might also be applicable in knowledge-intensive firms in other countries, since the studied companies were acting on a global market. Many of their business partners were from other countries (USA, Japan, and so on), and most of the interviewees had international work experience. Also, in terms of strategy, human resources organization, and management, Swedish firms are to a large extent influenced by international research as well as by international consultancy firms operating in Sweden.

WHAT KNOWLEDGE-INTENSIVE WORKERS SAY

In this and the following sections I will report some of the findings from the study. In this section I have analyzed the interview data from the perspective of a weakening organizational situation, according to Weick (1996)—see discussion above—trying to answer the question whether we can see clear signs of knowledge-based careers. In the following section, I will discuss the importance of tacit knowledge in knowledge-intensive work and raise the question to what extent companies are creating arenas or processes that enable the development and spread of tacit knowledge. Then the interactive nature of knowledge-intensive work is analyzed, and the question is raised whether knowledge-intensive companies are managed with regard to the need for community rather than agency in knowledge-intensive organizations. Finally, the potential clash between the strong managerial construction and the still much weaker knowledge-based construction is discussed, with its potential effects on knowledge-intensive companies.

Creative, knowledge-based careers versus organizational norms

Are we, then, already in a weakening situation? Do KIWs engage in creative, knowledge-based careers, and to what extent will this weaken the traditional career system and established company policies? Data from the study indicate that KIWs have weak visions of knowledge-based careers, that they nevertheless do experience them, and that, at an organizational level, traditional careers are reinforced because of strong managerial constructions.

KIWs' visions of knowledge-based careers. On an explicit level (what the interviewees articulated when speaking about career matters), KIWs were quite unaware of their changing career situation in the context of a boundaryless and knowledge-intensive organization. They did not seem to have a common language or a common identity as knowledge workers, and they were not particularly articulate, either about what a knowledge-based career might look like, or about what consequences or possibilities of making a knowledge-based career might be.

On the contrary, most of the interviewees stressed that they were not so much into 'the career thing' themselves. In fact, the word career might even have a negative connotation, an established company path, leading to managerial positions—that is, a part of the 'strong' system. 'The life of a KIW' was rather defined as a 'non-career', as illustrated by the following interview statement: 'If you want to make a career, you should follow the established career pattern. You have to be a project leader and a generalist, then you might be promoted, but this means you have to leave the specialist area. And God knows if you will ever be able to return again.'

KIWs' experiences of knowledge-based careers. On an implicit level, on the other hand, when not using the word 'career' but instead speaking of important aspects of work and personal development, the interviewees' statements clearly indicate that they use knowledge-based strategies for personal development. In this sense, a career is 'the accumulations of information and knowledge embodied in skills, expertise and relationship networks' (Bird 1996: 150). The content of a career is located in what is learned, in perspectives that are acquired or changed over time. A career plateau is not when you stay at the same job, but when you are not learning.

The interviewed KIWs were literally magnets of knowledge—they tended to 'gravitate' toward creative and knowledge-maximizing settings (that is, new problems or new aspects of earlier problems, customers, or colleagues with interesting knowledge). In most cases, their careers might be viewed as knowledge expeditions rather than stepwise shifts of status:

It is all about learning. Not the kind of learning that you get from attending courses—if there should be any courses in this field I would probably have to give them myself... It is rather about the kind of learning that comes from working on interesting and difficult problems. To develop, I need to work for a company where they have that kind of problems.

Reinforcement of traditional careers. However, at the organizational level, the weakening, transformational scenario still seemed to be quite remote. It is possible that a local strong system—that is, a 'new paradigm' or a new social construction—has just recently started building up around knowledge-based careers at the individual or team level. But, in general, the official HRM policies and competence strategies of the firm are more suited to reinforce traditional managerial careers, or to regulate classical conditions of employment, than to take full advantage of the skills, energy, and superb networks that are the contribution from the KIWs.

One explanation seems to be the existence of another 'local system' that is very healthy and strong but works almost in the opposite direction—namely, the managerial system, or managerial construction (Sandberg 2001). Managerial roles are often clearly defined, the managerial language is quite well developed (almost growing into a professional language of its own), and the managerial career patterns are easy to understand. There are reasonably clear expectations on how to behave as a manager, and the managerial 'scripts' are reinforced by a 'toolbox' containing methods and techniques that further reinforce the managerial role (Södergren and Söderholm 2001).

Data from the interview study thus suggest that, to the KIWs themselves, the idea of a knowledge-based career is still a weak social construction, whilst the classical managerial career pattern is a strong construction. Therefore, at the organizational level, traditional careers are still being reinforced, and an educated guess is that this imbalance will remain for at least some years to come. In the following sections I will discuss some further aspects of these competing organizational logics, one weak and the other strong.

TACIT KNOWLEDGE IN KNOWLEDGE-INTENSIVE WORK

Data from the study indicated that knowledge-intensive work is loaded with tacit knowledge, to an even higher degree than might have been expected (see also Morris 2000). KIWs in the study frequently expressed the importance of tacit knowledge in their work, mostly without using the term explicitly, since 'tacit knowledge' is not yet a widespread notion in the corporate world. Instead, it is referred to as gut feeling, business intuition, experience, educated guesses, beliefs, suspicions, inklings, and hints. The tacit dimension can also be referred to as something that goes beyond formal competence: 'Competence? Well formally we are all competent. But the difference is that some of us have the knowledge that sort of is in between facts. The kind of competence that makes it possible to see beyond...'.

What then is tacit knowledge according to research literature? Tacit knowledge, following Polanyi's classical work (1967), is the knowing that we cannot tell explicitly.

Moreover, according to Polanyi, tacit knowledge has a specific from–to direction. The individual's attention is directed from formal facts, details, and so on, to the underlying meaning, practical implications, and thus deeper understanding of a field. Polanyi exemplifies this with a skilled pianist, who easily becomes 'paralyzed' if he or she pays too much attention to the finger settings, but creates great art, if he or she dwells on the musical experience. His or her attention is directed from the technical details to the result, the music. In a similar way, a skilled doctor will be more able to make his or her diagnosis if he or she moves from formal knowledge such as symptoms, test results, and so on, to the patient as an individual who is going to become healthy.

All kinds of professionals use tacit knowledge, Polanyi argues, and very often to make the most fundamental choices—for instance, to identify the right problem or to recognize a good solution (sometimes even before the problem has been identified).

But the tacit dimension is not always possible to evoke. Tacit knowledge has many roots, and, according to Polanyi, important ingredients are empathy and indwelling—that is, really to understand the situation or the person presenting a problem, being deeply present and engaged in the problem. A sense of meaning and direction and the presence of positive emotions will also make the mobilization of tacit knowledge easier. This is also in accordance with modern research on the importance of emotions and 'emotional intelligence' when making logical analyses (Goleman 1995; Pert 1997).

From recent debate on competence in work life, one might have had the impression that tacit knowledge is the opposite of explicit knowledge—you can have either one or the other. However, Polanyi (1967) clearly shows that this is not the case; on the contrary, the more formal knowledge you have, the better the basis for tacit knowledge. But he concludes that it is not until you internalize these theories that you are able to make new discoveries—when you no longer see the theories as theories, but use them to create meaning of a higher order. Tacit knowledge is mobilized when you 'live' your knowledge.

Therefore, working on the tacit dimension of knowledge can create feelings of being out in the blue, being vague, or even 'irrational'. 'We can't explain why we had to follow this track—we just knew we had to', one respondent said, smiling rather sheepishly, referring to how a new technique had been formed some years previously, a technique that was about to make an almost revolutionary breakthrough in the company.

This embarrassment may be a sign that tacit knowledge is not really accepted as 'true' knowledge. Polanyi (1967) concludes that it is a widespread misbelief that details are true just because they are more tangible. It is, instead, empathy, or dwelling in other persons or problems, that creates full knowledge. While specialists work with combinations of explicit and tacit knowledge, the managerial system focuses on the explicit dimension.

Tacit and explicit knowledge

Nonaka (1991) and Nonaka and Tekuchi (1995), building on the notion of tacit knowledge, have suggested four types of interplay between tacit and explicit knowledge in the knowledge-creation process. These are:

- *Socialization* (tacit–tacit). Tacit knowledge is transferred to build another person's tacit knowledge (for instance, via apprenticeship).
- *Articulation* (tacit–explicit). Tacit knowledge is formalized or made explicit.
- *Combination* (explicit–explicit). Explicit facts or theories are exchanged and combined.
- *Internalization* (explicit–tacit). Explicit knowledge is made a part of a person's tacit knowledge.

Data from the study indicate that KIWs are to a high degree using all four types of knowledge creation. However, most important to them, are situations where two (or more) specialists work together, where they both must mobilize their respective tacit dimension. This is an exchange of tacit knowledge that goes somewhat deeper than Nonaka's term socialization, since it is not the case of an apprentice learning from the master, but rather a meeting of the tacit knowledge embedded in equally qualified minds.

Such a situation is likely to occur when specialists work together on a problem that enables mutual development of meaning as the work proceeds. An exchange of tacit knowledge is also likely to occur when KIWs are engaged in a common process of enactment or, in Polanyi's terms, when they share a joint attention to a specific goal.

The managerial system's focus

Of particular interest is then: to what extent are knowledge-based companies able to handle the growth, mobilization, and spread of tacit knowledge inside and outside the firm? Observations from the companies in the study, as well as my previous research on learning and change in organizations (Södergren 1997), give the impression that both managerial and HRM practices are quite far from focusing on the tacit dimension (see also Baumard 1999).

Instead, many firms seem to be developing managerial techniques and control systems that give priority to the explicit dimensions of knowledge. The development of competence profiles focuses primarily on formal, not tacit, skills and abilities. Reward systems focus mainly on formal merits. Systems for knowledge management—for instance, those introduced by well-known consultancy firms—also focus on the combination and spread of explicit knowledge. In recent work on measuring the knowledge dimension—for instance, intellectual capital (see Edvinsson and Malone 1997)—the development of numerical values of skills and competencies is emphasized (see also Södergren and Söderholm 2001).

If Polanyi (1967) was right about the vulnerable nature of tacit knowledge, the use of social engineering techniques to focus on specific parts or details of complex knowledge may even destroy some of the tacit dimension, instead of bringing further clarity to the matter: 'Scrutinize closely the particulars of a comprehensive entity and their meaning is effaced, our conception of the entity is destroyed' (Polanyi 1967: 18–19). In summary, a crucial task in a knowledge-based firm seems to be to create arenas, career patterns, and a learning climate that will enhance the 'joint mobilization' of tacit knowledge.

Understandably, though, this may also be a difficult process, both for managers operating from a more rationalistic logic, but also for the KIWs who are working under an unclear and seldom outspoken logic. The interviews show that tacit knowledge is not always regarded as something real or justifiable, sometimes not even in the eyes of the person who owns it. Moreover, the mobilization of tacit knowledge may be more time-consuming, since it relies on a more reflective mode, which is not entirely congruent with companies' current striving to cut costs and reduce lead times.

It can also be difficult, since a genuine dialogue between tacit fields of knowledge might be a very unexpected, emotional, and sometimes frightening process, since new knowledge always changes its creator (May 1975). As Weick (1996) points out, learning is about being vulnerable.

Weick also reminds us that Karl Deutsch's definition of power was 'the ability not to have to learn'. If stated publicly in a modern organization, Deutsch's definition would probably be firmly rejected, since such an attitude is not in accordance with modern leadership policies. Still, one might suspect that, in dealing with both managerial and specialist careers, firms have a tendency to reward the master, not the learner, and the exploitation, rather than the exploration.

In the process of creating viable conditions for knowledge-based careers, we probably need therefore to create a different definition of power. Power is the ability to learn all the time. To be able to lead a knowledge-creating process, you have to understand the openness and vulnerability that are present in a learning situation. And you need to be a learning partner rather than somebody controlling other people.

THE INTERRELATED NATURE OF
LEARNING PROCESSES

The study also shows that knowledge-intensive work is to a high degree based on personal relations and frequent interactions between the KIWs and their environment. Somewhat contrary to my initial beliefs—that highly specialized employees would be more interested in their personal development, and more individualistic in their approaches to learning—the interviewees, almost without exception, stated that advanced learning and knowledge creation have to take place through collaboration, in dialogue with others and as a collective and interactive process.

The KIWs seemed to share an intuitive awareness that the 'true' knowledge creating lies in the links between individuals. Knowledge creation is an interactive process, and the receiver of information is equally important to the process as the sender.

This interrelational perspective on learning is also congruent with recent literature—for instance, research on professions (Freidson 1986), organizational learning (Senge 1990; Isaacs 1999; Senge *et al.* 1999), social constructionism (Sandberg 2001), classical psychological theory on creativity (May 1975), studies of boundaryless careers (Arthur and Rousseau 1996*a*, *b*), theories on self-designing processes (Weick 1979, 1996) and relational marketing (Reichheld and Teal 1996).

I will discuss some theoretical implications further below, but first some glimpses from the KIWs' perspective on the interactive nature of learning summarized under five different themes: (1) continuous role redefinition, (2) team learning, (3) learning along the flow, (4) learning via networks, and (5) leadership as a support for learning.

Continuous role redefinition

The work of a KIW seems to entail a more or less continuous redefinition of professional work roles. The stories told by the interviewees showed that the same individual very often has different professional roles in different work contexts. In one situation, they may be the leading experts, while in another just giving a marginal contribution to a work activity. In some cases, they may act as a project leader, in others they are just members of the team. At times they also need to engage in hands-on production or implementation activities. Their organizational status might also vary; the same individual might in one case have formal authority toward others in the organization, while in another case serve as an adviser. Their role towards the customer may also vary, from very close collaboration as partners, to the role of a negotiating counterpart.

It was striking to hear how frequently, informally, and seemingly without friction the KIWs could enter quite different work roles, often without even reflecting upon it. Compared to experience from my earlier research on managers and traditional employees, I could not help noting this almost constant role redefinition. From time to time, it may also be unclear whether the KIWs' professional identity or their organizational identity should guide their behavior—for instance, in cases where their individual interpretation of the ethical principles of their profession collides with strategic decisions taken by top management.

Constant role redefinition might also be an example of boundaryless careers in the terms of Arthur and Rousseau (1996a), but in this case 'boundaryless' without shifting employer.

The varying professional roles also seem to be an interesting source of learning, since a shift in work role also means a shift in perspectives. In terms of interactive learning, it is a 'source of learning between yourself and yourself', as one interviewee put it, and continued: 'I might observe myself acting from different positions, thereby not only adding to the factual knowledge, but also learning more about how different expectations and different environments affect my work.'

Team learning

'My favorite organization? My team. Definitely my team. I would be nothing at all without my team,' one technical engineer stated in an interview.

During the interviews the team organization emerged as a true favorite work form when learning and knowledge creation are the task. And further analysis of the material shows that the team is predominantly used as a learning device.

A good team should, not surprisingly, consist of individuals with different, but interrelated, skills and competencies. It is an interesting matter, though, how to identify 'interrelated' skills. It seemed to be very important that the gap between different people's respective skills is wide enough to add value, but narrow enough to make bridging possible. It also seemed to be of importance for the KIWs to get access to each other's tacit knowledge. One way of achieving this is to work together for quite a long time, as observed by the following interviewee: 'You need to get close enough to each other as individuals, to get insights into the essence of a knowledge area that you need for a task, but are not able to develop yourself.'

Learning along the flow

When speaking about the company or organization as a whole, the interviewed KIWs tended to prefer process-based or work-flow-based organizations, where it is possible to follow the value-added chain or production process, from innovation to implementation. Many interviewees liked the idea of being able to follow 'their' product or solution all the way—'you have to see what happens to it in reality'. Contrary to what might have been suspected, most interviewed KIWs were truly interested in customers—but not primarily, as their company marketers might have hoped, to develop unique selling points or competitive advantages, but rather as a real-life experiment: 'Of course customers are interesting. They are interesting because they represent the final interaction between a product, system or solution and the people who are going to use it or benefit from it.'

Learning via networks

The KIWs also regard their personal networks as a great source of learning. Since this finding is in accordance with earlier theory (see e.g. Bird 1996; DeFillippi and Arthur 1996; Raider and Burt 1996; Stein 1996; Baumard 1999), I will just let a few interview statements illustrate three ways of using personal networks: networks for knowledge validation, networks for staying ahead, and networks for action, problem solving, and business development.

When you work via the Internet, and get access to more and more relevant information, research findings, and so on, you might think you need less personal contacts. But I think, actually, it is the opposite way around. Since you come across more and more data, it is more important than ever that you have a strong personal network. You have to be able to call somebody in the right position to get a validity check. Are the authors serious? Can we trust these findings?

I use my network as a private university. If I speak with the right people long enough, I might get conversant on a subject, that might have taken me years if I were to find it out for myself by reading books...And when a field of knowledge is emerging there are no seminars or educational programs, so you have to speak with people. Courses will not be organized until the knowledge already is beginning to mature...

Networks are really strategic and they are definitely capable of organized action. I have several examples of important business problems that were solved for free, just because I knew the right person. Some of my networking has led to quite profitable business solutions. But of course this kind of contact has to be reciprocal. If you exploit your contacts beyond what is considered to be fair, you will soon find yourself, very gently, and very subtly, cut out from the really important discussions.

Networking can also have a tacit dimension, something that is latent, resting in an organization, waiting to be of use, as illustrated by the following interview statement:

My job is to create an invisible web of knowledge concerning the Y-area. The idea is that we cannot know in advance what applications might come up. But if certain key people know about this way of working, they will probably evoke it the day they need it. It is very difficult to foresee when and where this demand will occur. It is like planting seeds. You never know which ones will grow.

Thus, knowledge creation is a process, the result of which is likely to occur at some place other than the initial place of knowledge generation. KIWs can sometimes make a more important contribution when spreading rather than gathering knowledge. Therefore, the most important contributions might also be the most difficult to trace.

Leadership as a support for learning

One question posed in the study concerned what kind of leadership would be desirable in a knowledge-intensive environment. Data from the interviews indicate the following.

- In spite of the high degree of personal autonomy in knowledge intensive work, KIWs perceived leadership to be very important.
- Leadership at the local level was the most crucial to create a learning climate.
- At the local level, KIWs stressed the relational, rather than the trans-actional, dimension of leadership as being the most important.

Although there was no widespread dissatisfaction with managers ('we do communicate', 'we have open doors'), there also seemed to be some room for improvement. And the direction of improvement was clearly toward more genuine dialogue and more interactions around the knowledge area. Interestingly enough, among the things that were not asked for were clearly stated goals, clear responsibilities, more structure, or better quantitative feedback. Rather, the ideas on what leadership could be or how they could act to handle a process of knowledge creation included the following.

- 'They should ask the right questions, not deliver answers.'
- 'They should support the individuals' learning processes.'
- 'A leading member of the team.'
- 'Being a part of the learning process, not observing from the outside.'
- 'Tutor', 'partner', 'coach', 'mentor'.
- 'Primus inter pares' (the first among equals).
- 'A processor, not a professor.'
- 'Keep less distance.'
- 'Not so much prestige!'

The requested leadership roles seemed to have much in common with some 'alternative' leadership roles suggested in earlier literature—for instance, 'consultative leadership' (Sandberg and Targama 1998), 'servant leadership' (Greenleaf 1977), or 'communion leadership' (Senge et al. 1999).

From a career perspective it is also interesting to note that the idea of becoming a manager is less attractive, the more decoupled from the learning process managerial activities are perceived to be, as illustrated by the following short example.

A top manager in one of the companies mentioned that he was worried that so many people with important key competencies were kept outside the strategic dialogue: 'The strategic information is only transmitted and discussed among the managers. Then it is their job to transfer the information to next level. I guess we miss that, sometimes.' A KIW in the same company confirmed this picture—he was not on the send-list to receive strategic information. But he formulated the conclusion the other way around: 'You cannot help feeling sorry for the management. They are cut out from the most strategically important dialogue—the one which occurs at the organizational core.'

THE GAP BETWEEN KNOWLEDGE-INTENSIVE WORK AND MANAGERIAL PRACTICE

The results from the study presented above thus indicate that there might exist a gap between the emerging, but still weak, KIW perspective versus the presently much stronger classical and rationalistic managerial perspective.

If these findings are correct, they also suggest that there is a need for creative forms of management, new career patterns, and human-resource (HR) activities with the purpose of creating organizational conditions better suited for knowledge-intensive work. The direction needed seems to be toward more focus on the tacit dimension as an important part of knowledge creating, and more focus on interaction and collaboration rather than further individualization and fragmentization in organizations.

In this section some theoretical as well as practical implications of the gap between knowledge-intensive work and managerial practice will be further discussed.

Relations versus transactions

In earlier research on careers, distinctions have been made between transactional and relational contracts between employer and employees (Rousseau 1990; Mirvis and Hall 1996). A transactional contract is defined in terms of money in exchange for the completion of a specific task in a given time. A relational contract, on the other hand, is not time bound, 'rather, it establishes an ongoing relationship between the person and the organization' (Mirvis and Hall 1996: 247).

Weick (1996) uses the related terms of 'agency' and 'communion' to describe the degree of individualism versus collaboration in knowledge creation. Agency is the more individualistic dimension and evokes images of self-assertive individuals who want to be judged by concrete achievement, people who try to take control of their environment and show independence. They also tend to have feelings of outer rather than inner development and of separation rather than affiliation (Weick 1996: 46).

Communion, on the other hand, is about tolerance, trust, being oriented to the present and non-contractual cooperation. Referring to Marshall (1989), Weick also notes that communion is very closely related to the notion of learning, and involves, for instance, flexibility, openness, and the acceptance of change. Communion sees itself as part of a wider context of interacting influences. Action based in communion may be significant, but largely invisible and difficult to disentangle. It may mean work forms where a person shapes the environment for others, or engage in mutually empowering relationships (Marshall 1989; Weick 1996). Communion is seldom fully recognized, and therefore not formally rewarded.

It can be observed from the discussion above that the different forms of learning through interaction identified by the interviewed KIWs (teamwork, networking, working along the flow, role redefinition, and close interaction with leaders) are of a relational rather than a transactional nature, and focus on communion rather than agency. Crucial in knowledge creation is not that you 'buy and sell' knowledge but that you 'live' your knowledge together with others, with whom you also interact in creating your world. Thus, personal qualities such as trust and interpersonal skills become important.

A problem from the perspective of knowledge-intensive workers seems to be that established policies and practices in large companies seldom support the relational dimension of knowledge-intensive work. The classical managerial social construction tends to favor agency rather than communion, and transactions rather than relations.

Examples of this are HRM activities aimed at developing individual competence profiles, rather than reinforcing team learning, as well as the focus on individually based wages and bonuses. Some KIWs also discussed problems that occurred when working together with colleagues in other departments, when managers might not always encourage work across organizational boundaries that does not contribute immediately to their own unit. To initiate work outside one's own domain, thus, might meet with disapproval.

Managers versus KIWs

Thus, we can see that the still weak but emerging knowledge-based construction runs contrary to the managerial construction when it comes to focus on agency versus communion, as well as the focus on explicit versus tacit

Table 3.1. Two conflicting perspectives on the essence of work

Issue	Managerial perspective	Knowledge-intensive worker's perspective
Power	Formal authority	Knowledge-based power
Competence	Explicit knowledge favoured	Tacit knowledge important
Structure	Important to respect boundaries	Important to cross boundaries
Degree of strength in the system (Weick)	Strong situation, norms well established	Weak situation waiting to be constructed
Time	is money	is learning
Professional roles	Fixed	Unclear, flexible
Collaboration focus	Agency	Communion
Career style	Change in hierarchical position	Knowledge-based career

knowledge. There is also an imbalance in the perspective on power, career pattern, time allocation, and the need for clear structures. These findings are summarized in Table 3.1.

It is important to note that in a sense the managerial system is also a local, self-designing system, reinforcing itself via the development of a 'managerial language', the establishment of norms, and so on. If the contents of Table 3.1 are correct, then there is a risk that the gap between the managerial system and the KIWs' work is widening, leading to possible conflicts and decreasing efficiency in knowledge-creating organizations.

Needed: a new form of dialogue

One interesting question is how to develop a new construction for the management of KIWs, and how such a construction process could occur. Fig. 3.1, (suggested by my colleague Lars Fredriksson), shows three possible ways in which the scenario can evolve.

As can be seen in Fig. 3.1, one way is to just let the transformation happen (arrow 1) and let the KIWs and 'the boundaryless world' be the driving force. If (or when) a new 'knowledge-based' construction becomes strong enough among the KIWs, it will weaken the organization and force the managerial system to adapt, in the way suggested by Weick (1996). Companies will have to create new career opportunities, reward systems, employee contracts, and so on to be able to attract and retain KIWs.

Another way is to make managerial initiatives, to 'invent' new managerial techniques that will be suitable for managing KIWs (arrow 2). If the managerial construction changes, so will the role of the KIWs.

A third way is to try to find the short cut (arrow 3). This can probably be accomplished only via a 'joint venture' between managers and KIWs. The 'third

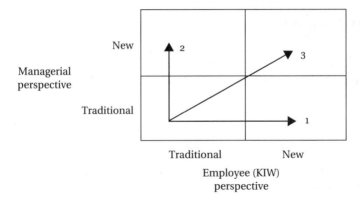

Fig. 3.1. Transformation of the managerial system when managing KIWs.

way' is likely to be achieved only via a genuine dialogue, where both parties are willing to share their respective basic assumptions and mindsets. This kind of dialogue needs to be closely linked to the business and the specific form of knowledge creating that is actually taking place in the company. Basic values and norms need to be discussed as well as the interests of companies, managers, and KIWs.

Of the three ways I can observe both no. 1 and no. 2 taking place in Swedish companies today. Arrow 1 is represented by many small, often IT-related companies, whose employees often work in a boundaryless world—at least as long as the demands on ever increasing shareholder value have not forced the small companies to merge into big conglomerates. A development according to arrow 1 can also be observed in large companies, driven by demands or even threats from KIWs, demanding new working conditions. So far, however, we have seen more of decoupling, with conflicts as a consequence, rather than mutual evolution.

In some firms, managers work according to arrow 2, trying to adapt managerial praxis to a learning context under labels such as 'learning organization', 'knowledge management', 'management of intellectual capital', and so on. In many cases, though, these methods seem to fail, since they are not taken too seriously by the KIWs.

Unfortunately, today I see very few proactive and joint approaches in accordance with arrow 3. I sincerely hope, though, that this is a passing stage, since, personally I am quite convinced that many knowledge-intensive organizations would be better off if they could find ways to reinforce and develop competence-based strategies, knowledge-based careers, and a leadership that maximized learning and knowledge creation. Since the strategies of tomorrow are based on the innovation and learning processes that occur today, I believe this is a strategic issue that will affect the long-term competitiveness for knowledge-intensive firms.

CONCLUSION

In this chapter I have described a tension that might exist in knowledge-intensive organizations between a strong and well-established managerial system, on the one hand, and an emerging, but still weak, knowledge-based work logic, assumed by knowledge-intensive workers (KIWs), on the other. I have also tried to illustrate that the work of a KIW is characterized by the following aspects:

- In highly specialized work the most important knowledge dimension is the tacit, rather than the explicit, knowledge.
- KIWs' creation of knowledge takes place via a multitude of interactions and personal relations, across organizational and professional boundaries, rather than via individual learning processes.
- The professional roles of KIWs can be described as very flexible and constantly changing knowledge expeditions, rather than clear, hierarchical positions.

A dilemma in the studied companies has been that the established managerial construction—that is, the ideals, values, and established practice about how to manage an organization—is focusing on a rather opposite set of norms. For instance, managerial praxis as well as HRM policies favor explicit rather than tacit knowledge. Individual performance is rewarded, rather than relational learning processes, and job descriptions are assumed to be clear, not vague. The creative, individually designed career path that focuses on learning rather than shifts in hierarchical positions is not given too much attention, which is why some of the interviewed KIWs also preferred to speak about their professional development as a 'non-career'.

The logic of a career as a knowledge creation process is still, as Weick (1996: 45) put it, 'waiting to be constructed'.

REFERENCES

Alvesson, M. (1995), *Management of Knowledge Intensive Companies* (Berlin: de Gruyter).
Arthur, M. B., and Rousseau, D. M. (1996*a*), 'The Boundaryless Career as a New Employment Principle', in M. B. Arthur and D. M. Rousseau (eds.), *The Boundaryless Career: A New Employment Principle for a New Organizational Era* (Oxford: Oxford University Press), 3–20.
——(1996*b*), 'A Lexicon for the New Organizational Era', in M. B. Arthur and D. M. Rousseau (eds.), *The Boundaryless Career: A New Employment Principle for a New Organizational Era* (Oxford: Oxford University Press), 370–82.

Baker, T., and Aldrich, H. E. (1996), 'Prometheus Stretches: Building Identity and Cumulative Knowledge in Multiemployer Careers', in M. B. Arthur and D. M. Rousseau (eds.), *The Boundaryless Career: A New Employment Principle for a New Organizational Era* (Oxford: Oxford University Press), 132–49.

Baumard, P. (1999), *Tacit Knowledge in Organizations* (London: Sage).

Berger, P., and Luckmann, T. (1966), *The Social Construction of Reality* (New York: Anchor Books).

Bird, A. (1996), 'Careers as Repositories of Knowledge: Considerations for Boundaryless Careers', in M. B. Arthur and D. M. Rousseau (eds.), *The Boundaryless Career: A New Employment Principle for a New Organizational Era* (Oxford: Oxford University Press), 150–68.

DeFillippi, R. J., and Arthur, M. B. (1996), 'Boundaryless Contexts and Careers: A Competency-Based Perspective', in M. B. Arthur and D. M. Rousseau (eds.), *The Boundaryless Career: A New Employment Principle for a New Organizational Era* (Oxford: Oxford University Press), 116–31.

Edvinsson, L., and Malone, M. S. (1997), *Intellectual Capital: The Proven Way to Establish your Company's True Value by Finding its Hidden Brainpower* (New York: Doubleday).

Freidson, E. (1986), *Professional Powers* (Chicago: University of Chicago Press).

Gardner, H. (1993), *Creating Minds* (New York: Basic Books).

Goleman, D. (1995), *Emotional Intelligence: Why it can Matter More than IQ* (New York: Bantam Books).

Greenleaf, R. K. (1977), *Servant Leadership: A Journey into the Nature of Legitimate Power and Greatness* (New York: Paulist Press).

Gunz, H. P., Evans, M. G., and Jalland, R. M. (2000), 'Career Boundaries in a "Boundaryless" World', in M. A. Peiperl, M. B. Arthur, R. Goffee, and T. Morris (eds.), *Career Frontiers: New Conceptions of Working Lives* (Oxford: Oxford University Press), 24–53.

Hirsch, P. (1987), *Pack your own Parachute: How to Survive Mergers, Takeovers and Other Corporate Disasters* (Reading, Mass: Addison-Wesley).

Isaacs, W. (1999), *Dialogue and the Art of Thinking Together* (New York: Doubleday).

Kunda, G. (1992), *Engineering Culture: Control and Commitment in a High-Tech Corporation* (Philadelphia: Temple University Press).

Marshall, J. (1989), 'Re-Visioning Career Concepts: A Feminist Invitation', in M. B. Arthur, D. T. Hall, and B. S. Lawrence (eds.), *Handbook of Career Theory* (New York; Cambridge University Press), 275–91.

May, R. (1975), *The Courage to Create* (New York: W. W Norton).

Miles, R. E., and Snow, C. C. (1996), 'Twenty-First-Century Careers', in M. B. Arthur and D. M. Rousseau (eds.), *The Boundaryless Career: A New Employment Principle for a New Organizational Era* (Oxford: Oxford University Press), 97–115.

Mirvis, P. H., and Hall, D. T. (1996), Psychological Success and the Boundaryless Career', in M. B. Arthur and D. M. Rousseau (eds.), *The Boundaryless Career: A New Employment Principle for a New Organizational Era* (Oxford: Oxford University Press), 237–55.

Mischel, W. (1977), 'The Interaction of Person and Situation', in D. Magnuson and N. S. Endler (eds.), *Personality at the Crossroads* (Hillsdale, NJ: Erlbaum).

Morris, T. (2000), 'Promotion Policies and Knowledge Bases in the Professional Service Firm', in M. A. Peiperl, M. B. Arthur, R. Goffee, and T. Morris (eds.), *Career Frontiers: New Conceptions of Working Lives* (Oxford: Oxford University Press), 138–52.

56   BIRGITTA SÖDERGREN

Nonaka, I. (1991), 'The Knowledge-Creating Company', *Harvard Business Review*, 6: 96–104.

Nonaka, I., and Tekuchi, H. (1995), *The Knowledge-Creating Company* (New York: Oxford University Press).

Peiperl, M. A., and Arthur, M. B. (2000), 'Topics for Conversation: Career Themes Old and New', in M. A. Peiperl, M. B. Arthur, R. Goffee, and T. Morris (eds.), *Career Frontiers: New Conceptions of Working Lives* (Oxford: Oxford University Press), 1–19.

Pelz, D., and Andrews, F. (1966), *Scientists in Organizations* (New York: John Wiley).

Perrow, C. (1996), 'The Bounded Career and the Demise of the Civil Society', in M. B. Arthur and D. M. Rousseau (eds.), *The Boundaryless Career: A New Employment Principle for a New Organizational Era* (Oxford: Oxford University Press), 297–313.

Pert, C. (1997), *Molecules of Emotion: Why you Feel the Way you Feel* (London: Simon & Schuster).

Polanyi, M. (1967), *The Tacit Dimension* (London: Routledge).

Raider, H. J., and Burt, R. S. (1996), 'Boundaryless Careers and Social Capital', in M. B. Arthur and D. M. Rousseau (eds.), *The Boundaryless Career: A New Employment Principle for a New Organizational Era* (Oxford: Oxford University Press), 187–200.

Reichheld, F. F., and Teal, T. (1996), *The Loyalty Effect: The Hidden Force behind Growth, Profits and Lasting Value* (Boston: Harvard Business School Press).

Rousseau, D. M. (1990), 'New-Hire Perceptions of their Own and their Employer's Obligations: A Study of Psychological Contracts', *Journal of Organizational Behavior*, 11: 389–400.

Sandberg, J. (2001), 'The Construction of Social Constructionism', in S.-E. Sjöstrand, J. Sandberg, and M. Tyrstrup (eds.), *Invisible Management* (London: International Thomson Business Press), 1–27.

—— and Targama, A. (1998), *Ledning och förståelse: Ett kompetensperspektiv på organisationer* (Management of Conception) (Lund: Studentlitteratur).

Senge, P. M. (1990), *The Fifth Discipline: The Art and Practice of the Learning Organization* (New York: Doubleday).

—— Kleiner, A., Roberts, C., Ross, R., Roth, G., and Smith, B. (1999), *The Dance of Change: The Challenges to Sustaining Momentum in Learning Organizations* (New York: Doubleday).

Södergren, B. (1997), *På väg mot en horisontell organisation* (Toward a Horizontal Organization) (Stockholm: EFI).

—— (forthcoming), *Kunskapsarbetaren: Om villkoren för specialister i arbetslivet* (Work Life According to a Knowledge Intensive Worker).

—— and Fredriksson, L. (1998), *Ledarskap i en lärande organisation lärdomar och idéer* (Managing a Learning Organization) (Stockholm: Arbetsgivarverket).

—— and Söderholm, J. (2001), 'Managing Positions or People?', in S.-E. Sjöstrand, J. Sandberg, and M. Tyrstrup (eds.), *Invisible Management* (London: International Thomson Business Press), 240–56.

Starbuck, W. (1992), 'Learning by Knowledge-Intensive Firms', Conference Paper presented at Knowledge Workers in Contemporary Organizations, Lancaster, 2–4 Sept.

Stein, J. (1996), *Lärande inom och mellan organisationer* (Learning in and between Organizations) (Lund: Studentlitteratur).

Stewart, T. (1997), *Intellectual Capital: The New Wealth of Organizations* (New York: Doubleday).

Sveiby, K.-E. (1994), *Towards a Knowledge Perspective on Organization* (Stockholm University: Univ. Edsbruk Akademitryck).

Tolbert, P. S. (1996), 'Occupations, Organizations, and Boundaryless Careers', in M. B. Arthur and D. M. Rousseau (eds.), *The Boundaryless Career: A New Employment Principle for a New Organizational Era* (Oxford University Press), 331–50.

Weick, K. E. (1979), *The Social Psychology of Organizing*, 2nd edn. (Reading, Mass.: Addison-Wesley).

—— (1996), 'Enactment and the Boundaryless Career: Organizing as we Work', in M. B. Arthur and D. M. Rousseau (eds.), *The Boundaryless Career: A New Employment Principle for a New Organizational Era* (Oxford University Press), 40–57.

Werr, A. (1999), *The Language of Change: The Roles of Methods in the Work of Management Consultants* (Stockholm: EFI).

Westelius, A. (1996). *A Study of Patterns of Communication in Management Accounting and Control Projects* (Stockholm: EFI).

4

Chalk Lines, Open Borders, Glass Walls, and Frontiers: Careers and Creativity

HUGH P. GUNZ, MARTIN G. EVANS, AND
R. MICHAEL JALLAND

There is a caricature of career boundaries that goes as follows. Boundaries in the world of work, everyone knows, are bad things. They block the diffusion of ideas, and they inhibit learning and personal reinvention by preventing people from experiencing new work environments. Boundaries reduce creative potential. If creative or innovative solutions to problems occur when the problem is viewed through several frames of reference,[1] and boundaries enclose similar frames, boundary crossing should result in multi-frame perspectives. Creativity, therefore, clearly must suffer in a bounded world, and be unleashed in an unbounded one. New career models in which people develop competencies not bound to any one organization must take over—indeed, are doing so—from older, traditional forms that produced Whyte's 'organization man' (1956).

Careers, then, should become as boundaryless as Welch's General Electric (GE) (Slater 1993) if creativity is to be maximized. Or so the rhetoric goes. Like most rhetoric that sweeps quickly to prominence, there is a good deal of sense in it. Indeed, in many ways we are exploring what, for anyone who has taken an interest in career structures and management development, is familiar territory. Hall's seminal concept (1976) of the 'protean' career, involving regular personal reinvention, has been around for some time. Nor is there anything at all new in the notion that bringing outsiders into an organization—often called 'new blood'—brings with it fresh thinking. Bouchet (1976), for example, showed that there is a positive relationship between the diversity of experience on a company's board, and the likelihood that the company has followed a strategy

---

[1] This is Koestler's definition (1964) of creativity.

of diversification—admittedly sometimes with disastrous consequences. So one purpose of this chapter is to explore some of the ways in which removing career boundaries releases creativity by enhancing the 'repository of knowledge enshrined in the individual's career' (Bird 1996: 325).

We shall, however, also be arguing a case for balance. Boundaries, we believe, have their uses as well as their hazards. Of course, few proponents of the 'boundaryless career' would recognize the caricature painted in the first paragraph of this chapter as anything close to their vision. Indeed, the term, as used in, for example, Arthur and Rousseau's definitive collection of essays (1996) introducing the concept, really refers to an absence of *organizational* boundaries in the structuring of careers. It was certainly not a general call to sweep away all career boundaries, and, as we shall see, there are many different kinds of career boundary that can be imagined. Our basic point is simply that removing career boundaries involves a trade-off: on the one hand, there are benefits in terms of creativity, but, on the other, there are costs. It is the trade-off between stability and change, between deepening the existing competencies within a given group or changing the mix of competencies to encourage creativity and innovation. Our aim is to make it legitimate to talk about career boundaries, to enable a more dispassionate account of what they are, how they differ, and when and under what circumstances they enhance or inhibit creativity.

It will be evident by now that the 'creativity' with which we are concerned in this chapter is the kind addressed in this volume by, for example, Södergren, Alvarez and Svejenova, and Jones. Although boundarylessness has the potential to produce wonderfully creative careers (see e.g. Parker, Chapter 7), our approach is avowedly instrumental: we shall be exploring the way different kinds of career boundary might affect the creativity of the social systems that the boundaries delineate and penetrate. In that sense, we continue to explore a theme that has been of interest to us for some time: that of the relationship between careers and strategies (Gunz and Jalland 1996; Gunz *et al.* 1998). To return briefly to Koestler's perspective, we assume that creativity is enhanced by the multiple viewing frames made available when boundary crossing is enhanced, and inhibited when people stay within rigid, impermeable boundaries. If creative decisions are subject to the 'garbage-can' phenomenon, then problems, solutions, people, and occasions for decision occur in organizations. Career boundaries influence the kinds of problems that people recognize and the potential variety of solutions they consider. But we shall be arguing that there are two sides to the issue, and that boundary crossing has its costs as well as its benefits.

Boundary crossing has been with us for as long as career boundaries have existed, and it is easy to forget how common it can be, particularly in certain industries and during certain historical periods. For example, industries with many small firms—such as the advertising industry or the pre-Second World War textiles industry in the UK—can experience a great deal more inter-firm

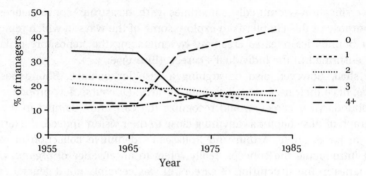

Fig. 4.1. Number of moves between employers, British managers, 1955–1985.
Source: Nicholson and West (1988).

mobility than do industries consisting of large firms with large internal labor markets (Gunz 1989). Notice here that it is size of firm rather than environmental needs that is driving the inter-firm mobility. In the case of advertising, a side benefit is the influx of new ideas, but in textiles, mobility simply served to reinforce the status quo. This mobility can change over time, too. Nicholson and West (1988) report data from a series of studies of members of the British Institute of Management (BIM) that show a dramatic increase in the number of firms managers had worked for at the end of the 1960s (Fig. 4.1). By the early 1970s—thirty years ago—the proportion who had worked for five or more employers (that is, had had four or more moves) had increased from 11 per cent in 1960 to nearly one in three. Most people, then, will have experienced boundary crossing, either in person or vicariously. They are also likely to have experienced some of the costs: moving can be traumatic, and nobody likes losing a productive colleague, if only because of the costs and risks associated with finding a replacement, not to mention the loss of firm-specific knowledge that accompanies his or her departure.

Our aim in this chapter is to explore some of the costs and benefits of career boundaries, particularly as they apply to ways in which boundary crossing might be linked to creative outcomes. We shall approach the issue by exploring the question of what a career boundary is. We shall develop a model that distinguishes between two kinds of boundary crossing, each with its own implications for creativity. All boundary crossing, in other words, is not equal.

WHAT IS A CAREER BOUNDARY?
WHY MIGHT WE HAVE THEM?

There are recognizable patterns to the way people flow through social structures over the course of their working lives. Perhaps the most familiar managerial career streams, as we shall call them here (Gunz and Jalland 1996), can be seen within the kind of large organization that recruits mainly into positions at the bottom of its hierarchy. One set of streams may follow what is often thought of as the traditional pathway up through successively higher hierarchical levels, while others might wind their way around the organization as junior managers, broadening their experience of different parts of the operation (Gunz 1989). Streams can also join firms within an industry; they may be geographically defined; they may connect different positions within a specific occupation; and so on. The potential variety of kinds of career stream is vast and growing as new forms of career appear (Arthur and Rousseau 1996).

Career boundaries define the 'edges' of these streams, giving them their shape. Firms with a single entry point for their supply flow (Sonnenfeld and Peiperl 1988)—the most extreme examples being the Japanese Keiretsu—have career boundaries surrounding them, separating them from the rest of the business world. Traditionally, so did companies such as IBM, although these boundaries were rarely completely hermetic: people often left such companies, typically to join smaller ones, which thereby benefited from the excellent technical and managerial training that these people brought with them. However, until recently it was uncommon for anyone to be brought into companies like IBM or Procter & Gamble at middle or senior levels. Moreover, it has been argued that a consequence of this was a more coherent strategic behavior on the part of the firm because of the greater knowledge and understanding of the company's charter and operations that insiders brought with them (Collins and Porras 1994).

A different, more permeable, career boundary surrounds firms that hire people in at every level of the organization. In so doing, these firms exploit their greater labor market pool to trade strategic continuity and a strong and idiosyncratic culture for more innovativeness and greater strategic flexibility.

Career boundaries come in many different forms. Schein's conical model (1971) of organizational careers, for example, distinguishes between three: hierarchical, functional, and inclusional. The first two follow the lines of the organization chart; the third is more subtle: it marks distinctions between levels of inclusion in the power structure of the organization. People cross inclusion boundaries as they join 'in' groups with greater influence in the running of the firm. As with boundaries surrounding organizations, these internal boundaries can vary greatly in their permeability from firm to firm. For example, Ouchi and Johnson (1978) suggest that the average number of functions experienced by a North American CEO is 2.5, compared to his Japanese counterpart's 11.5. Career boundaries can surround organizations, firms, departments (head office staff departments), organizational levels, occupations (lawyers, airline pilots, electricians, actors), or countries (in many, it can be extremely difficult for foreigners to get work, or, if they have it, to move from the job they are authorized to hold).

Formally, a boundary is an imperfection in the labor market, observable by the relative lack of movement that takes place between groups of roles on either side of the boundary. In other words, a career boundary is a 'line' across which people move less frequently than they do between roles *not* separated by a career boundary. As we have just seen in the discussion above on organizational boundaries, they differ in *permeability*. Some are highly impermeable, allowing virtually no movement; others permit almost as much movement as there is within the career streams enclosed by the boundary. The less permeable a boundary—in other words, the less movement there is across it—the more 'visible' (that is, readily detected) it becomes.

The kind of boundarylessness argued for by writers such as Arthur and Rousseau (1996) is about making boundaries more permeable, not doing away with them. On the contrary, it is hard to imagine a world in which there was a total absence of career boundaries. It would be one in which there was no constraint to movement of any kind as a result of, for example, geography, political boundaries, education, professional qualification, experience (or its lack), organizational membership, as well as the less readily admitted to, but nevertheless real, distinctions of age, race, ethnicity, sex, or religion.

Not only are career boundaries of some kind inevitable; it could be argued that they play an important role in maintaining the stability of social systems, as a simple illustration shows. Suppose (Fig. 4.2) a vacancy is created in a given role set (the role marked with an asterisk): perhaps someone retires, resigns, or dies. It is likely that the vacancy will be filled by someone moving from another role, in so doing creating another vacancy. This is filled by someone else, who creates yet another vacancy; and so on, until the chain is broken (in the figure, the role marked with a dagger). This might be because the last vacancy is filled by someone coming from outside the boundary surrounding the entire role set, or perhaps because the vacant role disappears for some reason: the work is no longer needed, or a reorganization disposes of it (Pinfield 1995). The sequence of events that we have just described is called a 'vacancy chain' (White 1970), and Fig. 4.2 illustrates an alarming implication of such a chain, which is

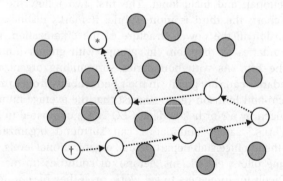

Fig. 4.2. Vacancy chain with no internal career boundaries.

unconstrained by boundaries. Once a vacancy has been created, there is no way of knowing which other roles will be affected: virtually any role within the set could find itself falling vacant as a result, which makes life very difficult for everyone in the role set. For example, if the role set in question were a firm, nobody would know whether a reorganization in the accounts department might trigger the loss of a key product manager. This is an example of one of the ways in which career systems exhibit the 'butterfly effect', in which tiny changes set off unpredictable consequences—a concept attributed to E. N. Lorenz, although there is some doubt about this attribution (see Cross 1996).

In practice, of course, any given role set will have some career boundaries that constrain the chains. In the example in Fig. 4.3 only the part of the role set within the second career stream from the left is affected by the vacancy; the other three carry on as before: life is more manageable and predictable than in the boundaryless condition.

This highly simplified example glosses over many useful features of more permeable boundaries, some of which we return to below. Most notably, it ignores the obvious point that moving to something new and different can be invigorating and developmental to the person making the move, and good for the organization as well. Our aim is simply to make the point that it is easy to overlook the benefits that spring from constraints on career movements: to put it in a crudely functionalist way, without some form of constraint, the impact of vacancies within the organization becomes extremely unpredictable and difficult to manage.

Interestingly, an echo of this point can be detected in Kauffman's modeling (1993) of the genome. The problem he addresses is that of understanding how the mutation rate observed in DNA produces observed rates of evolution. He modeled DNA using binary NK networks (networks with N nodes, each connected to an average of K other nodes) and found that they behaved as if they had boundaries within their state space. State space is the 'space' into which

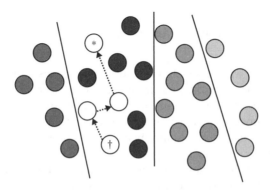

Fig. 4.3. Vacancy chain with internal career boundaries.

all possible states of the system fit; in other words, it is an imaginary multi-dimensional space, where the dimensions are the critical dimensions that define the state of the network. As the network changes ('mutates'), it moves across the state space. The boundaries that Kauffman observed in the state space of his NK networks created 'islands' such that networks tended to stay within the 'islands' for most of the time. Most mutations produced minor change to the overall state of the network, which kept it within a given 'island'; only very occasionally would a mutation move the system to another 'island'. In the absence of these boundaries, the system risks dramatic and unpredictable change in response to most, if not all, mutations. If this were the case, there would be too little continuity to reproduction, preventing the operation of the natural selection responsible for evolution. Kauffman is suggesting, in other words, that boundaries emerge spontaneously from the nature of the complexity of the genome and that these boundaries are necessary to the genome's evolution.

Thus far we have argued that career boundaries are both inevitable in some form, and that it is not hard to uncover reasons for them being functional. Without them, uncertainty can rise to hard-to-manage levels. Our account has been, however, at a very general level. We have hinted at the variety of types of career boundary that may be observed; next, we take a more analytical approach and develop a model of career boundaries.

CLASSIFICATION OF CAREER BOUNDARIES

The examples we gave earlier in this chapter were of many different kinds of boundary: between firms, between technical specialties, between hierarchical levels, and even between in-groups and out-groups. We now turn to an analytic exploration of these different kinds of boundary. We shall explore boundaries from two perspectives, which we shall call *technical* and *institutional*.

Technical factors and career boundaries

The most obvious way in which a boundary may be created is when it separates roles that are very different from each other. Theoretical examples of these distinctions can be seen in Lawrence and Lorsch's concept (1967) of differentiation between organizational units, and Offe's concept (1976) of task continuity versus task discontinuity between different levels in a hierarchy. Practical examples abound in a typical modern hospital with its myriad of different occupations: doctors and orderlies, nurses and nurse practitioners, dieticians and ward clerks, surgeons and physiotherapists. Stark differences appear in the nature of the work done by doctors and orderlies and in the education, qualifications, and experience needed for each role, so a highly impermeable career boundary separates these two groups of roles in a hospital: orderlies do not expect to become physicians without going to medical school first. Here, we focus on the *technical* basis for the career boundary. If we were to focus solely on the technical aspects of the career boundary, we would expect two kinds, which we call here *frontiers* and *chalk lines*.

A frontier is an impermeable career boundary that separates different kinds of job. Frontiers separate doctors from other occupations in a hospital because their job is so different from any other in the organization that nobody expects to cross the frontier (without, that is, qualifying as a doctor); similar boundaries surround most other highly skilled technical and professional occupations. Frontiers may surround the kind of traditional Procter & Gamble-like organizations we discussed above, in which recruitment is entirely at junior levels, if the reason for this is that the organization's work is unique. For example, all members of the UK Fire Service start their careers as firefighters because of the belief that nobody can take command in a fire department unless he or she has learned the basic skills and technology of firefighting.

The second type of boundary, the chalk line, separates groups of roles that do not differ very much from a technical point of view. Gouldner (1958) described a career pattern he called 'cosmopolitan', characterized by practicing the same occupation for a series of different employers in the way that professional engineers and software specialists often do. So cosmopolitans make their careers by crossing a series of chalk lines, moving from one organization to another but practicing the same occupation in each. There are usually contractual consequences that flow from changing employers, and probably a new group of people to get to know, but the work done by, for example, a software engineer or product manager is recognizably similar wherever it is being done. So chalk lines are permeable because there is little if any technical barrier to movement across them. Our cosmopolitan example describes interorganizational chalk lines, although they can be found within organizations as well. For example, a product manager who transfers between two divisions of the same firm is, in our terms, crossing a chalk line.

Thus far, our account has been straightforward: people do not move between groups of dissimilar roles (frontiers) but they do move between groups of similar roles (chalk lines). But were we to take our medical example a little further, we would discover that the technical perspective provides only a partial explanation for the formation of career boundaries. There is more similarity between doctors and graduate nurse practitioners than there is between doctors and orderlies—nurses are now trained to carry out a great many medical procedures that hitherto were the realm of the doctor—but the career boundary between them is in practice just as impermeable. Medicine is an example of a class of occupations, many of which carry the label 'profession' in Anglo-Saxon societies, which have powerful barriers to entry only partially connected to the technical requirements of the position (Daniels 1975).

Career boundaries are also created by *institutional* processes that may or may not have their origins in what we have called here technical factors.

Institutional factors and career boundaries

Several distinct kinds of institutional factor influencing the emergence of career boundaries can be discerned. Among the most significant are those concerned with contracts of employment, external jurisdictions, social attitudes, labor organizations, organizational size, and boundaries of inclusion. Examples of the institutional factors creating career boundaries include the following.

- *Contracts of employment.* Technical specialists in high-technology firms are often required to sign contracts of employment that control the extent to which they can move to competing firms. Firms impose these restrictions in order to protect the intellectual capital that is carried in the heads of their employees. Employees evade these barriers in four ways: (1) at the beginning of their employment through tough negotiation that results in such restrictions being omitted from their employment contract; (2) at the end of their employment by developing intellectual property that does not fit with the strategic direction of the firm, so they are permitted to leave and set up an entrepreneurial venture (for example, William Gore was refused support for GoreTex by Dupont); (3) by moving to firms that do not compete in the same industry; or (4) by moving to start up firms of such insignificance that the original company perceives no threat to their activities.
- *External jurisdictions.* Jurisdictions limit movement of otherwise highly qualified people across national borders. For example, a country such as Canada has its taxis driven by physicians and professional engineers who trained elsewhere but are prevented from practicing their professions. This is ostensibly because of the need to check the people's qualifications and language abilities, but often in practice because the places available in the relevant professions are relatively few. This is not something that individuals and firms can do much about directly. Nevertheless, we do see individuals evading this boundary through illegal immigration, marriages of convenience, and sponsorship by relatives. Indirectly, firms can lower these barriers through lobbying or industry pressure: for example, demands on the US Congress to increase the immigration quota for computer programmers and analysts. On a larger scale, such boundaries are becoming more permeable through international treaty, such as, for example, those among the European Union or North American Free Trade Association member countries.
- *Social attitudes.* Only recently have women begun to overcome barriers preventing them from practicing medicine or law, serving in combat roles

in the military, and being blocked by glass ceilings in managerial hierarchies. These boundaries begin to crumble only as social attitudes change. They change when one or more pioneering members of the discriminated class show that they are very effective in carrying out the duties of the position.

- *Labor organization.* Labor contracts often specify demarcations between different jobs that have their origins in a technical distinction that has long since disappeared in practice. These boundaries may be among the most difficult to cross, as they appear to be task related.

- *Organizational size.* Large organizations may have reasons for trying to limit the movement of their employees that have nothing to do with the technical requirements of the job. For example, a large international consulting firm finds it hard to keep its consultants in Canada because of the much greater compensation package they get in the firm's US offices, so the firm does its best to block these moves administratively. A related phenomenon can be seen in most large companies in which it becomes known that the most interesting career opportunities require a presence in their head office. It can be hard for people in the outlying locations to overcome the various formal and informal barriers that allow them to make this move. These boundaries are sometimes relaxed if the organization views a person as indispensable and so engineers a desirable move to keep the person. Individuals can sometimes evade the boundary by resigning their current position and, after a short interlude elsewhere, applying for and being hired at a more desirable location. For example, a faculty member employed by one of the suburban campuses of a large Canadian state university resigned his position, took a job at a major US university, and after a year was rehired to the Canadian university's central campus.

- *Boundaries of inclusion.* Inclusion boundaries separate the powerful and the less powerful in organizations (Schein, 1971). For example, every Prime Minister has an inner cabinet for key policy advice. Similarly in every university there are many Deans, but only a few—and not necessarily those of the most powerful unit—have the ear of the President or Vice-Chancellor. These boundaries are the most difficult to see, even though they are very impermeable (an exception to our argument that strong boundaries are very visible). They are very much under the control of the in-group, and the criteria for crossing are usually not widely publicized. As a consequence, managers wishing inclusion operate on a system of trial and error. Some inclusion comes from competence, but some comes from 'being the right type' (Eton School held the royal warrant as 'cabinet-maker' to the Queen) and some from having a mentor who is part of the in-group. Accordingly, in order to improve their chances of inclusion, out-group employees work hard, try to figure out the political situation at more senior levels, and attempt ingratiating tactics.

Contrasting institutional and technical factors

The distinction we have drawn here between the perspectives we have called technical and institutional is not, of course, a clean one. For example, barriers such as those preventing foreign doctors from practicing in a new country have a technical basis, but institutional forces are also evidently at work as well: the incoming doctors pose a competitive threat to those already practicing. However, the two perspectives play a useful role in reminding us that career boundaries are both technical and social facts. It would be as foolish to ignore the need to protect patients from unqualified medical charlatans as it would to ignore the social processes that have created the professions in the form they currently display in Western societies (Saks 1983).

The examples we have just given, of the way institutional factors block movement between otherwise similar kinds of role, are different from chalk lines and frontiers. The glass ceiling (Corsun and Costen 2001; Lemons and Parzinger 2001) is a familiar and useful metaphor to describe the plight of qualified people prevented by some ascriptive characteristic such as sex from reaching senior levels in an organization. Here we extend the metaphor to that of the *glass wall*, the boundary that separates groups of roles that are technically similar but between which there is little movement.

If glass walls separate similar roles, it is also the case that people can, and do, move between very different kinds of job. One of the firms studied by Gunz (1989), for example, had many examples of moves of this kind—for example, an information systems manager who became a senior chemical plant maintenance engineer, despite not having any engineering training. Technical dissimilarity, here, does not seem to be a barrier to movement; indeed, executives in firms with this kind of career boundary, with career logics Gunz labels *constructional*, are moved across the firm to give them broad experience of the company's operations and how they all fit together, to prepare them for senior roles in due course. We call this type of career boundary an *open border*: people cross the border regularly, even though the territory on the other side is very different and, quite possibly, new to the border-crosser.

Figure 4.4 summarizes these four types of career boundary. Two dimensions differentiate between them, both of which we have already introduced. The first, *similarity*, we use in the technical sense we introduced above. The second, *permeability*, is a simple concept but with complex causality. A focus solely on technical explanations of boundary formation would, as we have seen, result in only two kinds of boundary: chalk lines and frontiers. Introducing an institutional perspective implies that there is no simple correlation between similarity and permeability, but rather that the two dimensions in practice are orthogonal. Thus, boundaries between similar jobs can be impermeable, and those between dissimilar jobs can be permeable.

		Similarity between work roles on either side of boundary	
		High	Low
Permeability of boundary to movement	High	Chalk line	Open border
	Low	Glass wall	Frontier

Fig. 4.4. Types of career boundary.

CHANGING ONE KIND OF CAREER BOUNDARY INTO ANOTHER: GLASSCUTTERS AND PASSPORTS

Now that we have established a model of career boundaries and career boundary crossing we can return to the theme we introduced at the beginning of this chapter—namely, that creativity is enhanced by boundary crossing. We can now restate this assertion in a more analytical way, because we have a model that differentiates between two very different kinds of impermeable boundary, frontiers and glass walls. We have argued that permeability is not simply a function of technical similarity or dissimilarity between roles, but that it is also socially constructed. In other words, that permeability can be manipulated using institutional processes. Our focus will be on the implications of doing this: of using institutional processes to convert frontiers into open borders ('issuing passports'; see Table 4.1), and to convert glass walls into chalk lines ('using glasscutters'[2]). We shall explore the extent to which they have different implications for impeding creativity, but also the extent to which making them permeable brings with it costs to people and organizations. In practical terms, the question we are trying to answer is this: when, mainly from the perspective of the career manager (someone charged with or choosing to plan career progression in their organization), might it be good to issue glasscutters, when passports, and when neither?

We shall examine these ideas by drawing on examples of using glasscutters on intra-firm and inter-firm glass walls, and issuing passports to help people cross intra-firm frontiers. These are, of course, only a small subset of the number of possible career boundaries that can be encountered, and they have a strongly organizational bias, but they will suffice within the limits of the space available to us to indicate the utility of the approach.

---

[2] Anyone who has used a glasscutter knows that it is not the most effective way of opening up a glass wall. We hope the reader will forgive us for a somewhat inaccurate metaphor, but we thought that a more precise one, such as a brick, had overtones that might get in the way.

Table 4.1. A classification of boundarylessness

Type	From	To	Tool
I	Glass walls	Chalk lines	Glasscutter
II	Frontiers	Open borders	Passport

Glass walls to chalk lines: using glasscutters

Glass walls are institutionally created career boundaries between roles that are not technically very different. Their main obstacle to creativity is the way they inhibit the diffusion of ideas or constrain the choice of people available to fill particular roles, and the main cost associated with using glasscutters to turn glass walls into chalk lines is the obverse: the costs of diffusing ideas and of losing people. We gave a number of examples above of glass walls—between one high-technology firm and another, between jurisdictions, and so on—and described some of the ways people break through them. Next, we look at two examples of the impact of glasscutters, on glass walls (1) within firms and (2) between firms.

Within-firm glass walls. These kinds of glass wall (which we shall call here 'internal') are typically barriers created by the organization, although they sometimes result from larger societal forces. For example, when firms exclude women or members of minority groups from managerial jobs they are almost certainly behaving in accord with some social or religious norm. Cutting through glass walls is achieved by interventions and changes to social processes so that institutional barriers become more permeable. Many firms have successfully introduced diversity awareness programs. Other firms have worked long and hard to reduce demarcation practices. Glass walls are often eroded rather than shattered.

While it may be the case that turning glass walls (eventually) into chalk lines will help ideas spread around the firm, there are other, quite possibly less costly, ways of handling this issue. Indeed, the prototypical 'boundaryless organization', Jack Welch's GE, is precisely about this: the norms within the firm, and roles such as that of its Chief Learning Officer (Steve Kerr), are directed at moving ideas throughout the company. One of the worst sins an innovative manager can commit in GE is to be unable to point to examples of his or her innovations having been emulated elsewhere in the firm (Kerr 2000).

Internal glass walls also limit the choice of people available to fill given roles. If there are arbitrary reasons that prevent otherwise capable people from being seen as candidates for a given job, it becomes harder to find good people. Furthermore, the good but unconsidered people may well become frustrated; it is, it turns out, worse to be aware of a career opportunity that one feels qualified to take but arbitrarily prevented from taking than it is not to know about it at all (Gunz and Gunz 1994).

We have already seen examples of the kind of costs that can be incurred by breaking down internal glass walls. The consulting firm to which we referred, for example, would have found it much more expensive to maintain an effective Canadian operation if there were no glass wall between it and its US organization, because it would have had to match its Canadian compensation packages to its US ones (a solution increasingly, and expensively, being adopted by Canadian organizations in both private and public sectors). Companies that do indeed abandon international glass walls (if they ever had them) can find themselves facing the problem of the transient. A number of US companies, for example, use their European or Canadian operations as staging posts in which high-potential managers are given experience as CEOs before (assuming all goes well) they are transferred to more senior positions in the United States. The national operations in question become resigned to the notion that they will see a succession of transients in their top job, with implications for continuity (Collins and Porras 1994).

Between-firm glass walls. Perhaps the most celebrated example of glass walls being replaced by chalk lines (or, more accurately in this case, of chalk lines being found where glass walls might have been expected) is Silicon Valley (SV). Saxenian (1994) shows how innovation flourished in SV in a way that it did not amongst the otherwise comparable electronics firms along Boston's Route 128, because SV firms are surrounded by chalk lines and Route 128 firms are surrounded by glass walls. SV companies have thrived because of the free flow of highly skilled labor between very similar firms, taking ideas from one company to the next. In part, this is due to the origins of the industry as a community of like-minded individuals working together to solve technical problems at so-called 'homebrew club' meetings. On the other hand, firms located along Route 128 have cultures that value and reward loyalty to the company. These walls result in labor immobility and an insularity that seems to have resulted in a slower rate of innovation. As a consequence, electronic firms in Massachusetts have experienced competitive failure in a fast-growing industry. It may be that this culture was influenced by the military secrecy imposed upon early firms in the area (for example, Raytheon). These differences in career mobility are akin to those found by Burns and Stalker (1961) in terms of organization structure in the UK post-war electronics industry. In SV the assumption is that, over time, there will be reciprocation: my ideas will flow to another firm, but eventually ideas will flow back to me from some other firm in a richly interconnected network.

A second reason often given for the central role the extraordinarily permeable chalk lines that surround SV firms played in SV's development is the way they allow new firms to spring up virtually overnight. A group of entrepreneurs seized with an idea will leave their current employers at the drop of a hat, set up their own new firm, and draw skilled help into it from other firms before anyone has realized what is going on. The availability of venture capital is also vital to this process, of course, but virtually all accounts of the area identify the role of chalk lines (without, of course, using that term) as critical to SV's growth.

Even in quintessentially chalk-line industries, however, there can be virtually impenetrable frontiers between particular occupational groups. Any industry that depends on short-term projects is likely to experience considerable mobility as people move from one project to the next (Gunz *et al.* 2000), especially if the occupations are specific to that industry (so that these people are not able to work outside the industry without abandoning their training and experience). For example, the film industry has chalk lines between projects, so that people are continually on the move between production companies as one film is finished and another starts up (Jones 1996). However, it is an extremely tough industry to break into, requiring great persistence on the part of people wanting to establish themselves, only very few of whom actually succeed. In addition, there are impermeable boundaries between specific occupations: for example, few, if any, people now make it from camera operator to actor. So project-based industries such as films have chalk lines within them, but many frontiers as well. The costs associated with wielding glasscutters on inter-company glass walls can, however, be high. Again, SV provides an impressive exemplar. If it is easy to encourage people to move to start a new enterprise, it is very hard to keep them: firms spend incredible resources on finding people and trying to hang on to them. Indeed it has been argued (Cohen and Fields 1998) that the very high mobility is a consequence of the very high stress levels people experience working in the frenetic atmosphere of SV companies. One reason that people keep moving, according to this argument, is in a constant quest for a less stressful working life.

Other indications that there are costs to inter-firm chalk lines come from a study of Canadian biotechnology firms (Gunz *et al.* 2000), which seem to have boundaries much more closely resembling glass walls despite being in a high-technology sector. Factors appear to include (1) long project lengths, so that there is not a constant pressure from projects continually coming to an end making people think about job seeking; (2) geographical dispersion: unlike SV, the industry is geographically dispersed so that, although there are areas of concentration, moves between firms are a much more significant affair than moving to a firm two blocks away; (3) high levels of secrecy, making free movement of skilled employees a problem; and (4) being a regulated industry so that a detailed audit trail is needed for all pharmaceutical development.

To summarize, evidence from a number of sources suggests that, despite the SV experience—or, perhaps, because of some of it—glasscutters need to be used with caution on inter-firm glass walls. Under the right circumstances they may well release creativity, but they have their costs, too.

Frontiers to open borders: issuing passports

Within-firm frontiers. The issues surrounding passports are to do with the dilemma we raised earlier, that of choosing between stability and change. Typically this presents itself as a choice between, on the one hand, changing the mix of competencies to encourage innovation and creativity and, on the other, deepening the existing competencies of the firm's members. Frontiers— and here we focus on intra-firm frontiers—are the boundaries created by real technical differences between jobs. If we wish for the organization to improve its innovative capacity, then issuing passports will be a good idea. When people cross technical boundaries, they bring their old frames of reference with them. This enables them to see existing problems in new, and perhaps innovative ways. The interaction between them and their peers who may have grown up within a single 'silo' has the potential to generate creative solutions to those problems—solutions that satisfy those several frames of reference.

The multi-frame perspective is also used by general managers. It may be presumptuous to argue that the role of general manager is an innovative one. Nevertheless it does require being able to view the activities of the organization in the round. Accordingly, this is a second reason for the issue of passports. A problem faced by any organization divided by frontiers is that people make their careers largely, if not completely, within a particular functional or business area. These are the career logics Gunz (1989) calls, respectively, command centered and evolutionary; they develop experts in functional or business areas. But this does not prepare them for corporate-level roles; for this, they need broad-based multifunctional competencies and an overview of how the organization fits together as a whole. To redress this, firms move people around across different functional areas to develop them (the constructional career logic), converting the frontiers into open borders.

The danger of developing this broad perspective is that there is a tilt to the other horn of the dilemma: the deep skills that may be required to perform effectively in a function or in a particular business are not developed. There is a great danger that people become jacks of all trades, and masters of none. Furthermore, in their desire to avoid becoming 'stuck' in any one part of their company, they avoid developing any real attachment to their unit and its success. Critics of this style of management argue that the object that becomes real to these managers is their career, not their unit (Mant 1983). The answer, of course, is that organizations need some of each: specialists and generalists. Passports in organizations need to be issued selectively.

Between-firm frontiers. Frontiers between firms are in many ways the default labor market condition: career boundaries exist because of dissimilarities in requirements and work roles, even within the same industry. Operations executives are unlikely to be hired to head up marketing. To cross both firm and functional boundaries simultaneously is, in our view, a fairly unlikely event. Firms hiring from outside are usually looking for some track record in the type of job for which they are recruiting, thus they are unlikely to choose someone with a totally different set of experiences. Individuals seeking to move are similarly likely to seek a move where they can use their current repertoire of skills and abilities. It is often too big a stretch to learn new skills and a new culture at the same time; and crossing firm boundaries at a senior level is fraught with difficulty. As a result, we do not see much possibility of the simultaneous use of the passport and the glasscutter. Rather we would expect that such use would be sequential. A person wanting to move to a new company in a new role would either: try to move to the new role in his or her current company as a prelude to moving to the new company (in this way, a track record in the new role is developed), or move to the new company in his or her current role and then try to engineer a move to the new role having demonstrated proficiency in the old role.

CONCLUSION

In this chapter we have been exploring an idea. If creativity is about exposing old problems to new ways of thinking, then careers—the movement of people between work roles over the course of their working lives—become an essential social mechanism for engendering creativity. So career boundaries become of interest, because they are imperfections in labor markets that define points at which potential creative input is blocked. But they are of interest anyway, because it is hard to conceive of labor markets that lack any kind of boundaries: life like that would be virtually unlivable, and certainly impossible to make sense of.

We have, therefore, explored two sides of career boundaries: their benefits to creativity and their costs. Career boundaries—which we divided into four categories: chalk lines, glass walls, open borders and frontiers, defined by two dimensions: similarity and permeability—can be breached, if they are impermeable in a technical sense, by socially reconstructing them in ways we labeled using glasscutters and issuing passports. Using examples of intra- and inter-organizational glass walls and frontiers, we explored some of the ways in which glasscutters and passports can stimulate creativity and some of the costs in so doing. We offer the model of career boundaries in this chapter as part of the lexicon of a language for describing the structure of careers in a way that is both theoretically interesting and practically helpful.

REFERENCES

Arthur, M. B., and Rousseau, D. M. (1996) (eds.), *The Boundaryless Career: A New Employment Principle for a New Organizational Era* (New York: Oxford University Press).

Bird, A. (1996), 'Careers as Repositories of Knowledge: A New Perspective on Boundaryless Careers', *Journal of Organizational Behavior*, 15: 325–44.

Bouchet, J.-L. (1976), 'Diversification: Composition of the Top Management Team and Performance of the Firm', EGOS Conference on the Sociology of the Business Enterprise, Oxford.

Burns, T., and Stalker, G. M. (1961), *The Management of Innovation* (London: Tavistock).

Cohen, S. S., and Fields, G. (1998), 'Social Capital and Capital Gains, or Virtual Bowling in Silicon Valley', Working Paper 132, Berkeley Roundtable on the International Economy Working Paper Series, Berkeley, Calif.

Collins, J. C., and Porras, J. I. (1994), *Built To Last: Successful Habits of Visionary Companies* (New York: Harper Business).

Corsun, D. L., and Costen, W. M. (2001), 'Is the Glass Ceiling Unbreakable?: Habitus, Fields, and the Stalling of Women and Minorities in Management', *Journal of Management Inquiry*, 10/1: 16–25.

Cross, M. (1996), 'The Butterfly Effect', http://www.cmp.caltech.edu/~mcc/chaos_new/Lorenz.html.

Daniels, A. K. (1975), 'Professionalism in Formal Organizations', in J. B. McKinley (ed.), *Processing People* (New York: Holt, Reinhart, & Winston).

Gouldner, A. W. (1958), 'Cosmopolitans and Locals: Toward an Analysis of Latent Social Roles II', *Administrative Science Quarterly*, 2: 444–80.

Gunz, H. P. (1989), *Careers and Corporate Cultures: Managerial Mobility in Large Corporations* (Oxford: Basil Blackwell).

—— and Gunz, S. P. (1994), 'Professional/Organizational Commitment and Job Satisfaction for Employed Lawyers', *Human Relations*, 47/7: 801–28.

—— and Jalland, R. M. (1996), 'Managerial Careers and Business Strategies', *Academy of Management Review*, 21/3: 718–56.

—— Evans, M. G., and Jalland, R. M. (2000), 'Career Boundaries in a "Boundaryless" World', in M. A. Peiperl, M. B. Arthur, R. Goffee, and T. Morris (eds.), *Career Frontiers: New Conceptions of Working Lives* (Oxford: Oxford University Press), 24–53.

—— Jalland, R. M., and Evans, M. G. (1998), 'New Strategy, Wrong Managers? What you Need to Know about Career Streams', *Academy of Management Executive*, 12/2: 21–37.

Hall, D. T. (1976), *Careers in Organizations* (Pacific Pallisades, Calif.: Goodyear).

Jones, C. (1996), 'Careers in Project Networks: The Case of the Film Industry', in M. B. Arthur and D. M. Rousseau, *The Boundaryless Career: A New Employment Principle for a New Organizational Era* (New York: Oxford University Press), 58–75.

Kauffman, S. A. (1993), *The Origins of Order: Self-Organization and Selection in Evolution* (New York: Oxford University Press).

Kerr, S. (2000), Presentation to the Organization Science Winter Conference, Keystone, Colorado, Feb.

Koestler, A. (1964), *The Act of Creation* (New York: Macmillan).

Lawrence, P. R., and Lorsch, J. W. (1967), *Organization and Environment: Managing Differentiation and Integration* (Boston: Harvard University, Graduate School of Business Administration, Division of Research).

Lemons, M. A., and Parzinger, M. J. (2001), 'Designing Women: A Qualitative Study of the Glass Ceiling for Women in Technology', *SAM Advanced Management Journal*, 66/2: 4–11.

Mant, A. (1983), *Leaders We Deserve* (Oxford: Basil Blackwell).

Nicholson, N., and West, M. (1988), *Managerial Job Change: Men and Women in Transition* (Cambridge: Cambridge University Press).

Offe, C. (1976), *Industry and Inequality* (London: Edward Arnold).

Ouchi, W. G., and Johnson, J. B. (1978), 'Types of Organizational Control and their Relationship to Emotional Well Being', *Administrative Science Quarterly*, 23: 293–317.

Pfeffer, J., and Leblebici, H. (1973), 'Executive Recruitment and the Development of Interfirm Organizations', *Administrative Science Quarterly*, 18 (Dec.), 449–61.

Pinfield, L. (1995), *The Operation of Internal Labour Markets: Staffing Actions and Vacancy Chains* (New York: Plenum).

Saks, A. M. (1983), 'Removing the Blinkers? A Critique of Recent Contributions to the Sociology of the Professions', *Sociological Review*, 31/1: 1–21.

Saxenian, A. L. (1994), *Regional Advantage: Culture and Competition in Silicon Valley and Route 128* (Cambridge, Mass.: Harvard University Press).

Schein, E. H. (1971), 'The Individual, the Organization and the Career: A Conceptual Scheme', *Journal of Applied Behavioural Science*, 7: 401–26.

Slater, Robert (1993), *The New GE* (Homewood, Ill: Irwin).

Sonnenfeld, J. A., and Peiperl, M. A. (1988), 'Staffing Policy as a Strategic Response: A Typology of Career Systems', *Academy of Management Review*, 13/4: 588–600.

White, H. C. (1970), *Chains of Opportunity* (Cambridge, Mass.: Harvard University Press).

Whyte, W. H. (1956), *The Organization Man* (New York: Simon & Schuster).

5

Designing Creative Careers and Creative Lives through Reduced-Load Work Arrangements

MICHELLE L. BUCK, MARY DEAN LEE,
AND SHELLEY M. MACDERMID

When we first think of creativity, we may think of artists or scientists, and paintings or writings or patents or dramatic breakthroughs. We may think of sources of inspiration, bold moments of creative insight, or specific outcomes of creativity. We may think of famous creative individuals. In these cases, creativity might be considered something that is unusual, unexpected, novel, and different from the norms for the given context. Using this perspective, another stream of creativity emerges, although perhaps more gradually, in the careers and lives of many professionals and managers in organizations. This creativity emerges over time, as the individuals and their organizations pursue new paths, not limited by precedent and traditions, but in response to changing needs and changing contexts. Indeed, Bateson (1989: 3, 9) speaks of people's creativity in 'composing a life', and about 'life as an improvisatory art... in which commitments are continually refocused and redefined'.

In the midst of changing needs of the workforce, and the dynamic landscape of organizational life and the global business context, employees' motivations, career paths, and visions of themselves and their lives are in flux. As part of this, individuals and organizations are increasingly experimenting with alternative

This research was made possible by financial support from the Alfred P. Sloan Foundation (Mary Dean Lee and Shelley M. MacDermid, Co-Principal Investigators), and from the Social Sciences and Humanities Research Council of Canada (Mary Dean Lee, Principal Investigator). We are grateful for the assistance of other members of the research team, including Margaret Williams, Carol Schreiber, Leslie Borrelli, Sharon Leiba-O'Sullivan, Minda Bernstein, Stephen Smith, Pamela Dohring, and Lucy Ford. We are also grateful to the over 350 women and men who were participants in the study, and shared their time and insights with us, and to the organizations that allowed us access.

work arrangements, such as flexitime, job sharing, telecommuting, or part-time work (Catalyst 1997; Scandura and Lankau 1997; Epstein *et al.* 1998; Mirchandani 1998). Consider the following work arrangements of professionals and managers who are voluntarily working part-time.

An economist working as a manager in an oil company works a 75 percent load. Her work arrangement varies according to seasonal demand, such that she works three days a week, or 60 percent, for most of the year, except for the two weeks around quarter's end when she works full-time to help her department accommodate the heavy workload at that time.

A senior manager in a consulting firm works approximately 8 a.m. until 3 p.m. each day. She is a mother of three children and has used a variety of different work arrangements in the past. Most recently she has coordinated her departure time primarily according to a ferry schedule, rather than according to the work itself or the schedules of her colleagues.

A senior manager in a technology company views her reduced load as enabling her to weave her work and life into a patchwork quilt that is constantly changing and suits her perfectly. She does not have set hours, but rather keeps track to make sure that, at the end of the year, she is giving the company its due, but not more.

A program manager in another technology firm has had many different work arrangements over the past years, including full-time work, part-time work, telecommuting, and job sharing. He currently works a 75 percent load, but has no typical weekly schedule of hours, in the office or at home. His wife also works part-time in her job in an educational institution, and they together allocate their time according to a life philosophy that time should be divided relatively equally among work, family, and community service.

The working hours of these individuals, and their work arrangements, deviate from perceptions of what might be categorized 'traditional' job arrangements and schedules, particularly at high-ranking professional levels. They certainly represent flexibility, but, perhaps more importantly, these work schedules reflect just the tip of the iceberg of much larger stories of individuals who are creatively designing their careers and their lives. These cases are individual snapshots in an unfolding drama of a larger trend, an increase in the number of professional and managerial workers who are pursuing alternative work arrangements as a way of creatively balancing multiple priorities in their lives.

This trend seems to be occurring for a variety of reasons. From an individual's perspective, many employees feel increasing demands both at work and at home. Increasing international competition, market volatility, and advances in technology pressure companies to need more work from employees and at a faster rate than ever before. Simultaneously, the professional and managerial workforce increasingly includes women and members of dual-career or single-parent families, resulting in extra demands and less time at home and with family. Furthermore, many employees are searching for ways to find a sense of balance in their lives, and are seeking work or a way of life that offers a sense of meaningfulness and personal fulfillment. In response to changing priorities and seemingly overwhelming demands at both work and home, many individuals face the stark reality that traditional career paths and traditional ways of dividing work and non-work life are no longer consistent with the lives they lead, or the lives they want to be living. As a result, many employees are challenging the status quo by requesting alternative work arrangements. In addition to these individual reasons, organizations are also increasingly willing to experiment with alternative work arrangements. In their efforts to reduce costs, increase productivity and innovation, and maximize profitability, firms place high priority on attracting and retaining top talent in a tight labor market and know that they must increasingly respond to employees' needs and requests in order to remain competitive.

In seeking alternative work arrangements, individuals pursue creative options of how and where they spend their work time, and they seek freedom and flexibility in how their time is allocated between work and non-work life. In the myriad forms of alternative work arrangements, a common theme is the employees' efforts to change their working conditions, to depart from the status quo and find a new path, in order to create circumstances that are more consistent with the vision of the life they desire. This pursuit of alternative work arrangements involves a creative process and innovative spirit of generating new possibilities in response to a changing world. Indeed, there is sometimes nearly a longing or yearning for something more, for something different. Creativity is needed to forge new paths and to discover and create new possibilities.

This chapter examines a group of employees who are creatively redesigning the balance of their work and non-work lives. More specifically, we look at the use of creativity among a sample of eighty-two professionals and managers in forty-two firms in the United States and Canada who are voluntarily working part-time, and being paid less, to balance multiple priorities in their careers and personal lives. These are individuals who are innovative in crafting a work arrangement by addressing how and where and when they work. In so doing, they may deviate from traditional job designs and career paths in organizations, and offer inspiration and possible foreshadowing of ways in which professional and managerial work and careers may transform to accommodate the shifting demographics and shifting needs of the workforce. We say that these individuals are 'creative' in their efforts because they are pursuing non-normative solutions to challenges and changing circumstances. That is, they are voluntarily pursuing non-traditional and often unique job design and career paths. Their arrangements were often novel and sometimes groundbreaking within their organizations.[1]

---

[1] On average, about 10 percent of employees in the organizations of our sample worked part-time, but many of our targets were among the higher ranking of the part-time workers in their organizations.

This analysis draws from a large-scale qualitative study of reduced-load work arrangements. The study aimed to gather descriptive information about how these arrangements were working out, from the perspective of multiple stakeholders. In this chapter, after describing the sample and methodology used, and some highlights of the findings, we intend to use the case studies of these professionals and managers to identify some key factors contributing to the creative redesign of work and career paths. What does it take for new forms of work arrangements to emerge? What conditions particularly enable a creative integration of professional and personal life?

Our study suggests that the success of innovative work arrangements is multiply determined by numerous variables. Consequently, we believe that an understanding of the genesis and success of creative careers and creative lives requires an examination of three factors: the *individuals* involved (What are the characteristics of the professionals and managers in reduced-load work arrangements?), the *organizations* involved (What are the characteristics of the work units and companies in which part-time professionals and managers in our sample work?), and the *interaction* between the two, as represented by the negotiation of the reduced-load work arrangement between the individual and the firm. This multifaceted approach is consistent with the work of several researchers of creativity (Gardner 1993; Csikszentmihalyi 1996; Amabile 1998). In particular, several scholars emphasize that, despite society's tendency to focus on the creative individual, an understanding of any creative endeavor is not complete without also examining the role of the context and other key players in the creative individual's life.

For example, Csikszentmihalyi (1996) repeatedly claims that creativity involves more than the individual. He says that creativity 'arises from synergy of many sources and not only from the mind of a single person. It is easier to enhance creativity by changing conditions in the environment than by trying to make people think creatively' (1996: 1). Emphasizing the importance of context, Csikszentmihalyi proposes that creativity is an interactive process including an individual person, the domain or discipline in which that person is working, and the surrounding 'field' of gatekeepers who evaluate and give approval about the quality of performance or other potentially creative output.

Similarly, Gardner (1993) highlights the roles of three equivalent factors in his definition. He says that 'the creative individual is a *person* who regularly solves problems, fashions products, or defines new questions in a *domain* in a way that is initially considered novel but that ultimately becomes accepted in a particular *cultural setting*' (1993: 35). Both Csikszentmihalyi and Gardner argue that 'nothing is, or is not, creative *in and of itself*. Creativity is inherently a communal or cultural judgment' (Gardner 1993: 36), because, to be considered creative, an entity must be accepted and validated by others and produce a change in an existing community or culture. Because 'social confirmation is necessary for something to be called creative' (Csikszentmihalyi 1996: 25), an analysis of creative performance, jobs, or careers must encompass more than the individual person involved. Likewise, Amabile (1998) concurs that managerial practices and an organization's environment can significantly influence employees' intrinsic motivation, and, ultimately, their creativity. In our analysis of factors that contribute to the creative design of reduced-load work arrangements, we will consider the individual, the organizational characteristics and context (representing the domain or cultural setting), and the negotiation of a request for part-time work between employee and organization (representing the process of evaluation and social confirmation from critical gatekeepers, namely senior managers or human-resource (HR) representatives who have authority to approve or deny reduced-load work arrangements in their organizations).

SAMPLE AND METHODOLOGY

A qualitative study of reduced-load, or part-time, work in the United States and Canada examined the cases of eighty-two managers and professionals working less than full-time (for example, working four days a week, rather than five) by choice, with an accompanying reduction in compensation, for family and/or lifestyle reasons. The study was designed to document how these arrangements came to be, and how they were working out, from the perspective of multiple stakeholders. Each case included interviews with the target manager or professional, his or her senior manager, a co-worker, a spouse or partner, where applicable, and an HR representative of the organization. Managerial participants were those responsible for the work of three or more direct reports. The forty-six managers were project managers, line managers, or those responsible for managing professionals in a support function, such as Director of Finance. The thirty-six participants in professional-level jobs were individuals with specific expertise or skill who were functioning in individual contributor roles in their organizations, in areas such as research and development, marketing, engineering, finance, human resources, and communications.

Participants were recruited using a variety of strategies, including personal contacts with HR and work/life administrators, 'cold calls' to employers, and direct mail solicitations to members of organizations. We sought to include a wide range of cases along dimensions such as the type of job, the size and industry of the company, reasons for pursuing reduced-load work, and the degree of load reduction. Based on existing estimates of the extent of men's participation in reduced-load work at the professional and managerial level in North America (Catalyst 1997), we aimed for 10–20 percent of our sample being men.

About 90 percent of the target professionals and managers were female, and about 90 percent had children. The reduced-load arrangements had been in existence about four years, on average, at the time of the study, and

Table 5.1. Demographic information: target employee sample

Demographic variables	Professionals ($n = 36$)	Managers ($n = 46$)
Percent female	87	92
Mean age	39.5	38.3
Mean salary ($)	48,576	63,535
Mean spouse/partner salary ($)	70,577	93,167
Percent with postgraduate degree (%)	58	45
Mean number of years on reduced load	4.76	3.79
Mean percent load reduction (%)	69	73
Mean current hours/week	30	34
Mean previous hours/week	49	51
Mean years experience before reduced load	13.5	13.6
Mean age of youngest child	5.3	4.5
Mean age of oldest child	7.9	7.1

respondents were generally experienced in their firms, having been with the employer for a mean of thirteen years. Table 5.1 provides additional demographic information about the sample. Interviews were conducted in forty-two companies, representing a wide variety of industries and functional areas. No more than four cases of part-time professionals and managers came from any one firm. Table 5.2 identifies additional information about the industries represented. Most participating companies were quite large, averaging 48,000 workers, although they ranged in size from 170 to 240,000 employees. On average, the workforces were 46.4 percent female, 15.6 percent unionized, and 10.9 percent part-time.

Managers and professionals who were parents reported that they pursued the reduced-load arrangement in large part, although not only, for family reasons. About one-third of parents reported that having children had changed their life priorities, making them less willing to structure their whole lives around their jobs. Most expressed strong commitment to their careers, but also a sense that their work and life at home were at least as important. Some participants knew they would want to pursue a part-time arrangement in advance of the birth of their child, or very shortly after the birth. For others, there was a more gradual shift in plans, either involving an increasing need to find more balance in their lives, to find a new way of working and a new way of living, or involving a shift in identity, and a desire for a career path that was more consistent with a new self-image. Those respondents without children typically requested reduced-load work in order to achieve a greater sense of balance in their lives, allowing them to have time to pursue hobbies, religious activities, or community service, or in response to concerns about their health and stress levels. In most cases, participants were able significantly to reduce

Table 5.2. Demographic information: employer sample

Industry	Number of organizations in employer sample ($n = 42$)	Number of cases in the industry
Manufacturing	12	23
Financial	7	17
Telecommunications	5	10
Professional/management services	4	9
Consumer goods	3	5
Health-care services	2	3
Non-profit	3	3
Pharmaceuticals	2	4
Natural resources	2	3
Hotel and food services	2	5

their amount of time at work, to a mean of 32 hours a week, compared to a mean of 50 hours when they were full-time.

The reduced-load arrangements were pursued in a variety of ways. About 15 percent of the respondents changed employers, usually because they had been unable to arrange a part-time position with their previous employer. About 13 percent of the sample continued to fulfill the same responsibilities on a part-time basis. The remaining managers and professionals either moved into a new or pre-existing part-time job or gained formal reconfiguration of their current job. By far the most common strategy for pursuing a reduced-load arrangement was to approach the senior manager involved, either informally or with a formal written proposal. In about 15 percent of the cases, the senior manager initiated the idea as a means of keeping a valuable employee whom the manager thought would otherwise leave. Respondents who did not initiate the plan with their senior managers usually found positions via corporate intranet or their own personal or professional networks.

Data were collected in one-to-one, confidential interviews with the target professional or manager, and with his or her spouse or partner, the target's senior manager, a peer-level co-worker, and an HR representative from the company. Ninety percent of the interviews were face to face, conducted by a member of a team of seven researchers, while the remainder took place on the telephone. The interviews with target respondents lasted about one and a half hours, while all other interviews lasted about forty-five minutes. All interviews were audio-recorded and transcribed verbatim for analysis. Over 350 interviews were conducted in total. The interviews were semi-structured, including questions on the following topics:

- the structure of and reasons for the reduced-load work arrangement;
- how the job was restructured to accommodate the reduced-load schedule;

- perceptions of the challenges and difficulties involved in restructuring the job;
- perceived costs and benefits of reduced-load work from multiple perspectives;
- factors important in making the arrangements more or less successful.

Usually, one interviewer gathered all data for one particular case. Data were collected between August 1996 and March 1998.

In addition to the interviews with stakeholders, questionnaire surveys were sent to the direct reports of target managers in the sample, but these were completed anonymously. Of the 253 direct reports of the forty-six managers in the study, 218 were sent questionnaires to be returned to the researchers (questionnaires were not sent to direct reports in three cases where the reduced load had recently ended, and the addresses of all subordinates were no longer known, and in one case because of administrative error on the part of the interviewer). Overall, 72 percent ($n = 153$) of the surveys were returned, and in twenty-two cases this included 100 percent of the direct reports. In the survey, respondents indicated their assessment of the manager's overall effectiveness, and their level of agreement with statements about the effects of their manager's reduced-load work arrangement on (1) their own work experience; (2) their relationship with their boss; and (3) the work unit as a whole.

Following the collection of data for a particular case, the interviewer wrote a 'reflective memo' to summarize main themes and to include a global rating of the overall success of the part-time arrangement. Using interview transcripts, direct report questionnaires, and any personal field notes and observations, the interviewer extracted material related to pre-identified categories, including logistics and negotiations of the arrangements, pros and cons, facilitating and hindering factors of success, managerial strategies, gender ideology, organizational characteristics of the firm, and HR policies. Taking all of the data into account, the interviewer generated an overall success rating, integrating the perspective of all stakeholders. First, the perspective of the target worker was considered: to what extent did he or she fulfill his or her objectives of going on reduced load, and how satisfied was he or she with the perceived benefits, relative to the perceived costs and trade-offs, from personal and career perspectives? Secondly, the organizational perspective was evaluated in terms of the extent to which the senior manager, co-workers, and others in a work group reported positive outcomes. Thirdly, the family perspective considered the impact of the reduced-load work arrangement upon children, family life, and/or the couple's relationship. Finally, we examined the consistency across all stakeholders in all three perspectives in reporting positive or negative consequences of the work arrangement. On a scale of 1 to 9, a '1' indicated consistently negative outcomes reported across stakeholders, while a '9' indicated consistently positive outcomes. Two members of the research team rated each case, and any differences were discussed and resolved.

HIGHLIGHTS OF RESULTS

Results from this study have been reported elsewhere (see Lee *et al.* 1999, for a full report of findings; also Buck *et al.* 1999; Lee *et al.* 2000; MacDermid *et al.* 2001), but we present a selection of highlights here in the context of employees' endeavors to creatively design their work and their lives.

High levels of success from multiple perspectives

On average, the cases examined in this study were considered highly successful from the perspective of multiple stakeholders. The majority of cases (62 percent) were in the High Success category (rankings of 7–9 on the scale described above), 31 percent were in the Moderate Success group (ratings of 5 or 6), and 7 percent received a Low Success rating. There was no significant difference in the overall success ratings of managers' and professionals' reduced-load arrangements. It should be noted that this sample was not randomly selected, and is not necessarily representative of all part-time professional and managerial employees. Nevertheless, the high rate of success in this sample is significant in that it highlights the possibility of high levels of success in creative job arrangements, across a wide range of types of jobs, firms, and industries.

Additional indicators of success include the following.

- Managers and professionals gained an average of 18 hours per week by working reduced load.
- Direct reports' ratings of their part-time managers' overall effectiveness averaged 7.2 out of 9 (with 1 indicating 'very ineffective' and 9 indicating 'very effective').
- Senior managers reported that targets' individual work performance was generally maintained or improved.
- Senior managers reported no significant negative impact on work unit performance.
- 91 percent of participants reported being happier and more satisfied with work–home balance.
- 90 percent of participants reported positive effects on their children: better relationships, and more time with them.

Career advancement slowed, not stopped

A common concern about working reduced load is the potential negative impact upon career development. Some respondents in this study worried that they would be perceived as less committed or be stigmatized by working part-time. However, while most, but not all, respondents believed they had made some career trade-offs, about two-thirds believed that their career progress had not been stopped. Furthermore, about 35 percent of the managers and professionals in the sample had received promotions while on reduced load. For another 33 percent of the sample, their bosses reported that the company was still investing in these individuals and expected them to advance in their careers.

Variability in the structure of the reduced-load arrangements

The way in which the workload of the target professionals and managers was reduced, and the ways the arrangements were structured, varied among individuals. For many of the employees, the amount of work was reduced by cutting the number of clients or projects, by extending deadlines, or by trimming less important aspects of the job. Others had reduced their level of responsibility, often by moving away from managing people or interacting with clients, in favor of more project-oriented work. These means of reduction were accomplished in one of several ways:

- a new position, either already existing, or created for the target employee;
- the same job, reconfigured to eliminate certain responsibilities or projects;
- the same job, compressed into less time;
- same job with reduced client load;
- job sharing.

The above descriptions of different approaches indicate the initial position of the alternative work arrangement. It is important to note that many of these employees had been on reduced load for many years, and during that time had had numerous adjustments and changes to their work arrangement. Some started by working three days a week, and later moved up to four days a week, or vice versa. In fact, many employees and senior managers reported a period of experimentation and 'tinkering', until they found the right amount of work and best schedule to meet the demands of both the work unit and family circumstances. Considerable creativity was often used to devise arrangements that would provide 'win–win' solutions to the needs of the company and the individual.

Reduced-load work not a short-term phenomenon

Some participants initiated their reduced-load arrangement as a temporary situation, but many of them grew quickly accustomed to and appreciative of the greater balance in their lives, such that they no longer saw it as short term. The targets in the sample had been on reduced load for an average of 4.4 years. Furthermore, at the time of the study, only 10 percent planned to return to full-time in the next three years. For many, a creative alternative in a work arrangement became an attractive lifestyle that fulfilled multiple work and non-work related needs.

Personal outcomes: changes in the use of time at work and at home

By reducing their work hours from a mean of 50 hours per week before, to a mean of 32 hours per week in the part-time arrangement, these managers and professionals often had a more intense awareness of how time is used, an actual change in how time at work is used, and a heightened sense of making every moment count. At work, the reduced-load employees and other stake-holders reported that these workers had a high level of focus and concentration, and an ability to identify priorities and work efficiently. They often skipped activities considered to be non-essential, and displayed a high level of experimentation and creativity in delegating work, drawing boundaries, and communicating with a boss about workload and opportunities.

Organizational outcomes

From the perspective of work groups in the organizations, direct reports were quite satisfied with the performance and supervision of their managers who were on reduced load. About half of the co-workers of part-time professionals and managers were rated as highly supportive of the arrangement, while another 25 percent were not supportive. Some of these co-workers reported that the work not covered by the target ended up as extra responsibility for them.

From an organizational perspective, respondents in all stakeholder groups perceived more positive than negative outcomes. Reported benefits included:

- improved recruitment and retention efforts;
- advantages to managers, such as staffing flexibility;
- enhanced corporate image;
- increased loyalty and motivation among the part-time employees and among some full-time co-workers;
- opportunities for organizational learning.

Respondents in the organizations also reported some potential concerns:

- managing hassles and logistics (scheduling complications, task allocations, and performance evaluation);

- perceived inconsistencies with workaholic cultures;
- managing precedent and subsequent requests for more alternative work arrangements.

FACTORS CONTRIBUTING TO THE CREATIVE DESIGN OF REDUCED-LOAD WORK ARRANGEMENTS

Most respondents, across all stakeholders, felt that numerous factors contributed to the success of the reduced-load work arrangements, rather than any single factor. To gain the best understanding of the creative redesign of work and careers, we must look at a number of variables. In particular, and mirroring the approaches of creativity scholars outlined earlier, we draw upon a social psychological perspective (Ross and Nisbett 1991) suggesting that, in order to understand the behavioral phenomenon in question (in this case, the reduced-load work arrangements), we must consider the person, the situation, and the interaction between the two. In the context of this study, that means we must examine the characteristics of the target professionals and managers, the characteristics of the organizations with employees in reduced-load work arrangements, and the negotiation interaction between individuals and organizational representatives.

Characteristics of the individual

Of the top twelve factors contributing to the success of the reduced-load arrangements cited by all stakeholders, eight of these are related to the individuals working reduced load, suggesting that the workers themselves are perceived as largely responsible for making the arrangements work. While reasons for success may not be the same as the variables that are sources of creativity, it may be helpful to understand the profile of those employees successfully working in this way. These reported characteristics and behavioral strategies of the individual include:

- concentrated, highly focused work style;
- strong performance record;
- unique skill set in high demand;
- flexibility;
- high level of hard work and commitment;
- entrepreneurial style of taking initiative;
- strong, clear personal values;
- ability to manage communication seamlessly.

In addition to these factors, many of the target professionals and managers seemed to have engaged in considerable self-reflection, generating a keen sense of awareness of personal priorities, and a level of comfort with trade-offs. Furthermore, in many cases, these individuals could articulate a personal redefinition of career success. They often commented that they felt they were striving for something different from some of their peers in their organizations. They did not feel bound by traditional notions of 'climbing the ladder' as a basis of career success, nor did they necessarily even want this same path. This level of self-reflection seems to be linked with an ability to engage in creative pursuits, in the sense that the ability to design a different path must be preceded by an awareness of the gap between traditional desires and their own, and the willingness not to be bound by traditional norms or standards.

For example, one individual said:

To me, success has changed over the course of my career. But I would say that at this point in my life, it is achieving a certain amount of financial stability . . . and achieving a sense of contribution and satisfaction in what I do. So that says I couldn't make a lot of money and not enjoy what I was doing. Like, I would have to have both. But the success piece of it, I don't need the prestige and power, I just, I am quite able to contribute, lead, make a difference on a team environment. So I mean I have not desired to be president of [company name].

Another said:

Career success? It has got to do with making a contribution to the organization that I am in and the company at large, really having an impact, feeling that something I'm doing isn't just pushing a pencil but that there are things that I can see and touch and feel that I know that I contributed towards making them what they are. And then there is a personal element of it, too, which is that I do it in a way that is really very honorable. That I keep my work, that I am a person of commitment, that I fulfill my commitments, that I treat people well, fairly. That's it: that I do the job, and that I do it in a particular way.

Another manager said that, for her, career success involves

mostly having fun and constantly learning. So it has a lot to do with people I'm working with. So if you really enjoy the people you are working with, everybody is learning and growing and you're having fun. Which is pretty much all the jobs I've had have been like that. And I never really had a plan, ever. I never had a plan to get a Ph.D. It just felt good at the time. I was having a good time, I was really interested in what I was doing. And so it was just fun. I never had a plan to come and work here. I never had a plan to be a manager.

Many of the reflections of part-time managers and professionals in the sample indicated an awareness of their own ideas of success and their own priorities in work and non-work life, and a willingness and desire to pursue different directions. They often indicated that they went in directions they had not originally planned, but in directions that seemed to reflect what they needed and who they felt themselves to be. Drucker comments on the importance of self-reflection and awareness of personal priorities in saying that 'successful

careers are not planned. They develop when people are prepared for opportunities because they know their strengths, their method of work, and their
values. Knowing where one belongs can transform an ordinary person... into
an outstanding performer' (Drucker 1999: 67). By extension, we might add that,
in the cases of some of the part-time professionals and managers, 'knowing
where one belongs' and clearly knowing one's priorities can lead to creative
alternatives that may not be predictable or traditional, but that fit one's needs
and priorities.

Characteristics of the organization

The individuals on reduced-load work arrangements significantly contributed
to making the arrangements work, but they alone are not the full equation. To
understand creative endeavors, we need to look not only at the individuals
involved, but also at the environment in which they work, or the domain or
cultural setting, as creativity researchers suggest (Gardner 1993; Csikszentmihalyi
1996). In this study, respondents in all stakeholder groups commented that
work group factors and organizational characteristics were important in facilitating the success of alternative work arrangements of the targets. Among
work group factors, they said that a supportive boss and competent and supportive peers and subordinates were important for successful arrangements.

A supportive boss was the most frequently mentioned of all facilitating
factors (individual, work group, and organizational levels), indicating respondents' belief that, no matter how competent or creative the individual, a
supportive boss was critical. This support could be manifest in terms of the
initial approval of the reduced-load arrangement, but also, critically, in sustained support over time. Some bosses actively worked to make sure that
important meetings were not scheduled for the target's day off, or looked for
ways to make the arrangement work for all relevant stakeholders. In her
research on the factors that foster creativity in organizational settings, Amabile
(1998) says that 'supervisory encouragement' is one of the pivotal elements,
especially in *sustaining* creativity over time. She comments that 'managers who
kill creativity do so either by failing to acknowledge innovative efforts or by
greeting them with skepticism. In many companies... new ideas are met not
with open minds but with time-consuming layers of evaluation, or even with
harsh criticism.... [Some managers] look for reasons to not use an idea instead
of searching for reasons to explore it further' (Amabile 1998: 83).

In addition to a supportive boss, a strong team approach in the work unit
was also frequently mentioned as a facilitating factor in the success of the
reduced-load work arrangement. Among the managerial cases it was found that
there was a great deal of 'cross skilling' among the direct reports and a well-
established norm of peers helping and supporting each other in order to meet
organizational goals, even before the alternative work arrangement began.

We also found, in addition to the immediate work group and boss, that characteristics such as an organizational culture of employee-centered values and widely publicized work-life policies or programs were important in supporting and sustaining the reduced-load work arrangement. Organizational culture is a broad term that includes a wide array of meanings. Respondents most consistently commented on two aspects of organizational culture: values and work norms. When it was clear that employers really valued people as the most valuable resource, then reduced-load work arrangements were more likely to be successful. However, valuing people meant not just through words in a mission statement, but through: a long-standing history of taking tough actions to avoid lay-offs; investing in ongoing training and development; or taking seriously the connection between employees' quality of work life and organizational performance, by acknowledging employees as whole people with important duties both on and off the job.

A second value viewed as highly conducive to alternative work arrangements was flexibility, or adaptability to change. Organizations that were 'quick on their feet' to react to market trends or employee demands or whatever were seen as more likely places for successful, and creative, alternative work arrangements. In this kind of climate, ongoing fine-tuning or adjustments could be made more easily in the work arrangements in response to changing conditions in the work unit and/or the family, if needed.

As for work norms, there was a consistent view that innovative work arrangements were not likely to be successful in organizations where 'face time' was considered the most appropriate measure of productivity. On the contrary, in organizations where performance was judged on the basis of results rather than the number of hours being expended, or the amount of time seen in the office, there was a greater possibility of integration and success of alternative work arrangements. In these situations, the organizations were more open to alternative ways of getting work done, so long as the work actually did get done. A competitive advantage may emerge from this stance, because it removes constraints on the strategies employees may propose for maximizing organizational performance. In other words, *flexibility* in how, when, or where work is accomplished enables *creativity* in generating new options.

Another frequently mentioned organizational-level characteristic was the existence of widely publicized work–life or work–family policies and programs. However, it is important to note that these policies and programs did *not* exist in about one-third of the cases, so policies and programs are apparently helpful, but not necessary, for the success of creative work arrangements. Where there *were* specific formal policies about reduced-load work, approval always required 'buy-in' on the part of the senior manager of the individual requesting to work less, illustrating the importance of the interaction and the negotiation between the individual and the organization. Also, there was a great deal of variation in the kind of work–life policies and programs found. For example, some involved rigid rules and procedures that were viewed as serving to discourage experimentation with different ways of working. In other cases, a restrictive tone in the employee handbook carried an underlying message of mistrust. Finally, some organizations provided very detailed, highly specific policies, perhaps even labeling what jobs could or could not be done on a reduced-load basis. Other organizations intentionally kept their work–life policies more broad and general. These variations in the use of policies and programs were often reflective of variation in more general themes of organizational culture and values, which are critical in sending messages to employees about what possibilities for creativity will be encouraged, tolerated, or discouraged. Amabile (1998: 84) comments that 'creativity is truly enhanced when the entire organization supports it. Such support is the job of an organization's leaders, who must put in place appropriate systems or procedures and emphasize values that make it clear that creative efforts are a top priority.'

In order to better understand the organization-level response to alternative work arrangements in our present study, we examined the forty-two organizations, rather than the eighty-two cases of individual employees, to identify different 'paradigms' of implementation and interpretation of these reduced-load work arrangements (Lee et al. 2000). These paradigms emerged from an iterative process of grouping organizations according to similarities in predominant themes in the interview data around: (1) rationale given for approving the alternative work arrangements; (2) factors described as facilitating or hindering the realization or success of the reduced-load experiments; and (3) organizational outcomes. Eventually, the organizational groupings could be interpreted as representing three distinct patterns of response, negotiation, and enactment, which we labeled: accommodation, elaboration, and transformation (see Fig. 5.1). These terms were chosen because they suggest different responses to an external stimulus (request for reduced-load work) and subsequent modes of learning. 'Accommodation' suggests a firm making the most minimal adjustment in response to a request for a different way of working. In organizational learning terms, it means treating such a request as a random, non-standard event not worth development of new routines. 'Elaboration' connotes going further in investigating and even developing new routines in response to a new phenomenon, but without giving up the basic, status quo way of organizing and structuring work and careers. 'Transformation' implies a company's greater willingness to move away from the status quo and actively to use an external stimulus, like a request for reduced-load work arrangements, as an opportunity to find new ways of working. In organizational learning terms, transformation involves more exploration and more acceptance of disruptive, non-routine behavior. There is an underlying assumption that the organization must adapt and realign itself continuously. Reduced-load work arrangements become a springboard for thinking about new ways of defining and organizing work or rethinking career paths and reward structures for a changing workforce.

	Accommodation	Elaboration	Transformation
Negotiation context	* Guided by individual situation—reluctant	* Guided by policy and culture	* Guided by individual situation and culture
Responsibility	* Onus on target	* Policies and programs plus target	* Shared by target and senior manager
Employer rationale	* Financial benefits * Increased productivity * So firm does not lose a highly valued individual	* Retention * Help firm meet diversity goals * Get on work–life bandwagon	* Business needs * Organizational adaptation * Recruitment and retention
Employer posture	* Acquiesce and contain	* Institutionalize and manage	* Experiment and learn

Fig. 5.1. Organizational paradigms of reduced-load work.

Source: Lee *et al.* 2000.

These paradigms can thus be viewed as representing organizational level variability in creativity, or responsiveness to change in the external environment and challenges to the status quo. The paradigms illustrate how firms respond to the ongoing tension between continuity and change and between the motives of exploitation of routines and exploration of disruptive, non-routine behavior (Crossan *et al.* 1999; Weick and Westley 1996). For example, the accommodation firms' method of implementing and interpreting reduced-load work arrangements demonstrates high exploitation: the intent is to increase efficiencies and productivity and continue established routines. Individual cases of alternative work arrangements are treated as exceptions and as minor anomalies that can be dismissed, or, indeed, accommodated, but always with an eye on containment. In fact, it was often the case in accommodation firms that reduced-load work arrangements remained secret, in fear that, if news of them spread, the logistics of managing exceptions to the rule would become overwhelming.

On the other hand, transformation firms demonstrate a high level of the exploration aspect of learning, with reduced-load work requests being greeted with openness and as an opportunity for experimentation, even though such requests represent disruptive, non-routine behavior and challenge the status quo. In some transformation firms, senior managers talked about using reduced-load work arrangements as an opportunity to learn about how to manage more customized or non-standard work in general, in order to adapt to the changing values and lifestyles of the new 'Generation X' professionals in the labor force.

Beyond the three paradigms of organizational response to reduced-load arrangements, success in creative career arrangements, more generally, seems to require that the principals and the organizations realistically appraise their risks and opportunities. It is unrealistic to expect that every possible bump in the road with an alternative work arrangement can be anticipated and resolved in the initial approval and agreement setting up the arrangement. Organizations that foster success of innovative work arrangements may have been more likely to expect to make adjustments from time to time to adapt arrangements to the changing configuration of needs and concerns of the stakeholders involved.

Negotiation interactions between individuals and organizations

In order to understand the genesis and evolution of creative careers and creative lives, it is important to examine not only the role of the individual and of the domain or organizational context, but also the process by which the alternative arrangements came to be accepted in their particular context. Gardner (1993) and Csikszentmihalyi (1996) claim that creative endeavors are not just different from existing norms, but must survive a process of social validation and acceptance, signaling that change has actually occurred in a particular setting or community. Gardner emphasizes that creative designs must be *accepted*, and Amabile (1998) claims that business creativity, in particular, must be 'useful and actionable'. Furthermore, Csikszentmihalyi suggests that part of creativity is having something evaluated and approved by 'gatekeepers' in the relevant domain. In our study of part-time professionals and managers, the process of evaluation and validation can be represented by the negotiation and approval process between the target individual and representatives of the organization, most often the senior manager or HR representative. One variable that seems to increase the likelihood that a reduced-load work arrangement will be accepted, and therefore enhance creativity, is a fundamental *focus on the underlying interests*, rather than positions, of the parties involved (Buck *et al.* 1999). Furthermore, reduced-load arrangements that were negotiated with *a sense of joint accountability* for making the arrangement work were especially likely to lead to opportunities for learning and innovation (Lee *et al.* 2000).

In negotiations, *interests* are the underlying needs, concerns, and fundamental issues. They are distinct from the *positions*, or claims, that parties say that they want (Lax and Sebenius 1986; Ury *et al.* 1988; Fisher and Ury 1991). For example, an individual may approach her boss with a request to work four days a week, with Fridays off. This would be the particular position that she is planning to negotiate. But that request alone does not necessarily indicate her underlying interests, or the reasons *why* she attempts to negotiate a particular position. The interest may be the desire to accompany her daughter to special school activities that occur each Friday. Alternatively, the interest could be a more general desire to reduce working hours in order to reduce stress, with no particular need for a particular day of the week, or even particular hours, as long as overall work hours and workload are reduced.

Negotiations frequently involve discussions of desired positions, without distinguishing the underlying interests (Ury *et al.* 1988; Fisher and Ury 1991). Based upon our linguistic habits and conversation style, it is deceivingly easy to articulate positions, rather than the interests behind those specific requests. This is significant, because particular positions often cannot be fulfilled, but underlying interests may be able to be fulfilled in a variety of ways. For example, if the employee described above has an underlying interest of reducing stress in her life, but the position of not working Fridays is not feasible for her organization, her interest may be able to be accommodated with a variety of other work schedules. The distinction between negotiating positions versus negotiating interests becomes important because negotiation based upon interests increases *flexibility* and opportunities for creative alternatives. Negotiating based upon positions is more likely to lead to a conclusion of 'yes, this can work, and the request is approved', or 'no, this can't work, and the proposal is denied'. In contrast, identification of underlying interests is more likely to trigger a mindset of 'how can we make this work?' and foster conversations searching for creative ways to fulfill interests.

In the context of negotiating alternative work arrangements, a focused attention on the underlying interests, and a willingness to experiment with a variety of different ways in which individuals' and organizations' needs can be fulfilled, contribute to the ultimate success of the work arrangements (see also Friedman *et al.* 1998, for a discussion of win–win approaches to work–life issues). Furthermore, requests for part-time arrangements are more likely to be *accepted* and supported when they integrate the individual's and organization's needs, thereby meeting Gardner's and Csikszentmihalyi's criteria of social confirmation of creative endeavors.

Of the organizations examined in the present study, recall that those in the transformation paradigm (Lee *et al.* 2000) were most likely to use requests for reduced-load work arrangements as opportunities for innovation and organizational learning. In these cases, the negotiation context was characterized by a sense of joint responsibility between employees and the organization for making the arrangement work, rather than the individual employee experiencing the full 'burden' of satisfying the needs of all stakeholders. An organizational culture of joint responsibility enhances creativity, innovation, and, ultimately, change, by motivating multiple stakeholders to bring different perspectives, to devise new options, and to experiment with alternative ways of working. In general, the way that reduced-load work arrangements are negotiated sheds light upon opportunities for creative careers and creative employment relationships.

FUTURE DIRECTIONS

We conclude by considering the extent to which the creative design of work and careers, as expressed in the cases of reduced-load work arrangements among managers and professionals, are independent cases, or whether they might set precedents, or lead to a spreading of creativity. From an individual perspective, it seems clear that those who have found that reduced-load work has helped them maintain career and family commitments so far are enthusiastic about continuing to be able to 'customize' their work arrangements into the future. Many of our target managers talked about their creative ideas for adapting their work arrangements over time according to their changing needs and the changing needs of their families, for example as pre-schoolers become school age, or as a spouse's employment situation shifts, or as an elderly parent becomes sick and needs more attention, and so on. These individuals also acknowledged the importance of the corporation's shifting priorities too, and the fact that they might need to look for a position in a particular part of the company or with a progressive-minded boss, if they wanted to continue to work less and with more flexibility than the standard work arrangement. In general, however, these individuals seemed highly confident that they could work something out, because they felt the alternative work arrangements so far had worked well and been well received. They felt they had been successful at continuing to add value in their job, while also gaining more time for themselves and their families.

From an organizational perspective, the evidence is equally strong that experimentation with alternative work arrangements provides organizations with an opportunity for learning, innovation, and improvisation. A number of senior managers in a variety of host organizations told us that the reason for approving reduced-load work arrangements among professionals and managers is not just a mechanism for retention, or good public relations, or promoting productivity by being a more 'family-friendly' firm. Rather they viewed these individual requests as just the beginning of a major trend toward more customized, non-standard work arrangements with individually negotiated terms in general. One Vice-President said:

We need to find a way for this to work for SN not just to help her solve her unique challenges related to career and family. Because behind SN is another highly talented female and behind her another, and behind her a 'Generation X' man, etc. We have to figure out how to provide alternatives and manage more individually negotiated work arrangements if we want to move forward and be ready to meet the staffing challenges in our industry in the 21st century.

We also found specific examples in Transformation firms of how reduced-load work was just a building block in a larger on-going effort to open up traditional career path structures. For example, one firm discovered that its part-time work policy, which dictated that professionals who made that choice had to step off the 'Hi Potential' track, was losing some of its best and brightest to competitors, after 8–10 years of experience and significant company investment in training and development. So the policy was revised to create a place 'in-stream' for 'Hi Potentials' to work less for periods of times. An executive in another firm mentioned that his company was considering turning all promotions above a certain level into individually negotiated deals rather than rigid offers with standard parameters, partly because of the different priorities among the candidates for managerial positions these days, depending on family situation and financial needs and desires. For example, during certain points in their lives, some executives might want to limit travel or avoid work involving time-sensitive deadlines. Or they might want to arrange for a different mix of compensation that facilitated savings for children's university education.

Another example of how reduced-load work can be a stimulus to creative thinking and imagining about careers can be seen in the quote below from an executive in a high-tech company who was supervising a professional with an alternative work arrangement. She was asked about the career potential of this professional and what effect reduced-load work might have:

'Could she be Vice President working four fifths? Hard to say, but the real question is does she have the experience required, is she 'armed' to succeed at the next level. And after all, the critical issue at that level is reachability, because you are gone travelling, at least 25 percent of the time anyway, and even at full-time you have to delegate and worry about reachability. So isn't it just an extension of some of these more normal parameters taken to just a little bit more extreme case?'

Reduced-load work arrangements can be viewed as examples of organizational learning moments, or 'small wins', in Weick and Westley's terms (1996), but they may have bigger effects in the long term. They note that grassroots sorts of experiments or explorations that appear *ad hoc* and insignificant on the margins can sometimes precede and pave the way for more revolutionary and systematic change in an organization. As such, examination of reduced-load work arrangements among managers and professionals provides insight into ways that individuals are creatively designing their careers and their lives, and the ways that organizations may creatively adapt and evolve in dynamic environments.

REFERENCES

Amabile, T. M. (1998), 'How to Kill Creativity', *Harvard Business Review*, (Sept.–Oct.), 77–87.

Bateson, M. C. (1989), *Composing a Life* (New York: Plume Books).

Buck, M. L., Leiba-O'Sullivan, S., Lee, M. D., and MacDermid, S. M. (1999), 'Individual Negotiations as Catalysts for Organizational Change: The Case of Negotiating Alternative Work Arrangements', paper presented for the Annual Meeting of the International Association of Conflict Management, San Sebastian, Spain.

——Lee, M. D., MacDermid, S. M., and Smith, S. (2000), 'Reduced Load Work and the Experience of Time among Professionals and Managers: Implications for Personal and Organizational Life', in C. L. Cooper and D. Rousseau (eds.), *Trends in Organizational Behavior*, 7 (New York: John Wiley).

Catalyst (1997), *A New Approach to Flexibility: Managing the Work/Time Equation* (New York: Catalyst).

Crossan, M. M., Lane, H. W., and White, R. E. (1999), 'An Organizational Learning Framework: From Intuition to Institutionalization', *Academy of Management Review*, 24: 522–37.

Csikszentmihalyi, M. (1996), *Creativity: Flow and the Psychology of Discovery and Invention* (New York: HarperCollins).

Drucker, P. (1999), 'Managing Oneself', *Harvard Business Review* (Mar.–Apr.), 64–74.

Epstein, C. F., Seron, C., Oglensky, B., and Saute, R. (1998), *The Part-Time Paradox* (New York: Routledge).

Fisher, R., and Ury, W. (1991), *Getting to Yes: Negotiating Agreement without Giving in.* (Harmondsworth: Penguin).

Friedman, S. D., Christensen, P., and DeGroot, J. (1998), 'Work and Life: The End of the Zero-Sum Game', *Harvard Business Review*, 76/6: 119–29.

Gardner, H. (1993), *Creating Minds* (New York: Basic Books).

Lax, D. A., and Sebenius, J. K. (1986), *The Manager as Negotiator: Bargaining for Cooperation and Competitive Gain* (New York: Free Press).

Lee, M. D., MacDermid, S. M., Williams, M., Buck, M. L., Schreiber, C., Borelli, L., Leiba-O'Sullivan, S., Smith, S., Bernstein, M., and Dorhring, P. (1999), 'Reconceptualizing Professional and Managerial Careers', technical report prepared for the Alfred P. Sloan Foundation, New York.

——— and Buck, M. L. (2000), 'Organizational Paradigms of Reduced Load Work: Accommodation, Elaboration, Transformation', *Academy of Management Journal*, 43/6: 1211–26.

MacDermid, S. M., Lee, M. D., Buck, M. L., and Williams, M. L. (2001), 'Alternate Work Arrangements among Professionals and Managers: Rethinking Career Development and Success', *Journal of Management Development*, 20/4: 305–17.

Mirchandani, K. (1998), 'No Longer a Struggle: Teleworkers' Reconstruction of the Work–Non-Work Boundary', in P. J. Jackson and J. M. VanderWielen (eds.), *Teleworking: International Perspectives* (London: Routledge), 118–35.

Ross, L, and Nisbett, R. E. (1991), *The Person and the Situation: Perspectives of Social Psychology* (New York: McGraw-Hill).

Scandura, T. A., and Lankau, M. J. (1997), Relationships of Gender, Family Responsibility and Flexible Work Hours to Organizational Commitment and Job Satisfaction', *Journal of Organizational Behavior*, 18/4: 377–91.

Ury, W. L., Brett, J. M., and Goldberg, S. B. (1988), *Getting Disputes Resolved: Designing Systems to Cut the Costs of Conflict* (San Francisco: Jossey-Bass).

Weick, K.E., and Westley, F. (1996), 'Organization Learning: Affirming an Oxymoron', in S. R. Clegg, C. Hardy, and W. R. Nord (eds.), *Handbook of Organizational Studies* (London: Sage), 440–58.

II

CREATIVE CAREERS ENACTED

This section is the province of the individual career actor. It describes the creativity and adaptiveness so many individuals exhibit when reinventing their work or restarting their careers. Much has been written about the need to take responsibility for one's own career and to be proactive in so doing, but it is not always easy to see how. Here, four contributions—again, from four very different perspectives—go beyond the simple maxim of owning one's career to show how career actors not only pursue this approach but also make sense of it within a broader context. How can career actors be sufficiently individualistic, without losing touch with the collective institutions through which much work happens? Without being able to plan careers with any certainty, how can we nonetheless be purposeful and effective? How can we confront career disappointments in a way that is constructive for both ourselves and the institutions or customers we seek to serve? We experience four sets of answers, and are invited to consider the extent to which they affirm or challenge one another.

Gray Poehnell and Norm Amundson introduce us to the concept of 'CareerCraft' as a means to respond to the greater levels of creativity that the contemporary business climate seems to demand. The metaphor of craft, which the authors illustrate through the example of weaving, provides the underlying insight into the incorporation of all three components of function, skill, and creativity. Seen in this way, the component of creativity can be seen to involve career actors feeling more engaged, energized, and empowered. They are engaged through the process of being more creative, energized through the creative tension that their visions generate, and empowered through the freeing of mental blocks and the opening of new choices. The authors demonstrate how their ideas can be promoted through workshop activities designed for people who are experiencing radical organizational change.

Polly Parker looks at contract workers, those who undertake temporary rather than permanent job assignments, and suggests we can learn from the creativity in those workers' adaptations. In particular, she looks at the internally perceived, subjective careers of 'leased executives' (LEs) or 'interim managers' and finds a pattern of integration across their career investments. The LEs' investments in personal autonomy and project success are complemented by parallel investments in their own on-the-job learning. Temporary work relationships are complemented by enduring family and community attachments, and these lend continuity to the LEs' careers. These 'zig-zag' careers suggest a new career form, combining temporary project assignments into a coherent learning-driven career. Parker invites us to see the LEs' careers at the cutting edge of new employment practice, and therefore prototypical of career arrangements for the future.

Jeffrey Sonnenfeld focuses on how creativity in career behavior can stem from adversity. Citing F. Scott Fitzgerald's 'curse' that there are 'no second acts' in American lives, he explores the careers of victims who have subsequently challenged the curse. Common barriers that the victims face include loss of self-esteem, danger of burnout, loss of influence, frustrated opportunities, collateral impact on loyal friends and family, and cultural resistance to reclaiming one's former success. Sonnenfeld suggests how victims can in turn respond through case studies of what he calls 'resilient leaders'. The responses fall under five categories: fight not flight, recruiting others into battle, rebuilding heroic stature, proving your mettle, and rediscovering the heroic mission. Although the argument is illustrated by reference to business leaders, the author's invitation is for each of us to consider how we may respond creatively to adversity, and how we may thereby become strengthened rather than weakened by our subsequent career behavior.

The international assignment can be a particularly potent trigger to adaptation and career creativity. Douglas (Tim) Hall, Guorong Zhu, and Aimin Yan describe how being thrust into a foreign environment can oblige us to relearn the most basic rules of thought and behavior. As a result, the assignee often experiences deep personal transformation: new behaviors and a new identity. However, the authors note how these changes often fail to provide for successful adaptation at the assignment's conclusion, because the employing organization is blind to what has taken place. This often results in the person's experiencing frustration and lack of recognition—and ultimately in exit from the organization. The experience also sends signals to others that beget negative career outcomes in the wider organization. The authors argue that there is much untapped potential in the creative personal transformations resulting from the kind of potent challenges that international assignments represent. They conclude with a call for more effective relationships to help the transformed returning 'hero' maintain his or her identity—and membership in the organization.

For all of these authors, three themes seem to stand out. One theme concerns having the personal skills to behave creatively in one's career, to avoid reliance on traditional 'ladders' for success, and thereby to be better able to interact with and succeed (on one's own terms) in a rapidly changing world. A second theme that is either explicit or implicit in all of the chapters involves dealing with adversity. This is in contrast to, and more confrontational than, the traditional term for dealing with career discontinuity—namely, transition. The prediction of adversity, perhaps recurrent adversity, over the course of one's career also invites us to build a better tool kit, and to keep it ready, rather than simply to be ready to suffer occasional career disruptions. A third theme is that our organizations and institutions are not yet well equipped to support more creative career behavior. People seem to be on their own, to a great degree, rather than being able to anticipate much support from the employment systems in place. The emphasis here is on doing what we can despite the inadequacy of the career systems that host us. However, we can look ahead to Parts III and IV of this book to anticipate how those employment systems may be changing.

6

CareerCraft: Engaging with, Energizing, and Empowering Career Creativity

GRAY POEHNELL AND NORMAN AMUNDSON

It is our intention in this chapter to explore the value of looking at career issues from the perspective of 'craft'—the 'art of career' more than just the 'management of career'. Such an approach emphasizes the synergism of creativity, skill, and practicality as essential components in 'crafting' careers.

It can easily be demonstrated that 'management' is the predominant metaphor or paradigm for career. Consider the terminology used for career activities and concepts: career management, career development, labor market, marketing oneself, human-resources (HR) development, assessment, decision making, action planning—these reflect the perspective of 'management'.

People engage in 'career management' and, thereby, seek to 'manage their careers' in ways that are most effective. Such a perspective has many strengths, not the least of which is that it brings order and structure to what can be a very subjective process.

Suppose, however, that career activities were viewed from the metaphor of 'craft' rather than 'management'. As Tom Wujec (1995: 133–4) points out,

metaphors and their relatives—similes, analogies, parallels, allegories, symbols, allusions—are much more than figures of speech. They are the architects of our conceptual system; they build scaffolds of ideas. We usually think of a metaphor as a statement which expresses one concept in terms of another. . . . Each metaphor provides a new perspective, a new set of associations and fresh creative tension and energy. Consider how switching metaphors gives us new ways of examining an idea.

We would suggest that examining career from this new paradigm of 'craft' will indeed be a source of new perspectives, new associations, and fresh creative tension and energy, which will prove to be invaluable in the face of current career realities. Certainly this is consistent with the concept of a 'sense-making' metaphor put forward by Inkson in Chapter 2.

In a workshop that we offer on the theme of CareerCraft, we conduct an activity on word associations for 'management' and for 'craft'. Workshop participants start by listing the first five words that come to mind when they think of 'management'. They then list the first five words that come to mind when they think of 'craft'. The debriefing of the activity reveals that people often have quite different associations for these two words. When thinking of 'management', people think of words such as organize, step-by-step, planning, controlled, bureaucracy, marketing, logical, focused, realistic, driven, product-ive, cognitive, action oriented, decisive, conservative, guiding influence, disciplined, regulated, order, policy, vision, leadership, 'suits', responsibility, creativity, business, structure, slow, and power. 'Craft', on the other hand, suggests words such as craftsmanship, skillful, expertise, creative, beauty, hands-on, messy, practical, magical, artistic, personal, passionate, feelings, specialist, competence, proficiency, inventive, imaginative, functional, noble, stimulating, original, fun, flair, love, and well wrought. Clearly these two terms, craft and management, seem to focus on some different areas of function.

We believe that 'craft' complements 'management'; it does not replace it. A quick glance at the previous lists of associations shows some overlap. The paradigms of 'management' and 'craft' are not mutually exclusive. A focus on CareerCraft and creativity seems to be well timed in view of much of the new literature within the business field. Businesses are embracing creativity con-cepts with a new vigor as they face growing complexities. Consider the fol-lowing quote by Weaver (2000: 16):

Creativity is moving up the list of essential business skills needed to survive and succeed in the fast and complex new economy. Many books and articles in the *Harvard Business Review* and other business magazines urge us to pay more than lip service to the creative process. Why is creativity getting all of this attention? Because the rules of the new economy are changing, not only quickly, but fundamentally. We are on new and shifting ground with no clear path and no one to show us the way. We have to make it up.

Just as the world of business is fundamentally changing and concepts such as creativity are seen to be essential for survival, so too the world of career is fundamentally changing and concepts such as creativity are gaining momentum. It is in the light of this need that viewing career from the per-spective of craft is so important. The new insights and approaches suggested by such a perspective can have a powerful effect upon those who wish to craft their careers.

CareerCraft is a new paradigm for a new career reality. Feller (1995) speaks in terms of a major structural change in the workplace, nothing short of a 'new psychological contract' with workers. This new career reality must be seen in the context of a global economy characterized by global economic competi-tion, technical innovation, smart technology, advanced telecommunications, and changing demographics. In contrast to the old workplace, where the entitlement ethic emphasized primarily loyalty, endurance, and hard work, the ever-changing workplace is now characterized by more fluidity, less job security, fewer full-time positions, more temporary staff, more competitiveness, flexible and customized production, increasing emphasis on being more self-directed in lifelong learning and career planning, more multi-skilled workers, broader responsibilities, more flexible supervisors who act as 'coaches', fewer supervisors, greater teamwork, more emphasis on performance rather than seniority, the sharing of risks by both the employer and the workers, and the need to be able to solve problems and create new opportunities. These new career realities are illustrated throughout this book by the case studies presented by several authors (Södergren, Chapter 3; Buck, Lee, and MacDermid, Chapter 5; Parker, Chapter 7; Alvarez and Svejenova, Chapter 10; Jones, Chapter 11; Ensher, Murphy, and Sullivan, Chapter 12; Higgins, Chapter 15).

Gelatt (1991) argues that we should understand this new reality in terms of 'chaos', and emphasizes that the new approach must be that of 'positive uncertainty'. He calls for a more holistic approach utilizing the creative tools of flexibility, optimism, and imagination and for decision-making processes that are flexible and creative in nature. Both left brain and right brain must be called into action. People must be able not only to cope with change but also to create change.

Michell, Levin, and Krumboltz (1999) expand on this idea and use the term 'planned happenstance' as a reflection of current career reality. 'Planned happenstance' emphasizes that people need to be able to create, recognize, transform, and incorporate chance or unplanned events into opportunities for learning and for career development. This calls for the development of five skills: curiosity, persistence, flexibility, optimism, and risk taking (Michell *et al.* 1999: 117–18).

Within the new rapidly changing career reality, the resulting uncertainty may prevent people from managing their careers in the traditional sense; but within the context of CareerCraft, they will be able to use this uncertainty as an ally to success. Watts (1996: 46) sums it up well when he states, 'Careers are now forged, not foretold.'

SO WHAT IS CAREERCRAFT?

Craft may be defined as a noun—an art, trade, or occupation requiring special skill, especially manual skill; skill; dexterity; cunning; deceit—or a verb—to make or manufacture an object or objects with great skill and care (Costello 1995).

The definition for craft places emphasis on ability or skill, on care, on artistry, on ingenuity. The definition for 'manage', on the other hand, places more emphasis on control. The dictionary definition for 'manage' is as follows: to bring about or succeed in accomplishing; to take charge of, supervise; to dominate by tact, flattery, or artifice; to control in action or use (Costello 1995).

The concept of 'craft' can also be explored by looking at any number of crafts being practiced today. Such an exploration will provide a deeper understanding of craft than simple definition. The first author (Poehnell) has devoted considerable time to weaving, as well as other creative pursuits. This interest in craftsmanship was a deliberate attempt to increase right-brained (creative) thinking. After more than twenty years in a rather constricted academic environment, Poehnell found that it was time to find an activity that promoted a hands-on experience of creativity. Much of what was learned about craft and creativity in weaving may also be applied to career. To illustrate, Else Regensteiner (1970) gives a very eloquent description of weaving as a craft. This description captures the spirit and multifaceted nature of craft:

Weaving has many faces: it is a craft, a medium for working directly with fundamental materials to create joyful mixtures of textures and colors, to feel the accomplishment of mastering the tools and learning the steps, and to explore the discipline of fine craftsmanship. It is an art, an expression of our time, which can have the brilliance of a painting, the dimension of sculpture, the shape of invention, and the form of imagination. It is functional, intimately related to us through our daily use of fabrics. It is an industrial product made speedily by the power loom, but unchanged in its basic construction of interlocking threads, and it is as individual as its creator will make it. It is a tool for the educator and a technique for the therapist; it is romantic and sober, ancient and contemporary.

As with all crafts, fundamentals and theory must be learned before the full range of creative possibilities can be embraced. But invention can start together with learning, and technical perfection does not have to be dull.   (Regensteiner 1970: 7)

This reflection on the craft of weaving could easily be adapted to be a reflection on the craft of career. For example, CareerCraft also works to combine fundamental materials (such as skills, interests, and so on) to create career goals that reflect the wonder of a person. Tools and processes must be mastered. As we have already noted, in today's labor market, there is certainly the opportunity to create and invent. Career is both corporate (there are elements that most if not all people must deal with) and yet as unique as each individual. Career may certainly be used to help both teach and heal people. It is also ancient and contemporary. Though mastery of the fundamentals and theory of career will help people embrace the full range of career possibilities, it is equally true that people do not have to be perfect to start and that learning can take place as people begin to craft careers.

Let us explore this new paradigm in more depth. First, we will look generally at the characteristics of CareerCraft and then more specifically at creativity as it applies to career.

CHARACTERISTICS OF CAREERCRAFT

It is possible to group the characteristics of craft under three broad categories: function, skill, and creativity. These three broad categories may also be applied to CareerCraft. Herr (1999), when discussing the career, economic, educational, and psychological effects of advanced technology, indicates that all three of these concepts are essential for all people who are to be properly prepared for careers in the new economy. He refers to the need for career to be functional when he states that 'in the global economy, workforces will be required that have the capability to be *productive* and *purposeful* at all levels of the occupational structure'. He goes on to state that effective careers will also need to reflect both skill and creativity:

Unless a workforce can function with quality and efficiency at the levels of *creativity*, *invention*, and *innovation* as well as the implementation and application levels, in services delivery and in goods production, the occupational structure becomes increasingly divided into the haves and have nots and is encumbered by an underclass of persons who have neither the skills nor the motivation to be trained and retrained as emerging jobs require *new skills* and ways of being productive. (Herr 1999: 36–7; emphasis added)

Function

One fundamental difference between traditional craft and pure art is that craft is purposeful and practical—that is, the product of craft has a function. In the craft of weaving, for instance, one may make a scarf, a blanket, a rug, a tablecloth, or a garment; even if these may be stylized, they are still viewed as practical objects intended for practical use. This is part of the uniqueness of craft—its combining of creativity and beauty with the everyday practical things of life.

Robert Landa (1998), writing on another craft, that of graphic design, emphasizes that 'Graphic designers are creative artists who solve practical problems' (1998: 7). So too the people who craft their careers are in a sense creative artists who must solve many practical problems on the way to success. In today's evolving labor market, there certainly needs to be a synergism between creativity and practicality. People must generate new ideas of self, of career options, of ways to market themselves, of problem solving, of creating and recognizing opportunities, of doing work; but all of these ideas must ultimately pass through the checkpoint of practicality.

Skill

Craft also suggests skill and is associated with concepts such as workmanship, expertise, and dexterity. It involves learning to use the right materials, tools, and processes effectively to produce the desired product. When Poehnell began to weave, it was not enough just to buy a loom and some yarn. He had to learn about materials (for example, various fibers and yarns and their characteristics; there is a vast difference between a fuzzy mohair, a luxurious alpaca, a smooth silk, and a bumpy cotton novelty yarn). Tools (for example, looms, warping boards, ball-winders, bobbin-winders, reeds, pick-up sticks, shuttles, sley reeds, and so on) had to be purchased and mastered. Then came the actual processes of learning to handle yarn, drafting a pattern, measuring warp, setting up the loom, dressing the loom, winding shuttles, actual weaving, finishing the weaving, and so on. The craft is one that can be started with very little skill but that requires a lifetime of learning to master.

As people craft careers, they must bring together the appropriate materials: skills, interests, values, personality, support from significant others, education and learning experiences, work and leisure experiences, and labor market opportunities (Amundson and Poehnell 1996, 1998). But tools and processes must also be mastered. The use of self-assessment tools, books, Internet resources, résumés, cover letters, interview skills, and so on must be applied with career processes (self-assessment, career exploration, decision making, action planning, personal development, job search, job maintenance).

Creativity

Finally, craft suggests creativity and many related concepts: beauty, individuality and uniqueness, passion, being open to uncertainty, taking risks, being flexible, drawing on inner resources both spiritual and intuitive, drawing on both left and right brain. A craft such as weaving requires much more than the mastering of all the technical specifications of materials, tools, and processes. These must be combined in a creative process that produces a unique article of beauty and function. The same is true of career.

CREATIVITY AND CAREER

For the purpose of this chapter, we will focus on three key ways in which creativity may enhance career. Creativity helps people to engage more holistically in the entire career process. A creative approach also energizes people and their career development. Finally, creativity empowers people.

Arthur, Inkson, and Pringle (1999) illustrate the place of creativity in career through the metaphor of economic theater—the stage on which people enact their working lives. In the old economy, the emphasis was on scripted plays in which people performed their parts with little opportunity for creativity. However, the new economy is better represented by improvisational theater in which creativity and innovation are integral to the active actor participation and quality performance. Actors feel engaged, energized, and empowered as they creatively craft each performance in a dynamic fashion.

Engage

Amundson (1998) argues that our approaches to career must be characterized by 'active engagement' as opposed to an approach where the counselor does most of the work and the client is essentially passive in the process. Traditional conventions commonly held regarding career and career counseling techniques and practices should be challenged and, if necessary, replaced in favor of new conventions that support a career approach in which people are no longer passive but active and fully engaged in the process of career. He suggests that both career counselors and clients will do this as they 'use their full range of creativity and imagination...with a full measure of intensity' and greater flexibility (1998: 26–7).

Arthur, Inkson, and Pringle (1999) also emphasize the concept of people being active in forging new opportunities and dealing with constraints. Their extensive interview-based research study highlights the importance of engagement with and enactment of career behavior upon the host environment. People who were interviewed were influenced by drive and creativity and actively chose their career paths.

Such a view is supported by Csikszentmihalyi (1991, 1997), who has researched and written extensively on the 'psychology of optimal experience' or the concept of 'flow' and how it relates to creativity and everyday life. 'Flow' is simply the experience people have when they fully experience life. Csikszentmihalyi (1997) argues that the 'autotelic' people (that is, those 'who generally do things for their own sake, rather than in order to achieve some later external goal') are those who will engage with life most fully rather than consuming life with passivity. He sees creative people as typically fitting this profile.

Csikszentmihalyi (1997: 107–8) presents such creative engaged people as those who

give some of the best examples of how one can shape work to one's own requirements. Most creative persons don't follow a career laid out for them, but invent their jobs as they go along. Artists invent their own style of painting, composers their own musical styles. Creative scientists develop new fields of science, and make it possible for their successors to have careers in them. There were no radiologists before Roentgen, and there was no nuclear medicine before Yalow and her colleagues pioneered that field. There were no auto workers before entrepreneurs like Henry Ford built up the first production lines.

He then argues the reverse: that, if people were to do the same things as the creative autotelic person, they would also experience the same full experience of being totally engaged in their life, including their career. We may not all be artists or inventors, but we may engage in life, in career, and reap the benefits. 'Obviously very few people can start entirely new lines of work; most of us will follow the job description of conventional careers. But even the most routine job can benefit from the kind of transforming energy that creative individuals bring to what they do' (1997: 107–8).

Left mode	Right mode
Verbal	Non-verbal
Analytic	Synthetic
Symbolic	Concrete
Abstract	Analogic
Temporal	Non-temporal
Rational	Non-rational
Digital	Spatial
Logical	Intuitive
Linear	Holistic

Fig. 6.1. A comparison of left-mode and right-mode characteristics.
Source: Edwards (1989: 40).

This 'active-engagement' approach is fundamentally holistic in nature. It calls for a balance of left and right brain; of mental, physical, spiritual, emotional aspects. Consider Betty Edwards' comparison of left-mode and right-mode characteristics (Fig. 6.1). It is clear that both modes of thinking and working are needed to succeed in today's changing labor market. For example, people need not only to analyze issues they face but also to be able to see the big picture as they put the various pieces into a whole. They need to deal with abstracts but just as importantly they need to recognize relationships. In the active engagement model suggested by Amundson (1998), metaphors play a prominent part in assisting clients and counselors to understand and, if necessary, reframe their situations. As was suggested above in the discussion on 'planned happenstance' and 'positive uncertainty', there will be many times when people will need to rely on non-rational or intuitive approaches to their problems.

Energize

Craft not only engages; it energizes. Csikszentmihalyi (1997) identifies an important characteristic of people who are actively engaged in life: 'their psychic energy seems inexhaustible' (1997: 123). This is certainly true both in the craft of weaving and in career. When a weaver is actively engaged in weaving, there is an intriguing paradox; there are the feelings of being very restful and relaxed yet very alive and energized by creative energy. When one holds a finished project in one's hands, there is an excitement that makes the entire process worthwhile no matter the challenges involved in making it happen. The same can be said for the energizing effect of creativity in CareerCraft. As people are actively engaged in crafting careers, they can experience the excitement of solving problems and discovering new opportunities. All the challenge of the process is eclipsed by the joy of finding meaningful employment.

The dynamic involved in the energizing effect of creativity is explored by Fritz (1989) in his book on *The Path of Least Resistance*. His basic theory is that the creative tension between people's present reality and people's vision generates creative energy. Fritz argues that there is a waste of energy as people attempt to change their patterns of behavior by non-creative approaches such as compensating for circumstances or oscillating between reacting and responding to external circumstances. The creative orientation, in contrast, creates energy by the structural tension between two major components: vision (the result one wants to create) and current reality (what one now has). This structural tension is 'the armature of the creative process', the energy source for the creative process. As creators in whatever area we choose, including career, we establish tension, use tension, play with tension, orchestrate tension, and resolve tension in the direction chosen (Fritz 1989: 116–17).

In the area of career, this has a very practical application. Rather than potentially viewing present circumstances as a barrier to future career goals, it is possible to be energized by the tension these two poles create. In the language of 'planned happenstance', present circumstances may be viewed as opportunities for creative movement toward stated goals.

Empower

Empowering by freeing from mental blocks and habits. Creativity not only engages and energizes; it also empowers. This empowerment may be looked at from two different directions. On the one hand, creativity empowers people by freeing them from mental blocks or habits that have been hindering them from creating, recognizing, or attempting new alternatives. On the other, it empowers people by assisting them to make new connections, see new perspectives, consider new possibilities, and be open to make new choices.

Fritz (1989) advocates that there are two fundamental orientations to life— one passive, the other active. One, the reactive-responsive orientation, 'contains the basic presumption that [people] are powerless' because, when they habitually react or respond only to circumstances, the power clearly lies outside them, in the circumstances. 'Therefore, because the power does not reside in [them], [they] are powerless and the circumstances are all-powerful' (Fritz 1989: 21). The other, the creative orientation, presumes that people do not allow themselves to be controlled by circumstances but work from a locus of power within themselves.

When people are buying a piece of weaving, say a scarf, then they are restricted by the ones that are available. When someone weaves a scarf, the boundaries may be as wide as his or her imagination. Though there may be some limitations based on equipment or experience, the weaver has the power to weave to his or her full potential and then to upgrade equipment or experience as needed.

One of the biggest challenges for some in their career pursuits is that they carry with them mental blocks or habits that control their thoughts, decisions, and actions. These may revolve around incomplete or inaccurate views of the current labor market or of themselves personally.

Creativity enables people to be set free from such blocks. Von Oech addresses this task in his humorous yet insightful book, *A Whack on the Side of the Head* (1990). He argues that people often develop beliefs or attitudes that were useful at some point in their lives. These beliefs can become unconscious conventions that form an untouchable status quo. As a result, even though new circumstances may arise in which they need to be creative and generate new ways to do something, they are unable to do so because they are prevented by beliefs that have solidified into mental blocks and entrap them into certain thought and action patterns. Von Oech identifies ten of these 'mental blocks': the right answer; that's not logical; follow the rules; be practical; play is frivolous; that's not my area; avoid ambiguity; don't be foolish; to err is wrong; I'm not creative.

He further argues that

'Often we have integrated these mental blocks so well into our thinking and behavior that we are no longer aware that we're being guided by them. They have become habits. The danger of habits is that a person can become a prisoner of familiarity. The more often you do something in the same way—whether it's cooking a meal or managing a project—the more difficult it is to do it in any other way. You get stuck in how you already think about things'.   (Von Oech 1990: 12–14)

Amundson (1998) suggests that people seek career counseling because they feel 'stuck'; they are unable to imagine a new future for themselves. In offering assistance, the foundational need is to rekindle imagination and reframe thought structures. In the rapidly changing labor market described above, such mental blocks are particularly dangerous. Ready-made answers designed for a different work world or inadequate views of themselves block people from recognizing or generating opportunities to go off the beaten path in new directions.

Von Oech (1990: 14) suggests that we occasionally need a 'whack on the side of the head to shake us out of routine patterns, to force us to re-think our problems, and to stimulate us to ask the questions that may lead to other right answers'. Such 'whacks' may come in all kinds of forms and may be completely unexpected; Von Oech's first example of such a whack is interestingly the jolt of getting fired from a job.

Within the CareerCraft concept where people are alert to 'planned happenstance', even the shock of being fired from a job can be turned into a positive opportunity. By challenging preconceived ideas that have become mental blocks, it is possible to break free, to be empowered to think new thoughts, make new decisions, and follow new paths.

Empowering by opening up new connections, new perspectives, new possibilities, and, thereby, new choices. This leads us to the positive side of creativity's empowering approach. Not only does it empower by freeing people from mental blocks, it also empowers by opening up new connections, new perspectives, new possibilities, and, thereby, new choices.

Siler in his book *Think Like a Genius* (1999: 76–81) demonstrates that creativity is not to be equated with artistic talent or the like; these are merely areas in which creativity is applied. Creativity is more basic and can be applied in all areas. He defines creativity as 'any unconditioned response or interpretation'. He makes an important distinction between 'choice' and 'habit'. 'Habit' is like a 'long narrow highway'; 'choice' is like a road with 'a fork in it'. 'Habit' refers to those conditioned responses that people normally follow in any given situation (for example, Pavlov's dog); by its very nature it does not require much creativity because the path of response is already determined. 'Choice', however, requires creativity because it helps people to see that there are forks in the road ahead, alternative ways to respond. Siler argues that creativity is the principal agent of change. It enables people to become effective by helping them to break out of ruts, conditioned responses, old patterns, habits, and to see new possibilities. New alternatives lead to new choices and choice is an essential aspect of empowerment.

The generation of new ways of thinking or new alternatives or new choices can be accomplished in several different ways. Michael Michalko (1998) organized an elite team of NATO intelligence specialists and academics to research, collect, and categorize all known inventive-thinking methods and then later applied these creative-thinking techniques in the private business sector. He argues that creative thinkers, such as geniuses, 'think productively, not reproductively. When confronted with a problem, they ask themselves how many different ways they can look at the problem, how they can rethink it, and how many different ways they can solve it, instead of asking how they have been taught to solve it' (1998: 2). This is in sharp contrast to those who think reproductively and solve problems by looking to the past and repeating what has been done before. He illustrates this by presenting the problem-solving processes of geniuses throughout history. For example, Leonardo da Vinci believed that until one perceived something from a minimum of three different perspectives, one did not yet have a basis for understanding it. A true and complete knowledge comes from the synthesizing of these different views.

Another approach to generating alternative ideas has been developed by Hall (1995), who encourages creativity through the use of stimuli. Stimuli take people out of their normal frame and reference. Such an approach maximizes brain power and productive creativity, as opposed to the problem of 'brain drain' in which people exhaust their mind trying to come up with new ideas. The potential for this technique to be applied to career is almost limitless when you consider how often brainstorming of ideas is employed (generating career options, potential contacts, and so on).

In our workshop on CareerCraft we have adapted the following exercise from Hall (1995) to illustrate how the introduction of a simple set of stimuli can greatly increase effective idea generation. Consistently workshop participants come up with many more ideas for the second problem.

> Problem 1
>
> You want to expand the demand for the elastic bands from your factory. Come up with as many ideas as you can in 5–10 minutes.

> Problem 2
>
> You want to expand the demand for the balloons from your factory. Come up with as many ideas as you can in 5 minutes. (As a stimulus, participants are given balloons and are also provided with a random list of words from a magazine.)

The second problem utilizes many more stimuli and this addition seems to enhance the creative process.

Finally, note that creativity may even be applied to job maintenance. Gordon MacKenzie (1998), in his simple yet perceptive book *Orbiting the Giant Hairball: A Corporate Fool's Guide to Surviving with Grace*, shows how to maintain creativity within a corporate structure in such a way that both the person and the corporation benefit. 'Orbiting is responsible creativity: vigorously exploring and operating beyond the Hairball of the corporate mind set' (1998: 33). MacKenzie's argument is that through creativity one can find the fine balance between benefiting from all the resources that the organization has to offer without losing the individuality that makes one a unique asset to the organization or without reacting to bureaucracy in such a way as to fly out in space and thereby become unprofitable to all concerned.

ILLUSTRATING CAREERCRAFT WITHIN ORGANIZATIONAL CHANGE

To illustrate various components of the CareerCraft model practically, we will report our experiences with the staff and management of the Canada–Saskatchewan Career and Employment Services (CSCES). The creation of this service organization brought together employees from three different groups with distinct work cultures. An expanded mandate (not just social assistance recipients or employment insurance clients but now all provincial residents) called for a fundamental shift in philosophy and, therefore, in services. Staff and management needed to do more than manage this change; they needed to craft both a new organization and, at a personal level, new careers within the new organization.

Before we examine in more detail the application of CareerCraft to the CSCES, it will be helpful to provide some additional background. First, the organization made a concerted effort to develop a new collaborative management structure. As with many mergers, however, the initial results were disappointing and an initial needs assessment (Reekie 1998) revealed considerable organizational turmoil. Reekie's report (1998) called for 'relevant, additive, contemporary and engaging professional development activities which would provide support for staff transition, integrate three different work cultures and shape a common vision based on collaborative problem-solving'. The authors, in partnership with the Canadian Career Development Foundation, were contracted to address the organization development and professional development needs identified by Reekie.

A workshop series entitled 'Building Career and Employment Services Learning Organizations' involving three different workshops was developed and delivered to approximately 200 staff and management. The workshops addressed the need to craft both the new organization as well as personal careers in the midst of transition. Specifically, the three workshops focused on the themes of Building a Common Culture, Building a Learning Culture, and Building an Active Engagement Culture. In each workshop an attempt was made to have wide geographical representation (that is, from each of the five major regions) and from every level of the organization (that is, from administration support to upper level management). If these workshops were to succeed in helping the staff and management craft a new organization, they also needed to reflect the three concepts of craft—to be practical, skill oriented, and very creative.

We will overview how the concepts of function, skill, and creativity were worked out in the workshops as a whole and then more specifically in each of the three workshops. First, everything had to be very practical. Since the CSCES offices opened on the same day that the new organization officially came into being, the staff and management faced the very practical task of creating 'on the go' while they were already interacting with clients. They had neither the time nor the patience to listen to theory that did not work. Therefore, the content and approach of the three workshops were carefully chosen to address the practical issues they faced.

Secondly, at every level, the workshops encouraged the participants to enhance their skills. Because of the expansion in their client base and the fundamental shift in their service approach, they needed to transfer all the skills they had mastered in their previous organizations and supplement them with new tools and processes. They needed to clarify and understand who their new clients would be, what services they would provide, and the most effective ways to deliver those services. For example, a major shift needed to be made from a directive approach in counseling to a collaborative one that encouraged greater autonomy and responsibility on the part of the increased client base. Clients were now to be encouraged to be self-directed in their career pursuits. This meant fundamental changes in the way services were being delivered. Resource rooms with extensive print and computer resources were added. Staff needed to master these resources in order to assist clients at whatever level of service was required: from demonstrating how to use a particular résumé program on the computer, or surfing the Internet, to providing in-depth personal counseling.

Finally, since much of new service approach was perceived to be such a radical shift by many, it was essential that the workshops modeled the creativity they sought to promote. The workshops continually encouraged the staff and management to challenge their own conventional thoughts and practices at all points and to be open to generating and accepting new ones. In many respects, these workshops challenged them to grasp the interactive nature of learning and to be open to the concepts of continuous role redefinition, team learning, learning along the flow, learning via networks, and leadership as a support for learning (Södergren, Chapter 3).

Creativity was especially important throughout the workshops for a second reason: by the time people came to the workshops, months had gone by since the CSCES offices had opened, and some were resistant, many were demoralized, and most were feeling very pressured, ineffective, and exhausted. In order to overcome any resistance or inertia, we needed to find ways to engage and energize them personally and corporately. Finally, the workshops needed to empower them. Many struggled with a passive cynicism that fostered a mindset that it was all someone else's fault and there was nothing they could do, or, if there was something they could do, it would not make any difference anyway. Thoughts, feeling, attitudes, and actions needed to be challenged; and, where necessary, positive ones reinforced, mental blocks removed, and new thought processes and actions embraced. The workshops sought to energize, engage, and empower them by giving them new perspectives on their past, on their present, and on their future. As they were assisted to recognize and even to generate new opportunities, they began to acknowledge a new awareness of their ability and responsibility to make a difference.

Let us briefly examine how the concepts of CareerCraft worked themselves out in each of the workshops. The first workshop, Building a Common Culture, focused on the developmental needs for both the new emerging organization and the staff involved as a result of the merging of the founding groups. Before the merger, staff may have exhibited a high level of commitment and competence. When they were members of distinct organizations, they may have seen each other as colleagues and friends who coordinated programs with each other, cooperated on special projects, and shared many of the same challenges. After the merger, however, many felt vulnerable during the time of transition and expressed uncertainty about how they would manage their own career paths in the new organization.

To assist them at both the personal and the corporate level, the metaphor of the 'journey' was used to help them begin the process of identifying their own personal 'journey' within the organization; this very practical and yet creative approach helped them reframe their experience of the merger in positive terms (Bridges 1991; Barger and Kirby 1995; Simon and Tocher 1998). They were encouraged to identify personal and professional skills they had utilized in previous times of change and could draw on for the present changes. New tools were provided to help them identify where they were on the 'journey' of change and to help them work with the changes in a more effective manner. For example, many were unsure whether or not they wished to stay with the new organization or not; but they were also unsure how to process their thoughts and feelings. A new tool *Career Crossroads* was developed to help them deal with their confusion and to empower them to take control of their own careers (Poehnell and Amundson 2001). *Career Crossroads* focused on seven factors (match, direction, influence, boundaries, wholeness, duration, risk) that needed to be considered and evaluated in making the decision whether to stay with the current organization or whether it was time to go.

The process of melding groups that have qualitatively different cultures, histories, philosophies, and methodologies required the staff to function with co-workers who may have been socialized to make different assumptions and to respond in ways that would not have been acceptable in the old organization. Therefore, prior to any subsequent competency training, this first workshop also needed to focus on crafting a shared vision and a unified set of assumptions, beliefs, and values. It sought to incorporate the best from the merging organizations, while ensuring that the process valued each individual. Through a process of collaborative visioning and problem solving, the participants were encouraged to be creative as they worked through a number of policy statements that helped them clarify and integrate their personal mission with the organization's.

The second workshop, Building a Learning Culture, provided opportunities for the workshop participants to work in learning teams to define the key principles that would guide CSCES toward becoming a learning organization (Senge 1990; Senge *et al.* 1999). Participants also focused on their roles as learners and coaches for each other and worked with learning tools and procedures to develop personal learning plans. For many of the participants this was an entirely new approach to a career and employment services organization; again they had to deal with mental blocks and be open to doing things differently. They were also challenged to rethink all their skills and to identify which ones were essential in delivering services in a learning context. As they grasped the possibilities of forming a learning organization and the part they could play in it, the workshop participants gained a new sense of excitement and empowerment.

The third workshop, Building an Active Engagement Culture, addressed the practical need for training in new approaches to helping clients in the new expanded context. It utilized a creative experiential approach designed to overview some of the key principles of an active engagement approach and to assist participants in applying these ideas both personally and professionally. The active engagement principles include an emphasis on imagination, creativity, and flexibility embedded within a more dynamic communications approach. Traditional conventions were challenged along with some of the dynamics underlying the helping relationship. The principles of active engagement were applied to all aspects of the new service model adopted by the CSCES. This new model called for the staff to work with clients in a manner that recognized their level of self-directedness and encouraged them to develop greater autonomy.

Function, skill, and creativity were certainly at the center of the third workshop. Several creative yet very practical intervention strategies were highlighted. These approaches were drawn from each stage of the helping process and included use of metaphors, solution-focused questioning, the wheel, the individual style survey, pattern identification, team building, physical action, and so on (Amundson 1998).

These workshops and subsequent activities by participants certainly illustrate the concept of CareerCraft. As was mentioned earlier, the staff and management are involved in the process of crafting a new organization and, in many cases, new careers as well. The results of these workshops have been powerful and challenging. The input from all the staff and management on organizational issues such as the organizational mandate, the new service model, programs and services, quality service goals, and professional conduct were compiled into a Canada–Saskatchewan Career and Employment Services 'Workbook' (2000). This workbook forms the starting point for the next stage in organization development in which decisions will be made regarding further restructuring of the way services are promoted and delivered, the formalization of formal policies and procedures, and the continuing development of staff and management. This next stage has already begun and the future looks promising.

As a result of these workshops and the ongoing change process, many of the staff and management were able to examine their own personal experience of the merger, their own personal mandates, and their involvement in the new organization. Generally, over the year or so since the workshops took place, we have seen a radical change among a staff whose members were very discouraged, largely isolated from each other, and very unsure of whether they had a role to play in influencing the organization. The same members now have a much greater sense of being connected, and a more positive attitude toward their ability to make the organization and their own personal careers succeed, in spite of all the challenges they face.

CareerCraft is a complementary paradigm to 'career management'. This alternative perspective is especially suited to the challenges and opportunities of a rapidly changing and very uncertain labor market. A greater emphasis on CareerCraft will encourage practicality, the development of skills, and the embracing of creativity and innovation in the pursuit of career-related activities. Approaching career from a creative orientation will engage, energize, and empower people as they seek to craft careers for themselves and find success as a result.

REFERENCES

Amundson, N. E. (1998), *Active Engagement: Enhancing the Career Counselling Process* (Richmond, BC: Ergon Communications).

——and Poehnell, G. (1996), *Career Pathways*, 2nd edn. (Richmond, BC: Ergon Communications).

———— (1998), *Career Pathways: Quick Trip* (Richmond, BC: Ergon Communications).

Arthur, M. B., Inkson, K., and Pringle, J. K. (1999), *The New Careers: Individual Action and Economic Change* (London: Sage).

Barger, N. J., and Kirby, L. K. (1995), *The Challenge of Change in Organizations: Helping Employees Thrive in the New Frontier* (Palo Alto, Calif.: Davies-Black).

Bridges, W. (1991), *Managing Transitions: Making the Most of Change* (Reading, Mass.: Addison-Wesley).

Canada–Saskatchewan Career and Employment Services (2000), 'Workbook: A "Building Career & Employment Services Learning Organizations" Workshop Product', unpublished manuscript.

Costello, R. B. (1995), *Random House Webster's College Dictionary* (New York: Random House).

Csikszentmihalyi, M. (1991), *Flow: The Psychology of Optimal Experience* (New York: HarperCollins).

—— (1997), *Finding Flow in Everyday Life* (New York: Basic Books).

Edwards, B. (1989), *Drawing on the Right Side of the Brain*, rev. edn. (Los Angeles: Jeremy P. Tarcher).

Feller, R. W. (1995), 'Action Planning for Personal Competitiveness in the "Broken Workplace" ', *Journal of Employment Counseling*, 32: 154–63.

Fritz, R. (1989), *The Path of Least Resistance: Learning to Become the Creative Force in your Own Life*, rev. edn. (New York: Fawcett Columbine).

Gelatt, H. B. (1991), *Creative Decision Making* (Los Altos, Calif.: Crisp Publications).

Hall, D. T. (1995), *Jump Start your Brain* (New York: Warner Books).

Herr, E. L. (1999), *Counseling in a Dynamic Society: Contexts and Practices for the 21st Century*, 2nd edn. (Alexandria, Va.: American Counseling Association).

Landa, R. (1998), *Thinking Creatively: New Ways to Unlock your Visual Imagination* (Cincinnati, Oh.: North Light Books).

MacKenzie, G. (1998), *Orbiting the Giant Hairball: A Corporate Fool's Guide to Surviving with Grace* (New York: Viking Penguin).

Michalko, M. (1998), *Cracking Creativity: The Secrets of Creative Genius* (Berkeley, Calif.: Ten Speed Press).

Mitchell, K. E., Levin, A. S., and Krumboltz, J. D. (1999), 'Planned Happenstance: Constructing Unexpected Career Opportunities', *Journal of Counseling and Development*, 77: 115–24.

Poehnell, G., and Amundson, N. E. (2001), *Career Crossroads: A Personal Career Positioning System* (Richmond, BC: Ergon Communications).

Reekie, F. (1998), 'Conceptualizing Professional Development with Can–Sask Career Centre Staff', unpublished manuscript, Regina.

Regensteiner, E. (1970), *The Art of Weaving* (New York: Van Nostrand Reinhold).

Senge, P. M. (1990), *The Fifth Discipline: The Art and Practice of the Learning Organ-ization* (New York: Doubleday).

——Kleiner, A., Roberts, C., Ross, R., Roth, G., and Smith B. (1999), *The Dance of Change: The Challenges to Sustaining Momentum in Learning Organizations* (New York: Doubleday).

Siler, T. (1999), *Think like a Genius: Use your Creativity in Ways that will Enrich your Life* (New York: Bantam Books).

Simon, A., and Tocher, M. (1998), *Brave Work: A Guide to the Quest for Meaning in Work* (Ottawa: Canadian Career Development Foundation).

Von Oech, R. (1990), *A Whack on the Side of the Head: How you Can Be More Creative*, rev. edn. (New York: Warner Books).

Watts, A. G. (1996), 'Toward a Policy of Lifelong Career Development: A Transatlantic Perspective', *Career Development Quarterly*, 45: 41–53.

Weaver, J. (2000), 'Creativity', *Community Banker*, 9/1: 16–19.

Wujec, T. (1995), *Five Star Mind: Games and Puzzles to Stimulate your Creativity and Imagination* (Toronto: Doubleday Canada).

7

Creativity in Contract Workers' Careers

POLLY PARKER

Contract workers—people who undertake temporary rather than permanent job assignments—create their own careers. They do so by eschewing traditional models of either organizational or occupational careers, giving rise to an emergent pattern of work arrangements that is creative, and, according to the workers' own subjective criteria, successful. Although the careers of contract workers appear to be different from most people's careers, the micro-building blocks or job assignments from which the careers are derived may not be so different. What appears to be different is the creative act—what Bateson (1994: 10) describes as the ability 'to attend to something new, or to see the familiar in a new way'—in putting sequences of jobs together. Contract workers' behavior is consistent with recent calls in career theory to depart from traditional career models and to adopt 'new viewpoints on what we once took to be familiar' (Arthur and Rousseau 1996: 370).

Adopting Bateson's approach to creativity as a point of departure, this chapter reports on a study of careers of contract workers. These workers enact their careers according to their own subjectively defined criteria for success. These criteria provide the 'new viewpoints' of interest to career theory, although the contract workers themselves are not necessarily aware of creating anything new. Taken separately, each contractor career may seem unremarkable—merely personal improvisation to an individual situation. However, when these careers are studied collectively, we can see patterns. These patterns may be illustrative of the broader improvisation process involved in responding to the uncertainty experienced in contemporary employment (Bateson 1994).

Valuing contractors' careers for their creativity in process, rather than viewing them as simply deviant from compartmentalized models of successful careers in our society, can alter our perception. Instead of seeing several individuals making their own way through the world, we can learn from personal adaptations—that is, from responses to being 'called to join in a dance whose steps must be learned along the way' (Bateson 1994: 10).

My hope is that the telling of contract workers' stories may broaden both our views of careers and the vocabulary with which careers are discussed. My further hope is that the telling may raise awareness of the inherent limitations of normative career models by situating them in a wider range of available alternatives (Bateson 1994). Against such a backdrop, creativity is indeed evident in the careers of contract workers, as they combine and arrange their work in a manner that shuns traditional wisdom.

FLEXIBLE ORGANIZATIONS, FLEXIBLE WORKFORCE, FLEXIBLE CAREERS

The restructuring of organizations in recent years has replaced many stable structures with more flexible structures. In an environment characterized by competitive threats, challenges, and continuous change, it is increasingly difficult for organizations to predict what skills they will need. One strategy for them to obtain flexibility is to rely increasingly on a contingent workforce of contractors and casual workers (Von Hippel 1988). The growth of the contingent workforce has been a feature of the growth in the use of flexible staffing arrangements.

The conventional wisdom of careers as sequences of 'jobs' is threatened by alternative ideas such as those of Bridges (1995), who suggests that the rise of knowledge work over industrial work, and the unpredictability of locations of production, have caused the 'de-jobbing' of the workplace. The new environment makes every worker potentially a contingent worker. Workers affected are not only lower-paid and unskilled workers, but also skilled, experienced professionals commanding high salaries (Casey *et al.* 1997). Managers and professionals who could once reasonably have expected roles in the 'core' of their organizations, with predictable, upwardly mobile careers, increasingly find themselves on the 'periphery'.

The desire for flexibility is individually as well as organizationally driven. Individuals *seek* contingent work arrangements. Boden (1999) notes that nonpecuniary characteristics, including flexibility of schedules and personal/family obligations, were cited by both men and women as compelling reasons for seeking contingent work. Eaton and Bailyn (2000) also cite the inherent interdependence between the spheres of work and the whole of life precipitating the desire of increasing numbers of workers to bring about a better balance between the two spheres.

Irrespective of whether the shift is by choice or by force, the changes in the business environment result in a growth in numbers of part-time workers, temporary employees, limited-term contract workers, and consultants—that is, contingent workers. A common definition of a contingent worker is one whose contract of employment or service is explicitly temporary and dependent on appropriate tasks continuing to be available. One estimate suggests that one in four American workers have become contingent workers (Albrecht 1998), with eight million participating as independent contractors. An earlier UK survey reported that the flexible workforce amounted to almost 40 per cent of the total workforce (DFEE 1993).

This 'casualization' or 'contingentization' of the workforce makes explicit the move from (long-term) relational to (short-term) transactional psychological contracts (Rousseau and Libuser 1997). These changes have been criticized because of the erosion of career benefits inherent in traditional employment (Allan and Sienko 1997), and the parallel erosion of the loyalty, commitment, and institutional memory on which many organizations depend. This kind of criticism reflects traditional career thinking, but it may not do justice to the creative opportunities the changes introduce.

It is ironic to consider that the characteristics of the contingent workforce were evident in work patterns before the industrial era, when laborers' work was characterized by low security and high risk, and they 'worked when work was available' and had 'no contracts of employment' (Peiperl and Baruch 1997: 13). The agricultural laborers of the past have their counterparts in the unskilled casual factory workers, cleaners, and fast-food workers of the present. They serve to remind us that the world of 'boundaryless careers' (Arthur and Rousseau 1996), in which skilled professionals exercise high mobility to develop their marketable skills, has its downside in the likely exploitation of those whose skills have little open market value.

Notwithstanding these potentially negative effects, the contingent workforce is likely to continue to grow (Filipezak *et al.* 1995; Kosters 1997). One effect is likely to be the destabilization of the careers of many individuals, making it more difficult for them to conceptualize and plan their careers around 'organizational' or 'occupational' career principles that have in the past been central to their sense of identity and security. Mapping individual creativity in emerging careers reveals patterns that indicate that sequences of roles will be increasingly based around projects, assignments, or contracts of finite duration, sometimes conducted simultaneously in 'portfolios' (Handy 1990). The changes will weaken the influence that employing organizations have on individual career development. Moreover, they may render obsolete notions such as 'career planning' and 'planned personal development' as they have traditionally been conceived.

Levels of career ambiguity previously known to only a minority of members of the workforce become normative for contingent workers. Furthermore, the organizational support on which the traditional employee would often rely is not available. While the 'strong situations' (Mischel 1977) that in the past provided external structure for individuals' career behavior are weakening for all members of the workforce (Weick 1996), among contingent workers the weakening is especially dramatic. The career becomes more clearly the property and responsibility of the individual, yet is harder to conceive of as a career. The objective career, defined in terms of formal roles, salary progression, and organizational and social status, becomes more ambiguous. The subjective career, defined in terms of personal meanings and aspirations, takes on a new character. Archetypes of careers implicit in developmental theories (e.g. Super 1980), vocational theories (e.g. Holland 1985), and human-resource (HR) theories (e.g. Beer *et al.* 1984) become harder to sustain. With fewer or weaker external structures creating career paths for the individual, the individual increasingly has to create his or her own career. For career theorists, the mapping of the career patterns of today's contingent workers—both skilled and unskilled— becomes a pressing task.

Only a small number of studies have explored the nuances of contingent work as an alternative to traditional employment (Davis-Blake and Uzzi 1993; Pearce 1993; Rousseau 1997). Moreover, most of those studies have emphasized the *objective* career, as seen from the standpoint of society—for example, in focusing on the deprivation of job security. Very few studies have considered the *subjective* career—that is, the career as it is seen by the contingent workers themselves (Mallon and Duberley 2000). It is likely, of course, that being a contingent worker may for some alternate with a broader pattern of more traditional employment. The rise in contingent work means that many current contingent workers will have started their careers in more permanent employment before being displaced, or before choosing to change their status. Whatever their histories, workers, and contingency workers in particular, appear to be demonstrating creativity in both of Bateson's senses. That is, they are attending to something new (contingency work) and seeing the familiar in a new way (making a career out of contingency work).

LEASED EXECUTIVES

In this chapter I map out the subjective career self-perceptions of contingent workers known in New Zealand as 'leased executives'. (The term in the USA is 'interim manager'). Leased executives (LEs) are contract workers with professional and managerial qualifications and experience who are leased through an agency to work on temporary assignments and projects in a client organization. This arrangement enables the client organization to access high-level business skills on a temporary basis while absolving itself from any long-term responsibility for the individual. However, it must pay a premium salary to the LE as compensation for job insecurity, as well as a fee to the agency.

Such an arrangement may be beneficial to cover the temporary absence of a permanent employee, the completion of a special project, or the solution of a short-term problem. Organizations that seek to minimize the inflexibility and risk inherent in carrying a large 'core' workforce, or that forecast rapid and unpredictable changes in the skill sets required to remain competitive, may find it attractive to use LEs as a substantial part of their ongoing staffing. Extensive LE use means solving the classic 'make or buy?' decision with regard to scarce human resources through a new solution—'Rent!'

A complicating (or facilitating) factor in the employment conditions of LEs is the role of agents in 'match making' and supporting their employment opportunities. The intervention of the agency makes the normal 'two-way' employment relationship between a client organization and an LE a three-way one, involving agency–organization and agency–LE relationships as well as an LE–organization relationship. All of these contracts appear to be essentially transactional rather than relational—that is, they are grounded in a formal view of the work to be formed, rather than in a more informal trust-based approach (Rousseau 1995).

While it is common for LE contracts to be extended beyond the original time and scope negotiated between organization and agency, or for LEs to complete serial contracts in the same organization (Inkson *et al.* 2001), the relationship of the LE with the agency normally outlives that with the organization. The agency's interest in the LE's career is arguably stronger and longer term in focus than that of the client organization. The agency may seek to preserve good relationships with valued LEs in order to induce the LE to give the agency preference over other LE agencies in his or her choice of future assignments. The agency therefore retains a proprietary interest in the LE once he or she has commenced the assignment, and also following its completion. Thus the agency may assume some traditional employer characteristics in its relationship with the LE—for example, in the support it provides during assignments and in social and personal development activities it provides to the LEs on its books. These activities also enable the agency to enhance its reputation in the labor market for these executives and attract more of them to its lists. However, all parties recognize that the LE is basically a free agent who owes no particular loyalty to either agency or organization.

Agency efforts usually fall well short of any ideal relational contract and the LE typically has to take a major responsibility—including financial responsibility—for his or her own career development. The agency–LE contract contains no assurance of continuous, or even regular, employment, merely the support mentioned above and the promise to make the potential LE aware of suitable opportunities. In the long term, however, the sequences of LEs' contracts are assembled into careers. Yet, whereas 'normal' job-based careers enable the considered development of identity and career purpose through long-term commitment to specific settings, the LE must assemble a career based on multiple, temporary, relatively disengaged encounters with several agencies and many organizations.

Since a typical assignment lasts six to twelve months and there is no certainty of new assignments to follow, the formulation of career objectives and the creation of career paths by LEs is problematic. How do they create a sense of identity for themselves, safeguard their security, and progress their development? Is there a temptation to become 'typecast' by applying similar specialist expertise in each successive project rather than trying to ensure that each one brings novel challenges and extends career-relevant learning? Are LEs able to utilize networks and contacts developed across a range of employment situations to advance their careers? These issues are important not only to the LEs in question, but to prospectively larger coming generations of contract and temporary workers.

A RESEARCH SAMPLE

The empirical evidence presented here is drawn from a larger study of LEs in which three kinds of data were collected: individual semi-structured interviews; individual 'intelligent career card sort' data (described below) to elicit the subjective career, and focus group data in which participants reflected on their aggregated card sort responses. The semi-structured interviews provided insights into the basic career histories, identities, and attitudes of sample members. These results have been reported in detail elsewhere (Inkson *et al.* 2001), but I will draw on these data to present additional background information about the sample of LEs. Then I will briefly explain the *intelligent career* perspective, and the related card sort technique, before turning to emphasize the elicitation of intersubjective career data—that is, the shared meanings generated through focus group discussions.

The LEs in question were sampled from the lists of a major agency in the Auckland area. At the time of the research the list of potential LEs contained approximately 300 names. A target of 50 LEs was sought through random sampling. Of 77 LEs with whom contact was initiated, 27 declined or did not return calls. The 50 participants who agreed to take part were interviewed at their homes by a trained interviewer. The sample of 50 was 68 per cent male and 32 per cent female. The mean age was 43.5 years, but the men were significantly older on average than the women (mean 46.5 versus 36.7), presumably because of the relatively recent entry of large numbers of women to the professional/managerial work in question. Fifty-six percent of the sample cited finance or accounting as their main area of expertise, the other most common areas being general management, sales and marketing, and human resources. Information-technology specialists were handled by a different division of the agency and were not included in this study.

The median time since a person first engaged with LE work was three years, and 79 per cent had been LEs for five years or less. This is presumably due to the relatively recent growth of the contingent workforce in general and the LE concept in particular. Thus, nearly all the LEs had served extensive periods of non-contingent employment prior to their first contract. The most common reason given for being an LE was career turbulence, most often caused by lay-off from previous positions, but in some cases by dislocation because of travel, or family relocation. Typically, LEs reported first adopting LE status not as a clear career decision but as a temporary expedient in a situation where permanent jobs were not available. However, in many cases they found that the change suited them, and increasingly they pursued further LE contracts as a means of maintaining a lifestyle that they liked.

ELICITING SUBJECTIVE CAREER DATA

The subjective dimension of career involves the private meaning of work and occupational choice according to the interpretation of the career actor (Savickas 1997). Engaging with the subjective career involves getting people to focus on identifying and talking about areas of personal concern so that individual meaning emerges from reflection on individual career situations. This necessitates combining emotive, affective, imaginal, and conceptual dimensions of the person as well as cognitive ones (Heron 1992), thus promoting whole-person learning. Eliciting the subjective career requires a different interaction between the person and the counselor from traditional career 'guidance', which involved matching the characteristics of the person with occupational roles (Herr 1996), often with the aid of formal assessment instruments (for example, the Strong Interest Inventory). From both theoretical and practical perspectives, the limitations of this approach are becoming increasingly evident (Savickas 1996).

The work reported in this chapter is grounded in a distinctive perspective of career—namely, the *intelligent career* (Arthur *et al.* 1995), which stands in contrast to more traditional views. The intelligent-career framework reflects much of what others are calling for in the new economy—for example, for people to know their aspirations and strengths, and to be reflective and adaptive in order to succeed in a changing environment (Drucker 1997). Comprised of three 'ways of knowing' called *knowing-why, knowing-how*, and *knowing-whom*, the intelligent career focuses on the subjective interpretations of the career actor over objective interpretations of others (Arthur 1994).

Knowing-why incorporates themes of individual motivation, values, and the construction of personal meaning and identity. *Knowing-why* also encompasses attitudes to family, community, and other non-work aspects of life that affect career choice, adaptability, and commitment. Each of these aspects changes over time, as experiences, interests, and family situations change.

Knowing-how reflects an individual's career relevant skills and understanding that underlie current work behavior. While these areas of expertise provide the medium of exchange between employee and employer, they may also be used as a lever to invest in new areas for people who wish to use or develop a broader set of skills and knowledge than their present job demands. Continuous *knowing-how* development enhances career opportunities through increasing individual employability.

Knowing-whom includes the relationships people maintain and invest in to provide career support, promote the transmission of reputation, and provide access to information. Work-related relationships include internal company contacts, as well as supplier, customer, and broader industry contacts. People also have personal connections through family, friends, fellow alumni, and professional and social acquaintances that are also likely to grow over time.

The explicit identification and integration of three ways of knowing provides greater holism with respect to the person than traditional approaches to sub-jective career phenomena. The intelligent-career perspective also allows for a more flexible approach to the person's participation in multiple employment settings, including companies, occupations, and industries. Such participation enables development of each of the three ways of knowing, which may be considered as different forms of non-financial cultural, human, and social, 'career capital' (Arthur *et al.* 1999).

The intelligent career card sort

An assessment instrument known as the intelligent career card sort (ICCS) was developed specifically to elicit the subjective career data (Parker 1996). The ICCS consists of three subsets of up to forty cards reflecting the three ways of knowing previously described. That is, the *knowing-why* cards are concerned with a person's motivation, identity, and the balance of work and family; the *knowing-how* cards are concerned with a person's areas of skill and expertise; and the *knowing-whom* cards are concerned with a person's relationships. A person selects seven cards from each of the three sets and ranks them. An individual process then clarifies the meaning each item has for that person. The assumption underlying the ICCS is that people select cards reflecting their unique subjective careers. Further conversation draws out the distinctive interpretation a person attaches to each card.

A variant of the above argument may be applied at the group level of ana-lysis. At the group level (for example, LEs) interest lies in the commonality among subjective phenomena—that is, in the level of intersubjective agree-ment among the group's members. The seven most popular items are ranked by the subject according to the frequency of selection and relative importance for each of the *knowing-why*, *knowing-how*, and *knowing-whom* categories. The results are then discussed in focus groups, chosen to be representative of the larger group (Parker 2000). The resultant scale of weights runs from 0 (no selections) to 2 (unanimous selections of the item with top ranking). In practice the emergent weights fall in a range from 0–1.

Intersubjective data are different from aggregated individual data (Daft and Weick 1984). The purpose of the focus groups is to elicit intersubjective data by asking focus group participants to focus on their shared understanding. Intersubjective data may also reveal the presence of 'career communities'— that is, the largely voluntary community attachments people make to provide career support and continuity (Parker 2000). Career communities contribute to our understanding of career growth by making explicit the reflexivity between the individual and the multiple communities in which they participate.

ELICITING INTERSUBJECTIVE DATA: THE CASE OF LEASED EXECUTIVES

Intersubjective data for LEs were gathered from three focus group discussions. Members of two focus groups of LEs had completed the ICCS. A third group of LEs who worked for the same agency had not completed the initial ICCS. The author and a co-facilitator were present at all three focus group discussions to monitor the group dynamic during the discussions, and to verify the accuracy, analysis, and interpretation of the data collected.

The results reported below are organized around the *knowing-why, knowing-how*, and *knowing-whom* distinctions embodied in the ICCS methodology. Following that, the interplay among the three ways of knowing will be discussed.

Knowing-why

Table 7.1. sets out the weighted scores and frequency measures for the principal ICCS *knowing-why* items chosen by sample members. In the discussion that follows, emphasis is placed on the highest ranked-items.

The item most endorsed by the LEs was *I like to gain a sense of achievement from my work*, yet there was considerable difference as to what 'achievement'

Table 7.1. Aggregated *knowing-why* scores: leased executives

Item	Weighted score
I like to gain a sense of achievement from my work	0.99
I want to be challenged in my work	0.85
I like having a choice about the work that I do	0.62
I like being directly responsible for the results of my work	0.62
I like being involved in new business opportunities	0.46
I want to contribute to innovation at work	0.42
I want employment to support my lifestyle	0.42

meant. For example, there was a tension as to whether achievement was defined by the LE or by the client company. Several LEs mentioned the value of clearly defined projects, because they led to clear expectations and outcomes. Yet, the question was: 'Is the outcome set by the company sufficient to meet the achievement needs of the LE?' The project-based focus and its specificity were seen as motivating factors in LE work. The main sense of achievement came from solving problems at the core of project activities. There was a perceived contrast between 'value-adding' project-based work and the relatively routine work LEs associated with regular employment.

The achievement theme was closely related to the accountability inherent in *I like being directly responsible for the results of my work*—the fourth most endorsed item. There was a shared appreciation of the value of the authority they were afforded. Participants said that clients assumed that LEs required less supervision and would use their initiative to complete the task. Thus 'we are seen as independent' and 'we are expected to achieve the results for them' meant that 'we have more power to get ideas out there than permanent employees'.

A corollary of the independence of LEs was the welcome separation from organizational politics within the client company. The LEs agreed that 'we can avoid that stuff'. Company politics was seen as a 'cloak and dagger activity that distracts you from the work'. LEs felt that being removed from politics enabled them to maintain the integrity of their role. 'We have to be able to tell them what we see without worrying about whose toes we step on.'

The second item was *I want to be challenged in my work*. There was agreement that the nature of leased executive work was challenging. 'You wouldn't be a leased executive if you didn't like challenge.' One elaboration concerned the overall unfamiliarity of the workplace: 'You have to go into an organization not knowing anyone, having to ask where the photocopier is and work out how it all is and things like that.' Another elaboration covered the larger challenge of an unknown environment: 'Yeah, it is a challenge before you even start the job—many people couldn't do that ever in their lives.' Participants had a strong sense of shared fortitude that they enjoyed sharing with one another.

I like having a choice about the work that I do was frequently mentioned. However, many participants compared their own subjective criteria for choice and by implication career development with those defined by others. For example, 'people ask you what you do and you say, "I am a contractor". Then you realize that you don't have a "job" or medical insurance or a car park. You're not moving up a ladder or achieving anything that others can recognize.'

There was agreement that LEs should be selective about the assignments they accepted. 'You choose to be challenged by the contracts you choose.' However, sometimes choice seemed to be a luxury secondary to the need for work. A sense of realism was apparent: 'ho-hum contracts bore me out of my mind.' One participant balanced integrity and pragmatism thus: 'Overall, I have made a choice about something, and there are occasions when I am perhaps doing something that I would probably prefer not to do but I know that it is actually part of the overall choice that I have made, therefore, it is all right.' There was perceived to be a 'trade-off' between performing well, and learning and staying at the cutting edge of their occupation.

Wider choices involved the selection of the LE role. 'The choice may be about staying on—some jobs are for temps on trial and when you do a good job they offer you a permanent one—I never take them though!' No LEs wanted to stay permanently with any client. Being asked to become permanent was common yet apparently viewed with skepticism.

A further salient aspect of choice was choice in relation to the item *I want employment to support my lifestyle*. The LEs considered that their employment status conveyed benefits using the additional flexibility to develop a better balance between work and home life. Their defense of their non-traditional position was strong: 'Choice for me is really about do I want to live my job all day every day or do I want a job where I can get good financial rewards and only have to work eight hours a day?' Men as well as women believed that flexibility was critical.

In sum, the pattern that emerged from the *knowing-why* selections illustrates a strong motivation for LEs to engage in project-based work. Each person contracted work in order to integrate, in his or her own way, work and non-work activities. LEs' needs for achievement, challenge, autonomy, and learning were largely met through project arrangements. They broadened their career perspectives to pay attention simultaneously to non-work, and to issues of balance between work and family. They narrowed their focus from 'company' or 'job' perspectives to a 'project' perspective. The company was thus sidelined in the LE's career thinking.

The excitement of improvisation lies in amalgamating work experiences into a coherent whole. Close-up views of contingent assignments may suggest mere fragments of work, yet a broader vision shows that each assignment contributes to a *knowing-why* career theme involving 'the bits and pieces stitched into improvisations' (Bateson 1994: 10). The bits and pieces become unified by an underlying preference for project-based careers.

Knowing-how

Table 7.2. sets out the weighted scores and frequency measures for the principal ICCS *knowing-how* items.

The highest ranked item was *I am open to fresh ideas*. The discussions revealed strong links between this theme and the project orientation discussed in *knowing-why*. Each project was perceived to be not just a problem to solve but also an opportunity to acquire fresh ideas, and a conduit for knowledge exchange and learning. 'What you bring in is fresh ideas to the client company

Table 7.2. Aggregated *knowing-how* scores: leased executives

Item	Weighted score
I am open to fresh ideas	0.82
I want to work on successive projects instead of a continuous job	0.77
I enjoy working in job situations from which I can learn	0.72
I enjoy working as part of a meaningful project	0.72
I enjoy working with people from whom I can learn	0.71
I seek to improve my range of business skills	0.64
I am becoming a more strategic thinker	0.46

but you must take up fresh ideas as well or you dry up.' Thus the LEs perceived themselves not simply as experts downloading knowledge into client companies, but as partners in a reciprocal exchange and synergistic development of personal and company knowledge.

Participants compared different ways of performing the same task in order to decide which worked best. They recognized that this is possible only after several assignments within one industry. However, repeated application of the same skills was usually seen as precluding broader development. Discussion was again related to project work and also addressed the fourth item *I enjoy working as part of a meaningful project*. For example, 'I am always giving them fresh ideas but I am also in there exploring—partly for my own personal gain.'

A minority position emphasized the utility of *knowing-how* skills already in place: 'I find I don't have enough time to (develop new expertise). At the end of the day, the company is in trouble with cash flow and they want my expertise—I've been doing this for twenty-five years.' However, this position was challenged: 'Yeah, but I realized that I always needed to be on my toes and I couldn't sit back and let things stay the same.' 'I learned that if I wanted to be more creative I had to learn from others in each assignment.' The exchange echoed the tension between performance and self-development mentioned under *knowing-why*.

LEs mentioned the limited time and money available for self-development. Although they opted for a lifestyle that allowed a better balance between work and family than was possible with permanent employment, some were reluctant to allocate any non-work time to training. Also, 'the time you take out is dollars (taken from) your pocket'. This was one of the few areas in which permanent employees were perceived as having a better deal: 'Employees are paid for the time off and someone pays for the course.' However, others felt that learning was inherent in the way projects were done: 'You develop new skills each time.'

I want to work on successive projects rather than a continuous job reinforced the other arguments about the challenges of working as an LE. 'The appeal is in the change'; 'I couldn't stand to be in the same job doing the same thing day in and day out'; 'It relates to choice' (which recognized LEs' appreciation of the flexibility they had); 'I like to be in this industry and within that I have an expertise that feeds my choice'; 'I do not pass my use-by-date this way'.

The importance of learning as a source of further *knowing-how* expertise was emphasized by the third item, *I enjoy working in job situations from which I can learn*. Ongoing learning strategies were discussed. The LEs were explicit about their interest in picking up fresh ideas outside the work environment. Some described discussions with self-employed friends purposely oriented to generating broader perspectives. 'Sometimes the best ideas are ones where you transfer the knowledge from other experiences—or other people's experiences.' The focus groups were themselves treated as learning opportunities.

In sum, the discussion on *knowing-how* reinforced the strong motivation from *knowing-why* in favor of project-based work. The skills the participants applied in different contexts reinforced their identity as specialists, yet learning demanded being open to fresh ideas and adopting different approaches to familiar problems. The LEs recognized a fundamental tension between doing a good job for the client and learning new things for themselves. There are risks of becoming stereotyped through the repetition of similar projects; and of failing to invest in formal learning to accompany informal learning on the job.

Bateson (1994: 6) suggests creativity involves weaving 'fine threads of novelty' into the fabric of our unfolding lives. The career behavior of the LEs shows that novelty being incorporated in the way they thread both expertise and learning through projects that they undertake. Being an expert and simultaneously being open to fresh ideas also reflects an inherent ambiguity in the LEs' unfolding careers. However, Bateson (1994: 9) suggests that 'ambiguity is the warp of life, not something to be eliminated'. The ambiguity undertaken by LEs appears worth preserving, and offers a heuristic for other workers to consider.

Knowing-whom

Table 7.3. sets out the weighted scores and frequency measures for the principal ICCS *knowing-whom* items chosen by sample members.

Table 7.3. Aggregated *knowing-whom* scores: leased executives

Item	Weighted score
I develop and maintain relationships with family	1.17
I maintain relationships to keep old friends	0.96
I cultivate relationships with customers or clients for my work	0.50
I develop and maintain relationships with previous employers	0.41
I spend time with people from whom I can learn	0.38
I cultivate relationships to make new friends	0.37
I develop relationships with people outside my company members	0.34

The highest ranked item of any set was *I develop and maintain relationships with family*. This confirmed a pattern of participants' holistic approach to life signaled in the earlier *knowing-why* section. It also connected directly to a recurrent review of their lifestyle, particularly the importance of family and its balance with work. For example, 'I have decided that family is more important than work', and 'I can spend more time with my family this way'.

For most participants the decision to avoid the full-time corporate scene had both positive and negative aspects. For example, 'I miss some of the corporate niceties now that I don't travel much. However, I have a much better relationship at home.' The support gained from family was described as being particularly important for 'advice, guidance and that sort of stuff'.

The next item selected was *I maintain relationships to keep old friends*. This item was perceived by many to describe an extension of their families. Thus, LEs' significant networks were not those directly involved in the LEs' day-to-day work. Participants' relationships with old friends provided a major support network that reflected the effort invested in these relationships over time.

The high relative significance of the first two items was also reflected in the time and energy expended in discussion of them. Relationships with family and friends were continuous, whereas work relationships were discontinuous, even for those who socialized with work colleagues. For example, 'moving between companies means that old friends become far more important'; 'a shift from being a permanent employee to a contractor allows you to focus on family'. The autonomy LEs were afforded within client companies (see *knowing-why*) gave them 'more negotiating power' to take time off. 'They know you'll be back and will do the work.' This attitude increased their self-confidence about negotiating terms of employment.

I cultivate relationships with customers or clients for my work and *I develop and maintain relationships with previous employers* both seemed high on LEs' agendas, but only if they respected and/or liked the people involved. The aspect of choice was again important. The maintenance of relationships was reported to be due to a genuine regard for the person rather than an instrumental desire to secure career benefits. 'I do develop relationships with those I get on well with, and I get work from that, but that is not the reason I do it.'

In sum, the *knowing-whom* discussions illustrated that participants drew career support and built reputation through various networks that transcended any particular work setting. They found reinforcement in their relationships with others similarly (or self-) employed. However, they also separated their family and friendship networks from what they saw as necessary but more instrumental work relationships. Indeed, the insistence on the importance of friends and family, and on finding time to stay close to them, was a notable feature of the LEs' career behavior.

Despite not having one standard work environment, the LEs' discussions revealed multiple connections with others, rather than any sense of loneliness or disconnection in their careers. Bateson (1994: 89) suggests change and continuity often appear as 'two sides of the same coin'. The continuity gained from family and friends seemed to provide strength to sustain changes in the work aspects of LEs' lives.

INTEGRATION OF THREE WAYS OF KNOWING

From the LEs' focus group discussions a pattern was evident of inter-dependence among the three ways of knowing. The primary focus was on the bounded nature, in both time and scope, of the projects they worked on. The strong *knowing-why* motivation to work with a project orientation was supported by their particular areas of *knowing-how* expertise, and was used further to develop that expertise. Most LEs recognized that maintaining their expertise required remaining at the cutting edge of their field. Being open to fresh ideas and engaging in continuous learning were consciously effected through work on successive projects. Work opportunities in turn were linked with several *knowing-whom* relationships. Personal reputation was always at stake and interdependent with the broad knowledge and specialist expertise that facilitated smooth inter-project transitions. The reciprocity inherent in the exchange of expertise for new learning emphasized the integrity required in each assignment. The support of family and old friends was particularly important in the light of the transient nature of their employment.

At the heart of the intelligent career concept of *knowing-whom* is the idea of relationships—in fact, the term appears in most ICCS items. A relational approach to careers means more than looking at interpersonal relations, and sees the career as 'interactive with the person's entire environment' (Hall 1996: 342). The relational perspective focuses on the dynamics of *process* inherent in the engagement of knowledge and learning in context (Hosking *et al.* 1995). The perspective relates closely to social theories of learning that emphasize people's participation in sociocultural communities (Lave and Wenger 1991), and in turn to the concept of career communities (Parker 2000).

As people enact their careers, they shape and are shaped by the communities in which they participate (Weick 1996). By adopting 'peripheral vision' (Bateson 1994) they can simultaneously focus on the interdependence among the concepts of working, learning, and careers. They can also engage actively at both individual and community levels of analysis. The focus group data for all three ways of knowing revealed clear evidence of strong project community attachments, and an immediate base for developing new competencies. Other connections such as to the leasing agency and its other clients provided further reference groups against which the LEs could assess their project-to-project reputation. Furthermore, the strong, emphatically more stable, communities of family and non-work friends provided additional strength and support.

With the exception of their fundamental need for *knowing-how* opportunities to apply and extend their expertise, the LEs operated largely independently of employing organizations. The strength of their *knowing-why* desire to achieve, be challenged, and choose their work motivated the LEs to stitch together successive pieces of work into a repertoire of assignments. Their membership in relevant career communities supported their learning and reinforced their identities.

The evidence above indicates that membership in more than one community—and in particular in communities beyond the immediate workplace—provides support for career growth. Moreover, different community attachments can contribute to the development of different aspects of self. As investors in such career communities, LEs illustrate 'continuity and creativity in the ways ... [they] "compose" their lives' (Bateson 1994: 87). In seeing LEs weave career patterns that are different from traditional models, we might also wonder if they might be harbingers of broader patterns of career creativity in the future.

CONCLUSION

Leased executives assess their careers against subjective measures of success. Working as self-employed professionals, LEs assume responsibility for the development that they recognize is central to their continued employability. They are aware that project-to-project learning is the underlying dynamic of their careers. They are sensitized to take advantage of learning opportunities. Moreover, the LEs had either chosen to move to or stay with project-based work instead of holding permanent positions in the core of any organization. The LEs relied on their *knowing-how* skills and expertise to leverage their *knowing-why* preferences for autonomy and a balanced lifestyle, and to cultivate *knowing-whom* reputation in anticipation of future assignments. The strong project orientation afforded the LEs a separation between work and non-work activities. Participation in multiple career communities provided sites for growth and development by reinforcing their *knowing-why* motivations as well as their *knowing-how* areas of expertise. Their investment in work-related *knowing-whom* relationships appeared parsimonious but effective, and allowed room for important further investments in both friends and family.

Contract workers engaged through agencies to work on project assignments for successive companies seem like the antithesis of traditional career actors. The mobility that characterizes their work patterns used to be considered less as a career than as a series of 'jobs'. They are 'zigzag' people (Bateson 1994: 82) who deviate from the traditional career prototype. Their careers involve successive project cycles, and the transfer of experience from one cycle to the next. They reflect what Bateson (1994: 82) now suggests as the new 'norm of a successful life'—namely, one that 'involves repeated new beginnings and new learnings'. From this perspective, the LEs may be demonstrating a new career form. The movement from project to project nurtured by enduring community attachments outside the workplace does suggest a prototype for future career arrangements.

REFERENCES

Albrecht, D. G. (1998), 'Reaching New Heights', *Workforce*, 77/4: 42–8.

Allan, P., and Sienko, S. (1997), 'A Comparison of Contingent and Core Workers' Perceptions of their Jobs Characteristics and Motivational Properties', *SAM Advanced Management Journal*, 62/3: 4–9.

Arthur, M. B. (1994), 'The Boundaryless Career: A New Perspective for Organizational Inquiry', *Journal of Organizational Behaviour*, 15: 1–12.

——and Rousseau, D. M. (1996) (eds.), *The Boundaryless Career: A New Employment Principle for a New Organizational Era* (New York: Oxford University Press).

——Claman, P. H., and DeFillippi, R. J. (1995), 'Intelligent Enterprise, Intelligent Careers', *Academy of Management Executive*, 9/4: 7–20.

——Inkson, K., and Pringle, J. K. (1999), *The New Careers: Individual Action and Economic Change* (Thousand Oaks, Calif: Sage).

Bateson, M. C. (1994), *Peripheral Visions* (New York: HarperCollins).

Beer, M., Spector, B., Lawrence, D., Quinn Mills, D., and Walton, R. (1984), *Managing Human Assets* (New York: Free Press).

Boden, R. J. J. (1999), 'Flexible Working Hours, Family Responsibilities, and Female Self-Employment: Gender Differences in Self-Employment Selection', *American Journal of Economics and Sociology*, 58/1: 71–83.

Bridges, W. (1995), 'A Nation of Owners', *Inc.*, 17/7 (May), 89–91.

Casey, B., Metcalf, H., and Millwards, N. (1997), *Employers Use of Flexible Labour* (London: Policy Studies Institute).

Daft, R., and Weick, K. (1984), 'Toward a Model of Organizations as Interpretation Systems', *Academy of Management Review*, 9/2: 284–95.

Davis-Blake, A., and Uzzi, B. (1993), 'Determinants of Employment Externalization: A Study of Temporary Workers and Independent Contractors', *Administrative Science Quarterly*, 38: 195–223.

DFEE (1993), Department for Education and Employment, *Labour Force Survey* (London: HMSO).

Drucker, P. (1997), 'The Future that has Already Happened', *Harvard Business Review* (Sept.–Oct.), 20–4.

Eaton, S. C., and Bailyn, L. (2000), 'Career as Life Path: Tracing Work and Lie Strategies of Biotech Professionals', in M. Peiperl, M. B. Arthur, R. Goffee, and T. Morris (eds.), *Career Frontiers: New Conceptions of Working Lives* (New York: Oxford University Press), 177–98.

Filipezak, B., Hequet, M., Picard, M., and Stamps, D. (1995), 'Contingent Worker Numbers will Grow', *Training*, 32/11.

Hall, D. T. (1996), 'Long Live the Career', in D. T. Hall and Associates, *The Career is Dead: Long Live the Career* (San Francisco: Jossey-Bass), 1–12.

Handy, C. (1990), *The Age of Unreason* (Boston: Harvard Business School Press).

Heron, J. (1992), *Feeling and Personhood: Psychology in Another Key* (London: Sage).

Herr, E. L. (1996), 'Toward the Convergence of Career Theory and Practice: Mythology, Issues, and Possibilities', in M. L. Savickas and W. B. Walsh (eds.), *Handbook of Career Theory* (Palo Alto, Calif.: Davies-Black), 13–35.

Holland, J. L. (1985), *Making Vocational Choices: A Theory of Careers* (Englewood Cliffs, NJ: Prentice-Hall).

Hosking, D.-M., Dachler, H. P., and Gergen, K. J. (1995) (eds.), *Management and Organization: Relational Alternatives to Individualism* (Aldershot: Ashgate Publishing Company).

Inkson, K., Heising, A., and Rousseau, D. M. (2001), 'The Interim Manager: Prototype of the Twenty-First Century Worker?', *Human Relations*, 54/3: 259–84.

Kosters, M. H. (1997), 'New Employment Relationships and the Labor Market', *Journal of Labor Research*, 18/4: 551–9.

Lave, J., and Wenger, E. (1991), *Situated Earning: Legitimate Peripheral Participation* (Cambridge: Cambridge University Press).

Mallon, M., and Duberley, J. (2000), 'Managers and Professionals in the Contingent Workforce', *Human Resource Management Journal*, 10/1: 33–47.

Mischel, W. (1977), 'The Interaction of Person and Situation', in D. Magnuson and N. S. Endler (eds.), *Personality at the Crossroads* (Hillsdale, NJ: Erlbaum).

Parker, H. L. P. (1996), 'The New Career Paradigm: An Exploration of 'Intelligent Career' Behaviour among MBA Graduates and Students', unpublished master's thesis (New Zealand: University of Auckland).

—— (2000), 'Career Communities', unpublished doctoral thesis (New Zealand: University of Auckland).

Pearce, J. L. (1993), 'Towards an Organizational Behaviour of Contract Laborers: Their Psychological Involvement and Effects on Employee Co-Workers', *Academy of Management Journal*, 36: 1082–96.

Peiperl, M. A., and Baruch, Y. (1997), 'Back to Square Zero: The Post-Corporate Career', *Organizational Dynamics*, 25/4: 7–22.

Rousseau, D. M. (1995), *Psychological Contracts in Organizations* (Thousand Oaks, Calif.: Sage).

—— (1997), 'Organizational Behaviour: The New Organizational Era', *Annual Review of Psychology*, 48: 515–46.

—— and Libuser, C. (1997), 'Contingent Workers in High Risk Environments', *California Management Review*, 39: 103–23.

Savickas, M. L. (1996), 'A Framework for Linking Career Theory and Practice', in M. Savickas and W. B. Walsh (eds.), *Handbook of Career Counseling Theory and Practice* (Palo Alto, Calif.: Davies-Black).

—— (1997), 'The Spirit in Career Counseling: Fostering Self-Completion through Work', in D. P. Bloch and J. R. Lee (eds.), *Connections between Spirit and Work in Career Development* (Palo Alto, Calif.: Davies-Black), 3–25.

Super, D. E. (1980), 'A Life-Span, Life-Space Approach to Career Development', *Journal of Vocational Behaviour*, 13: 282–98.

Von Hippel, E. H. (1988), *The Sources of Innovation* (New York: Oxford University Press).

Weick, K. E. (1996), 'Enactment and the Boundaryless Career: Organizing as we Work', in M. B. Arthur and D. M. Rousseau (eds.), *The Boundaryless Career: A New Employment Principle for a New Organizational Era* (Oxford: Oxford University Press), 47–57.

8

Creative Resilience and the Mastery of Career Adversity

JEFFREY A. SONNENFELD

Few careers can be mapped as an unbroken chain of success. There is an endless array of career frustrations that can seem so insurmountable that they are demoralizing. Regardless of whether the setbacks are the consequence of terminations, lay-offs, false accusations, missed promotions, plateauing, burnout, reduced responsibility, disappointing colleagues, uninteresting work, unpleasant clients, unsuccessful assignments, failed projects, abusive bosses, cruel co-workers, or other such sources, the resolution requires new behaviors and fresh perspectives.

A person's established portfolio of skills is unlikely to be sufficient to overcome what he or she experiences as unfamiliar barriers. This may be especially so when one feels personally humiliated, professionally diminished, and vocationally blocked. Creative new approaches to adversity must be summoned.

These setbacks, however, can be not just recoverable but in fact even redemptive. Leaders and artists face common barriers in their career ascent and their recovery from career descent. Psychologists and anthropologists have long discovered the common qualities of creativity, which unify the careers of artists and leaders. Rank *et al.* (1989) described 'the urge to create' that drives their shared superhuman levels of accomplishment as the manifestation of their common quest for immortality. Joseph Campbell (1949/1990) revealed the links between the storyteller and the subject or the mythmaker and the hero across cultures and through the ages. Campbell showed through his 'monomyth of the hero' that, following a separation from society and subsequent triumphs over a series of trials, recovery from adversity was the next universal critical life stage in defining the heroic character.

More recently, Howard Gardner (1998) in his book *Extraordinary Minds* advanced a set of traits shared by all truly great achievers across professions. Gardner, focusing on four extraordinary historic figures, Wolfgang Mozart, Virginia Woolf, Sigmund Freud, and Mahatma Gandhi, postulated that the key to their success was not raw intellectual horsepower, fortunate circumstances, or boundless energy. Rather, Gardner pronounced three qualities of super-achievement among artists and leaders across cultures: (1) they have a special talent for identifying their own strengths and weaknesses; (2) they are skilled at accurately analyzing the events in their own lives; and (3) they can convert into future successes those inevitable setbacks that plague every life.

Such skill at introspection and resilience is a combination of the creative disposition and the creative environment. The admonition of F. Scott Fitzgerald (1941, p. 163) that, in American lives, there are 'no second acts' haunts creative careers, leadership careers, and naturally the leaders of creative fields. The flameout of early career superstars in drama and the arts such as Kurt Vonnegut, J. D. Salinger, Alan Jay Lerner, Arthur Miller, Judy Garland, and Orson Wells overshadowed their later careers. Others such as John Irving, Mike Nichols, Robert Altman, Carlos Santana, and John Travolta successfully managed to reignite the flames of their careers in bold challenge to Fitzgerald's curse.

This paradox is similarly found in such creative industries as information technology and communications media. Brilliant creative leaders such as HBO's pioneer Michael Fuchs, Sony USA's CEO Mickey Schulhoff, or Apple's visionary past CEO John Scully have hardly been heard from since they left their high public perches. At the same time, media moguls like USA Network's Barry Diller triumphed over setbacks at the helm of enterprises such as Twentieth Century Fox and QVC to reveal irrepressible energy and skill.

TRIPPING ALONG THE PATHS TO CREATIVE CAREERS

The needed creative career resilience tasks can, ironically, be even more difficult for those in creative fields. The concept of the self-determining protean career should flourish in creative environments (Hall and Mirvis 1996). In fact, perhaps the opportunities for infinite reinvention may hit a ceiling for those seemingly most fortunate in creative businesses owing to the fleeting nature of the currency of reputation these leaders require.

Furthermore, psychologists have noted that the shared 'urge to create' may be a common quest for immortality. The drive for recognition is an essential element for leadership in creative businesses as well as for artists. In his book *The Frenzy of Renown*, literary scholar Leo Braudy (1986) has argued that society always generates a subset of individuals eager to live their lives in the public eye. These people court or at least endure recognition on a grand scale in the belief that fame will ultimately liberate them from suffocating conventional expectations akin to idiosyncrasy credits (Hollander 1964).

The currency of celebrity allows artists a cushion for greater risk taking as well as commercial success and elusive material luxury (Braudy 1986). As for leaders, after initial early career compliance with the group norms and expectations of their constituents, the leader is permitted to depart from these norms without jeopardizing his elevated status in the group. Groups allow their leaders considerable freedom for innovation in order to act in the presumed best interests of the group (Hollander 1964).

THE DOUBLE-EDGED SWORD OF GREATNESS

Such elevation and celebrity, however, are never guaranteed to be permanent. The vulnerable nature of reputations in creative and leadership roles ultimately creates common barriers for the career recovery of artists and leaders. When a devastating career setback hits such superachievers, their resources and situations create a double-edged sword as they fight to recover their career. Known for enormous success, they now see themselves and see that others see that they have failed. They have lived very public lives analyzing external challenges yet now must confront personal loss in a way that draws more heavily upon internal diagnosis. As action-oriented individuals, they do not tend to be the most reflective. Their success has reinforced a confidence in their own world view. Now that vision may have been shattered. So used to dispensing wisdom to others, they may not be as comfortable with accepting the help and guidance of others. Accustomed to self-reliance, prominent creative figures may not find it easy to ask for help.

The costs of career adversity to accomplished, creative people are enormous. First, they must come to terms with the mindset of now being the victim. The victim must deal with: being a very proud person who has just suffered enormous loss of *self-esteem*, the danger of *burnout* from the emotional drain on energy and spirit (Freudenberger 1974; Freudenberger and Richelson 1980; Golembiewski 1986), the sudden loss of *influence* and respect from others in the victim's world, and the frustration of seeing life's *opportunities* pass by as access to the tournament of top-quality career slots is denied (Rosenbaum 1979).

Next, the victims must be aware of the impact on their own support system. There is unanticipated *collateral impact* on the lives of innocent close third parties such as loving family members, loyal friends, and frightened co-workers (Gutek *et al.* 1981; Lee and Kanungo 1984).

Lastly, the victims must consider the special properties of the work culture typifying their profession or industry (Sonnenfeld and Peiperl 1988; Sonnenfeld 1989). The creative industries, classified as 'baseball teams', such as fashion, software, entertainment, media, and advertising are noted for fluid career paths across many employers, as are the turnaround situations classified as 'fortresses', which have a preference for mobile turnaround types. Those classified as 'clubs' and 'academies' have been shown to favor loyalty and have historic preference for those who rise up from within.

Setbacks for those in internally fueled career systems, such as the 'old economy' clubs and academies, would appear to be far more difficult. The book *Indecent Exposure: A True Story of Hollywood and Wall Street* (McClintick 1982) demonstrates the resilience possible in 'baseball teams'. This book shows how Columbia Pictures chief Alan Hirshfield was forced out at Columbia Pictures in the wake of a scandal over check forgery after he had hired, fired, rehired, and again fired the head of movie production who brought him down, David Begelman. After immediately assuming a courtesy position at Warner Brothers for a year, Hirshfield gained a top job at Twentieth Century Fox.

Similarly, the book *Hit and Run* (Griffin and Masters 1996) profiles new starts at other 'baseball teams'. It demonstrates how two film producers with limited background, by leveraging a hit film into the top jobs at Sony Pictures, cost Sony $800 million in a settlement with their former employer Time Warner. By the time they were fired in 1994, Sony reported a loss of $3 billion on a string of failed expensive films over the five years. They returned to produce for Warner Brothers.

At the same time, all creative environments are not Hollywood, where celebrity often counts for more than integrity of reputation. It could be argued that, in fluid external labor markets, leaders and creative individuals must rely even more upon the sterling nature of their reputations, since there is no common calibration of excellence and common pool of performance knowledge that one is more likely to have in the internal labor markets of clubs and academies.

Blending the accumulated experience of resilient leaders with relevant dispositional and situational bodies of scholarship suggests that the challenges to career recovery can be clustered into five sets of tasks:

* fight not flight: acknowledging and redirecting the stress;
* recruiting others into battle: showing concern for the collateral victims;
* rebuilding heroic stature: spreading the true nature of the adversity;
* proving your mettle: regaining trust and credibility;
* rediscovering the heroic mission: clearing the past and charting the future.

FIGHT NOT FLIGHT: ACKNOWLEDGING AND REDIRECTING THE STRESS

A first challenge is to acknowledge career losses and admit the consequences. Often we deny our setbacks because of the impact on our status within the groups that can define our identity. We may think that friends, neighbors, family, and co-workers have not noticed. We may also deny the losses because of how they erode our self-esteem. Job loss has been ranked as number eight among the most stressful events in life—just after death of family members, jail, and personal injury or illness (Holmes and Rahe 1967). Similarly, the loss of title and role clarity are destructive workplace stressors as well (Cooper and Payne 1988, Cooper 1983).

Sadly, our society conspires with the victim of career distress to hide the losses. Others around us are embarrassed by our loss of face. Since stress is the perception of helplessness in dealing with serious demands, we should be seizing control at just the time our therapeutic society often counsels retreat and vacation. There is no such thing as objective stress existing on its own. We respond stressfully only to people, places, and events; our response is dependent upon our perceptions of the adequacy of resources to deal with the stressors (Matheny and Cupp 1983). The common advice that the career distress victim gets of 'taking some time off' is in fact avoidant behavior rather than competency-building behavior. The oft-prescribed vacation may not 'clear the head' but exacerbate feelings of exclusion and diminished career mastery—thus escalating the stress.

Instead of retreat, the victim of career adversity should confront the adversity. Engagement is necessary rather than submission. Research on psychological hardiness in responding to stress suggests that victims must regain control, make commitments to external events, respond to challenges, be willing to take a radical approach, and essentially become blind to their fears (Kobassa 1979; Maddi and Hightower 1999).

Coping with stress is often incorrectly defined as accommodating the stress. It is common to counsel those suffering career losses to reduce the *importance* of the stress they feel by 'putting things in perspective' or 'finding gratification in non-work pursuits'. These may be fine life choices, but not as a consequence of denial, avoidance, projection, and withdrawal. Similarly, superficial efforts to reduce the *effects* of stress through exercise, diet, meditation, or support groups are rarely enough by themselves. Instead, it is worthwhile to examine ways of reducing the *source* of the stress, perhaps through direct confrontation (Schuler 1984).

It is not easy to confront the source of stress directly, because people often lack sufficient resources and preparation for such engagement. For example, the sterling reputation of Henry Silverman was badly tarnished when Cendant, his once soaring enterprise, fell into a tailspin. The original business, Hospitality Franchising, was composed of a cluster of travel and relocation businesses such as Days Inns, Rama Hotels, Howard Johnson Hotels, Avis Rent-a-Car, Century 21, and Ramada Hotels. The revenues of this empire spiraled upwards, with 20 percent plus growth rates and constantly escalating stock prices—from 4 in 1992 to 77 in 1997, when a scandal hit.

The megamerger of Hospitality Franchising with a direct marketer called CUC led to the firm being renamed to Cendant in late 1997, and the unfurling of Silverman's reputation. Cendant's stock plummeted 46 percent, losing $13 billion in market capitalization when a series of massive improprieties emerged from a series of investigations. Apparently fraud had led to three years of inflated earnings of $700 million.

A proud, self-made man, Silverman was crushed by these events. Although his father had run a commercial finance company, Silverman wanted to be known for his own accomplishments rather than through any inheritance. He had cut his teeth in the deal business working with several notorious corporate raiders and blue chip investment bankers. In building his own empire, Silverman had acquired a reputation for diligence and savvy that melted in the heat of the CUC scandal. A near-debilitating anger and humiliation eroded his self-esteem. 'My own sense of self-worth was diminished,' he commented.

Associates cautioned him from letting himself become consumed by the failure. For example,

[Fellow financier] Darla D. Moore recalls a dinner shortly after the scandal broke. She was seated next to Silverman, and as guest speaker Henry Kissinger got up to speak she looked at her friend, who seemed suddenly quite gray. 'As bad as it seems, nobody has died,' she leaned over to whisper to him, 'but if you don't get some relief [from the pressure], you'll be the first to go.'   (Barrett 2000: 128)

With psychiatric guidance, Silverman redirected the rage outside of himself. His daily schedule was punctuated with rigorous aerobics, tennis, and weight-lifting. In just a year, he increased his bench press weight from 65 to 150 pounds. On top of this sublimation, however, Silverman redirected his anger through a determination to regain his credibility. His method was to define himself as a victim and not the villain. Silverman directly implicated CUC's top leadership and sued its accountants, Ernst & Young. The recent criminal indictments of CUC's former leaders, Walter Forbes and E. Kirk Shelton, seem to have brought Silverman some sense of vindication (*Bloomberg News* 2001). Now, at last, Silverman felt he could reach out to investors and point to the true culpability for the great losses: 'We had to keep our mouths shut for the past two years. The worst thing would be to tell investors a story that isn't a story' (Colarusso 2001).

Until these indictments, Silverman minimized the need continually to explain and thus relive the situation, by limiting his family's social engagements, withdrawing to the comfort of friends such as financiers Leon Black and Darla Moore. Meanwhile he stabilized Cendant by selling non-core businesses to repurchase 20 percent of the outstanding shares to boost the stock price. Silverman began reviewing smaller acquisitions, and finally he worked to regain credibility through alliances with firms like John Malone's Liberty Media in e-commerce deals. By the spring of 2001, Silverman could point with pride to steady returns and 'strong-buy' recommendations from several leading analysts (Colarusso 2001).

RECRUITING OTHERS INTO BATTLE: SHOWING CONCERN FOR THE COLLATERAL VICTIMS

In addition to feeling the need to redeem himself before shareholders, Silverman felt responsible for the ways his situation affected his family, his co-workers, and his friends. His efforts to bring others into his campaign are not unusual.

By enlisting the assistance of others, it is possible to attend to the needs of the innocent bystanders who suffer from a victim's career crisis. This helps to show appreciation for, and replenish the resources of, the support system that is so critical for coping with stress. This reinforcement from trusted advisers is also of great value for candid feedback. Gardner's observation (1998) that resilient exceptional people have a talent for self-awareness is true, in part, because these people energetically use personal networks in both their ascent and their recovery from setback. The trusted advisers the victim consults help through more than consolation alone. The trusted advisers hold up a candid mirror for self-reflection and help brainstorm the range of next steps.

Without doubt, no leader's resilience more falsifies F. Scott Fitzgerald's denial of second acts in American careers than that of Bernard Marcus, Chairman of The Home Depot, and his co-founder CEO, Arthur Blank. They had been fired by Sandy Sigoloff as the leaders of Handy Dan's Home Improvement Stores, a unit of Daylin which they ran. Sigoloff, an infamously tough turnaround manager, was often referred to as 'Ming the Merciless.' Marcus revealed what he believed motivated Sigoloff to fire them:

He really wanted credit for turning Daylin around, saving it from the creditors, saving it for the shareholders, saving it from bankrupcy. But the only Daylin division that had a great cash flow was Handy Dan—my Division...The day I knew I was finished with Sandy Sigoloff was the day the Daylin board of directors discussed succession. One Sigoloff-appointed board member said, 'I don't know why there is any question about succession here, since you have your obvious successor right in this room, Bernie Marcus'...A quick glance at Sigoloff's ashen face told me that that was never going to happen. And the very notion that some on the board supported the idea made me a genuine threat to Sigoloff. The situation between us just went from really bad to dire. (Marcus and Blank 1999: 32, 33)

Marcus accurately suspected that not only was he the prime target of Sigoloff's wrath, but so were his top lieutenants, Arthur Blank and Ron Brill, who were also dismissed in separate rooms and in rapid succession. 'Ron, like Arthur and me, never knew what hit him.' Marcus believed that further damage was done when Sigoloff released a statement to the press at Friday afternoon's deadline to ensure a prompt unanswered publication. Marcus explained, 'But it was far worse than just the loss of a couple of well-paying, high-profile jobs, or a few embarrassing newspaper stories. Sigoloff was primarily after me; for Arthur and Ron, it was more a matter of guilt by association. We all had painful experiences telling our family and friends what happened' (Marcus and Blank 1999: 34).

Marcus added that, subsequent to their dismissal, Sigoloff attempted to vilify the victims further by suggesting to the authorities that there had been some infractions in labor organizing efforts. Marcus and Blank insist that such allegations were invented and were never found to have merit by the authorities, but were trumped up to humiliate and disable them from retaliating.

Marcus and his team remained loyal to each other. A close friend, the financier Ken Langone, encouraged him to pursue his dream of creating a different type of home improvement store, advising him, 'This is the greatest news I have heard...You have just been kicked in the ass with a golden horseshoe' (Marcus and Blank 1999: 37). Langone immediately joined him as a primary financial backer of The Home Depot. Similarly, when he turned for solace to another retail pioneer, his friend Sol Price, co-founder of the Price Club, he found support and inspiration: 'Over dinner, I told Price how Sigoloff turned me out. There was a lot of self-pity on my part. Why did this happen to me? I was drowning in my sorrow, going several nights at a time without sleeping. For the first time in my adult life, instead of building, I was more concerned with surviving' (Marcus and Blank 1999: 39). Price asked Marcus if he believed he had talent and if he thought that he had 'the ability to build something, to create. Do you feel good about yourself?' (Marcus and Blank 1999: 40). It was soon evident that, with such rallying of support, his distress created a new professional opportunity.

Marcus found that his colleagues and friends believed in him and eagerly joined him in battle. Their infectious enthusiasm encouraged many others to join the campaign. His concept comprised stores that were immense warehouses catering for do-it-yourself home-repair enthusiasts, providing greater selection, superior customer service, a highly trained staff, and direct purchasing from the manufacturer. The founders relocated from Los Angeles to Atlanta and opened their first store in 1979. By 1990 they had 17,500 employees with sales of $2.7 billion. By 2001 they had sales of $58 billion and 160,000 employees. They also had roughly 1,000 superstores, with each store stocking more than 40,000 types of home improvement supplies. The founders stayed together through the building and leadership succession, to become some of the wealthiest people in the world. In 1996 Arthur Blank succeeded Marcus as CEO, with Marcus as Chairman. The Home Depot continued to grow and replaced Sears on the coveted Dow Jones stock index list. Then in 2001, while their corporate reputation was still number six in the nation on Fortune's list, Marcus and Blank recruited Robert Nardelli from a top post at General Electric to become CEO and move the firm to a new stage of life (Diba and Munoz 2001). They still rally around the motto born in crisis, 'We take Care of the Customer and Each Other.'

REBUILDING HEROIC STATURE: SPREADING THE TRUE NATURE OF THE ADVERSITY

In the above example, it was clear that Bernie Marcus did not escape to the comfort of sycophantic cronies to nurse his hurt, but rather turned to friends and colleagues who challenged him, inspired him, and joined him. Great leaders acquire a larger-than-life heroic persona. When that is deflated, when the audience disappears and the co-workers are no longer around, leaders can lose their identity. They do not find contentment merely being one of the crowd. Great leaders, like great artists, cultivate a personal dream that they share with the public. If the dream is accepted, the leader becomes renowned, but if it then becomes a public possession it may ultimately be discarded by the public (Sonnenfeld 1988). The leaders may then suffer the loss of both a private dream and a public identity. As people rallied around Marcus, they allowed him to regain his familiar role. They rallied because they still believed in him and in his heroic identity. They were able to rally because Marcus told them the truth and gave them something to believe in. When a hero stumbles, the constituents are confused as to how that happened, given the larger-than-life presence the hero held.

Just as Marcus took his story to friends, investors, employees, and now to countless readers, so have others who have discovered the need to repair their armor. John Eyler, the chief executive of Toys 'R' Us, was fired at a large clothing retailer on Christmas Eve without even a chance to clarify his benefits or severance. He feels what was critical to his resilience was that he did not let the situation define him to others, because, if it had done so, 'I might have started to doubt myself as well.' Before getting the chance at the enormous Toys 'R' Us chain, Eyler seized a chance to rehabilitate his reputation by accepting the leadership of the smaller but upmarket FAO Schwarz toy chain for eight years. By January 2001, one year into the new job, Eyler had built on a strong record of success at FAO Schwarz to lead the troubled Toys 'R' Us back to cutting-edge retail service concepts, sharply increased profits, and a doubled stock price. In one year he had remodeled 225 of the 710 superstores, at almost $1 million per store, and saw sales growth double as a result (DeGross 2001). He made imaginative partnerships with The Home Depot and Universal Studios for toys, along with one with Amazon.com to run its Toys 'R' Us Internet business. He is planning to open a new huge marquee Times Square store, which will trumpet to all, with a 60 foot Ferris Wheel that should serve as a great symbol of the ups and downs of life. The image of Toys 'R' Us had fallen on hard times. It was seen as a fallen star itself: stodgy, stale, and in decline. It was through Eyler's own sterling reputation for creativity, fairness, and profitability that he was able to entice some of the most dynamic companies in retail, entertainment, and technology to join him as partners. Eyler would not let one setback brand him a failure and repackaged himself as a winner, taking on challenges in stages to prove his correctness.

The value of reputation as a corporate and a personal asset has long been recognized by scholars. A reputation is built through experience, performance, and affiliations (Staw *et al.* 1983; Elsback and Sutton 1992; Fombrun 1996). When it is damaged, it can be restored through painstaking efforts of explanation and proven actions. In essence, the victim of reputation loss must circulate an explanation of the setback that must embrace several critical elements for successful image restoration: (1) making clear denials of culpability; (2) shifting responsibility for the mishap; (3) reducing the offensiveness of the act; (4) maintaining the appearance of reasonableness of behavior (Jones and Nesbitt 1971); and (5) offering acceptable motives (Scott and Lyman 1968). Marcus' explanation of the Handy Dan termination by Sandy Sigoloff well demonstrates these dimensions.

Turning to yet another great retailer, Leonard Roberts, the CEO of Tandy/ Radio Shack, was previously fired as CEO of Shoney's restaurants. Renowned throughout his life as a maverick, he married at age 17 while in high school and became a father at 19. Roberts obtained several grain patents and a law degree, becoming head of the food service division of Ralston Purina. In 1985 he left to become CEO of the troubled Arby's roast beef restaurant chain. At Arby's Roberts engineered a profound turnaround through a combination of team management, aggressive marketing, and new product development. In 1989 he escaped a difficult controlling owner who faced his own legal challenges to run the $1.5 billion Shoney's chain of 1,600 restaurants. Roberts led a sweeping overhaul in customer service and franchise relations. Store design, purchasing, and marketing were rebuilt completely and quickly. In just three years, Shoney's profits went from $15.5 million to over $50 million.

Nonetheless, Roberts was the first CEO to be recruited from the outside and some powerful elements of the old culture rejected him. Many viewed Roberts' firing from Shoney's as a political revolt of the old guard against Roberts' style (Romeo 1993). *The Wall Street Journal*, in fact, carried a scorching story that some board members felt Roberts had gone too far with his affirmative action efforts just six weeks after Shoney's had settled a $105 million racial discrimination lawsuit. The founder, Raymond Danner, was quoted to have told one manager that 'you've got too many niggers here. If you don't fire them, I'll fire you.'

Roberts was unable to offer public comment as part of his $2.9 million severance package, but word of his skills got around. Some recruiters thought that his battle at Shoney's made him too controversial. However, when in 1994 Tandy CEO John Roach began hunting for a successor, he was quickly drawn to Roberts' moral courage as well as his general management skills. Thus, he took the risk of appointing Roberts, a lifelong restaurateur, as president of the 7,100 store electronics retailer. (Palmeri 1998).

In 1998 Roberts succeeded Roach, and pioneered creative store-within-a-store partnerships with suppliers such as Sprint, RCA, Compaq, Microsoft, Blockbuster, Verizon, and Excite@thome. At the same time, he had to dismantle several large divisions that he had inherited, which were draining resources. For example: McDuff Electronics acquired in 1985 was sold in 1997; Incredible Universe superstores launched in 1992 were sold in 1997; and Computer City opened in 1992 was sold to CompUSA in 1998 (Grant 2001). These divisions were created to compete against 'big-box' competitors, but they diverted from the more cozy RadioShack shopping experience. The strategic repositioning and alliances led to a stunning 18 percent annual growth rate in operating income over Roberts's, first four years. As with Eyler, Roberts found his now widely revered reputation to be a key asset in the repositioning of the company and in forging these strategic alliances.

PROVING YOUR METTLE: REGAINING TRUST AND CREDIBILITY

It is not always easy to find the opportunities to prove oneself in the way that Roberts, Eyler, Marcus, and Silverman have done. Artists and performers require their work to be shown, but other forces control the galleries, museums, performance halls, and films that are required to provide access to their trades. Regularly, actors hear that they are too old, musicians that they are passé, and artists that galleries will no longer present their work. Similarly, even chief executives face gatekeepers to showcase their skills.

It is easy to be considered last year's model. Once you are painted with the brush of controversy, the ready pool of rising stars will make it hard for you regain your footing. Regardless, following profound setbacks, leaders must demonstrate that they still have the skills that have made them great. Roberts, Marcus, and Silverman all eagerly jumped back into action to prove they retained the talents that had built their careers.

A competitive real-estate tycoon, Donald Trump was always driven to win, even in the rivalry with his father, Fred, who was also a real-estate developer. Trump remarked, 'I'm lucky Manhattan wasn't his thing. If he had come to Manhattan, he would have been very successful, but to do my own thing I would then have had to go somewhere else' (Blair 2001). Although his accomplishments far outstripped his father's, the name Trump could easily have gone the way of other real-estate titans of the 1980s such as the Reichmann brothers and Robert Campeau.

Donald Trump joined the family real-estate business after graduating from Wharton in 1968. By his twenties he was already considered New York's paramount developer. Trump's name was whispered in the same breath as that of the legendary William Zechendorff. He erected his Trump Tower at the age of 36, considered the tallest, most expensive reinforced concrete structure in the city. The Trump name appeared garishly on virtually all his building projects.

Nevertheless, by 1990, he was caught in a real-estate crunch with a crushing $975 million debt (Rutenberg 1996). Banks that had once been eager to lend him money were now eager to get it back. He was forced to sell his signature yacht, his Boeing 727, his helicopter, and a twin-tower apartment block in

Florida. Several of his properties were put into 'pre-packaged bankruptcy', and he was forced to surrender control of the Trump Plaza. Even his salary and personal living expenses were dictated by the banks (Morrison 2001).

A dozen years later, his net worth was reportedly back to $3.5 billion, his casinos were booming, and he was wheeling and dealing in real-estate development just like before (CNN 1998). Both he and financial analysts consider the resurgence of his Atlantic City casinos, Trump Plaza, the Taj Mahal, and Trump's Castle, as the source of his comeback (Tomkins 1994). In addition to the disposal of personal assets, however, he made his much-derided ego and celebrity a bankable asset. His book *The Art of Comeback* in 1997 was a proud follow-up to his brazen book *The Art of the Deal* a decade earlier. With $7 billion in sales and 22,000 employees in 2001, his empire has continued to grow. He has acquired the GM Building and half of the Empire State Building, and at the time of writing was building the world's tallest residential building, the ninety-storey Trump World Tower.

Perhaps an even more impressive comeback is that of the 1980s iconic financier Michael Milken. Many have viewed Milken's life as the essence of American myth. He was literally born on the Fourth of July 1946 to a modest California family. By the mid-1980s he was already a billionaire and one of the most feared and influential investment bankers in the world. Milken bypassed Wall Street snobs by building the moderate-sized, stodgy Philadelphia origin Drexel Burnham Lambert into the capital of high yield (junk bond) debt through a high-flying Los Angeles operation. By 1987, the value of high yield debt rose from almost nothing to about $200 billion. It moved from the fringes of finance to become a mainstream vehicle helping such entrepreneurs as CNN's Ted Turner, MCI's Bill McGowan, and New Corp's Rupert Murdoch build their enterprises.

The US Justice Department's investigations, led by Rudoph Giuliani as Attorney, moved Milken to plead guilty to six breaches of securities law. He was fined over $1 billion and sent to prison for two years, his reputation shattered— a lifetime ban preventing his return to the securities business. Many of the financial institutions holding the junk bonds went into financial distress. To add to this tragic saga, soon after leaving prison, Milken was told he had prostate cancer and had eighteen months to live.

Nevertheless, Milken survived. His cancer went into remission and he wrote several cookbooks for fighting cancer through diet. In 1997 he founded a cradle-to-grave learning company with his brother and Oracle chief executive, Larry Ellison. He had a consulting firm called Nextera and funded an economic institute called the Milken Institute. By 1999 CaP CURE charity had raised over $63 million for research into prostate cancer (*The Economist* 1999).

Milken was unwilling to wallow in grief or to accept any of the externally imposed constraints on his desire to create and regain prominence. As he returned to demonstrate his business acumen, so old and new partners rushed to join him.

REDISCOVERING THE HEROIC MISSION: CLEARING THE PAST AND CHARTING THE FUTURE

The quest for immortality that drives artists and leaders requires that they see a lasting legacy through their work. Even more troubling than the externally imposed barriers that confront exceptional people after setbacks are the self-imposed barriers that are due to shattered confidence or a lack of replenishment of ideas and energy. In many of the cases discussed above, this meant leaders lowering their image from where they left off. Marcus and Milken had to start again from scratch. Silverman and Trump had to rebuild their own wrecked empires, while Roberts and Hanaka assumed challenging environments that required learning new skills.

Michael Bozic, at the time of writing the Vice Chairman of Kmart, found that a career crisis can be liberating. In 1990 he was thrown out of the chief executive's throne of the Sears Merchandizing Group after twenty-eight years at the company. Many believed he had not been given full credit for his innovative triumphs at Sears, such as his Brand Central merchandizing concept, and in fact he was assumed to have taken a bullet for his boss, the slow-moving Chairman, Edward Brennan.

Following many months of job hunting, Bozic became the CEO of Hills Stores, a bankrupt discount retailer in Canton, Massachusetts—quite a come-down from the world's largest retailer. After reviving Hills back from near death, Bozic lost control of the company in a wild proxy battle of competing value-investors (Rouvalis 1995). Thus, after a successful turnaround there, Bozic left for Florida to lead the turnaround at Levitz furniture. Bozic left for Levitz with his world weary wit intact, announcing, 'No good deed goes unpunished.' In November 1998, Bozic became Vice Chairman and CEO-contender at Kmart (Coleman 1998).

Michael Bloomberg, elected in 2001 as the Mayor of New York City, became an overnight legend in communications, rising from the ashes of a failed career as a financier. Soon after he had been fired from Salomon Brothers in 1981, Bloomberg advanced a radical idea for providing market information. Bloomberg machines can be found everywhere from the Federal Reserve to the Vatican and the company delivers business information in 100 countries. His TV stations alone broadcast twenty-four hours a day to forty countries in seven languages. In 2001 his radio networks, publishing empire, online businesses, and wire service had revenues estimated at $2.5 billion and 4,000 workers (Lowry 2001).

Born on Valentine's Day in Medford, Massachusetts, the son of an accountant, Bloomberg calls himself the David who challenged the Goliath of financial news. Before he was fired by Salomon Brothers, he had flourished for fifteen years within this firm—the only employer he had ever had. The night he was fired, he bought his wife a sable jacket, saying, 'job or no job we are still players' (Bloomberg 1997: 17). The next morning he settled down to work at his customary 7 a.m. to launch Bloomberg Inc. with his $10 million of severance. He gave away $300 million of his emergent net worth of $4 billion in just four years (Lowry 2001).

Finally, no reflections on resilience can be complete without acknowledging the fabled return of Apple founder Steve Jobs. At the age of 22, in 1977, Jobs created the PC boom at the first major trade show of personal computers. By 1980 Apple had gone public and Jobs was worth $220 million—still a year before IBM entered the PC market. In 1985, at age 32, two years after being forced out of the firm he had created at age 21, he founded Next with five devotees from Apple to build a powerful computer to be used in university instruction. His NeXTStep Cube product flopped but his NeXT Step OS survived (Carlton 1997).

Then, in 1996, he sold the company back to Apple for $425 million and persuaded the then Apple CEO, Gil Amelio, to bring him back as a 'consultant' as part of the deal and to make NeXTStep OS the core of its OS strategy (Stoller 2001). Jobs showed open disdain for Amelio around the office and derided many of his management team members (Pollack 1997). After Amelio had resigned in July 1997, Jobs agreed to become interim CEO. He cut many of the projects he had inherited and introduced triumphant new products like the iMac, G3 desktops, and PowerbookG4 laptops that helped increase the Apple market share by 10 percent. By spring 2001, Jobs was announcing that his new 'Mac OS X is the most important software from Apple since the original Macintosh operating system in 1984 that revolutionized the entire industry'.

Not every accomplished creative person can drop back and start anew. In his late twenties and thirties, Alan Jay Lerner wrote or co-wrote great Broadway classics like *Brigadoon, Paint your Wagon, Gigi, My Fair Lady*, and *Camelot*. By his fifties and sixties, he felt his creative genius was suffocated by his own creations. 'The older a writer gets, the harder it is for him to write. This is not because his brain slows down; it is because his critical faculties grow more acute. If you're young, you have a sense of omnipotence. You're sure you're brilliant. Even if youth is secretly frightened, it assumes an outer assurance, and plows through whatever it is' (Freeman 1986: 1). It was not his public that held him to punishing standards. The taskmaster was himself. By contrast, many we have profiled optimistically believe what Nietzche said: 'what does not destroy me, makes me stronger.' Through heavy life demands, these exceptional people are actually strengthened rather than weakened by the triumph over their adversity.

REFERENCES

Barrett, A. (2000), 'The Comeback of Henry Silverman', *Business Week*, 13 Mar., 128–50.

Blair, G. (2001), *The Trumps: Three Generations that Built an Empire* (New York: Simon & Schuster).

Bloomberg, M. (1997), *Bloomberg on Bloomberg* (New York: John Wiley).

Bloomberg News (2001), 'Cendenat Former Executives Forbes, Shelton Indicted', 28 Feb.

Braudy, L. (1986), *The Frenzy of Renown: A History of Fame* (New York: Oxford University Press).

Campbell, J. (1949/1990), *The Hero with a Thousand Faces* (Princeton: Princeton University Press).

Carlton, J. (1997), *Apple: The Inside Story of Intrigue, Egomania, and Business Blunders* (New York: Times Books).

CNN (1998), Cable News Network, *Lou Dobbs Moneyhour*, 8 June.

Colarusso, D. (2001), 'Wall St is Pondering Cendant's Fresh Start', *New York Times*, 22 Apr., B-9.

Coleman, C. (1998), 'Kmart Lures Bozic away from Levitz to be Vice Chairman, CEO Contender', *Wall Street Journal*, 18 Nov., B-10.

Cooper, C. L. (1983), *Stress Research: Issues for the Eighties* (New York: John Wiley).

——and Payne, R. (1988), *Causes, Coping, and Consequences of Stress at Work* (Chichester: John Wiley).

DeGross, R. (2001), 'Toy Story', *Atlanta Journal Constitution*, 25 Mar., Q-1.

Diba, A., and Munoz, L. (2001), 'America's Most Admired Companies', *Fortune*, 19 Feb., 64.

The Economist (1999), 'Michael Milken, Comeback King', 350/8112, 27 Mar., 34.

Elsbach, K. D., and Sutton, R. (1992), 'Aquiring Organizational Legitimacy through Illegitimate Actions', *Academy of Management Journal*, 35: 699–738.

Fitzgerald, F. S. (1941), *The Last Tycoon: An Unfinished Novel.* (New York: C. Scribner & Sons).

Flores, A. I. (1999), 'Sports Authority Takes Steps to Whip Itself into Shape', *Wall Street Journal*, 28 July, B-4.

Fombrun, C. J. (1996), *Reputation: Realizing Value from the Corporate Image* (Boston: Harvard Business School Press).

Freeman, S. G. (1986), 'Alan Jay Lerner, the Lyracist and Playright, is Dead at 67', *New York Times*, 15 June, 1, 36.

Freudenberger, H. J. (1974), 'Staff Burn-out', *Journal of Social Issues*, 30: 159–65.

——and Richelson (1980), *Burn-Out: The High Cost of High Achievement* (New York: Doubleday).

Gardner, H. (1998), *Extraordinary Minds* (New York: Basic Books).

Golembiewski, R. T. (1986), 'Contours In Social Change: Elemental Graphics and a Surrogate Variable for Gamma Change', *Academy of Management Review*, 11/3 (July), 550–66.

Grant, L. (2001), 'Radio Shack Uses Stategic Alliances to Spark Recovery', *USA Today*, 26 Mar., B-1.

Griffin, N., and Masters, K. (1996), *Hit and Run* (New York: Simon & Shuster).

Gutek, B., Nakamura, C., and Nieva, V. (1981), 'The Interdependence of Work and Family Roles', *Journal of Occupational Behavior*, 2, 1–16.

Hall, D. T., and Mirvis, P. H. (1996), 'The New Protean Career: Psychological Success and the Path with a Heart', in D. T. Hall and Associates, *The Career is Dead: Long Live the Career* (San Francisco: Jossey Bass), 15–45.

Hollander, E. P. (1964), *Leaders, Groups, and Influence* (New York: Oxford University Press), 117–127.

Holmes, T. H., and Rahe, R. N. (1967), 'The Social Adjustment Rating Scale', *Journal of Psychosomatic Research*, 11: 213–18.

Jones, E. E., and Nesbitt, R. E. (1971), 'The Actor and the Observer: Divergent Perceptions of Cause and Behavior', in E. E. Jones, D. E. Kanouse, H. H. Kelly, R. E. Nesbitt, S. Valines, and B. Weiner (eds.), *Attribution: Perceiving the Causes* (Morristown, NJ: General Learning Press).

Kobassa, S. (1979), 'Stressful Life Events, Personality, and Health: An Inquiry into Hardiness', *Journal of Personality and Social Psychology*, 37: 1–11.

Lee, M. D., and Kanungo, R. (1984) (eds.), *The Management of Work and Personal Life* (New York: Praeger).

Lowry, T. (2001), 'The Bloomberg Machine', *Business Week*, 23 Apr., 76–84.

McClintick, T. (1982), *Indecent Exposure: A True Story of Hollywood and Wall Street* (New York: Morrow).

Maddi, S. R., and Hightower, M. (1999). 'Hardiness and optimism as expressed in coping patterns', *Consulting Psychology Journal*, 51: 95–105.

Marcus, B., and Blank, A. (1999), *Built from Scratch* (New York: Times Books).

Matheny, K. B., and Cupp, P. (1983), 'Control, Desirability, and Anticipation as Moderating Variables between Life Change and Illness', *Journal of Human Stress*, 9: 14–23.

Palmeri, C. (1998), 'Radio Shack Redux', *Forbes*, 23 Mar., 54.

Pollack, A. (1997), 'Can Steve Jobs Do it Again?', *New York Times*, 8 Nov., c-1.

Rank, O., Atkinson, C. F., and Nin, A. (1989), *Art and Artist: Creative Urge and Personality Development* (New York: Norton).

Romeo, P. (1993), 'What Really Happened at Shoney's?', *Restaurant Business*, 1 May, 116–20.

Rosenbaum, J. E. (1979), 'Tournament Mobility: Career Patterns in a Corporation', *Administrative Sciences Quarterly*, 22: 220–41.

Rouvalis, C. (1995), 'A Wild Ride', *Pittsburgh Post Gazette*, 2 July, c-1, c-6.

Rutenberg, J. (1996), 'Towering Comeback for Trump', *New York Daily News*, 7 Apr., 10.

Schuler, R. (1984), 'Organizational and Occupational Stress and Coping: A Model and Overview', in M. D. Lee and R. Kanungo (eds.), *The Management of Work and Personal Life* (New York: Praeger), 169–72.

Scott, M. B., and Lyman, S. (1968), 'Accounts', *American Sociological Review*, 33: 46–60.

Sonnenfeld, J. A. (1988), *The Hero's Farewell: What Happens when CEOs Retire* (New York: Oxford University Press).

—— (1989), 'Career Systems and Strategic Staffing', in M. B. Arthur, D. T. Hall, and B. S. Lawrence (eds.), *Handbook of Career Theory* (Cambridge: Cambridge University Press), 202–27.

—— and Peiperl, M. A. (1988), 'Staffing Policy as a Strategic Response: A Typology of Career Systems', *Academy of Management Review*, 13/4: 588–600.

Staw, B. M., McKenchnie, P., and Puffer, S. (1983), 'The Justification of Organizational Performance', *Administrative Sciences Quarterly*, 28: 582–600.

158 JEFFREY A. SONNENFELD

Stoller, P. M. (2001), 'On a New Face for the Mac', *The New York Times*, 5 April, Section G, 5.

Tomkins, R. (1994), 'Casinos Deal Trump a Fistful of Aces', *Financial Times*, 31 June, 14.

Trump, D., and Bohner K. (1997), *The Art of the Comeback* (New York: Random House).

—— and Schwartz, T. (1987), *The Art of the Deal* (New York: Random House).

9

Career Creativity as Protean Identity Transformation

DOUGLAS T. HALL, GUORONG ZHU, AND AIMIN YAN

In contemporary organizations, the need for individuals to be creative, to be adaptive, and to be engaged in continuous learning is self-evident (Arthur and Rousseau 1996; Hall and Associates 1996). The problem is, how does a person who is changing so frequently and so deeply at the same time maintain his or her own 'path with a heart', the inner compass, so that the changes serve the person's values and needs as well as the demands of the environment? In other words, can the protean careerist be adaptive and maintain or develop his or her identity in the process? This issue will be the focus of the present chapter.

Inkson's chapter for this volume discusses the power of metaphor in career analysis and identifies some strengths and weaknesses of the image of the 'protean career' (Hall and Associates 1996). The strength of this metaphor is its 'unusual vividness, the empowerment that it provides to the heroic individual career actor, and the value in today's rapidly changing careers arena of being able quickly to improvise new ways of working'. (Inkson, Chapter 2, p. 15). Thus, the protean career certainly seems to Inkson to be essentially a creative career. However, in Inkson's view, the weakness with the protean notion is

the failure of the pure protean career to take account of career *history*. If the individual truly has the power to change to any form at any time, then such things as the accumulation of career skills and the nature of the job held prior to the change are irrelevant. This does not seem to be realistic. Every career is informed in some way by retrospective sense making (Weick 1996) or knowledge acquisition from that career's past (Bird 1996). No career can be more than partly protean. Proteus is, as it were, 'anchored'! (Inkson, Chapter 2, p. 15).

Work on this chapter was supported in part by the Executive Development Roundtable, School of Management, Boston University. The collaboration of Robert F. Morrison and the helpful comments of Michael Arthur and Mami Taniguchi on an earlier draft are gratefully acknowledged.

This is a good point. In the protean myth, the problem that Proteus caused for others was the fact that no one could pin him down to any one shape. And, as Inkson suggests, the risk for any modern protean careerist is that he or she might achieve great adaptability but lose his or her personal identity in the changes. This is a question that we will address in this chapter: how can a person become a creative, adaptive, self-managed protean careerist *and* maintain continuity of identity? (And by 'continuity' we mean a process by which the identity can change, but it changes in a way that maintains its connection with earlier stages of identity.) How can one change in a way that keeps one true to one's career history and basic values but still engenders a fundamental transformation of identity that is congruent with the new adaptive behavior unfolding over time and that is still integrated with one's earlier identity?

In this analysis of adaptability and identity, we will use the concrete example of a career experience that often triggers major personal transformation: the international assignment. We will use this example to show how potential career creativity is made possible by identity change. We will consider triggers to positive change and some outcomes that can result from creative career transformations associated with an international assignment. At the same time, we argue that natural forces in an organization can easily cause the loss of such creativity. These ideas have implications for employing organizations on how to capture the re-created or transformed human capital.

THE INHERENT CREATIVITY IN CAREERS: DEFINING CAREER CREATIVITY

Careers are by definition creative endeavors. Creativity in a work context has been defined in term's of a person's capacity for combining ideas in a unique way or for making unusual connections between ideas (Amabile 1988), and the ability to look beyond what one is doing now to new possibilities (Hare 1982; Hardaker and Ward 1987). Other researchers include the criterion of *effectiveness* (Delbecq and Mills 1991)—the new ideas should not just be novel, they should also work well. Thus, creativity implies something that is (1) *novel* in that person's career, (2) *self-invented* (that is, created by the person), and (3) an *effective* or successful response to the altered environment.

And let us consider the definition of 'career' in relation to this understanding of creativity: *the career is the individually perceived series of work-related experiences and attitudes that take place over the span of the person's life* (Hall 1976; 1996). (This is a definition of the career from the perspective of the individual. It is psychologically grounded and reflects the 'subjective' versus the 'objective' career.) Let us unpack that definition and see how it portends creativity.

First, the career is individually perceived. That is, the career is what the person construes it to be. We are reminded of the story of the baseball umpire's definition of what constitutes a ball or a strike: 'They ain't nothin' until I call 'em!' Increasingly, this self-constructed quality is coming to be seen as the good news in the new career contract: while there may not be clear career paths through organizations any more, this creates more openings and opportunity for the person to pursue the path with a heart, and to do so in his or her own unique way. As Karl Weick (1996) once pointed out, careers are 'eccentric predicates', and the enactment process is inherently individual and creative. Thus, the career is creative to the extent that it is self-invented—created by the individual.

Other elements of the definition of career are the words 'series' and 'work life'. What this means is that careers often unfold in erratic *episodes*, motivated by changes in the work environment. They tend to move in fits and starts. They take sudden left turns. These changes represent adaptive new directions for the person. They are not nearly as orderly as our traditional theories of career and adult development stages might suggest. In fact, contemporary careers might properly be viewed as a series of *learning cycles* over the person's life (Hall 1993, 1996; Hall and Mirvis 1996), as traditional boundaries to movement within and between organizations have become more permeable (Arthur and Rousseau 1996). This contemporary boundaryless career demands that the person become facile in multiple ways of knowing (*knowing-why, knowing-how, knowing-whom*, and so on (Arthur *et al.* 1995). Thus, instead of the career's being one long cycle containing stages such as exploration, trial, establishment, and so on, as the first author described careers in an earlier era (Hall 1976), the career today is made up of many short cycles or episodes lasting perhaps two, three, or four years, during which the person learns about and masters a new (to him or her) area of work.

Each episode in a career learning cycle might have an exploratory phase, a trial or testing period, a period of getting established, and a final stage of mastering the work. Then, whether for external reasons, such as new technology, market changes, and so on, or for internal reasons, such as personal or family needs and values, the person might 'get itchy' and start to explore some other terrain. Each cycle represents an attempted adaptation to changes in the work environment. For example, when electronic commerce was new and booming, a lot of people surged into the new business platform. Then in the wake of the dot-com tailspins around 2000 and 2001, IT professionals were jumping back to traditional companies. Thus, the career in the contemporary environment represents continual novelty to the person. This model of the career as creative learning episodes is shown in Fig. 9.1.

Another important quality of this definition of career is what it does *not* contain: any mention of an organization. Perhaps the most important aspect of the new career contract is that it is not with the organization; it is with the self and one's work. The path to the top has been replaced by the path with the

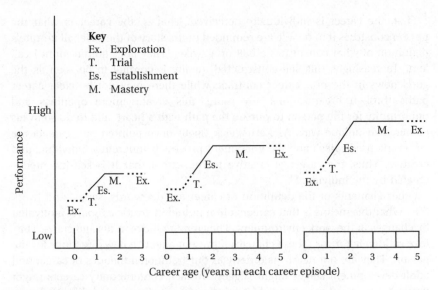

Fig. 9.1. The career as creative learning episodes.

Source: Adapted from Hall (1993: 15).

heart, as described by Herbert Shepard (1984/1995). This is another way in which the person creates the career.

Shepard used this term to describe success in terms of one's own unique vision and central values in life—in short, what we have called psychological success. Shepard (1984/1995: 172) also pointed out that the path with a heart encompassed one's own most-loved talents: 'These are the things that you can now or potentially could do with excellence, which are fulfilling in the doing of them; so fulfilling that if you also get paid to do them, it feels not like compensation, but like a gift.'

In this same paper, Shepard (1984/1995: 176) also discusses the skill of *developing multiple perspectives* as an important part of creatively discovering what he called one's 'genius':

[An] important quality of a worthwhile life is the perspective necessary to guide choices and to inform experience. If you have only one way of looking at the situation you are in, you have no freedom of choice about what to do. And if you have only one framework for understanding your experience, all your experience will reinforce that framework....If your perspective is differentiated—if you can see, for example, the potential of a new relationship to be either collaborative or adversarial—you enlarge your range of choices. Thus, if you are aware of 'the multiple potential of the moment', you will usually be able to make a choice that will make the next moment better for you and for the others in the situation.

To summarize, then, creativity as applied to the career is the ability of the person, on a dynamic and continuing basis, to engage in, and benefit from, lifetime learning; to conduct critical self-assessment and reflection of his or her strengths and capabilities in performing the current jobs; effectively to adjust his or her planned career path in response to changes in the internal and external environment, and to look beyond the current job experience and career goals to new opportunities both within and outside the current organization. Thus, there are several components in career creativity:

- lifelong learning and change;
- self-reflection and self-invention;
- effective revision of career goals and openness to new opportunities.

Examples of such creativity in a career can be found in every type of work. In the current volume Parker's rich description of the experiences of leased executives (Chapter 7) and Ensher, Murphy, and Sullivan's analysis of women in the entertainment industry (Chapter 12) provide nice illustrations of the constant personal exploration and learning in these career fields. And these particular fields give us a glimpse into the environment of many other career fields in the future.

UNDERSTANDING ADAPTABILITY AND ADAPTATION

Part of the creative complexity inherent in careers is that it deals with the continuous adaptations that take place as the changing person interacts with a changing environment. Each aforementioned 'episode' in a person's work history can be micro-analyzed as an adaptation process. And adaptation has many layers and components, as Morrison and Hall (2001) have shown. Their model of adaptation is shown in Fig. 9.2. Let us describe how this process operates.

Adaptability

First, there is an important distinction between *adaptability* and *adaptation*. Adaptability is the person's *capacity* to change. Adaptation is the actual *process of changing*. The person's capacity to change has two components. First, the person must have a motivation to change (adaptive motivation). This includes such things as psychological preparedness and readiness to change. In Lewin's force-field model, we would call this being unfrozen to change (Lewin 1958).

Motivation, however, is not sufficient. Secondly, there is a competence dimension. Some people, perhaps through prior experience or perhaps through inborn abilities, are more capable of changing than others (Morrison and Hall 2001). We call this dimension adaptive competence.

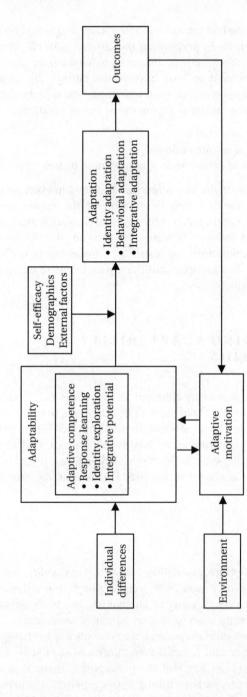

Fig. 9.2 A model of individual adaptation.

Source: Morrison and Hall (2001).

Response learning. The skills component of adaptability is also multilayered. Perhaps the most familiar aspect of this capacity is the person's ability to change his or her behavior in response to new demands from the environment. Morrison and Hall (2001: 17) call this quality response learning: 'Response Learning is the conscious predisposition to continuously scan and read external signals and to develop or update a diverse set of role behaviors so that they maintain an effective response to constantly changing environmental requirements and influence the environment.'

Identity exploration. Important as this behavioral flexibility is, it alone is not sufficient for a healthy adaptability. When fundamental changes in role behavior occur, they also create systemic influences on the person's sense of identity. Thus, to be truly effective with deep adaptability, the person must also be capable of 'identity exploration', which entails being able to learn about him or herself (for example, through feedback seeking, through truly listening to personal feedback, through reflective observation, and through learning from experience.) In other words, when a person changes, it is not just his or her behavior that changes, but his or her sense of self, as well. Morrison and Hall (2001: 9) define this quality as follows: 'Identity Exploration is the continual striving for a more complete and accurate fund of knowledge about the self to develop the potential to modify or maintain one's identity.'

Integrative potential. There is a third quality that is key to adaptive competence, as well. Not only does the person have to be capable of changing behavior and changing personal identity, but these must be done in such a way that the two are congruent or integrated. The changes must not only be responsive to the realities of the environment, but they should be true to him or herself, as well. Thus, we have a third element of adaptive competence, integrative potential: 'Integrative potential is the ability to continuously maintain congruence between one's personal identity and those behaviors that are timely and appropriate responses to the ever-changing demands of the environment' (Morrison and Hall 2001: 10).

In sum, then, we have the following 'formula' for adaptive competence:

adaptive competence = identity exploration + response learning + integrative potential.

We cannot emphasize strongly enough the importance of identity exploration as an element of a person's adaptive competence. To many people, adaptability is a matter of quick behavioral responses. Capacity for identity change related to these behavioral changes is not generally associated with adaptive capability. However, complete adaptive change has both a cognitive and a behavioral component, and if the person cannot change his or her thinking, especially the way he or she views the self (identity), the change is more of a matter of compliance than of internalization. Thus, for a behavioral response to be long lasting, it should be supported by a revised image of the self.

Adaptation

Adaptability alone, however, is not enough to generate creative career experiences and outcomes. While some people may be very adaptable and very creative, they may not in fact follow through and convert that adaptive capacity into actual adaptation or transformation.

To realize the potential creativity of the protean career, the individual must develop the adaptive competencies related to the management of self and career. The new career has become a continuous learning process. In particular, the person must learn how to develop self-knowledge (self-awareness) and adaptability. These have been called 'meta-competencies', since they are the skills required for learning how to learn (Hall 1986, 1996).

TRIGGERS OF CAREER CREATIVITY AND TRANSFORMATION

Under the appropriate conditions, a person with high adaptability will perform the appropriate behaviors and achieve adaptation. The question is, what triggers adaptation? One powerful kind of experience that can have this transformational potential is an *international assignment*. Let us look at the international assignment scenario to understand the adaptability and adaptation process.

Growth-triggering potential of the international assignment

International assignments as a means of leadership development are generally more challenging than domestic executive development. An international assignment exposes managers to novel situations and great uncertainty. What had worked previously for the manager in the domestic context does not necessarily work in this new international environment, forcing the person to adapt (Black and Gregersen 1999).

Often the international assignment involves a start-up or a turnaround process, which can provide wonderful stretching experiences (McCall *et al.* 1988) for development. Also, being suddenly immersed in a foreign context, where getting through the mundane activities of everyday life (having a telephone installed, hiring a new employee, getting directions while driving) is likely to be a struggle, is a powerful personal and professional role transition, requiring communication across language and culture boundaries. There are constant surprises, where the person is rudely brought up short and told that his or usual programs for behavior no longer apply. These daily challenges and upending experiences provide compelling personal feedback and force a person to examine situations and his or her own identity in a new way. Indeed, Osland (1995) uses the metaphor of the hero's journey (Campbell 1972) to describe the call to adventure, making the transition into an unknown, threatening world, overcoming incredible challenges, experiencing victory and thus personal transformation and spiritual rebirth.

And the person does not always deal with these tasks successfully. There are many setbacks and failures. And learning how to deal with these experiences is also another building block for development (McCall *et al.* 1988). This sort of surprise and sense making is part of the transition into any new role (Louis 1980), but the situations are orders of stronger magnitude when the boundaries crossed are international. And the more powerful the role transition, the more profound the identity changes will be.

As Inkson, Arthur, Pringle, and Barry (1997) point out, organizations are often blind to the personal and career transformations that occur in expatriate assignments, primarily because the assignment is usually framed in terms of the company's objectives (as part of a centralized human-resource (HR) activity). The causes of success or failure are generally attributed to the company, and the assignment is seen as a short-term staffing activity, separate from the longer-term career development process of the individual. In this chapter we hope to bring the career perspective that Inkson *et al.* call for to bear on the expatriation and repatriation process.

Expatriation strategies and their impact on career creativity

Creativity can be stimulated by flexibility on both sides of an international assignment—that is, in both the organizational and the individual plans of career development. In terms of the Mintzberg (1987) model of four aspects of strategy (intended versus emergent, unrealized versus realized), career development can be facilitated by incorporating each of these components. *Intended strategy* is the formal, required assignment in terms of job descriptions, tasks, and responsibilities to be performed by the employee while abroad, closely connected to the organizational purposes for the overseas assignment and the specific individual's career development within and outside of the organization. Despite the best intentions, *emergent strategy* happens. Given the uncertainty down the road, considering both the job's necessary adaptation to the local environment and possible organization changes, flexibility should be built in the expatriation and repatriation plan. No perfect expatriate assignment contract is possible and individuals should allow room to adjust its expectations facing the unexpected contingencies.

In response to what emerges, some plans have to be discarded. This is the *unrealized strategy*, the other side of the same 'flexibility' coin. Organizations should be willing to adjust performance assessment criteria and development plans for the individual. And the employee should not be held responsible for both the original and the adjusted performance expectations. On the other hand, development of the individual should take into account the new skills and competencies gained while adapting to environmental and organizational changes. Without discarding the obsolete objectives/expectations, the employee would be put in a position of fighting against ever escalating or conflicting expectations, a mission impossible. *Realized strategy* is '*consistency* in behavior, *whether or not* intended' (Mintzberg 1987: 12; emphasis in original). As this applies to the international assignment, the individuals should develop a career growth path that is flexible and adaptive. More so today than in the past, a clearly articulated career development plan is becoming increasingly difficult. This is consistent with the notion of a protean career, which is very much a self-invented, self-perceived process.

Let us consider an example. When one of the authors asked his eighth-grade daughter several years ago what career goals she would likely pursue, she replied clearly 'a medical doctor or a lawyer'. When he asked her the same question several days ago, she found it to be much more difficult to answer. She would not rule out an MBA and a business career now. (You can see a management professor father's influence!) This is interesting—our conventional theories would predict that one's goals become realistic and more clearly defined as time goes by and the person grows mature. But that is not the case. As one might ask in the case of grounded theory building, 'How can you build a theory when the ground is shaking?'

ADAPTATION AND CREATIVE CAREERS: THE THREAT TO IDENTITY

What, then, does this model of adaptability and adaptation have to do with creative careers? One implication is that adaptability alone is not enough to generate creative career experiences and outcomes. First, as aforementioned, there must be something to trigger an adaptive person into adaptation. It is the novelty in experiences and the deviation from strategic planning that provide the stimulating environment for adaptation. And there may be external factors, such as a role transition or an organizational change (for example, restructuring), that create trigger events for change. Secondly, while some people may be very adaptable and very creative, they may not in fact follow through on the triggers and convert that adaptive capacity into actual adaptation or transformation. It takes a level of *self-efficacy* or self-confidence to enable the person to take the risk of making a creative change. And there may also be some demographic enabling factors, such as access to resources like social networks (Higgins, Chapter 14), that motivate or support some people to engage in creative adaptations but not others who lack such resources.

But perhaps the most important implication of the adaptation model is that *career creativity and adaptation are not the same processes*. The adaptation model proposed by Morrison and Hall subsumes creativity (novelty, self-invention, and effectiveness), but it adds the important requirement that an adaptive response must be consistent with the person's identity. In other words, *creative career transformations must be integrated with identity*. That is, for an adaptation to be deep and complete, it has to reflect change at three levels. First, the behavior must change to fit with the demands of the new environment. And, secondly, the change cannot be just at the behavioral level. There must also be a concomitant change in the person's identity or sense of self; the person must personally value the new behavior and must incorporate the new behaviors into the self-image. And, finally, the behavior changes and the identity changes must be congruent and integrated with each other. If the behavior change and the identity change are somehow at odds with each other, this could leave the person feeling conflicted and inauthentic.

An example of a non-integrated change would be a person who led a turn-around in a troubled overseas business in an ethically questionable way. The person may have made changes that were very effective. These changes may have included laying people off and bribing local officials to let the company cut corners in meeting local regulations. And the person's skills may have changed to include being a shrewd, decisive, insensitive, and expedient leader, and these changes in the person could have been very creative (novel, self-invented, and effective.) But these personal qualities may be ones that the person does not value, and thus the new behaviors would not be integrated with the person's deeper sense of identity and personal value, the type of person he or she aspired to be. Thus, the person could be left feeling conflicted and inauthentic in the transformed state.

It is too easy for a person to become successful in an organizational sense and even in a psychological sense (that is, in terms of job satisfaction) and still lose sight of living out his or her most deeply held values and sense of personal identity. For example, Hall (1993) described the experience of Karen Camp, an account manager with responsibilities that spanned eight states. She was on a business trip just after her son Webb's first birthday. She called home—and learned from the sitter that Webb had just taken his first steps. Her reaction: 'I realized that his first year had gone by so quickly, I had been like a visitor in his life' (Hall 1993: 201).

One of the reasons a person loses sight of the path with a heart is that he or she may have pursued career creativity (that is, novel, self-invented, and successful career changes) without realizing that his or her most important value or needs might have changed. Early career and life choices may not necessarily be the best fit for a person in mid-career. As one shocked 42-year-old manager exclaimed in the middle of a self-reflective career planning exercise, 'Oh, no! I just realized I let a 20-year-old choose my wife and my career!' (Hall 1993).

The positive view of this is that we need to be attentive to the need for creative career transformations to include all three components of the adaptation process. The behavior must change appropriately, the identity must change, and those two changes must happen in a way that is congruent with the person's highest values. However, in most adaptation situations the main concern is usually with behavior. If the person meets the new role requirements, many organizational observers would think that the transformation was complete. We do not tend to focus on deeper changes in personal identity, and we are even less likely to inquire as to whether these identity changes are consistent with the new behaviors and are in tune with the person's core values. In short, we look for compliance, not with internalization of change.

EFFECTS OF CREATIVE CAREERS

Unleashing the genie from the bottle

What are the effects of this creativity and adaptability in a person's career? One very specific result of a creative career episode is that the person is now more likely to have another one at some point in the future! There is a learning process here, whereby the experience, self-image, and psychological success associated with being creative increase the person's motivation and competence to do it again (Hall 1986). In short, career creativity breeds further creativity. And then, for a repatriate returning home, if that creativity is not being appreciated and utilized, it is an ego-deflating experience. To illustrate, here is a report of a recent repatriate, describing the different way he was viewed abroad and the different sense of accomplishment that he had:

Yeah, expats returning is a, I don't know, it's a 70%–80% attrition rate.... You know, when you're out with the customer or out in the field, you do have more feeling of getting things done. You know? I'm trying to think of the proper term here, of *accomplishment*. You have more responsibility and people listen more to you than now. You're buried back here, and you know, it's a different story.

This shows that the very rewarding overseas experience of accomplishment and career creativity could be a 'genie-out-of-the-bottle' phenomenon when the person comes back home. Once the person has had the experience of being the agent of his or her own course through life and work, it is very liberating. He or she cannot go back to the previous, more constrained state. In the organization's view, the person may appear to be 'harder to manage'—perhaps turning down 'plum' assignments, or perhaps pursuing interesting tasks and challenges that are not the company's highest strategic priorities. In reality, however, what this means is that the alignment challenge for the organization just became more salient: it is now necessary to work collaboratively with the employee to find future assignments and a future path that provides *mutual* value, to both parties.

An example of this situation would be a person who took an expatriate assignment and found herself totally on her own to create a new business in her region. Initially, this might have felt like a total upending experience, with no organizational support, no guidance, and countless local obstacles. However, through persistence, exploration, learning, networking, and follow-through, she created a business out of nothing. And in the process she discovered inner resources and strengths that she did not realize she had. Out of this 'testing' experience, she emerged with a new identity as an insightful, strong, creative, and well-connected leader. Thus, she returns as the 'transformed hero' (Osland 1995).

One organizational effect of this adaptation and identity change would be that, as a transformed hero, she may no longer be content to return to the kind of position back home that the company had planned for her. Often the next assignment after repatriation is a staff role in the corporate headquarters, one that falls far short of her new, expanded capabilities. After becoming turned on to the excitement of starting up and successfully running her own business in this challenging international field environment, the 'genie' (read: hero) of the creative, entrepreneurial self is out of the bottle and cannot be put back in the form of a corporate staff position. When the person grows, the organization must respond with a next assignment that fits the new identity—or suffer the consequences.

As Inkson *et al.* (1997: 354–5) explain, the expatriate experience can be a creative (but generally invisible) development process for the person and for the organization:

career theory sees career development as an outcome of complex forces, including individual self-direction as well as organizational career frameworks (Arthur, Hall, & Lawrence 1989). There is much evidence that people 'sculpt' their own careers rather than allowing themselves to become corporate sculptures (Bell & Staw 1989). Individual career patterns create organizational patterns and inadvertently build company expertise and shape company structures (Weick 1996). The proactive role of the expatriate/repatriate in controlling her or his own life and in building company and cross-company expertise goes largely unacknowledged in the EA [expatriate assignment] literature.

Thus, a well-managed repatriation process can capture the creative lessons and personal transformations of the international assignment and make them part of a good corporate knowledge management process. Through this kind of experience, the unleashed genie can work his magic to the great benefit of the firm. This is when we *want* the genie to be out of the bottle, to spread the person's transformation throughout the organization.

Effects on others

Experiences like this are not lost on colleagues in the organization. What is troubling about this kind of experience is that it is very public and it sends a signal to others who are considering taking an international assignment. As Jones reports (Chapter 11), what others observe in a person's career experiences can communicate powerful *signals*—messages about what contributes to identity (*knowing-why*), performance (*knowing-how*), and networks and relationships (*knowing-whom*). And precisely because a key international assignment is in fact a *key* assignment, by definition it contains great visibility and potential for high impact on the organization. Unfortunately, the content of the signals emanating from the experiences of the repatriated employee often represents negative lessons to others. And, since career networks are becoming more potent in influencing an individual's career decisions (Higgins and Kram 2002), this just magnifies the impact of these signals.

Of course, when the story has a happy ending, the signals emanating therefrom can have correspondingly positive effects on the career motivations and plans of others in the career network. Unfortunately, an outcome like this is a rare organizational event. But this is precisely a type of creative career event that deserves future research.

Effects on the organization

And how can these creative career transformations affect the organization? We would argue that, given the systems properties of organizations toward homeostasis, the answer is usually 'not much'. Organizations, even creative ones, like stability and predictability. As Ensher, Murphy, and Sullivan found (Chapter 12), successful women executives in the entertainment industry had to marshal impressive personal resources (connections, networks, self-management skills) in order to impact their environments successfully. But, the good news here is that, if one uses these resources, it is possible to exert creative influence on an organization.

One way that the creative career experience can affect the organization is through an *organizational adaptation and knowledge management* process. The lessons from the expatriate's overseas experience can be utilized by the organization to create successful changes upon the person's return. Here is an example from our research of such a happy ending. The respondent, a recent repatriate, is describing a job that was created to support international field operations, based on the learnings that arose from his expatriate work:

It is the job that I've been wanting to do for a long time. The detail of that is, there has never been...someone coordinating the field technical issues here in Headquarters.

[This is a new role in this organization.] So there's never been someone here representing the interests of the people that today work for me. So I'm real glad to have this job, I think. From here, I can do a lot of good for those employees, and I can do a lot of good for the company by helping those employees do their job more effectively.

And, of course, the adaptive transfer of learning can occur in a more informal, individual way, as other people simply take advantage of what the repatriate has learned and brought back from overseas:

I'm glad that I did it. I think it will be useful to the company and I think that I contribute much more here because I can tell people what they need to do to service international markets, not just the US market, which was a limitation that I had before I could guess about international markets. I probably thought about them more than most other people did, even though I was a US employee. But now that I've been there, people come to me for advice and I'm able to render it more effectively.

And there can be more macro-effects of creative careers. Higgins (Chapter 14) found that the careers of individuals can affect organizations and industries. In particular, she found that the financial success of biotech start-up firms was positively related to the career histories and social capital of their founders. In fact, she found that the CEOs of twenty-one of the fifty biotech companies in her data set came from one health-care organization: Baxter Travenol. She attributes the creative effects of Baxter to three sources: (1) Baxter's entrepreneurial culture, (2) Baxter's organizational design (flat, decentralized, providing lots of autonomy and challenge), and (3) Baxter's social network (concentrated in Deerfield, Illinois, an atmosphere of camaraderie and intense interpersonal contact).

Thus, many of the positive effects of the Baxter culture led to strong career development (especially the meta-competency of adaptability) for its managers. And the strong, creative perspectives that they developed led, in turn, to the creation of a host of new entrepreneurial ventures. This is a powerful kind of organizational effect.

However, getting back to our original, rather pessimistic observation about organizational effects, these positive effects of the Baxter alums took place through the creation of new ventures, not through the changing of large, established organizations. It is easier for an individual to affect an organization at an early, entrepreneurial stage than at a later, larger, more mature stage.

Deep organizational ambivalence over creative individual change

Why is it harder for a creative careerist to influence a larger, more mature organization? *Simply put: organizations cannot handle fundamental personal change*. To explain, we see a dilemma here around the issue of career creativity.

On the one hand, the organization in principle values employee development, and it would generally prefer to have employees who are more developed rather than less developed. Yet, on the other hand, when the person develops creatively and adaptively, he or she becomes more independent, more pro-active in pursuing his or her own values, and more self-confident in turning down organizational overtures aimed at enticing him or her to do something that may not be of great personal interest. This is reminiscent of Chris Argyris' early work (1957) showing the inherent conflict between the goals of the organization and the needs of a psychologically healthy person. For its goal achievement purposes, the organization needs control, predictability, a focus on tasks and rationality rather than personal feelings, and a short-term, immediate-results time orientation. But a healthy person needs autonomy, a range of choices that may not always be predictable, a balance of feelings and rationality, and a longer-term time perspective. As the person develops, he or she becomes more of a free agent, and organizations have trouble dealing with free agents.

Inkson, Arthur, Pringle, and Barry (1997) help us understand this phenom-enon with their distinction between the expatriate assignment (EA) and the overseas experience (OE). In Australia and New Zealand, where the overseas experience is part of the culture, 'every year thousands of young people head overseas for a prolonged period of travel, work, and tourism' (Inkson *et al.* 1997: 358.) The OE is *not* a career development experience, and it is driven not by an organization but by the individual. Cultural experience is just as important as work, and the individual's curiosity and personal learning agenda are the primary motivating factors. Inkson *et al.* (1997) report several stories in which interviewees describe their OEs and what they learned from them. The fol-lowing themes emerged from the OE experiences in their sample:

- personally designed experimentation;
- personally designed apprenticeships;
- unlearning past experiences;
- discovering career identity;
- developing self-reliance;
- developing a clearer career focus;
- increasing self-employment (Inkson *et al.* 1997: 364).

As these themes suggest, the themes in the learnings from the OE experience represent the same kind of personal transformation that we have been describing as resulting from the expatriate assignment (EA). *But in our view this personal transformation generated by the EA is invisible to the company.* As Osland (1995) shows, learnings such as developing a new occupational or industry identity, greater confidence and self-reliance, a clearer career focus and identity, and increased concern for independence (if not self-employment) are some of the personal transformations that result from the 'hero's adventure' at the 'global frontier'. Inkson *et al.* (1997) report that, in contrast, the EA has a company focus, the goals relate to specific company projects, and the relevant career is the (organization's) company career, not the (person's) boundaryless or protean career. Thus, since these qualities of the EA are what the company 'sees' when it looks at the repatriate, since this EA focus is so strong and so figural, it is literally blind to the more person-centered OE-type outcomes from an EA.

Sadly, there is much untapped individual potential here. The effects of the individual's enhanced creativity and adaptability from the EA could be extremely positive if the organization were able to put the repatriate into a domestic assignment that would utilize this overseas development. This greater sense of self confidence, greater clarity of personal values, combined with proactivity and effectiveness, would mean that the repatriate would have a higher sense of what Shepard (1984/1995: 183) called 'resonance':

The term resonance...conveys the notion of being 'in tune' with other people and environments; it suggests the synergy and expansion of tone when your energy has joined with the energy of others. It also implies harmony. Harmony is a beautiful arrangement of different sounds, in contrast to mere noise, which is an ugly arrangement. Resonance, as used here, implies people's capacity to use their differences in ways that are beautiful rather than ugly.

Although managing such a 'high-resonance' person is a more difficult task for the organization than giving assignments to less self-aware, more agreeable employees, the reward is also much greater. When an assignment is mutually desirable, the resulting commitment and motivation from the employee are much higher, as the above quote suggests. And, presumably, innovative performance and retention would be correspondingly higher, as well.

This Shepard quote also gives us a hint of the effects of career creativity on others. It has become clear in recent years that one of the great sources of development at work is *relational* influence. We and our colleagues all live in one another's gravitational fields. If my colleague comes into work with a very positive tone, a balanced perspective, and a strong sense of resonance, her tone would affect my mood, and her resonance and perspective would represent a powerful model to me. I could not help but be affected by her contagious enthusiasm. On the other hand, if she came in feeling depressed and in conflict with (out of resonance with) her role, I would probably experience her as a 'downer'. As Bandura's work (1997) has shown, people can affect their colleagues' self-efficacy perceptions through social influences such as modeling, persuasion, and the creation of attitude-shaping experiences.

We would argue, then, that the creative and adaptive careerist would influence others toward greater career creativity through personal modeling, through occasional persuasion (for example, in a coaching or mentoring situation), and (for managers, say) by creating challenging and varied assignment experiences that would lead that person to greater career creativity.

Getting the creative change 'entered' in organizational systems

Another one of the dilemmas in this creative career process involves another aspect of the organization's fundamental ambivalence toward the person's development. Not only is the organization (here defined operationally as the organizational significant others, role senders in the person's career) uneasy about seeing the person adopt a new identity, but it is even more difficult formally to 'enter' this new identity into the formal organizational career management systems. By systems, we mean both the formal systems (succession planning, job assignment, performance review, and compensation), as well as the informal system (for example, the person's reputation in the eyes of senior management). Homeostasis, always a formidable force in organizational life, intensifies only when it comes to an employee's decision to shift paths and to become a new person in some way. The forces arrayed to keep her or him the 'same' person are massive and multiple. The primary reason for this is the fact that there have to be two sides to a role relationship. Thus, if one side changes, and if the change is 'seen', the other side must change accordingly. But, if the other side does not 'see' the first person's change, there is no need for the other side to change.

The changes that would be involved for the other party can range greatly. It may be as simple as the need to acknowledge the first person's change and to discuss it in some way. But this may also lead to an implied change in behavior by the second person—perhaps more flexibility, if the second person is the boss and the employee feels more empowered and wants more balance in life, or perhaps more active intervention to assist in getting the returnee a more challenging job assignment. Another possible change might be that, through modeling, the first person might induce in the second some previously suppressed urges for more career creativity of his or her own. These stirrings of greater autonomy and career self-direction may cause stress and may not be totally welcome. The result of these and perhaps other mixed reactions may cause the second person simply to avoid the returnee and any sustained conversation about his or her personal transformation.

CONCLUSION

While the creative elements of the boundaryless, protean career are becoming more visible in contemporary work life, they are not being universally welcomed. When the person's career changes in creative ways, the change is not only about skills and behavior. *To be truly adaptive, the creative career change should also include a new identity.* An identity is a social product—it is the way the person sees him or herself and is seen by others in the context of a given social role. Thus, there are two parties to the identity: self and others. If the self changes, then the others must change in some way as well. When the person experiences a creative career adaptation, this change necessarily makes demands on the organization for change as well. And organizations, being the homeostatic systems that they are, resist change, especially from the inside. (It is hard enough for organizations to respond to demands for change from the external environment, where most change originates. Internal pressures for change have less power and are easier to ignore or resist.)

However, there are many natural triggers to creative individual adaptations inside the organization, such as the transformational demands of international assignments. Such an experience provides a virtual natural 'laboratory' for studying personal identity transformation. By analyzing the personal experiences associated with expatriation and repatriation, we can see how protean adaptations can occur. We can also see what happens when the concomitant changes in personal identity either happen or do not happen. We conclude that, when identity changes occur that are integrated with the adaptive behavior, this represents the deepest and most positive form of adaptation.

The final step in an effective adaptation process is when the organizational environment also adapts in a way that accommodates this new identity of the individual. In the repatriation context, this means acknowledging and 'entering' the person's new identity in the formal and informal assignment, reward, and development systems of the enterprise. While we argue that this rarely happens, the fact is that these rare events sometimes do occur. We need more careful study of these responsive organizational accommodations to identity change, to let us tap more of the potential of creative protean careers.

REFERENCES

Amabile, T. M. (1988), 'A Model of Creativity and Innovation in Organizations', in B. M. Staw and L. L. Cummings (eds.), *Research in Organizational Behavior*, 10 (Greenwich, Conn.: JAI Press).

Arthur, M. B., and Rousseau, D. M. (1996) (eds.), *The Boundaryless Career: A New Employment Principle for a New Organizational Era* (New York: Oxford University Press).

—— Hall, D. T., and Lawrence, B. S. (1989) (eds.), *Handbook of Career Theory* (New York: Cambridge University Press).

—— Claman, P. H., and DeFillippi, R. J. (1995), 'Intelligent Enterprise, Intelligent Careers', *Academy of Management Executive*, 9/1: 7–20.

Argyris, C. (1957), *Personality and Organization* (New York: Harper & Row).

Bandura, A. (1997), *Self-Efficacy: The Exercise of Control* (New York: W. H. Freeman).

Bell, N. E., and Staw, B. M. (1989), 'People as Sculptors versus Sculpture: The Roles of Personality and Personal Control in Organizations', in M. B. Arthur, D. T. Hall, and B. S. Lawrence (eds.), *Handbook of Career Theory* (New York: Cambridge University Press), 232–51.

Bird, A. (1996), 'Careers as Repositories of Knowledge: Considerations for Boundaryless Careers', in M. B. Arthur and D. M. Rousseau (eds.), *The Boundaryless Career: A New Employment Principle for a New Organizational Era* (New York: Oxford University Press), 150–68.

Black, J. S., and Gregersen, H. B. (1999), 'The Right Way to Manage Expats', *Harvard Business Review*, 77/2: 52–63.

Campbell, J. (1972), *The Hero with a Thousand Faces*, reprint edn. (Princeton: Princeton University Press).

Delbecq, A., and Mills, P. (1991), 'Managerial Practices that Enhance Innovation', *Organizational Dynamics*, 24–34.

Hall, D. T. (1976), *Careers in Organizations* (Glenview, Ill.: Scott, Foresman).

—— (1986), 'Breaking Career Routines: Midcareer Choice and Identity Development', in D. T. Hall and Associates, *Career Development in Organizations* (San Francisco: Jossey-Bass), 120–59.

—— (1993), 'The New "Career Contract": Wrong on Both Counts', technical report, Executive Development Roundtable, School of Management, Boston University.

—— (1996), 'Protean Careers of the 21st Century', *Academy of Management Executive*, 10: 8–16.

—— and Mirvis, P. H. (1996), 'The New Protean Career: Psychological Success and the Path with a Heart', in D. T. Hall and Associates, *The Career is Dead: Long Live the Career* (San Francisco: Jossey-Bass), 15–45.

—— and Associates (1996), *The Career is Dead: Long Live the Career: A Relational Approach* (San Francisco: Jossey-Bass).

Hardaker, M., and Ward, B. K. (1987), 'Getting Things Done: How to Make Teams Work', *Harvard Business Review* (Nov.–Dec.), 112–20.

Hare, A. P. (1982), *Creativity in Small Groups* (Berkeley, Calif.: Sage).

Higgins, M. C., and Kram, K. E. (2002), 'Reconceptualizing Mentoring at Work: A Developmental Network Perspective', *Academy of Management Review*, 26/2: 264–88.

Inkson, K., Arthur, M. B., Pringle, J., and Barry, S. (1997), 'Expatriate Assignment versus Overseas Experience: Contrasting Models of International Human Resource Development', *Journal of World Business*, 32/4: 351–68.

Kegan, R. (1994), *In Over our Heads: The Mental Demands of Modern Life* (Cambridge, Mass.: Harvard University Press).

—— and Lahey, L. (2000), *How the Way we Talk Can Change the Way we Work: Seven Languages for Transformation* (San Francisco: Jossey-Bass).

Lewin, K. (1958), 'Group Decision and Social Change', in E. E. Maccoby, T. M. Newcomb, and E. L. Hartley (eds.), *Readings in Social Psychology*, 3rd edn. (New York: Holt, Rinehart & Winston), 197–211.

Louis, M. R. (1980), 'Surprise and Sense Making: What Newcomers Experience in Entering Unfamiliar Organizational Settings', *Administrative Science Quarterly*, 25: 226–51.

McCall, M. W., Jr., Lombardo, M. M., and Morrison, A. M. (1988), *The Lessons of Experience: How Successful Executives Develop on the Job* (New York: Lexington Books).

Mintzberg, H. (1987), 'Crafting Strategy', *Harvard Business Review*, 65/4: 66–75.

Morrison, R. W., and Hall, D. T. (2001), 'A Proposed Model of Individual Adaptability', unpublished technical report, San Diego.

Osland, J. S. (1995), *The Adventure of Working Abroad: Hero Tales from the Global Frontier* (San Francisco: Jossey-Bass).

Shepard, H. A. (1984/1995), 'On the Realization of Human Potential: A Path with a Heart', in M. B. Arthur, L. Bailyn, D. J. Levinson, and H. A. Shepard (eds.), *Working with Careers* (New York: Center for Research on Careers, Graduate School of Business, Columbia University), 25–46; repr. in D. A. Kolb, I. Rubin, and J. Osland, *Organizational Psychology: An Experiential Approach* (Englewood Cliffs, NJ: Prentice-Hall, 1995), 175–86.

Weick, K. E. (1996), 'Enactment and the Boundaryless Career: Organizing as we Work', in M. B. Arthur and D. M. Rousseau (eds.), *The Boundaryless Career: A New Employment Principle for a New Organizational Era* (New York: Oxford University Press), 40–57.

III

CAREERS IN CREATIVE INDUSTRIES

Within the so-called creative industries—across art, film, literature, and theater—the demand for creative products is inherently uncertain. Nobody really knows in advance whether a product will be accepted or not. However, because of the intense competition within these industries, time is of the essence and rapid decision making is vital. Most products are made under severe time constraints, but once made those products tend to last. Books, films, and works of art are commonly developed in response to pre-existing budgets or time-tables. These products are usually made under conditions of both speed and uncertainty, where creative action and commercial interests are inextricably linked. Also, hierarchies of prestige are pervasive, and people with higher prestige reap disproportionately higher rewards when compared to people of slightly inferior status. The exploration of creative careers has much to learn from the experiences of creative industries.

The first chapter in this section by José Luis Alvarez and Silviya Svejenova examines the creative trajectory a renowned Spanish film director Pedro Almodóvar, sustains with his brother and executive producer, Agustín. Through this examination the authors introduce and elaborate the concept of symbiotic careers. They note that the symbiotic career, in which two people jointly navigate the challenges confronting their creative endeavors, is a particular form of career trajectory that is frequently observed, but rarely investigated. Pedro Almodóvar's highly acclaimed creativity in making feature films appears enabled by his brother Agustín's role in taking up the more commercial and humdrum aspects of the business. The relationship between the two is marked by stable and affective trust and affection, and by a differentiation of tasks into responsibilities that each individual is comfortable handling. The authors make a distinctive contribution to the literature on creative careers by introducing, as well as sketching, the key features of this concept.

Next, Candace Jones looks at the role of signals in shaping career trajectories by integrating insights from information economics, social dramaturgy, and organization theory. Within creative industries, individuals are bound up in a political economy of signs and signals. Signs have to be understood, assimilated, and learned before they can be signaled to advance one's career. Jones contends that signals concern three elements: identity, which is an individual's vocabulary of motives, interests, and meanings; performance, which communicates a person's past track record and future potential, and relationships, which symbolize an actor's social capital. Jones also argues that, in order to shape the most favorable career trajectory, individuals need to be skilled at amplifying, attenuating, and deflecting signals as required by the context. Meanwhile, immutable signals concerning such things as gender, age, and ethnicity constrain people's mobility. The chapter leads us to consider how signals affect not only careers, but also their host industries.

In the last chapter in this section, Ellen Ensher, Susan Murphy, and Sherry Sullivan examine the employment experiences of successful women executives in the network and cable TV industry. Basing their work on interviews with fifteen informants, the authors synthesize a career model that predominantly features movement between and across organizational boundaries. Successful women executives also share in common a number of career-enhancing strategies related to self-management and emotional intelligence, such as the ability to network, build meaningful mentoring relationships, develop a nurturing leadership style, and become self-reliant. This chapter makes a number of contributions to the careers literature by providing important and rare empirical evidence about the nature of boundaryless careers and by highlighting the pioneering path carved out by successful women executives in the entertainment business. Like other chapters in this section, it also invites us to consider how careers may reshape the contexts within which they are embedded (a theme discussed in greater detail in the final section of this volume).

All three chapters in this section reflect the way individuals seek out others with complementary roles in order to cope with the environment's complexity. For example, Alvarez and Svejenova contend that the nature of the relationships between individuals with complementary skills will have a bearing on the creativity of what gets produced. Jones suggests that demand uncertainty, speed, and the need to collaborate with competent professionals cause industry participants to rely on signs and signals in making timely decisions. Decisions turn into actions, and ultimately into outputs, which then have a bearing on the reputation and subsequent careers of those involved. Ensher, Murphy, and Sullivan show that successful women executives within the entertainment industry are mindful about cultivating relationships with reputable individuals in order to advance their own careers. Collectively, these chapters reinforce the notion that careers in the so-called creative industries suggest the shape of things to come for other industries, as the demands for creativity multiply.

10

Symbiotic Careers in Movie Making: Pedro and Agustín Almodóvar

JOSÉ LUIS ALVAREZ AND SILVIYA SVEJENOVA

SYMBIOSIS . . . occurs naturally when an alga and a fungus grow together to form a lichen which differs from either plant. Each organism benefits from this close association. The fungus, which cannot produce its own food, gets its food from the alga. The alga gets protection from the fungus.

(*World Book Encyclopedia*)

I'm the sole owner of my career.

(Pedro Almodóvar[1])

I took a vital decision—to abandon my career... for love of Pedro... [and] to see the happiness and coherence of the career of a gifted person.

(Agustín Almodóvar)

Studies on painters (Greenfeld 1989; White and White 1993), writers (Anheier *et al.* 1995), and musicians (Hirsch 1972; Abbott and Hrycak 1990; Murnighan and Colon 1991) have cast light on creative careers. The film industry has also been a frequent field site, adding insights on creative career advancement and its sources, such as skills, knowledge, reputation, relationships, and roles (Faulkner and Anderson 1987; Baker and Faulkner 1991; Jones 1996; DeFillippi and Arthur 1998; Bielby and Bielby 1999).

Most of this research, however, has assumed individually pursued tracks within single career types. While multi-type careers have received only scant attention (e.g. Abbott and Hrycak 1990; Baker and Faulkner 1991; Menger 1999), united career trajectories have been largely left unattended, with few notable exceptions outside the career literature (e.g. Marshack 1998; Felipe 1999; Heenan and Bennis 1999).

---

[1] In Gritten (1999).

This chapter goes beyond traditional accounts of the career as an individual trajectory. It focuses on the paradox of unbinding creativity by binding up artistic and business tasks in a symbiotic career carried out by two people. It addresses two questions: why two people (an artist and her trustee) sustain a common career course, and how this symbiosis affects creativity.

The chapter deals with these questions in the following way. After both data and methods are highlighted, we move to defining creative careers by combining artists' peculiarities (traits, motivation, and choices) with structural markers (nestedness and duality of social structures). We come across a structural layer that is largely overlooked by the extant literature—independent production companies started by creative professionals for the purposes of their creative endeavors.

Next we explore the literature to uncover viable rationales for the introduction of this intermediate layer. Theoretical insights are combined and advanced in the form of propositions, which are illustrated with the case of the internationally acclaimed (and Oscar-winning) Spanish film director Pedro Almodóvar, whose trajectory is unreservedly supported by his brother, and executive producer of his films, Agustín.

Pedro Almodóvar is a maverick film director (Dale 1997) who has consolidated his innovative style and distinctive identity deviating from the conventions of acceptable practice in the Spanish cinema (Becker 1982). Maverick artists, constrained by the conventions, have to substitute their own collaborative networks for those that are unable or unwilling to facilitate the expression of their creativity and idiosyncratic vision.

In search of such creative freedom and control over artwork, Pedro and Agustín created the production company El Deseo. Since that company was formed, Pedro's artistic and commercial success as a filmmaker has been due not only to his unique gift and drive towards continuous learning and increased professionalism, but also to his brother's commitment to 'the dirty part of this business'—that is, the deal making and production.

Interweaving theoretical arguments and empirical findings, we arrive at a career pattern that has been largely overlooked by career scholars—a symbiotic career. With the term 'symbiosis' we depict how a couple (for example, an artist and his or her trustee) with a stable, affective, and trusting relationship engages in a common career path, which encompasses tasks that are highly differentiated and usually incompatible for being carried out by a single person, for the completion of a product or service (for example, artistic and business responsibilities in the production of art).

Through the symbiotic bonding, the artist reconciles the classical principal–agent tensions between producers and film directors (e.g. Fama 1980; Baker and Faulkner 1991), pursuing her expressive needs without opportunism or futile opposition, and consequently boosting her creativity by increased discretion over all aspects of artwork production. The alter ego gets professional (interesting job occupation) and personal (contribution to the self-realization of a talented artist) satisfaction. In our view, the distinctive contribution of this chapter lies precisely in shedding light on why two people sustain a joint career, and how this symbiosis allows creativity to flourish.

Next, we expand career–creativity links beyond those put forward in our propositions, providing some insights into the cultivation of nuclei of trust and affection and the nurture of weak ties for legitimacy and self-actualization. Finally, we outline the study's limitations and suggest avenues for further research and for possible extensions of our arguments to domains other than that of art.

We depict creativity as 'the ability to bring something new into existence' (Barron, quoted in Storr 1985) through 'creative efforts that strike the market as unusually distinctive, satisfying, and/or productive in opening new ground' (Caves 2000: 202). We approach creativity as a social activity (Becker 1982; Brass 1995), with the gifted person requiring collaborative support to produce and diffuse works of art. Apart from cooperation, and despite the tensions between creative tasks and 'humdrum commerce' (Caves 2000), art and business are espoused to deliver artwork to the market.

This chapter addresses the main theme of this book—the multifaceted link between careers and creativity—in several ways. First, it casts light on careers in creative industries (filmmaking in particular), 'in which the product or service contains a substantial element of artistic or creative endeavor' (Caves 2000: p. vii). Secondly, it accounts for the careers of extremely gifted people who undertake their creative endeavors largely at odds with the canons of acceptable practice (Becker, mavericks (1982)). Thirdly, it looks at careers as being creative endeavors (Poehnell and Amundson, this volume)—going beyond individualistic career patterns to a shared career path. Finally, at the crossing of creative careers and career creativity is the fascinating issue of creativity in the creation of support networks for producing and bringing to market innovative artistic work.

EXPLORING THE SYMBIOTIC CAREERS

This chapter is not an attempt to quantify the symbiotic career pattern. Rather, it looks for understanding of the antecedents and outcomes of this phenomenon by exploring two general research questions: *why* two people (an artist and his trustee) sustain a common career course, and *how* their symbiosis affects the artist's creativity.

'Why' and 'how' questions are mainly explanatory in nature, suggesting case studies as a feasible research strategy (Yin 1994). Case-oriented methods are holistic, treating the cases as whole entities rather than as collections of scores on variables, and thus allowing contextual understanding of the relations between the parts (Ragin 1987).

We center on a single case. One rationale for such a research strategy, claims Yin, is when it is a critical case that allows us to confirm, challenge, or extend well-developed theory. Though the framework this study proposes by linking insights from sociological and socio-psychological theories is rather incipient, it does develop propositions that could be checked against and/or illustrated with the particular case under consideration.

Our main case is the symbiotic trajectory a renowned Spanish film director, Pedro Almodóvar, sustains with his brother and executive producer, Agustín, which is nested in their own production company, El Deseo.

Multiple sources of evidence are used to disentangle the issues of interest for this study. Extensive open-ended interviews were conducted with two people from El Deseo: Agustín Almodóvar (managing director, and executive producer of Pedro's films) and Paz Sufrategui (press director). Further telephone conversations with them were used for clarification of details. A description of the case on the basis of the interviews and of rich secondary data was sent to both of them for approval, and their comments on the representation of events were taken into account.

Other highly regarded Spanish film directors or producers and/or their trusted collaborators were also interviewed in order to gain comparative insights into similar phenomena (see References for a complete list of interviews held).

An open-ended interview with the Deputy-Director of Protection of the Instituto de Cinematografía y de las Artes Audiovisuales (ICAA) (the Film Institute for Audio-Visual Arts reporting to the Ministry of Culture and responsible for developing and implementing the Spanish film industry regulation) provided a contextual flavor of the study, and access to film project archives, industry analyses, and institutional policy documents. Further contextual peculiarities were captured by interviewing a film critic and historian, and a film producer, who served as an expert adviser in the initial stages of the project.

Extensive secondary data included the complete press clips archive of El Deseo; published collections of interviews with reputable Spanish cinematographers, screenwriters, and art directors, commenting, among other things, on their relations and work with renowned Spanish film directors; memos on artistic and/or production decisions concerning film projects by Pedro and Agustín Almodóvar sent to the ICAA when applying for subsidies (publicly accessible in the Central Archive of the Spanish Ministry of Education and Culture, because of the regulated nature of the industry); professional biographies of renowned Spanish film directors, and so on.

Recently, even first-rank economists acknowledge that 'if one settles for information that is heterogeneous and largely qualitative, but nonetheless abundant, a great deal can be learned on the economic organization and behavior' of creative industries (Caves 2000: p. vii). To link abundant qualitative data to the propositions we advance, we use 'pattern matching'—relating pieces of information from the case to theoretical arguments (Campbell 1975). Pattern matching is one of the tactics suggested for addressing the issue of internal validity, which is about 'establishing a causal relationship, whereby certain conditions are shown to lead to other conditions, as distinguished from spurious relationships' (Yin 1994: 6).

Unlike the positivist tradition in case-study research (Eisenhardt 1989), however, we do not start with a preconceived framework. Rather, the issues of interest and the theoretical arguments emerged more in the style of grounded theory (Strauss and Corbin 1990) with a continuous traveling back and forth between theory and data.

DEFINING CREATIVE CAREERS

We delineate the field of creative careers by intersecting individual accounts (predominantly psychological) with structural arguments (grounded mainly in sociology of art and sociology of markets and organizations). Our focus, initially placed on the creative person's abilities and motivation in unfolding her creativity, is then embedded in a structural perspective, with further discussion on the paradoxical role of social and economic structures both to constrain and to enable artwork.

Creative people: traits, motivation, and choices

The peculiarities of creative people and their activities are no longer the exclusive terrain of psychologists (Storr 1985; Amabile 1996) and sociologists (Becker 1982; Menger 1999). Organizational scholars (Jones 1996), and even economists (Caves 2000), increasingly have a say about them. Below we explore some converging insights of this diverse literature, focusing on the traits, motivation, and choices of creative people in shaping their professional trajectories.

Passion and control. Understanding one's rationale for pursuing a particular career is a competence DeFillippi and Arthur (1994) denominate *knowing-why*. Scholarly work on artists has emphasized diverse 'why'-arguments for artwork and the occupational choices related to it, with recurrent themes being the passion for work and the need to control the creative process and outputs.

Artwork requires special and scarce *talent* (Becker 1982: 14). 'An artist is someone who is gifted in some way that enables him to do something more or less well which can only be done badly or not at all by someone who is not thus gifted' (Stoppard, quoted in Becker 1982). Still, talent alone is insufficient for a successful artistic trajectory.

Zeal for artistic accomplishment has to accompany it (White and White 1993; Caves 2000). Passion for work (Storr 1985; Jones 1996; Amabile 1997)—or 'labor of love' (Menger 1999)—encompasses the motivation to work on something 'because it is interesting, involving, exciting, satisfying, or personally challenging' (Amabile 1997: 39). It is nicely expressed by film director Sydney Lumet: 'Every picture I did was an active, believable, passionate wish' (Jones and DeFillippi 1996: 93).

Passion is complemented by a drive for control over artwork (Storr 1985; DeFillippi and Arthur 1999), 'providing an inner standard to which reference is made' (Storr 1985), likely to demand a higher performance, and to lead the artist to forswear compromise and to resist cooperating with humdrum partners (Caves 2000).

Artistic choices: professional integration and role versatility. Two important career choices of creative people concern their conformity to canons of acceptable practice, and the variety of artistic activities to handle.

Regarding *conformity*, artists may choose either to follow existing conventions (being integrated professionals—competent but uninspired workers), or else, to break them (becoming mavericks), which requires creating their own collaborative networks (Becker 1982).

Our main case, Pedro Almodóvar, is among 'the few European film-makers who have succeeded in rising above the "subsidy trap" mentality', and who 'are the human face of the industry and prove that however bureaucratic the world becomes, there will always be mavericks who stand out and make their voice heard' (Dale 1997: p. xi).

Further, Dale comments on the rupture with traditional artistic circles caused by Pedro's distinctiveness and success, evident in the 'considerable jealousy within the Spanish film community—where most film-makers have come up through the state system' (Dale 1997: 284). Pedro has been virtually ignored by the Spanish Film Academy, an omission only made good with the seven 1999 Goya Film Awards granted to his film *All about My Mother*.

Role versatility—introduced by Nash (1955/1970) and developed by Menger (1999)—captures the variety of activities performed by an artist simultaneously and/or successively to preserve agility and to increase control over valuable resources. Combinatorial patterns of occupational roles (director, screenwriter, producer) in filmmaking, for example, are seen as an adaptation or imitation strategy for accessing social, cultural, and material capital in the pursuit of a creative vision (Baker and Faulkner 1991).

The creative person's working time and earnings are divided among the creative activity itself, art-related work, and non-art-related work (Menger 1999). The *creative activity* encompasses tasks associated with preparing the artistic product (thinking, dreaming, searching for information, rehearsing, and practicing).

It may be complemented by *art-related work* (for example, teaching activities and management tasks in artistic organizations), which relies on artistic skills and qualifications but has no immediate contribution to artistic outputs. The creation and nurturing of networks of contacts—the *knowing-whom* career competence (DeFillippi and Arthur 1994)—could be positioned here. Through networking, creative people may get inspiration, ideas, and resources for their projects, and increase the legitimacy and acceptance of their artwork and/or themselves. A creative career may also include *non-art-related work* (for example, sales, clerical, or service jobs), whose primary function is to generate income.

Role versatility is definitely a feature of Pedro's idiosyncratic style. He combines his core occupation (film directing) with art-related, and initially even non-art-related work. When Pedro first came to Madrid, he took a variety of casual jobs followed by twelve years as a clerk for the Spanish telephone company. He was earning money to realize his creative ideas, which in this pre-professional period ranged from acting and Super 8 filmmaking to singing in a spoof punk-rock band and writing for underground magazines. The screening of his first commercial feature film on 16 mm coincided with the arrival of democracy in Spain.

Pedro enjoys being involved in a multiplicity of roles in the making of his films. Thus, apart from being a traditional artistic 'hyphenate' (industry jargon to denote the combination of screenwriter–director roles), and even at times covering the full combinatorial pattern (director–producer–screenwriter) in Baker and Faulkner's sense (1991), Pedro has also been directly involved as an artistic director, and even as an actor in his own movies.

Structural accounts of creativity: nestedness and duality

Approaching artwork as social activity (Becker 1982; Greenfeld 1989; White and White 1993), we have to raise issues of structural nestedness and duality, and assess their impact on creative careers. Nestedness accounts for the embedding of the core artistic activity into larger support structures, nested one within another, while duality emphasizes that structures both enable and constrain artwork.

Nestedness of creative careers: art worlds and artistic labor markets. 'Any influence by an artist depends upon his or her being embedded in a group', with the degree of inbreeding in social networks determining the level of influence (White and White 1993: p. xi). Each network, however, may be placed in a larger and more complex one (Perrow 1986). Actors are members of those nested collectivities, which constitute differential comparisons and identities for these individuals (Lawler 1992).

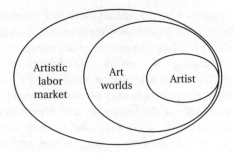

Fig. 10.1. Structural nesting of a creative career trajectory.

Figure 10.1 depicts a nested sequence inferred from selected structural studies on creative careers. In it, the artist embeds her career trajectory in *art worlds*—networks of people and processes of cooperation between them for the production of art (Becker 1982). Signaling an identity through aesthetic style and project choices is a way of differentiating oneself, but it also shapes the opportunities of the artist for current and future matches in the artistic labor market, placing him within specific market niches (Jones, Chapter 11).

Art worlds are usually assembled with inputs from the *artistic labor market*. A career in the film industry, for example, 'is a two-sided affair, sustained by entrepreneurs making distinctions among qualified artists; on the other side of the market, directors, cinematographers, screenwriters, composers, and other artists are making distinctions among film productions (and their producers)' (Faulkner and Anderson 1987: 889).

Uncertainty of matching could be curbed through repetitive exchanges with proven professionals (Faulkner and Anderson 1987), reputable talent agency intermediation (Bielby and Bielby 1999), independent production companies (DeFillipi and Arthur 1999), long-term contracts (in the early days of the Hollywood studios), or signaling strategies (Jones, Chapter 11).

Duality of social and economic structures: constraint and means for artwork.
Artists need structural support to produce art, usually in the form of art worlds (Becker 1982) or single-project organizations (Faulkner and Anderson 1987) selected from a larger pool of professionals available in the artistic labor market. Structures, however, both enable and constrain creative action (White 1992).

Structure constrains by blocking fresh action. In many accounts of creative careers, social forces are found to be harmful to creativity, among other things because they intervene in the final outcome of artwork, diminishing the creator's degree of internal control over her work (Amabile 1996). Artists have to be 'discovered' by entrepreneurial organizations—regulators of innovation—with power to influence the artist's fate (Hirsch 1972).

However, 'artwork...is a social phenomenon' (Greenfeld 1989), and, if artists find certain social structures constraining, they cannot simply abandon them and work on their own. They need to create their own group, or 'art world', through which to express their creativity. The way they do this will naturally influence the direction taken by their careers.

FORMING AN INDEPENDENT PRODUCTION COMPANY TO BUFFER CREATIVITY

Independent freelancers in the arts act like small firms building subcontractual relations with artistic organizations (Menger 1999). In this chapter we not only portray film directors this way. We focus on those who actually create their own production organizations.

Our main case is about the joint trajectory of the brothers Pedro and Agustín Almodóvar embedded in their own production company, El Deseo. El Deseo was registered on 14 June 1985, during a break in the filming of *Matador*, produced by Andrés Vicente Gómez, one of the most important Spanish film producers. By that time Pedro had already demonstrated his gift for telling stories and his enormous inner drive to express his internal and external world in a string of feature films.

In the nested structural sequence, an independent production company could be placed as an interface layer between the artist's trajectory and the art worlds for the production of his or her artwork. Furthermore, the creation of a new venture is in line with a larger (renewed) interest in action theories in understanding managerial careers. More flexible structures enable managers to shape them according to the activities they have in mind, and consequently to gain control over their careers (Weick 1996; Alvarez 2000). This means that, to 'restart the social clock' and 'buffer one chain of action from another', agents would decouple from constraining structural 'straitjackets' (White 1992).

Hence, it may be hypothesized that film directors start their own production companies to buffer themselves from restrictions on creativity imposed by traditional production organizations, and from the uncertainty of not being matched in the labor market.

The relationship between producers and creative professionals in film-making has never been easy, partly because of the need to match artists' expressive needs with producers' budget and time considerations. As Agustín noted, 'if from the very beginning Pedro had had a producer who had said "We have to favor...creativity because it is a treasure", El Deseo would never have existed'.

Another driver is artists' autonomous entrepreneurial impulse (DeFillippi and Arthur 1999). Menger (1999) maintains that parallels may be drawn between the careers of self-employed artists and those of entrepreneurs. Common attributes, he claims, are 'the capacity to create valued output through the production of works for sale... a strong sense of personal achievement through the production of tangible outputs, the ability to set their own pace'. Entrepreneurs are portrayed as looking for non-structured situations where control and independence can be asserted, so 'to design their own organizations, to create and structure organizations centered around themselves, often becomes the only alternative' (Kets de Vries 1995: 119–20).

Sharing these traits of the entrepreneurial personality, creators, too, resist external attempts to control their behàvior (Amabile 1996). For example, Woody Allen reports that being a writer or stand-up comedian is more enjoyable than being a filmmaker, where he is not in complete control of the outcome. Thus, 'independent film companies'—claim DeFillippi and Arthur (1999: 187)—'arose in part because successful film actors... sought more creative freedom and ownership rights to the fruits of their artistic labor'. Hence, creation of production entities by film directors could also be seen as an attempt to reduce external influence on art making by internalizing an important part of the control over the output. In the case of Almodóvar, it was his need to work with complete freedom, Paz Sufrategui, press director of El Deseo, acknowledged, that really pushed him to undertake the production venture with his brother.

Pedro's initiation in filmmaking in the 1970s was marked by his involvement in a multiplicity of roles: inventing the story, working behind and in front of the camera, adding the sound track, and so on. He was initially motivated by resource scarcity rather than solely by creative impetus, and so tight control became a hallmark of his idiosyncratic style.

As Alfredo Mayo, a famous Spanish cinematographer who has contributed to several of Pedro's films, explains: 'Pedro always tends to control everything... It's not that he shuts his mind to any suggestions people make, but... he has to see *exactly* what [a scene] is going to look like [on the screen]' (Heredero 1994: 459). In his work with actors, Mayo continues, 'what he does is first interpret and act out the scene himself, so that the actors can then imitate what he does...' (Heredero 1994: 460).

Independent production companies are particularly apt for maverick film directors whose style, vision, and so on are usually unacceptable to conventional art worlds. Pedro is just such a maverick film director, working at odds with the canons of traditional practice, and hence suffering exclusion by certain circles of the film establishment (Dale 1997). As Becker (1982) suggests, in such cases mavericks may have to create their own support structures to replace those unable or unwilling to service their unconventional style and vision.

The following proposition is a summary of the arguments presented so far:

Proposition 1

An artist starts his own production company in order to reduce social constraints on creativity, to have more control over his artwork, or to assemble his own art world.

The illustration provided by the Almodóvar case largely confirms our first proposition, with their production company being started because of a combination of factors.

Independent companies owned by artists internalize the art–business tension, encompassing both creative and business-related activities. In general, tension occurs when interdependent tasks for completion of a product have different orientations (Lawrence and Lorsch 1967). This dilemma results in classic principal–agent problems, where the producer's interests in ensuring the film is made on time and within budget are opposed to the artistic vision of the film director (Baker and Faulkner 1991).

The art–business tension additionally speaks to the issue of role versatility and combinatorial patterns of occupational roles (Baker and Faulkner 1991; Menger 1999). Baker and Faulkner, for example, argue that combinations of occupational roles that bridge commercial and artistic domains (for example, being producer–director–screenwriter, producer–director, or producer–screenwriter) simplify coordination and reduce agency problems but may also cause patterned ambivalence. Still, technological change and greater administrative load (among others) may encourage the separation of artistic and business domains.

Further, psychological accounts of artistic and business activities in art show important differences. For example, a creative person prefers complexity, asymmetry, and incompleteness, rejects facile solutions, waiting to arrive alone at a more satisfying synthesis (Storr 1985). This may contradict the scheduled and budgeted logic of business. Further, an artist need not be methodological and systematic, and often seeks to bend or break the rules (Cummings and Oldham 1997), which could contradict the repetitive and routine nature of deal making and production.

Analytical, problem solving, and decision/judgment-making skills, balanced learning habits and skills, command of basic facts, and proactivity (that is, a tendency to respond purposefully to events) are all qualities possessed by successful managers (Pedler et al. 1986). They are not necessarily compatible with the creative personality, which is better portrayed by words such as independence, originality, impulsiveness, and expansiveness (Storr 1985).

No doubt, there is also an area of overlap containing features that are relevant for both business and artistic tasks, such as emotional resilience, mental agility, and social skills and abilities (especially in the case of film directors, who create their films through people). Managerial tasks are relevant to directors, who organize, control, and direct resources for the project, motivate creative action, and handle stress and conflict (Morley and Silver 1977; Jones 1996).

Despite similarities, however, cognitive maps and technical and administrative requirements will tend to impede artists in any attempt to perform both artistic and business tasks. Hence, our second proposition is:

Proposition 2

Since a production company encompasses business tasks that require different cognitive maps and abilities from those required for artistic activities, the artist alone is unlikely to start/run a production company.

As Paz explained, 'Pedro is definitely not a businessman. He does not perform any kind of business tasks, neither is he interested in such issues.' He relies on his younger brother Agustín for the management of the company and the executive production of his films. In a similar vein, Cristina Huete, the wife of another reputable, Oscar-winning Spanish film director, Fernando Trueba, is also his executive producer and partner in their production company. This serves to confirm our second proposition that the director alone is unlikely to perform both artistic and business tasks. Further research, however, is required to disentangle the multiplicity, contextual appropriateness, and influence on artistic and commercial outcomes of the plausible combinatorial patterns between artistic and business roles.

As was argued earlier, the differing logic of art and business, together with the creator's need to 'to deliver himself wholly up to [art]' (Charles Dickens, quoted in Amabile 1996: 8), call for a partner to take charge of the business-related tasks in the production structure.

Creative binomials sharing artistic and business responsibilities date back to the dawn of filmmaking—the brothers Auguste and Louis Lumière. Other famous siblings are Paolo and Vittorio Taviani, Bernardo and Giuseppe Bertolucci, or Joel and Ethan Coen, the latter being described by Barry Sonnenfeld, cinematographer of several of their earliest titles, as 'a perfect and self-contained ecosystem of two persons' (Brown, quoted in Felipe 1999).

All these cases feature close, stable, affective, and binding relationships—expressive bonds in which the strength of the tie is a function of 'the amount of time, the emotional intensity, the intimacy (mutual confiding), and reciprocal service' (Ibarra 1993). Such relationships, Ibarra affirms, are both instrumental and expressive, and serve as 'systems for making decisions, mobilizing resources, concealing or transmitting information, and performing other functions closely allied with work behavior and interaction'.

Trust embedded in such strong, frequent personal relationships nested in wider networks is referred to as thick (Putnam 2000) or relational (Rousseau et al. 1998) trust. Under conditions of uncertainty and complexity, requiring mutual adjustment, characteristic of the film industry, sustained effective coordinated action is possible only where there is mutual confidence and trust (Thompson, quoted in McAllister 1995). Affective foundations of trust consist of the emotional bonds between individuals, and lead to expressions of genuine care and concern for the welfare of the partners (McAllister 1995).

Hence, we advance our next proposition:

Proposition 3

To handle the business and production aspects of artwork in a creativity-enhancing way, the artist needs a trusted person.

Pedro Almodóvar wanted to start his production company 'with somebody who was going to understand him intimately, from the essence, from the first idea of a film', explained Paz Sufrategui. Agustín's decision to support Pedro had a strong affective ground coupled with a strong belief in his brother's talent: 'I took a vital decision—to abandon my career...for love of Pedro... [and] to see the happiness and coherence of the career of a gifted person.' An indispensable condition for his complete dedication, he added, was his relationship with Pedro, based on fidelity, affection, and fraternity, and ultimately his 'love for Pedro'.

Agustín followed Pedro to Madrid, and Pedro introduced him to the cultural and social worlds of the Spanish capital. That strengthened their bonds and allowed Agustín to observe more closely and to take part in the creative worlds in which his brother was moving.

On a more instrumental level, Pedro needed Agustín's support to increase control over his artwork and to avoid the typical tension between art and business, exhibited in sterile opposition, mismatches of intentionality, or formal disagreement (Felipe 1999).

For Agustín, as he himself acknowledged, apart from the personal satisfaction of seeing the advancement of a gifted and loved sibling, his initiation into film production and the running of a production company offered a much more exciting and rewarding occupation than his previous one as a chemistry teacher.

Central to this chapter is a peculiar career pattern—a symbiotic career—which is left unattended by the traditional depictions of a career as an individual enterprise. The *World Book Encyclopedia* describes that in symbiosis 'an alga and a fungus grow together to form a lichen which differs from either plant'. In a similar way, the joint trajectory of an artist and her trustee, which may be further embedded in their independent production company, is different from that followed by the artist alone.

Both the artist and the trustee benefit from this association. On the one hand, the artist, who is unable and/or reluctant in most cases to have business responsibilities for the production of her art, receives support in these activities from her trusted partner. On the other hand, the partner enjoys a very interesting occupation, and also gets a personal satisfaction from helping a loved, and gifted person.

Our fourth proposition advances a definition of the symbiotic career, as an attempt to conceptualize it as a distinctive career pattern, which complements the individual career pattern in a typology of creative careers.

Proposition 4

A symbiotic career is a career trajectory sustained by a couple (for example, an artist and his or her trustee) with a stable, affective, and trusting relationship, who share highly differentiated tasks (for example, artistic and business responsibilities in the production of art) that are incompatible for being carried out by a single person.

Servicing Pedro's creativity in a symbiotic way is not an easy task. As Pedro has recognized publicly on several formal occasions, being his producer is a good business, but being his brother sometimes is not so easy. On receiving the 56th Annual Golden Globe Award for Best Foreign Language Film for *All about My Mother*, Pedro expressed his gratitude to his brother Agustín, the producer of his films, for 'doing the dirty part of this business'.

SYMBIOTIC CAREERS FOR BOOSTING CREATIVITY

Metaphors are the architects of our conceptual system (Poehnell and Amundson, Chapter 6), and by using them we cognitively appreciate and understand the world (see Inkson, Chapter 2 on the use of metaphors in thinking creatively about careers). In this chapter we employ the metaphor of symbiosis to emphasize the close association that exists between the career paths of two people, as well as the mutual benefits for those who sustain it. In addition, this joint path is an 'entity' itself that differs from either singular career, and raises motivations and outcomes, which cannot be pursued through independent trajectories.

The symbiotic metaphor is a cognitively appealing way of labeling not only peculiar, but also increasingly viable career patterns, which is applicable to a wide range of settings, especially with the increase in 'copreneurship' and 'coleadership'. Copreneurs are couples who choose to join forces and do something new together (Marshack 1998) in search for quality of life and/or as a response to downsizing, outsourcing, glass ceiling, or another career obstacle. Coleadership is associated with the emergence of a new Silicon Valley model of success, where a leader counts on the committed support of her deputy (Heenan and Bennis 1999).

Both trends (copreneurship and coleadership) pose the need to comprehend better the (symbiotic) pattern that makes them sustainable from a career point of view. The literature on entrepreneurial couples emphasizes the joint commitment of both partners (be they spouses, siblings, friends, etc.) both to the career and to the relationship, in a self-employed setting. The coleadership issues are seen more in relation to an egalitarian view of governance, where a deputy who is committed to the visionary, to the organization, or to a cause, co-runs the business, relieving the leader from core activities, for which he may not have the necessary time and/or abilities.

The symbiotic career is associated with recurrent exchanges with both instrumental and expressive incentives for the parties involved. In instrumental terms, the artist unbinds his creativity and gains control over the business and production side of art making by having it managed by a trusted partner. The trustee, on the other hand, enjoys an attractive professional occupation, which may bring recognition and awards if the support is provided to an extremely gifted artist.

According to recent developments of exchange theory, however, emotions and emotional processes can enrich exchange theorizing and research, which are focused largely on self-interest as a driver of relationships (Lawler and Thye 1999). Frequent exchanges may lead to relational cohesion—the relationship itself becoming a unifying force or an object of attachment (Lawler and Yoon 1993) because of the shared emotions and feelings it produces (Lawler and Yoon 1996). Emotions are integral to the process through which relations remain salient (Lawler and Thye 1999).

Research has found that positive affective states promote social interaction and creativity (Jones and George 1998). Further, it is widely acknowledged that trust enhances collaboration. Here, we focus on thick (Putnam 2000), or relational (Rousseau *et al.* 1998), trust derived from repeated interaction over time between trustor and trustee, which leads to the formation of attachments based upon reciprocated interpersonal care and concern (McAllister 1995).

Our fifth proposition summarizes the link between the career symbiosis and the boosting of the artist's creativity.

Proposition 5

The artist unbinds his creativity by binding the career of the trusted person to his own creative trajectory in a symbiotic way.

Pedro's creative style is a blend of detailed preparation and sweeping improvisation. Alfredo Mayo comments that 'though sometimes the filming is very well prepared and the details have been worked out with almost manic precision, he [Pedro] also improvises a lot and always incorporates new ideas...[and] when he has a whim or falls in love with something he fights and pursues it with insistence' (Heredero 1994).

In a general case, sudden changes and improvisation would require negotiation with the producer regarding feasibility, and may evoke conflict of interests, mismatch of intentions, and even sterile opposition. When the executive producer is committed in a symbiotic way to the film director's trajectory, however, he or she will try to understand the motivation behind the modification, and to service its requirements. This was emphasized both by Agustín (Pedro's executive producer) and by Cristina Huete (Trueba's executive producer).

Another creative peculiarity of Pedro concerns his filming style. Typically, directors will film without following the script sequence to economize on resources. Pedro, however, films his projects sequentially, which gives him more control over his artwork and additional freedom for sweeping changes and improvisation. Furthermore, he can go and edit any time of day or night, and also has responsibility for the final cut (Gritten 1999). As Gritten notes, 'with the clout to make any film he wants, he may wield more artistic freedom than any other European director. Agustín is devoted to keeping Almodóvar happy.' Hence creativity is boosted by the symbiotic director–producer relationship between the two siblings.

In confirmation of our propositions, the support of his brother and the back-up of their own production company give Pedro the freedom to carry out his projects without restrictions. The binding of Agustín to Pedro's trajectory in a symbiotic way in fact unbinds Pedro's creativity.

EXPANDING CAREER–CREATIVITY LINKS

In line with Becker (1982), we conceptualize mavericks as people who disobey the conventions of acceptable practice, and who because of that may face the unwillingness or inability of the existing art worlds to collaborate in the materialization of their artistic vision. Yet, we also deviate from Becker's original depiction of a maverick by relaxing some of its features.

First, we diverge from Becker in his claim that mavericks have initiated their careers in the establishment and have been trained in the conventions of the acceptable practice, finding them constraining to their expressive needs and creativity. While this could be true for maverick musicians, who constitute the bulk of cases Becker presents, and who may require some basic training in playing an instrument or in composing, painters or film directors are much less dependent upon formal rules and may perform artwork relying heavily on experimentation.

Another point in which our depiction differs from Becker's account is that we do not necessarily think that a maverick loses his extraordinary status with the wide acceptance and acclaim of his work. He may sustain a maverick identity, which cannot be easily imitated by the integrated professionals or its manifestations incorporated as established practice.

Despite this more relaxed depiction of a maverick artist, however, we find the artistic category, introduced and scrutinized by Becker (1982), extremely insightful for understanding the motivation to pursue a symbiotic career, embedded in an independent production company. In Fig. 10.2 we use the propositions advanced on the basis of our case to introduce these two

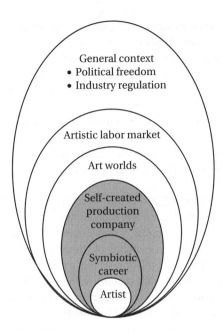

Fig. 10.2. Structural nesting of a creative symbiotic career.

additional intermediate layers—symbiotic career and self-created production company—in the nested sequence of social structures shown in Fig. 10.1. These two layers are buffers that allow the artist to increase control over the artwork, overcome constraints on creativity, and assemble proprietary art worlds for the completion of creative projects. Hence, they unbind the artist's creativity while at the same time binding him to the trajectory of a trusted partner.

Further, the issue of political and artistic freedom could enrich the nested sequence of the artist's trajectory as an outer layer embracing all the previous layers. It reflects the idea that labor market dealing, and the assembly of art worlds for filmmaking, could be patterned differently and allow for distinctive trajectories of creative people in democratic versus dictatorship contexts.

In this line, Pedro's dedication of his 1999 Cannes Best Director Award for his film *All about My Mother* to Spanish democracy is not surprising. Under Franco's regime, his films would not have been possible, and, as he himself admits, he would probably have ended up in Paris making alternative theater and writing novels in another language.

A similar enabling or constraining role is played by government regulation of the film industry. The Socialist government, which had been in power since 1982, was advancing money for independent film projects upon submission of script and budget. Thus, film directors—closer to the screenwriting function, and in some cases screenwriters themselves—had an incentive to start their own companies, and claim financing on their own.

The wave of new production companies set up by film directors in the 1980s in Spain further atomized and weakened the production sector. Most firms' stamina expired upon completion of the subsidized film project. El Deseo outlived the majority of those companies to produce a steady succession of films that won both artistic and commercial recognition in Spain and all over the world. The success of this company for creativity may be attributed to the talent and ambition of Pedro, but also to the unconditional support of his brother Agustín and of the nuclei of support committed to Pedro's vision, as will be seen later in this chapter.

The richness of the case of Pedro and Agustín Almodóvar reveals relevant career–creativity ties beyond those advanced in the propositions. They lie in two main directions. First, the symbiotic 'artist–trustee' formation is not sufficient to fulfill the creative and business needs of the film projects, and may require nesting in tightly coupled nuclei of support that extend the 'family' nature of the symbiosis. Secondly, there are art-related activities (largely of a networking character) that a film director has to perform personally to boost professional legitimacy and reputation, or to get inspiration and self-actualization.

Beyond symbiotic careers: cultivating nuclei of trust and affection

Pedro works through 'family' groups, his nuclei of trust and affection, which are part of the nested sequence depicted in Fig. 10.2. First is the biological family—his brother supports his career in a symbiotic way. Yet, however strong Pedro's relationship with his brother, an artist has to look further afield to assemble and maintain collaborative networks for particular film projects.

The biological family is extended to accommodate the team of El Deseo, woven through affective bonding to Pedro. As the director himself acknowledges: 'They're my second family, or they've already become my natural family, combined with the biological one.... It's a small team but one that has really made the company its own family... and we're happy to have Paz, Lola, Esther, Michel... because El Deseo is part of them' (Francia 2000: 33).

As these words indicate, the strong affective and trust-based relationship between the two brothers stretches out to include the members of the production team. The way the two brothers select the members of their team is critical to an understanding of how El Deseo sets itself apart. Initially, the company consisted of the two brothers and had no internal infrastructure to support the projects. Key professionals were 'brought in' on a project basis as a permanent production team was unaffordable.

Repetitive project-based exchanges with some professionals allowed the brothers to get to know them really well and to establish close affective and increasingly trust-based bonds with them (the move from cognition to affect-based trust in McAllister's terms (1995)). These people formed the core of the production company when the financial situation allowed for the creation of a permanent support infrastructure. Agustín summed up his *organization building strategy* as follows: 'I find a person and then I create the position for her.' Such was the case of the line producer and Agustín's 'right hand' Esther Garcia, or of the public relations director, Paz Sufrategui.

The team is united by love and respect for Pedro's talent, and is committed to servicing Pedro's gift and professional trajectory. It is a core unit that puts together the art worlds for the making of Pedro's movies.

In these art worlds, Pedro has the tendency to work repeatedly with actors and other professionals he appreciates and enjoys working with. For example, he 'cherishes the notion of a family of actors...forming the tightest stock company in movies. Nearly a dozen actors have appeared in three or more films' (Corliss 1999). This 'family' is also extendible to professionals such as Alberto Iglesias, who has put the music to three of Pedro's films so far, or to José Salcedo, editor of all Pedro's films.

Jones *et al.* (1998) distinguish between a collectivist strategy (constellations that are highly exclusive and stable over time) and an individualist strategy with an entrepreneurial logic (highly inclusive and involving a large number of firms that work together only rarely). Our case is a middle ground, blending features from both strategies. On the one hand, it is collectivist in the sense that Pedro tends to reconvene professionals in his consecutive projects. On the other hand, however, this reconvening is not driven by the need to nurture the collective identity of the constellation, but rather by his individual quest for a distinctive identity. We believe that, in a creative, innovation-driven enterprise, such cross-fertilization of these two strategies is feasible and may be beneficial if there is a strong visionary, who needs continuity of his stylistic peculiarity by recurrently bringing together certain professionals.

Thus, our study reveals, in line with emotional accounts of social exchange (Lawler and Yoon 1996, 1998; Lawler and Thye 1999), that a guiding principle in the transformation of an artistic vision into a work of art is the tightly woven affective network fully committed to the artist's creative ideas.

Beyond nuclei of trust and affection: nurturing weak ties for legitimacy and self-actualization

The Almodóvar brothers further stretch their strong, trust-based bonding to their inter-organizational relations. For example, El Deseo works with its main partners through a 'key-man clause'. As Agustín explains it, whenever they have to deal with a particular company, be it for distribution or promotion, they do so through a specific person, whose departure from that company means the end of the contractual relation between El Deseo and that company.

This is a very strong restriction that may lead to the loss of a client, yet it guarantees the necessary trust and differential service beyond what an ordinary firm would get. As Agustín put it, 'I am interested in the person, not in a box in an organization chart.' In his view, this is attributable to the world they come from—a modest village family, a visceral world in which personal relations and trust are important.

Counting on trusted and dedicated helpers to look after the art worlds that filmmaking requires, Pedro keeps control over these networks and enjoys the legitimacy and resources they may offer. He also saves energy and time to concentrate on the creative core of filmmaking.

However, even with the support of his brother, his team, his recurrent project collaborators, and the 'key men' in partnering companies, Pedro cannot devote himself entirely to inventing and directing films. That is due both to the nature of artwork, and to the peculiarity of Pedro's style. First, by its very nature, creative work in filmmaking requires spending time on other activities that feed the creative impulse. In the words of film director Fernando Trueba, people who want to be film directors 'have to live as much as possible, read all they can, and see a lot of movies' (Heredero 1999).

Apart from looking for fresh ideas, Pedro participates in promotional activities and award ceremonies to help build his and his films' image both in Spain and abroad. Recently, his film *All about My Mother* generated a hugely favorable response from critics and audiences, bringing him a spectacular number of awards, sometimes more than one a day (Francia 2000), and culminating in winning the ultimate prize of Hollywood, the Oscar for best foreign language film. The following quotation gives us an idea of the impact such undoubtedly art-related activities have on the director's core artistic activities: 'These are very, very intensive days and weeks in America, and all this kind of activity leaves me feeling empty and slightly depressed. I need to stay in touch with other new projects, and on the planes and in the hotels I intend to keep working on a new story I have in mind. But I can never find enough time, and that ends up frustrating me' (Francia 2000: 33).

So, it turns out that, even with a symbiotic career pattern and a personal production company as buffers, there are certain activities that cannot be 'outsourced' to trusted others and have to be performed by the director himself in order to enhance the diffusion and legitimacy of his artwork, though sometimes at the expense of his creative impulses.

CONCLUDING REMARKS

In this chapter we have sought to provide insights into an underexplored topic in the careers literature, that of symbiotic careers embedded in self-created opportunity structures, such as production companies. We explored motivations for starting up a company and binding trajectories in a symbiotic way, and mechanisms through which these social formations may allow outstanding artistic and commercial performance. The framework proposed for addressing these issues was illustrated by a single critical case—that of the internationally recognized Spanish film director, Pedro Almodóvar, who has his independent production company, co-partnered by his brother Agustín.

The fact that the data come from a single case allows for analytical generalization (from data to theory) but prohibits inferences regarding the entire population of Spanish film directors and/or production companies. Extra caution in interpreting the results is required because the case focuses on a renowned film director—that is, on a 'public' figure whose actions and image are constructed by and through the media. As previous studies inform, the reasons an actor gives discursively for acting in the way he does may diverge from the rationale he employs at the moment of acting (Giddens 1984: 4). Or, as Weick (1969) affirms, careers are sets of actions interpreted as such *ex post* rather than planned as a career *ex ante*.

We propose that constraints on creativity imposed by existing production structures generate dissatisfaction in talented film directors, who need freedom to express their vision. Still, the decision to start one's own company also depends on the availability of a trusted person, preferably a very close relative or friend, who is totally committed to serving the talent of the creative person. That is to say, for an artist successfully to embed her career trajectory in her independent production company, she may need to have entirely at her disposal the career of a trusted partner. In other words, the artist and the partner need jointly to develop a 'symbiotic' career.

This tight career coupling or symbiotic formation is insufficient on its own, especially if the creative person's artistic and commercial ambitions are large and at odds with the industry. The artist has to build up and nurture a nucleus of supporters based on trust and affection, which will include her production team; that is, she has to 'nest' the symbiotic career in an inspired and dedicated core team.

Each member of this core team is then responsible for creating and maintaining relations of trust and affection (though without the same intensity as the relations between the two halves of the symbiotic career) with people from various different domains that are relevant for filmmaking. This saves the creative person's energy and allows her to concentrate on art creation and self-actualization, while at the same time controlling a diversity of art worlds.

Even extremely gifted people cannot produce artwork on their own. They need the collaborators they themselves and/or their trusted partner draw into the project, cutting across social layers (that is, existing ties from the art worlds of previous projects, new ties formed through participation in events or through the artistic labor market, and so on).

The tight affective and trust-based nucleus the film director forms cannot maintain the director's artistic integrity and identity on its own. A further mechanism that he or she may resort to is role versatility—that is, combining artistic, art-related, and non-art-related work. Assuming that film directing is the main artistic activity, there are many art-related options left that increase the director's control over the artwork. She may get partly or completely involved in the scriptwriting, or she may take part in public promotional activities to enhance her visibility, professional legitimacy, and reputation, and aid the diffusion of her artwork. Ties may be established not only for publicity reasons, but also to satisfy the need for constant self-actualization and inspiration by discovering new experiences and meeting interesting people.

Taking this into account, it appears that despite creating tightly coupled affective nuclei around her, a film director cannot completely insulate herself from market uncertainty or non-artistic activities. Publicity may squeeze out creative energy but it also builds on reputation and access to novel ideas, people, and possibilities.

To deepen the account of creative careers and to move from the peculiarities of creative partnerships to the more general concerns of top management teams, further research is necessary. First, the nature of the symbiosis needs to be disentangled, with an exploration of the requisite variety of symbiotic alternatives (exhibiting differential sharing of tasks, or differing intensity of commitment to the symbiosis—complete or partial). Positive as well as negative forms of symbiosis should be depicted and their functional or dysfunctional implications understood at the level of the parties involved and the organization that the couple co-governs. Secondly, the sustainability of the pattern should be explored. In this direction, an interesting issue for further exploration is when a symbiotic trajectory acquires sufficient critical mass to reach a professional peak. Is the peak achieved through accumulated experience and/ or self-actualization, through having rich support networks, or both? Thirdly, scholarly attention could be directed to the dynamics of the symbiosis in different cultural contexts, as reliance on trust and affection may differ from one culture to another.

This study is only an incipient attempt to conceptualize an increasingly relevant career pattern, ubiquitous in arts (Felipe 1999), but also applicable to other settings. Ventures between couples are on the rise (Marshack 1998) and corporations, countries, and other entities increasingly realize that top leaders and their coleaders are essential complements (Heenan and Bennis 1999). We can therefore expect that the symbiotic career will be a distinguishable part of the pluralistic career landscape at the beginning of the twenty-first century (Anand, Peiperl and Arthur, Chapter 1).

The chapter can thus be seen as part of a larger effort to restore the belief that, by creating and changing structures to suit them to the activities they have in mind, managers can gain ownership of their own career trajectories.

REFERENCES

Abbott, A., and Hrycak, A. (1990), 'Measuring Resemblance in Sequence Data: An Optimal Matching Analysis of Musicians' Careers', *American Journal of Sociology*, 96: 144–85.

Almodóvar, P. (1999), *Todo sobre mi madre*, definitive edition of the screenplay (Madrid: El Deseo).

Alvarez, J. L. (2000), 'Theories of Managerial Action and Their Impact on the Conceptualization of Executive Careers', in M. Peiperl, M. Arthur, R. Goffee, and T. Morris (eds.), *Conversations in Career Theory: Insights and Trends* (Oxford: Oxford University Press), 127–37.

Amabile, T. M. (1996), *Creativity in Context* (Boulder, Colo.: Westview Press).

—— (1997), 'Motivating Creativity in Organizations: On Doing what You Love and Loving what You Do', *California Management Review*, 40/1: 39–58.

Anheier, H. K., Gerhards, J., and Romo, F. P. (1995), 'Forms of Capital and Social Structure in Cultural Fields: Examining Bourdieu's Social Topography', *American Journal of Sociology*, 100/4: 859–903.

Baker, W. E., and Faulkner, R. R. (1991), 'Role as Resource in the Hollywood Film Industry', *American Journal of Sociology*, 97/2: 279–309.

Becker, H. S. (1982), *Art Worlds* (Berkeley and Los Angeles: University of California Press).

Bielby, W. T., and Bielby, D. D. (1999), 'Organizational Mediation of Project-Based Labor Matters: Talent Agencies and the Careers of Screenwriters', *American Sociological Review*, 64/1: 64–85.

Brass, D. J. (1995), 'Creativity: It's All in Your Social Network', in C. M. Ford and D. A. Gioia (eds.), *Creative Action in Organizations: Ivory Tower Visions and Real World Voices* (Thousand Oaks, Calif.: Sage), 94–9.

Campbell, D. T. (1975), 'Degrees of Freedom and the Case Study', *Comparative Political Studies*, 8: 178–93.

Caves, R. E. (2000), *Creative Industries: Contracts between Art and Commerce* (Cambridge, Mass.: Harvard University Press).

Corliss, R. (1999), 'Loving Pedro', *Time*, 29 Nov., 59–60.

Cummings, A., and Oldham, G. R. (1997), 'Enhancing Creativity: Managing Work Contexts for the High Potential Employee', *California Management Review*, 40/1: 22–38.

Dale, M. (1997), *The Movie Game: The Film Business in Britain, Europe and America* (London: Cassell).

DeFillippi, R. J., and Arthur, M. B. (1994), 'The Boundaryless Career: A Competency-Based Perspective', *Journal of Organizational Behavior*, 15: 307–24.

—— —— (1998), 'Paradox in Project-Based Enterprise: The Case of Film Making', *California Management Review*, 40/2: 125–39.

—— —— (1999), 'Paradox Revisited: A Reply to Phelan and Lewis', *California Management Review*, 42/1: 186–91.

Eisenhardt, K. M. (1989), 'Building Theories from Case Study Research', *Academy of Management Review*, 14/4: 532–50.

Estevez, M. V. (1994), 'Dos o tres diferencias entre cine Norteamericano y cine Europeo', *Servicios de estudios BBV*, 3: 79–89.

Fama, E. F. (1980), 'Agency Problems and the Theory of the Firm', *Journal of Political Economy*, 88: 288–307.

Faulkner, R. R., and Anderson, A. B. (1987), 'Short-Term Projects and Emergent Careers: Evidence from Hollywood', *American Journal of Sociology*, 92/4: 879–909.

Felipe, F. de (1999), *Joel y Ethan Coen: El cine siamés* (Barcelona: Glénat).

Francia, J. I. (2000), 'Pedro Almodóvar', *Magazine, La Vanguardia*, 30 Jan., 26–33.

Fresneda, C. (2000), 'Almodóvar, más cerca que nunca del Oscar después de haber ganado el Globo de Oro', *El Mundo*, 25 Jan., 62.

Giddens, A. (1984), *The Constitution of Society: Outline of the Theory of Structuration* (Berkeley and Los Angeles: University of California Press).

Greenfeld, L. (1989), *Different Worlds: A Sociological Study of Taste, Choice and Success in Art* (Cambridge: Cambridge University Press).

Gritten, D. (1999), 'One for the Girls: Interview with Pedro Almodóvar for the *Telegraph Magazine*', 14 Aug.

Heenan, D. A., and Bennis, W. (1999), *Co-Leaders: The Power of Great Partnerships* (New York: John Wiley).

Heredero, C. F. (1994), *El Lenguaje de la luz: Entrevistas con directores de fotografía del cine español* (Madrid: Festival de Cine de Alcalá de Henares).

—— (1999), *Fernando Trueba: retrato de una mirada* (Madrid: Fnac).

Hirsch, P. M. (1972), 'Processing Fads and Fashions: An Organization-Set Analysis of Cultural Industry Systems', *American Journal of Sociology*, 77: 639–59.

Holguín, A. (1994), *Pedro Almodóvar* (Madrid: Ediciones Cátedra).

Ibarra, H. (1993), 'Personal Networks of Women and Minorities in Management: A Conceptual Framework', *Academy of Management Review*, 18/1: 56–87.

Jones, C. (1996), 'Careers in Project Networks: The Case of the Film Industry', in M. B. Arthur and D. M. Rousseau (eds.), *The Boundaryless Career: A New Employment Principle for a New Organizational Era* (New York: Oxford University Press), 58–75.

—— and DeFillippi, R. J. (1996), 'Back to the Future in Film: Combining Industry and Self-Knowledge to Meet the Career Challenges of the 21st Century', *Academy of Management Executive*, 10/4: 89–103.

—— Hesterly, W. S., Fladmoe-Lindquist, K., and Borgatti, S. P. (1998), 'Professional Service Constellations: How Strategies and Capabilities Influence Collaborative Stability and Change', *Organization Science*, 9/3: 396–410.

Jones, G. R., and George, J. M. (1998), 'The Experience and Evolution of Trust: Implications for Cooperation and Teamwork', *Academy of Management Review*, 23/3: 531–46.

Kets de Vries, M. F. R. (1995), *Organizational Paradoxes: Clinical Approaches to Management* (London: Routledge).

Lawler, E. J. (1992), 'Affective Attachments to Nested Groups: A Choice-Process Theory', *American Sociological Review*, 57: 327–39.

—— and Thye, S. R. (1999), 'Bringing Emotions into Social Exchange Theory', *Annual Review of Sociology*, 25: 217–44.

—— and Yoon, J. (1993), 'Power and the Emergence of Commitment Behavior in Negotiated Exchange', *American Sociological Review*, 58: 465–81.

—— —— (1996), 'Commitment in Exchange Relations: Test of a Theory of Relational Cohesion', *American Sociological Review*, 61: 89–108.

——— (1998), 'Network Structure and Emotion in Exchange Relations', *American Sociological Review*, 63: 871–94.

Lawrence, P. R., and Lorsch, J. W. (1967), *Organization and Environment: Managing Differentiation and Integration* (Boston: Harvard University, Graduate School of Business Administration, Division of Research).

McAllister, D. J. (1995), 'Affect- and Cognition-Based Trust as Foundations for Inter-personal Cooperation in Organizations', *Academy of Management Journal*, 38/1: 24–59.

Marshack, K. (1998), *Entrepreneurial Couples: Making it Work at Work and at Home* (Palo Alto, Calif.: Davies-Black).

Menger, P.-M. (1999), 'Artistic Labor Markets and Careers', *Annual Review of Sociology*, 25: 541–74.

Mickelthwait, J. (1989), 'A Survey of the Entertainment Industry', *The Economist*, 23 Dec., 3–18.

Morley, E, and Silver, A. (1977), 'A Film Director's Approach to Managing Creativity', *Harvard Business Review* (Mar.–Apr.), 59–69.

Murnighan, J. K., and Colon, D. E. (1991), 'The Dynamics of Intense Work Groups: A Study of British String Quartets', *Administrative Science Quarterly*, 36: 165–86.

Nash, D. (1955/1970), 'The American Composer's Career', in M. Albrecht, J. Barnett, and M. Griff (eds.), *The Sociology of Art and Literature* (London: Duckworth), 256–65.

Pedler, M., Burgoyne, J., and Boydell, T. (1986), *A Manager's Guide to Self-Development* (New York: McGraw-Hill).

Perrow, C. (1986), *Complex Organizations: A Critical Essay* (New York: Random House).

Putnam, R. D. (2000), *Bowling Alone: The Collapse and Revival of American Community* (New York: Simon & Schuster).

Ragin, C. C. (1987), *The Comparative Method: Moving beyond Qualitative and Quant-itative Strategies* (Berkeley and Los Angeles: University of California Press).

Rousseau, D. M., Sitkin, S. B., Burt, R. S., and Camerer, C. (1998), 'Not So Different after All: A Cross-Disciplinary View of Trust', *Academy of Management Review*, 23/3: 405–21.

Storr, A. (1985), *The Dynamics of Creation* (New York: Atheneum).

Stoppard, T. (1975), *Travesties* (London: Faber & Faber).

Strauss, A. L., and Corbin, J. (1990), *Basics of Qualitative Research: Grounded Theory Procedures and Techniques* (Newbury Park, Calif.: Sage).

Weick, K. E. (1969), *The Social Psychology of Organizing* (Reading, Mass.: Addison-Wesley).

——— (1996), 'Enactment and the Boundaryless Career: Organizing as We Work', in M. B. Arthur and D. M. Rousseau (eds.), *The Boundaryless Career: A New Employ-ment Principle for a New Organizational Era* (New York: Oxford University Press), 40–57.

White, H. C. (1992), *Identity and Control: A Structural Theory of Social Action* (Princeton: Princeton University Press).

——— and White, C. A. (1993), *Canvases and Careers: Institutional Change in the French Painting World*, rev. edn. (Chicago: University of Chicago Press).

Xaxás, X. (2000), 'Almodóvar de oro', *La Vanguardia*, 25 Jan., 31.

Yin, R. K. (1994), *Case Study Research: Design and Methods*, 2nd edn. (Applied Social Research Methods Series, 5; Thousand Oaks, Calif.: Sage).

Interviews

Almodóvar, Agustín, executive producer, El Deseo, SA, Madrid, 24 Nov. 1999, 1 Dec. 1999, and 9 June 2000.

Armas, Beatriz de, *Deputy-Director* General of Protection, ICAA, Ministry of Culture, Madrid, 29 Nov. 1999.

Capparós-Lera, J. M., film critic and historian, director of the Film-History Research Centre, and professor at the University of Barcelona, 20 Dec. 1999.

Huete, Cristina, executive producer, Fernando Trueba PC, Madrid (telephone interview), 12 May 2000.

Masclans, Angels, executive producer, Oberon Cinematográfica, SA, Barcelona, 3 Mar. 1999.

Pons, Ventura, director and executive producer, Els Films de la Rambla, Barcelona, 22 Dec. 1999.

Sufrategui, Paz, public relations manager, El Deseo, SA, Madrid, 24 Nov. 1999, 10 May 2000, and 9 June 2000.

11

Signaling Expertise: How Signals Shape Careers in Creative Industries

CANDACE JONES

Creative industries are 'goods and services' associated with 'cultural, artistic, or simply entertainment value' (Caves 2000: 1). In creative industries, each project or product is a unique and non-routine combination of inputs, demanding both creative skills and flexibility in the enactment of one's skills and careers. No two movies, buildings, or operas are alike, even if they draw heavily from a prior performance. Careers in creative industries such as film, music, fashion, architecture, and advertising are constructed around projects. The project is both the vehicle for creative output (for example, film, building, or ad campaign) and a participant's career, which is 'a succession of temporary projects embodied in an identifiable line of...credits' (Faulkner and Anderson 1987: 887). Projects involve matching processes whereby producers and buyers (White 1981) signal their interest in and qualifications to one another.

Signals include activities that showcase one's identity through prior projects (for example, commercial versus art films), competencies in skills and genres (for example, jazz rather than classical musician), and relationships (for example, beatnik crowd in poetry or population ecologists in sociological research). Signals also include attributes such as gender, race, nationality, and ethnicity and exchange parties make inferences about how these attributes will influence a match (for example, cross-national partnerships will require more work to avoid misunderstandings). Signals as activities and attributes convey information to others and as such are a form of strategic action, taking place under conflicts of interest and an eye toward consequences of decisions (Feldman and March 1981). Signaling as a form of strategic action is especially

An earlier version of this chapter was presented at the NYU Art and Commerce in Film conference, April 1998, the Sunbelt Social Networks Conference, Sitges, Spain, May 1998, and EGOS, Maastricht, Netherlands, July 1998. Paul DeLaat, Joe Galaskiewicz, and Joe Lampel provided helpful comments and insights. I thank Sharon McKechnie for her editing assistance.

relevant in creative industries where parties must solve problems, handle uncertainty, and fashion novel products during project engagements. By exploring how signals and signaling strategies affect project matches, we gain insight into how careers are constructed and how market niches and labor-market segmentation are enacted.

The goal of this chapter is to provide a theoretical model that integrates literatures from economics, sociology, and organizational theory to illuminate the signaling process and its influence on careers in creative industries. I identify the content of signals needed in creative industries, strategies for sending signals to enhance project opportunities and matches, and how this matching process of signaling shapes market niches, labor-market segmentation, and career stratification. The next section of the chapter outlines the guiding assumptions and defines the key terms, which form the model's theoretical foundations. The following section introduces the theoretical model, and illustrative examples, primarily from the film and architecture industries, are provided. Finally, conclusions and future directions for research are offered.

BACKGROUND: SIGNALS AND INDICES AS INFORMATION

Signals and indices as informational tools

Signals and indices are signs that convey information to others (Goffman 1959; Spence 1974). Signals, such as education, experience, and appearance, may vary from one 'performance' to the next, whereas indices, such as gender and race, are relatively fixed (Goffman 1959: 4; Spence 1974). A signal is multidimensional. For example, education conveys information about status by the institution attended, personal interest by the major chosen, and intelligence by the ranking achieved (for example, magna cum laude). Consequently, like language, the context in which the signal is used and its placement vis-à-vis other signals are critical for deciphering its meaning. Indices, in contrast, are observable attributes such as race, gender, age, and ethnicity, which are more difficult to alter from situation to situation.

Signals, such as 'cues, tests, hints, expressive gestures, status symbols' (Goffman 1959: 249), are used to predict behavior, value, or quality that is difficult to ascertain before it is experienced (Goffman 1959; R. Hall 1992; Darby and Karni 1973). When used repeatedly to make matches, signals develop into a signaling code and individuals invest in signaling reputations because that enhances communication about expected behaviors, qualities, or shared values (Spence 1974). Because signals are ambiguous, they are interpreted in the light of a person's past experiences (Spence 1974), and those who have more experience in attending to signals and seeing the outcomes of project choices are more likely to develop a tacit expertise in signaling.

Signaling as expertise

Signaling expertise in creative industries develops where (1) work is organized around projects with many diversely skilled participants who compete for project participation, (2) a lead firm or person organizes many of these projects over time, and (3) projects have relatively clear, timely feedback about their success (for example, a movie's commercial success, a building completed on time and on budget). When these conditions exist, signals can be used repeatedly to ease communication among parties, creating codes within an industry and reputations among players. In industries such as film and advertising with high turnover rates, signaling codes and reputations represent knowledge and expertise held by industry survivors, typically its most successful members. For example, Faulkner's study (1987) of Hollywood shows that only 7 percent of producers and directors made between 33 and 50 percent of Hollywood feature films during 1964–79. By deciphering the signaling code and discerning the signaling strategies, we see how industry members construct not only their careers, but also an industry.

Signaling as expertise involves both analysis and intuition (Prietula and Simon 1989). Analysis identifies and measures signals, tracking the relationship between a signal and desired outcome. For example, film studies have shown the importance of stars in predicting box-office rentals (Simonet 1980; Litman 1983; Sawney and Eliashberg 1996; Wallace *et al.* 1996). Thus, a star aligned with a project is an important signal to studios when funding and distribution are sought from them. As Robert Evans, CEO for Paramount during the 1970s, explained: 'A bare script with no "elements" [a director, a star or one of a handful of producers] usually remains on the shelf...the studio executive, whose job is usually to say no, will do just that' (in Squire 1983: 15). Intuition, in contrast, is often called a hunch or professional judgment and is honed through about ten years of intensive job experience (Prietula and Simon 1989). Mike Medavoy, Chairman of Tri-Star Pictures (in Squire 1983: 169), explains his cultivation of intuition:

I have always immersed myself in the work of the most active writers, directors, producers and principal performers, through seeing their movies, reading their screenplays and meeting with them personally. I also keep abreast of talent in the same way. That's the creative side. From the business standpoint, having negotiated or been responsible for the negotiation of countless talent and picture agreements, there are references to cash and expertise tucked away in memory that is always called upon. Formulas are connected to faces connected to credits. The creative and business disciplines blend via a sort of mental checklist which evolves over years and is the source of intuitive reactions when putting together a motion picture deal.

The quote above also highlights the contextual specificity of signaling expertise. The ability strategically to use and to decipher signals depends on an institutional context, defining the 'rules of the game' (North 1991). Signals and signaling tactics that are highly effective in one industry may be less effective in another industry because of institutional differences—differing rules of the game for what signals to use and how to use them.

SIGNALING AND CAREERS

Signals are context dependent; an industry defines what signals to use and how to use them. Thus, the first step in understanding signaling is to know one's context, since the misuse of signals may stall rather than spur a career. Although specific content of signals will vary by institutional context, creative industries are concerned with signaling content about identity, competency, and relationships—the *knowing-why*, *knowing-how*, and *knowing-whom* of signaling. In addition, parties develop strategies, such as status enhancement, reputation building, and impression management, to amplify, dampen, or deflect signals sent by or about them by framing how these signals are interpreted. Signaling content and strategies interact and are moderated by the more constant indices to define opportunity structures for participants.

Because parties match up with one another on relevant criteria sent through signals, buyers and producers are sorted into different salaries, classes, and jobs. This process creates market niches and labor markets. Each round of signaling, sorting out, and matching up generates new signals (for example, job experience, educational degrees, and so on) and revises strategies, which defines participants' opportunity structure and generates, through positive feedback, relatively stable market structures, career trajectories, and labor-market segmentation. These relationships are shown in Fig. 11.1. Each component of the model is discussed in detail below.

Signaling rules: the institutional and economic context of signals

Every person is embedded to various degrees in institutions (Baum and Dutton 1996; Dacin *et al.* 1999). An institution is defined by its 'rules of the game', which involve the informal and formal structures and enforcement mechanisms that humans 'impose upon one another' (North 1991). These rules of the game are reflected in an industry's macro-culture—widely shared norms and practices that guide actions and exchange relations (Abrahamson and Fombrun 1994; Jones *et al.* 1997) and are the basis for strategic action. Macro-culture contains knowledge about what exchange rules guide parties (Baker *et al.* 1998), how business and artistic symbols are manipulated, how claims on

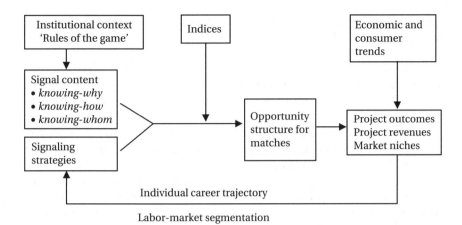

Fig. 11.1. Signaling and careers in creative industries.

artistic properties are invoked, and how others' reputations may be used (Baker and Faulkner 1991). In this way, institutional context shapes signaling content because 'information is not simply a basis for action. It is a representation of competence and a reaffirmation of social virtue' (Feldman and March 1981: 177). Institutional context through macro-culture defines what signals are appropriate and what signaling tactics conform to or violate industry expectations.

Signaling rules in creative industries are shaped by the dynamics of uncertainty, which are primarily due to sudden shifts in fads and fashions and product success (Peterson and Berger 1971; Hirsch 1972; Mariotti and Cainarca 1986; Faulkner and Anderson 1987). Thus, signals that reflect outdated consumer trends, overused genres, or a primary concern with artistic rather than commercial ends are seen as invalid by key institutional decision-makers. As Garud (1997: 87) points out, 'the more rapidly an environment changes, the more quickly does knowledge of what customers want become obsolete'. In this way, we expect that both the pace and the intensity of signaling among parties should match the level of uncertainty and pace of new product development in an industry. This pace should also influence the content of signals in an industry, such as showing that one's aesthetic style matches current market preferences.

Signaling content in creative industries

Signaling content provides cues about a player's identity, competency, and relationships. An identity showcases an individual's aesthetic style and creative skills. Competency is gleaned from a performance history that exhibits requisite skills and commercial viability. Relationships reduce uncertainty by certifying qualifications. These are the *knowing-why, knowing-how,* and *knowing-whom* of signaling.

Knowing-why: *signaling an identity.* Identity captures what is central, distinctive, and enduring about individuals and is reflected in career choices (McCall and Simmons 1978; Barley 1989; Hall *et al.* 1997). In this way, it is the basis for *knowing-why*—motives, interests, and meanings individuals have for pursuing a career (DeFillippi and Arthur 1994), which are often grounded in occupational roles and statuses and demand passionate involvement with one's work (Jones and DeFillippi 1996). As Parker (Chapter 7) points out in her research on contract workers, careers in these kinds of temporary engagements often demand that individuals define success for themselves and define who they are independently of an organizational attachment. In many creative industries, identities are reflected in one's aesthetic style and project choices. Aesthetic style relies on creative skills that are 'deeply and personally held forms of knowledge; they are rooted in an individual's values, commitment and beliefs about their craft, involving inexplicable issues of "good taste", intuitive leaps, and creative choices' (Jones and Walsh 1999: 10).

An identity that is clearly communicated to industry participants is also a means for differentiating oneself from competitors. Differentiation is a key aspect of developing a reputation (Fombrun and Shanley 1990). Aesthetic style defines an individual's approach to the medium, genre, and problem-solving techniques. Alfred Hitchcock's aesthetic style was defined, in large part, by a specific genre—the suspense thriller—and his style within this genre (Kapsis 1989). Project choice reveals the signaler's desire to target (or not) specific audiences and market niches. For example, Helena Bonham Carter's continued choice of British art film projects suggests little concern for commercially viable movies produced in Hollywood. Indeed, in evaluating the value of an Oscar for project pay, the *Wall Street Journal* suggested that 'to make it in the big leagues, she needs to trade her corsets for "Batman V" spandex' (Daspin 1998). Thus, industry participants create a distinct identity through their aesthetic style and project choices; they also locate themselves within specific market niches and shape their opportunity for current and future project matches by doing so.

Knowing-how: *signaling performance.* Performance reflects one's *knowing-how*—relevant skills, experience, and knowledge needed for competent performance in one's work roles and job assignments (DeFillippi and Arthur 1994: 309; Jones and DeFillippi 1996; Garud 1997). Performance is vital information that needs to be conveyed to key stakeholders when constructing a reputation (Fombrun and Shanley 1990). In creative industries, prior project performance, captured by project revenues, awards, or critical acclaim, signals one's potential to perform on a current project. Additionally, given the fads and fashions of creative industries, project performances that occurred recently are more valid as signals. For example, in a longitudinal study of screenwriters' careers, Bielby and Bielby (1999: 81) found that 'association with a project that has achieved great success in the contemporary marketplace signals the capacity to produce within currently fashionable genres, but participation in successful projects more than a few years old often signals just the opposite'. Thus, participants in creative industries who have more recent and greater project revenues, awards, or critical acclaim enhance their opportunity structure for current and future matches.

Knowing-whom: *signaling relationships*. Relationships in the form of collaborative skills and social capital comprise *knowing-whom*—'career relevant networks' (DeFillippi and Arthur 1994). Collaborative skills refer to interpersonal communication and mutual adjustment needed for highly interdependent tasks (Jones and DeFillippi 1996) and are critically important in highly creative collaborative tasks such as filmmaking. Alvarez and Svejenova (Chapter 10) describe how strong and trusting relationships form the basis of collaboration, creating 'symbiotic careers'. Social capital, on the other hand, refers to the resources created by and accessed through relationships (Coleman 1988; Burt 1992; Nahapiet and Ghoshal 1998) and facilitates locating project members with desired skills and behavioral attributes.

One form of social capital is extensive ties that provide access to resources and opportunities. Michael Medavoy, Chairman of Tri-Star studios, described the importance of 'relationships with many of the creative people in the business [that help in] selecting which movies we choose to make, figuring out what hasn't been done, making original choices' (Brouwer and Wright 1990: 10). Additionally, prior research shows that teams with more external contacts are more successful (Ancona 1990) and more productive (Katz 1982; Katz and Allen 1982; Trent and Monczka 1994). Another form of social capital is brokerage, where 'intermediary actors facilitate transactions between other actors' (Marsden 1982: 202). In film, talent agencies perform brokerage roles by linking creative talent with studios. Bielby and Bielby (1999) show how talent agencies 'certify' and 'signal' screenwriters' reputation; specifically, affiliation with a core agency earned a screenwriter 25 percent more employment opportunities and $50,000 more per year than similar screenwriters affiliated with peripheral agencies or with no representation. Thus, creative industry participants who signal collaborative skills and social capital, primarily through association with core talent agencies, enhance their opportunity structure for current and future matches.

Signaling content in many creative industries centers around three key aspects of information—identity, skills, and relationships. This information allows parties to sort and select those perceived as 'best matches' for a project. Signaling content is essential for understanding *why* parties choose one another. It also shapes what strategy is needed: do signals need to be amplified, dampened, or deflected? Signaling strategies, in contrast, explain *how* parties shape the information contained in signals, influencing the way this information is interpreted. We discuss signaling strategies next.

Signaling strategies: the art of amplification, reduction, and deflection

Signals are inherently ambiguous: the same signal may be used to convey multiple, often contradictory, meanings. For example, the length of time to complete a service or product may reflect either attention to detail for a quality product or inefficiency because of disorganized work processes. This ambiguity opens the door for strategic action—attempts to frame how signals are perceived so that others 'enact voluntarily one's own plan' (Goffman 1959). Generally, these strategies involve amplifying positive signals so recipients engage in halo effects by transforming the localized information into a global perception or dampening negative signals to contain damage to a localized area. Additionally, one may attempt to deflect a damaging signal through sending many positive signals, using contradictory signals to confuse, or heightening ambiguity about a signal to mask its meaning.

Several signaling strategies may be employed to define an event, person, or opportunity: status enhancement, reputation building, and impression management tactics. We examine these in more detail below.

Status enhancement. Status is one's hierarchical rank within some social grouping (Benoit-Smullyan 1944; Geschwender 1967) and typically involves 'being the object of many relationships that provide control over valued resources, authority and deference' (Knoke and Burt 1983: 199). Status plays an influential role in partner selection where quality is difficult to discern and outcomes uncertain (Podolny 1994). It is used for partner selection in more traditional industries such as investment banking (Podolny 1993, 1994), in the securities market (Baker 1984), as well as in the more creative industries such as the film industry (Faulkner 1987). When the skills and knowledge needed for partnering success are uncertain and intangible, objectively measuring them is difficult, if not impossible. Under these conditions, status is accorded to others based on the *perception* of holding the desired competencies. As Kilduff and Krackhardt (1994) show in their analysis of prominence within a firm, being perceived to have friends of high status was more important for predicting the parties' perceived job performance than actually having these friendships. In this way, status becomes an important means for managing perceptions.

Status enhancement strategies amplify a signal by giving it credence or legitimacy to be heard above competitors' signals (Rao 1994). For the recipient, status signals help sort the wheat from the chaff in prospective partners. Actors enhance their status signals by engaging in several different strategies: affiliation with high-status partners (Podolny 1994), recognition from high-status peers through winning status competitions, or indicators of material wealth or value.

The first of these strategies, affiliation with high-status associates, is an important signal of status providing prominence for the actor. Prominence is the 'extent to which an actor is involved in relations that make one an especially visible member in a particular social system' (Knoke and Burt 1983: 198). In essence, actors' status is defined by the status of their exchange partners. This is consistent with empirical observations. For example, Podolny (1994: 460) notes that 'affiliations and patterns of interaction become the basis for evaluation because they are presumed to be correlated with quality and yet are more observable than quality itself'. As discussed earlier, Kilduff and Krackhardt (1994) explicitly examined how perceived affiliations with high-status firm members boosted an individual's perceived performance by compatriots. A common strategy is to magnify the perception of high-status partners by engaging in 'name dropping' of prominent others. In terms described in the prior section, affiliations are concrete representations of quality, an intangible and elusive attribute.

A second status-enhancing strategy is to engage in and win status competitions such as Merit Awards in architecture, or Academy nominations and Awards in film. These awards signal a high level of competence and provide legitimacy by one's industry or professional peers (Rao 1994). These status awards are critical in the professions because status enhances client's perceptions of a professional's effectiveness (Miner *et al.* 1994) and generates esteem and recommendations from professional peers (Winch and Schneider 1993). Winning status awards opens up opportunities and provides a means for shifting to different market niches and labor-market segments. For example, Francis Ford Coppola explains how winning 'a Goldwyn Award for a screen play...set me up for my first alliance with the establishment [Hollywood]... On the basis of the Goldwyn Award I had won, Seven Arts offered me a job' (Baker and Firestone 1972: 54). At this point, he started making a lot of money and moved from the 'exploitation' market niche of horror, science fiction, and pornography films to working for the major studios.

A third status-enhancing strategy involves obtaining material indicators of one's status. In many industries this involves large salaries, perks, or corner offices. For example, actor Rod Steiger describes how status in film is gauged by pay: 'in Hollywood it all depends on your stature—who you are and how much you are being paid' (Baker and Firestone 1972: 117). Pay and perks can become contentious battlegrounds because of how they signal status, and thus influence perceptions of quality. Mike Medavoy, Chairman of Tri-Star Pictures (Squire 1983: 173), explains how: 'sometimes the talent and their representatives are insulted if they are not offered their last deal, even though that picture was a failure. As a matter of fact, they usually want more. Also, perks have become a new big problem in Hollywood. (The private jet is a "must" for stars today, almost more important than the deal—it's absurd.)' These strategies for amplifying status signals are a means for eliciting work on challenging projects, associating with highly skilled partners, and moving into and holding onto desired market niches.

Enhancing status through signaling strategies is often seen simply as reputation building. However, status and reputation are distinct constructs and, as such, can be inversely related. Status involves a partner's rank in the social group whereas reputation involves in-depth knowledge about a partner's attributes. One may have high status and a terrible reputation, as is the case with prima donnas. Reputation is discussed next.

Reputation building. Reputation is widely shared information (via third parties) about a person's character, skills, reliability, and other attributes important to exchanges (Jones *et al.* 1997). A women executive in film summarized a reputation as 'doing good work and not being too difficult' (Ensher, Murphy and Sullivan, Chapter 12, p. 242). Discerning these attributes about potential partners is critical in creative industries, where unique projects demand that parties work through problems and develop common understandings to accomplish their tasks. Reputation addresses not only the validity of signals but also their content. An individual's reputation is created by third parties that have deep knowledge of a party owing to prior exchanges (Granovetter 1985; Powell 1990; Uzzi 1997). By providing in-depth information about signals, reputation via third parties frames how signals are interpreted, and as such can moderate, negate, or even reverse their effects.

Reputation-building strategies involve the type and pattern of relations one pursues. The strength and pattern of these relations influence what information is spread and to whom; thus, relationships influence information flows, shaping how signals are framed by third parties. Strong relational ties, characterized by frequent interaction and positive affect (Granovetter 1973, 1982), provide greater control over information flows because parties share identities, expect fair dealing (Granovetter 1985), consider one another's needs and goals (Granovetter 1992), and exhibit behaviors such as trust, confiding, and information sharing (Uzzi 1997). Thus, reputational information from third parties that have strong ties tends to amplify positive signals while dampening and deflecting negative signals. For example, when a strong tie is asked about your technical experience, he or she may also tout your interpersonal skills and integrity to a potential partner. Strong ties may dampen negative signals by providing viable explanations to partners or deflect signals by shifting the focus from one signal to another—such as directing the conversation away from your poor credit rating to describing your recently released innovative product that has garnered national press.

Negative ties, those characterized by strong, negative affect, dampen positive signals by casting them in a negative light; this is called impugning or sullying another's reputation. For example, when someone has landed a prestigious contract, a negative tie might imply that it was won through bribery rather than merit. Negative ties also amplify negative signals by highlighting the informational content that supports a pejorative interpretation of the negative signal. Weak ties, those characterized by infrequent interaction and little emotional affect, disperse information widely and effectively (Granovetter 1973) but provide little control to an actor over informational content. Thus, as a reputation-building strategy, weak ties reach more people but are riskier, unless one exhibits pro-social behaviors consistently and has predominately positive signals. The consistent display of pro-social behavior means that one minimizes the potential 'dirt' about oneself that may be spread through third parties. Since few individuals are angels, weak ties may spread information that may be misconstrued or that one would prefer left private.

In addition, the pattern of ties, the extent of their structural embeddedness, influences information dispersion. Structural embeddedness is the extent to which a 'dyad's mutual contacts are connected to one another' (Granovetter 1992: 35). This means that an actor's primary and secondary ties are redundant; not only do you have the same friends, but their friends all have the same friends. Structural embeddedness is a function of how many participants interact with one another, how likely future interactions are among participants, and how likely participants are to talk about these interactions (Granovetter 1985, 1992). Structurally embedded ties are tightly knit, which provides greater control over behavior and predictability about information content. They also tend to produce convergent opinions as parties interact to discuss and compare common experiences. This enhances a signal's validity because 'there seems to be a general feeling that the most real and solid things in life are ones whose description individuals independently agree upon' (Goffman 1959: 87).

Control over the dissemination of signals can be strengthened if an actor spans a structural hole in the network/market niche. Structural holes involve a pattern of ties that is non-redundant (Burt 1992) so that participants in an industry or profession are segmented into cliques that an actor spans. In essence, structural holes segment information and potential partners into distinct market niches (cliques in network terms or audiences in Goffman's terms), allowing the actor who spans the holes, not the third parties, to control information. Goffman (1959: 49) suggests that this type of social structure reflects 'audience segregation', whereby 'the individual ensures that those before whom he plays one of his parts will not be the same individuals before whom he plays a different part in another setting. Audience segregation is a device for protecting fostered impressions.' Thus, the pattern of these relations influences who receives what signals and how they perceive these signals.

Another set of strategies that are widely used for influencing signals and how they are perceived are impression-management tactics, which we discuss next.

Impression-management tactics. Impression management is 'the process by which individuals change or manage several aspects of their behavior in order to create a positive impression on others' (Baron 1993: 204). Alvarez and Svejenova (this volume) describe how Pedro Almodóvar's participation in promotional activities and award ceremonies is an important part of building both his own artistic and his films' image for audiences. Goffman (1959) describes this process as unacquainted individuals gleaning clues from one another's conduct and appearance, enabling them to make judgments. Impression management is an important means for eliciting 'chemistry' (Nohria 1992) or 'sympathy' (DiMaggio 1992), which parties use to predict conflict, control, and ease of working together in their exchanges. Indeed, Nohria (1992) found that 'interpersonal chemistry' was an important component for participants in the 128 New Venture Group used for identifying leads and deciding to pursue further interactions that may result in inter-firm collaborations. Impression management is a vehicle for creating and maintaining personal bonds between parties and enhances the potential for future exchanges.

Impression-management tactics may be used strategically to amplify, reduce, or deflect signals. A key distinction between impression management and reputation building is that reputation building involves trying to manage information through third parties by the strength and pattern of ties, whereas impression-management tactics involve individuals manipulating their own behavior to influence another's perception of their signals. Impression-management tactics may be assertive or defensive (Stevens and Kristoff 1995). Assertive tactics such as ingratiation and self-promotion amplify positive signals by enhancing perceptions of the signal's positive attributes (for example, similarity, competence, liking), whereas defensive tactics such as excuses or justifications dampen negative signals by minimizing their impact.

Assertive tactics are comprised of two primary types: ingratiation and self-promotion (Stevens and Kristoff 1995). Ingratiation relies on norms of reciprocity and principles of homophily for its effectiveness, whereas self-promotion relies on a principle of meritocracy. Ingratiation tactics that rely on norms of reciprocity include behaviors of praising another to invoke reciprocal liking (Stevens and Kristoff 1995), or providing favors to invoke reciprocity so that the other will feel he or she has to return the favor sometime in the future (Gouldner 1960). Ingratiation tactics that rely on homophily—the tendency of individuals to affiliate with other individuals that are perceived to be similar in thoughts, behavior, and background (Lazerfeld and Merton 1954)—include opinion conformity, and expression of similar attitudes and values. Homophily has been shown to be an important predictor of interactions among parties (Ibarra 1993; Portes and Sensenbrenner 1993), and may be especially important in exchange conditions of high ambiguity and uncertainty. Ingratiation tactics amplify a signal through halo effects, where a positive experience on one attribute is translated into a global perception. Research on ingratiation tactics shows that parties who smiled more were thought to be more intelligent—although too many ingratiation tactics used simultaneously generate distrust in the recipient (Baron 1993). This distrust, suggests Spence (1974: 1–2), comes from assuming that the other party, 'knowing our interest in the matter, will rightly discount our signals rather heavily'. A key component of effective partnering is finding those parties who like one another (Nohria 1992); ingratiation facilitates this process when partners who like one another match up, forming market niches.

Self-promotion tactics magnify the possession of key attributes such as competence, social skills, and leadership (Stevens and Kristoff 1995). Self-promotion is achieved through three means: by claiming responsibility for positive outcomes, by embellishing one's contributions to positive events, or by describing how one overcame obstacles (Stevens and Kristoff 1995). Self-promotion amplifies positive signals by tapping into values for meritocracy where parties are pursued because they are perceived as the most qualified, which is an especially viable strategy in cultures like the United States or United Kingdom. Self-promotion facilitates the matching process of markets by sorting parties who have similar attributes and meritocracy levels. In this way, it influences the stratification of careers and labor markets based on differing levels of meritocracy.

Impression-management tactics influence the formation of market niches and labor-market segmentation by the way in which they shape the matching process among potential partners and potentially create stratification based on differing levels of perceived meritocracy. However, indices, such as age, gender, and race, may act as a drag on the effective use of signal content and signaling strategies previously discussed. Indices may exert a powerful influence on opportunities for matches, thus shaping how and what market niches are formed, who is stratified into what career trajectory, and exactly how labor markets are segmented. We discuss the role of indices next, followed by market niches and labor-market segmentation.

Indices: moderating effects on signals and signaling strategies

Indices moderate the ability of an individual to signal content and use signaling strategies effectively by providing a constant benchmark against which signaling will be evaluated. The critical indices for each industry may vary; however, discrimination within the USA has focused on race, gender, age, and religion. Bielby and Bielby (1999: 80), in their longitudinal study of screenwriters' careers, found that earning capacity 'decreased substantially with age, while minority and women writers have an estimated earnings capacity of approximately $30,000 to $35,000 lower than writers with otherwise identical demographic traits and years of industry experience'. Ensher, Murphy, and Sullivan (this volume) describe how women in Hollywood are underrepresented in some roles such as directors and directors of photography, whereas, in executive roles, women's representation increased 19 percent from the 1997–8 season to the 1998–9 season. As these findings suggest, for women, minorities, and older industry participants, indices shape career trajectories by restricting their opportunities for matches, where buyers and sellers exchange services and resources. In creative industries matches are seen concretely in who works on what projects and a career is defined by a series of projects.

Indices such as gender, race, or ethnicity influence access to opportunities, primarily because 'birds of a feather flock together'. This grouping and preference behavior shapes who resides in which market niches and in which segments of the labor market. For example, Popielarz and McPherson (1995) found that greater similarity on attributes among members reduced turnover and made groups more distinct from one another. Market niches may also reflect audience segmentation based on age, gender, or race. For example, a growing niche has been one aimed toward African-American or Latino audiences in film and television; this has resulted in an increased number but a restricted variety of projects, constraining career opportunities for those perceived to be in that particular niche. Grouping behavior based on similarity shapes opportunity structures. It can also transform previous constraints such as limited opportunities in film and television roles for Latino actors into opportunities, as US demographic shifts expand a market niche.

Signaling outcomes: market niches and labor-market segmentation

Market niches, especially in industries and services that are characterized by intangibles (for example, architectural design services, filmmaking, advertising), represent groupings or clusters of exchange partners who collaborate to perform complex work within distinct industry or professional areas of expertise, for somewhat distinct clientele. For example, within the commercial building industry there are distinct areas of building expertise with different clients such as courts and justice buildings primarily for local, state or federal governments, or commercial office space for real-estate developers (Jones and Lichtenstein 2000). Each specialty area represents a market niche within architecture that has unique building codes, works with different clients, and requires specific technical expertise. The same is true for film. These market niches in film are composed of Hollywood major studios, small independent art studios, African-American or Latino films, pornography, and other exploitation niches. Careers in project-based industries shape market niches and industry structure through the interactions of industry participants. In other industries, such as biotechnology, the career movement of personnel across firms shapes an industry by defining who becomes CEO of which new ventures. For example, Higgins (this volume) found that former Baxter employees played a disproportionate role in becoming CEOs of new biotech firms and taking them public. The matching of Baxter's former employees with new biotech companies has important implications for how the industry evolves.

The matching process by which partners form inter-firm clusters has long-term implications for participants when dealing with intangible resources and services. Since intangibles need to be represented by concrete signals, the most concrete signal is a final product (for example, film or building). The market niche in which one gains experience then showcases specific skill sets and shapes one's opportunity structure. Thus, initial experiences constrict or open up opportunities for work in different niches. In addition, status and image-management signaling promote stratification among potential players. Players are sorted into various levels depending on perceived importance, skill, pay, and so on. Thus, not only are niches based on end products (for example, in construction, a hospital versus a courthouse), but they are also stratified by positions within the niche and by the relative status of the niche itself.

The relationship between market niches and labor-market segmentation may be seen clearly in the US film industry, which is composed of a core populated by the major studios (for example, Columbia, Paramount, Universal). This core is inhabited by the elite, which has greater compensation, employment stability, and access to resources (Faulkner 1987; Jones and Walsh 1996). The semi-periphery is composed of mini-majors and B studios that make cheaper, less prestigious films primarily for the exploitation market. In contrast, the periphery, which is composed of 'fly-by-night' firms, inhabited by those who make one or two movies and then leave the industry (for example, pornography), involves lower-paying jobs, unstable employment, and limited access to resources. Jones and Walsh (1996) tracked the careers of 131 film subcontractors based on their work experience during 1977–9 within the industry. The initial position of subcontractors predicted their opportunity structure ten years later. Few who started out working for firms in the periphery (for example, exploitation films) made it into the industry core of higher-status firms.

This result can be explained in terms of signals. The experiences on films by lower-status firms were not seen, in general, as an adequate signal to move into a different niche, especially one at a higher level of stratification. These niches and labor-market segmentation are maintained through the matching processes that were described earlier. Since liking and similarity are influential in who gets matched with whom, preferential hiring of partners reinforces prior selections. Status competitions or success at the box office are a primary means available for parties to shift market niches and transcend labor-market segmentation. Status competitions alter the value of the current signal (for example, a movie with a B studio) through recognition from professional peers for quality. In addition, image-management tactics are critical for gaining initial opportunities, especially when one has little or no experience (Jones 1996), and are important for maintaining partnering choices. Finally, reputation-building strategies are important for defining niches, either by linking parties within niches into tighter clusters, or by segmenting these cliques from other cliques, both of which define the niche more clearly. Signals and signaling strategies, in these ways, lead to market niches and segmented labor markets. (For a more general framework of how careers shape fields, see Peterson and Anand, this volume.)

CONCLUSION

The purpose of this chapter has been to develop a model of signal content, signaling strategies, and their influence on careers, market niches and labor-market segmentation. We have explored what signals—identity, competency, and relationships—are important and how they may be used in creative industries. These signals may be amplified, dampened, or altered through three primary means: status enhancements, reputation building, and image-management tactics. In this way, signaling strategies influence the formation of market niches through matching processes, shape career trajectories through augmenting or diminishing signals, and generate labor-market segmentation through the creation of perceived differences and stratification based on attributes. Experience in these market niches and labor markets spawns a set of signals that shape an individual's career options in the next round of projects. In this way, the process creates stable social structures that influence but do not completely define opportunity structures for industry participants.

The chapter makes two contributions. First it integrates various economic, sociological, and organizational literatures to provide a simple yet comprehensive model of the signaling process. Secondly, it examines how signals and signaling strategies provide insight into career trajectories and labor-market segmentation.

The development of this model also opens up some directions for future research. At this point, very little work has been done on the content of signals and the dimensions of reputation that are required to complement one another for effective signaling to occur. For example, in architecture a key signal is excellent design. Yet it is unclear how architects signal design skills, and what reputational information accompanies this signal. This is a potentially ripe area for future research. In addition, research has tended to focus on either indices or signals but rarely examined their interaction. However, the interaction of the two may shape the strategies actors employ and which strategies are successful. By building a better understanding of their interaction, we may enhance predictions of market niches and labor-market segmentation. Finally, further study needs to be undertaken on signaling strategies. Few studies have examined how parties develop their signaling strategies. A longitudinal study that examines the processes of successful and unsuccessful signaling strategies would advance our understanding of the relationships between micro-strategy and macro-structure. Signaling strategies are critical for understanding how projects are formed and markets reproduced. This study of signaling content, signaling strategies, and market formation provides a wealth of opportunity for enhancing our understanding of how careers unfold and creative industries are constructed.

REFERENCES

Abrahamson, E., and Fombrun, C. J. (1994), 'Macrocultures: Determinants and Consequences', *Academy of Management Review*, 19: 728–55.

Ancona, D. G. (1990), 'Outward Bound: Strategies for Team Survival in an Organization', *Academy of Management Journal*, 33: 334–66.

Baker, F., and Firestone, R. (1972) (eds.), *Movie People* (New York: Douglas Book Corporation).

Baker, W. E. (1984), 'The Social Structure of a National Securities Market', *American Journal of Sociology*, 89/4: 775–811.

——and Faulkner, R. R. (1991), 'Role as Resource in the Hollywood Film Industry', *American Journal of Sociology*, 97/2: 279–309.

————and Fisher, G. A. (1998), 'Hazards of the Market: The Continuity and Dissolution of Interorganizational Relationships', *American Sociological Review*, 63: 147–77.

Barley, S. R. (1989), 'Careers, Identities and Institutions: The Legacy of the Chicago School of Sociology', in M. B. Arthur, D. T. Hall, and B. S. Lawrence (eds.), *Handbook of Career Theory* (Cambridge: Cambridge University Press), 41–65.

Baron, R. A. (1993), 'Impression Management by Applicants during Employment Interviews: The "Too Much of a Good Thing" Effect', in R. W. Eder and G. R. Ferris (eds.), *The Employment Interview* (Thousand Oaks, Calif.: Sage), 204–15.

Baum, J. A. C., and Dutton, J. E. (1996), 'Introduction: The Embeddedness of Strategy', in J. A. C. Baum and J. E. Dutton (eds.), *The Embeddedness of Strategy* (Advances in Strategic Management, 13; Greenwich, Conn.: JAI Press), 1–15.

Becker, H. S. (1982), *Art Worlds* (Berkeley and Los Angeles: University of California Press).

Benoit-Smullyan, E. (1944), 'Status, Status Types, and Status Interrelations', *American Sociological Review*, 9: 151–61.

Bielby, W. T., and Bielby, D. B. (1999), 'Organizational Mediation of Project-Based Labor Markets: Talent Agencies and the Careers of Screenwriters', *American Sociological Review*, 64/1: 64–85.

Brouwer, A., and Wright, T. L. (1990), *Working in Hollywood* (New York: Avon).

Burt, R. S. (1992), 'The Social Structure of Competition', in N. Nohria and R. Eccles (eds.), *Networks and Organizations: Structure, Form, and Action* (Boston: Harvard Business School Press), 57–91.

Caves, R. E. (2000), *Creative Industries: Contracts between Art and Commerce* (Cambridge, Mass.: Harvard University Press).

Coleman, J. S. (1988), 'Social Capital in the Creation of Human Capital', *American Journal of Sociology*, 94, suppl., s95–s120.

Dacin, M. T., Ventresca, M. J., and Beal, B. D. (1999), 'The Embeddedness of Organizations: Dialog and Directions', *Journal of Management*, 25: 317–56.

Darby, M. R., and Karni, E. (1973), 'Free Competition and the Optimal Amount of Fraud', *Journal of Law and Economics*, 16: 67–88.

Daspin, E. (1998), 'In Hollywood, Where you Sit is Where you Stand', *Wall Street Journal*, Eastern Edn., 231/55, 12 Mar., W4.

DeFillippi, R. J., and Arthur, M. B. (1994), 'The Boundaryless Career: A Competency-Based Perspective', *Journal of Organizational Behavior*, 15: 307–24.

DiMaggio, P. J. (1992), 'Nadels' Paradox Revisited: Relational and Cultural Aspects of Organizational Structure', in N. Nohria and R. G. Eccles (eds.), *Networks and Organizations: Structure, Form, and Action* (Boston: Harvard Business School Press), 1–22.

Faulkner, R. R. (1987), *Music on Demand: Composers and Careers in the Hollywood Film Industry* (New Brunswick, NJ: Transaction Books).

—— and Anderson, A. B. (1987), 'Short-Term Projects and Emergent Careers: Evidence from Hollywood', *American Journal of Sociology*, 92: 879–909.

Feldman, M. S., and March, J. G. (1981), Information in Organizations as Signal and Symbol', *Administrative Science Quarterly*, 26: 171–86.

Fombrun, C., and Shanley, M. (1990), 'What's in a Name? Reputation Building and Corporate Strategy', *Academy of Management Journal*, 33: 233–58.

Garud, R. (1997), 'On the Distinction between Knowing-how, Knowing-why and Knowing-what', *Advances in Strategic Management*, 14 (Greenwich, Conn.: JAI Press), 81–101.

Geschwender, J. A. (1967), 'Continuities in Theories of Status Consistency and Cognitive Dissonance', *Social Forces*, 46/2: 160–71.

Goffman, E. (1959), *The Presentation of Self in Everyday Life* (New York: Anchor Books).

Gouldner, A. W. (1960), 'The Norm of Reciprocity: A Preliminary Statement', *American Journal of Sociology*, 25/2: 161–78.

Granovetter, M. S. (1973), 'The Strength of Weak Ties', *American Journal of Sociology*, 78: 1360–80.

—— (1982), 'The Strength of Weak Ties: A Network Theory Revisited', in P. Marsden and N. Lin (eds.), *Social Structure and Network Analysis* (Beverly Hills, Calif.: Sage), 105–30.

—— (1985), 'Economic Action and Social Structure: The Problem of Embeddedness', *American Journal of Sociology*, 91: 481–510.

—— (1992), 'Problems of Explanation in Economic Sociology', in N. Nohria and R. G. Eccles (eds.), *Networks and Organizations: Structure, Form, and Action* (Boston: Harvard Business School Press), 25–56.

Gulati, R. (1995), 'Social Structure and Alliance Formation Patterns: A Longitudinal Analysis', *Administrative Science Quarterly*, 40: 619–52.

Hall, D. T., Briscoe, J. P., and Kram, K. E. (1997), 'Identity, Values and Learning in the Protean Career', in G. L. Cooper and S. E. Jackson (eds.), *Creating Tomorrow's Organization: A Handbook for Future Research in Organizational Behavior* (New York: Wiley and Sons), 321–35.

Hall, R. (1992), 'The Strategic Analysis of Intangible Resources', *Strategic Management Journal*, 13: 135–44.

Hirsch, P. M. (1972), 'Processing Fads and Fashions: An Organization-Set Analysis of Cultural Industry Systems', *American Journal of Sociology*, 77: 639–59.

Ibarra, H. (1993), 'Personal Networks of Women and Minorities in Management: A Conceptual Framework', *Academy of Management Review*, 18/1: 56–87.

Jones, C. (1996), 'Careers in Project Networks: The Case of the Film Industry', in M. B. Arthur and D. M. Rousseau (eds.), *The Boundaryless Career: A New Employment Principle for a New Organizational Era* (New York: Oxford University Press), 58–75.

—— and DeFillippi, R. J. (1996), 'Back to the Future in Film: Combining Industry and Self-Knowledge to Meet Career Challenges of the 21st Century', *Academy of Management Executive*, 10/4: 89–103.

—— and Lichtenstein, B. B. (2000), 'The Architecture of Careers: How Career Competencies Reveal Firm Dominant Logic in Professional Services', in M. Peiperl, M. B. Arthur, R. Goffee, and T. Morris (eds.), *Career Frontiers: New Conceptions of Working Lives* (New York: Oxford University Press), 153–76.

—— and Walsh, K. (1996), 'Boundaryless Careers in the US Film Industry: Understanding Labor Market Dynamics of Network Organizations', *Industrielle Beziehungen*, 4/1: 58–73.

—— —— (1999), 'Institutional Context, Career Competencies, and Knowledge Components: An Exploration of the US Film Industry', working paper, Boston College.

—— Hesterly, W. S., and Borgatti, S. P. (1997), 'A General Theory of Network Governance', *Academy of Management Review*, 22/4: 911–45.

Kapsis, R. E. (1989), 'Reputation Building and the Film Art World: The Case of Alfred Hitchcock', *Sociological Quarterly*, 30: 15–35.

Katz, R. (1982), 'The Effects of Group Longevity on Project Communication and Performance', *Administrative Science Quarterly*, 27: 81–104.

—— and Allen, T. (1982), 'Investigating the Not Invented Here Syndrome: A Look at the Performance, Tenure, and Communication Patterns of 50 R and D Project Groups', *R and D Management*, 12/1: 7–19.

Kilduff, M., and Krackhardt, D. (1994), 'Bringing the Individual back in: A Structural Analysis of the Internal Market for Reputation in Organizations', *Academy of Management Journal*, 37: 87–108.

Knoke, D., and Burt, R. S. (1983), 'Prominence', in R. S. Burt and M. J. Minor (eds.), *Applied Network Analysis* (Beverly Hills, Calif.: Sage), 195–222.

Lazarsfeld, P. F., and Robert K. Merton, R. K. (1954), 'Friendship as a Social Process: A Substantive and Methodological Analysis', in M. Berger, T. Abel, and C. H. Page (eds.), *Freedom and Control in Modern Society* (New York: Von Nostrand), 18–66.

Litman, Barry R. (1983), 'Predicting Success of Theatrical Movies: An Empirical Study', *Journal of Popular Culture*, 16: 159–75.

McCall, G. J., and Simmons, J. L. (1978), *Identities and Interactions* (New York: Free Press).

Mariotti, S., and Cainarca, G. C. (1986), 'The Evolution of Transaction Governance in the Textile-Clothing Industry', *Journal of Economic Behavior and Organization*, 7: 354–74.

Marsden, P. V. (1982), 'Brokerage Behavior in Restricted Exchange Networks', in P. V. Marsden and N. Lin (eds.), *Social Structure and Network Analysis* (Beverly Hills, Calif.: Sage), 201–18.

Miner, J. B., Crane, D. P., and Vandenberg, R. J. (1994), 'Congruence and Fit in Professional Role Motivation Theory', *Organization Science*, 5: 86–97.

Nahapiet, J., and Ghoshal, S. (1998), 'Social Capital, Intellectual Capital, and the Organizational Advantage', *Academy of Management Review*, 23: 242–66.

Nohria, N. (1992), 'Information and Search in the Creation of New Business Ventures: The Case of the 128 Venture Group', in N. Nohria and R. G. Eccles (eds.), *Networks and Organizations: Structure, Form, and Action* (Boston: Harvard Business School Press), 240–61.

North, D. C. (1991), *Institutions, Institutional Change and Economic Performance* (Cambridge: Cambridge University Press).

Peterson, R. A., and Berger, D. G. (1971), 'Entrepreneurship in Organizations: Evidence from the Popular Music Industry', *Administrative Science Quarterly*, 16: 97–106.

Podolny, J. M. (1993), 'A Status-Based Model of Market Competition', *American Journal of Sociology*, 98: 829–72.

—— (1994), 'Market Uncertainty and the Social Character of Economic Exchange', *Administrative Science Quarterly*, 39: 458–83.

Popielarz, P. A., and McPherson, J. M. (1995), 'On the Edge or in between: Niche Position, Niche Overlap, and the Duration of Voluntary Association Membership', *American Journal of Sociology*, 3: 698–720.

Portes, A., and Sensenbrenner, J. (1993), 'Embeddedness and Immigration: Notes on the Social Determinants of Economic Action', *American Journal of Sociology*, 98/6: 1320–50.

Powell, W. W. (1990), 'Neither Market nor Hierarchy: Network Forms of Organizing', in B. Staw and L. L. Cummings (eds.), *Research in Organizational Behavior*, 12 (Greenwich, Conn.: JAI Press), 295–336.

Prietula, M. J., and Simon, H. A. (1989), 'The Experts in your Midst', *Harvard Business Review* (Jan.–Feb.), 119–34.

Rao, H. (1994), 'The Social Construction of Reputation: Certification Contests, Legitimation, and the Survival of Organizations in the American Automobile Industry: 1895–1912', *Strategic Management Journal*, 15: 29–44.

Sawney, M. S., and Eliashberg, J. (1996), 'A Parsimonious Model for Forecasting Gross Box Office Revenues of Motion Pictures', *Marketing Science*, 15/2: 113–31.

Simonet, T. (1980), *Regression Analysis of Prior Experience of Key Production Personnel as Predictors of Revenues from High-Grossing Motion Pictures in American Release* (New York: Arno Press).

Spence, A. M. (1974), *Market Signaling: Informational Transfer in Hiring and Related Screening Processes* (Cambridge, Mass.: Harvard University Press).

Squire, J. E. (1983) (ed.), *The Movie Business Book* (Englewood Cliffs, NJ: Prentice-Hall).

Stevens, C. K., and Kristoff, A. L. (1995), 'Making the Right Impression: A Field Study of Applicant Impression Management during Job Interviews', *Journal of Applied Psychology*, 80/5: 587–606.

Trent, R., and Monczka, R. (1994), 'Effective Cross-Functional Sourcing Teams: Critical Success Factors', *International Journal of Purchasing and Materials Management*, 30/4: 3–11.

Uzzi, B. (1997), 'Social Structure and Competition in Interfirm Networks: The Paradox of Embeddedness', *Administrative Science Quarterly*, 42: 35–67.

Wallace, W. T., Seigerman, A., and Holbrook, M. B. (1993), 'The Role of Actors and Actresses in the Success of Films: How much is a Movie Star Worth?', *Journal of Popular Culture*, 17/1: 1–27.

White, H. C. (1981), 'Where do Markets Come from?', *American Journal of Sociology*, 8: 517–47.

Williamson, O. E. (1985), *The Economic Institutions of Capitalism: Firms, Markets, Relational Contracting* (New York: Free Press).

Winch, G., and Schneider, E. (1993), 'Managing the Knowledge-Based Organization: The Case of Architectural Practice', *Journal of Management Studies*, 30/6: 923–37.

12

Boundaryless Careers in Entertainment: Executive Women's Experiences

ELLEN A. ENSHER, SUSAN E. MURPHY, AND
SHERRY E. SULLIVAN

The typical configuration of careers has drastically changed in the last several decades. Driven by the forces of rapidly changing technology, global competition, and an increasingly diverse workforce, how careers are enacted has become increasingly varied (Arthur and Rousseau 1996; Hall 1996; Sullivan 1999). The largest growth in the US-workforce and many other workforces is in small businesses, particularly among women-owned organizations (Brush 1992; Wiatrowski 1994; Moore and Buttner 1997). This growth trend is reflected in the entertainment industry as greater numbers of women head independent production companies or entertainment support services entities (Coolidge 1999; Post 1999). In fact, 30 per cent of the new entrepreneurial ventures in the entertainment industry in Los Angeles County are headed by women (Dickerson 1997). The entertainment business depends on entrepreneurs, free-lancers, and contract workers; thus past researchers have suggested that this industry provides an excellent context in which to examine the boundaryless career (Jones 1996; Jones and DeFillippi 1996).

Specifically, we believe much can be learned about navigating this new boundaryless career environment by studying how creative executive women are helping to shape a creative industry. Gardner (1993: 35) defines a creative person as one who 'regularly solves problems, fashions products, or defines new questions in a domain in a way that is initially considered novel but that ultimately becomes accepted in a particular culture'. These women executives have creatively changed their careers as well as the industry in which they work in three major ways. First, because these women operate in a fast-paced environment that encourages risk taking, learning, and play (Leonard and

Swap 1999; Durant 2000), they are naturally more likely to choose or develop creative career paths. They have applied the skills, knowledge, and abilities they normally use to accomplish their jobs in the television and cable industries in original and useful ways to design their own non-traditional career paths. Secondly, because these women work in the male-dominated entertainment industry, many of them have broken away from traditional firms to create their own production companies or to engage in entrepreneurial endeavors. This freedom from the trappings of organizational rules, procedures, and politics permitted these women to focus on their passion to do good work and to connect with others with similar interests. They created organizations that encouraged new ways of thinking and new ways of designing work that permitted more balance between work and family demands. As these women succeeded, they inspired change in the way the industry did business by demonstrating the effectiveness of empowered workers, team-based, flexible leadership, and family-friendly organizations. Thirdly, these women have brought a female perspective to the industry and have pushed for more accurate representation of women both on and off the screen. These women have changed the type of programs being made by shifting emphasis from the female characters' physical attributes to their intelligence in order to provide a more realistic portrayal of women and how men and women interact. Off-screen, instead of focusing on traditional mentoring, these women networked with peers to form partnerships, share insider information, and provide support so that the influence of women in the entertainment industry continues to grow. In sum, these women executives have creatively altered traditional career paths, the way organizations and work in the entertainment industry are designed, and how women are represented on screen. We can learn important lessons from these women because their non-traditional career paths and choices may depict the future career patterns that many professionals will soon adopt.

BOUNDARYLESS CAREERS

The boundaryless career is one in which an individual travels career paths that are discontinuous and go beyond the boundaries of a single organization (DeFillippi and Arthur 1996). A boundaryless career is characterized by portable skills, knowledge, and abilities across multiple firms, personal identification with meaningful work, on-the-job action learning, the development of multiple learning and peer learning relationships, and individual responsibility for career management (see Sullivan 1999 for a review). This new career definition may more accurately capture the career experiences of women and may provide them with more and better avenues for career success (Sullivan and Mainiero 2000). Although women's focus on flexibility, skill adaptability, and empowerment may make them more suited to boundaryless environments, there have been very few studies that examine women's career experiences overall (Swanson 1992; Watkins and Subich 1995) and within the boundaryless career in particular (Sullivan 1999).

The entertainment industry is ideal for studying the boundaryless career, as it relies less on traditional organizational forms of careers and more on loosely structured, diverse networks of contributors (Sonnenfeld and Peiperl 1988; Miles and Snow 1994; Jones 1996). The findings on the status of women in the entertainment industry have been mixed. With the notable exception of Lauzen (1999), there have been very few longitudinal or empirical studies that have examined women's representation in the entertainment industry. Lauzen (1999) found that women who hold positions as an actress, director, or director of photography are still woefully underrepresented in these key jobs in comparison with their male counterparts. However, in other important roles such as producers or executive producers, women have either maintained their position or even made progress (Dickerson 1997; Ayres-Williams and Brotherton 1999; Parisi 1999). For example, there was a 19 percent increase in the number of female executive producers in the USA in the 1998–9—season as compared to the previous year (Lauzen 1999). While parity is still a long way from being a reality in terms of the full integration of women into key areas of the entertainment business, the successful experiences of women producers and executive producers contain some valuable lessons not only for women in entertainment but for women in management in general. It is surprising that few studies have focused on the entertainment business overall and women's boundaryless career experiences in particular.

The purpose of this chapter is to describe the boundaryless careers in the entertainment business by developing a model depicting career patterns of executive women as well as by describing strategies that enable executives successfully to navigate their careers. We begin by providing background information on the entertainment industry and the unique role that women play in this industry. Next, we describe our study participants and methods. We then introduce the career movement map and provide examples and anecdotes to highlight aspects of this model. Finally, we discuss specific career-enhancing strategies as well as practical and theoretical implications.

THE ENTERTAINMENT INDUSTRY

The entertainment business is a vital component of the US economy, foreign sales and exports of entertainment products totaled approximately $66.85 billion in 1997, more than any other industry sector (Krebs 1999). Regionally, the entertainment business was credited with extricating California out of its recession in the early part of the 1990s and is one of the state's largest employers (Lesher 1996; California Trade and Commerce Agency 2000). Approximately 250,000 jobs in Los Angeles County are based in the entertainment business and the number of jobs provided by this industry is on the rise (Dickerson 1997). The entertainment business and its related products are notable and controversial for their widespread influence not only on the USA, but also on worldwide culture. The entertainment business provides a rich context to draw from, as it operated successfully during the second half of the twentieth century in ways that preceded relatively recent business changes elsewhere (Balio 1985). These ways include a reliance on contingency workers, a constant need to respond quickly and efficiently to the mercurial whims of consumers, as well as the need to maintain a leadership edge in adapting to and integrating technology.

While the entertainment business has always been dominated by powerful men, women have also played an important role in this industry as it burgeoned in the early 1900s (Gansberg 1999). Women have made significant strides within some key positions, such as the executive ranks, in their ability to wield influence in Hollywood (Dogar and Diamond 1997; Sellers 1998; Parisi 1999). Perhaps this is due to their unique leadership style, their entrepreneurial talent, or their suitability for the career patterns found in entertainment. According to recent studies in leadership and entrepreneurship, women may be particularly well suited for a career within the entertainment industry for a number of reasons. Studies contrasting and comparing men and women's leadership styles found that generally women used a more democratic style of leadership than the directive style used by men (Eagly and Johnson 1990). These differences, however, were discounted because they were said to result from the demands of the task or job, or were the result of the stereotypes held by subordinates. Other work has uncovered particular motives and style preferences that women may use to their advantage. One of the first is related to women's desire to maintain and rely on relationships (Helgesen 1990). The second is the ability to exhibit behaviors of 'connectedness' essential in the interdependent and diverse work environments of today (Lipman-Blumen 1996). Connectedness refers to 'the use of the self and others as instruments for accomplishing goals... ethically and altruistically' (1996: 4). As pointed out in previous studies related to the entertainment business (Jones 1996), the ability to form relationships and effectiveness is indeed critical to success.

Recent years have seen a large increase in the number of women involved in entrepreneurial ventures. Some claim this increase stems from women's desire to move ahead in organizations and the only way they can accomplish this is by moving out of traditionally male-dominated organizations and developing their own businesses based on their own rules for success (Moore and Buttner 1997). Early thoughts about women entrepreneurs, for example, suggested that women do well in these roles when they have a high need for achievement, have an internal locus of control, and are likely to have had families engaged in entrepreneurial ventures (Bowen and Hisrich 1986). In addition, individuals who adopt entrepreneurial strategies may be at a competitive advantage in navigating a boundaryless career within the entertainment industry (Sullivan 1999). Moreover, because of the rapidly changing nature of organizational structures in the entertainment industry, women may be more suited to careers in this industry because of their more fluid career patterns. For example, Brush (1992) suggests that women entrepreneurs do not view their businesses as separate economic units, as do men, but instead perceive their businesses as part of an interconnected system of relationships that includes family and the community. Women business-owners, as opposed to male owners, tend to emphasize flexibility, team management, knowledge growth, and simultaneous management of work/non-work demands.

In summary, many of the external factors that dictate the nature of the entertainment industry appear to complement the values and motives that women bring to their careers. Throughout this chapter we will explore in greater detail just how these factors combine to provide a basis for success.

FIFTEEN EXECUTIVE WOMEN

The participants in this study were fifteen executive women with creative control, influence, and/or producing responsibility in the cable and network television industry in Los Angeles. These women represented a diverse group of successful entertainment organizations including networks such as ABC, NBC, CBS, cable stations and affiliates such as Disney Channel, Fox Family Channel, and independent production companies such as Pie Town Productions. Eleven of the women interviewed were full-time employees of their respective organizations and twelve of them had experienced at least a brief foray as an entrepreneur. These women all held high-status positions as vice-presidents, senior vice-presidents, or presidents of their respective organizations. Four of the women owned and managed their own independent production companies or were highly placed freelancers (that is, show-runners—the person in charge of managing a show, including hiring personnel, making creative decisions, and ensuring that the show stays on budget). The women in this study were all college educated and several had masters degrees in fields such as education or business.

The study participants were obtained in several ways. First, we used lists from our university alumni organizations. Thirty women appeared to be producers, production company owners, or production executives and were sent introductory letters that were followed up with personal phone calls. This method garnered only three contacts of the appropriate level who were interested in participating. We also used several personal contacts, which garnered two interviews. Obtaining an initial interview was often very difficult, as soliciting many of the interviewees took an exorbitant amount of initial phone calls and/or faxes (ten phone contacts prior to interviewing was not unusual). We were also challenged to run the gauntlet of assistants, public relations personnel, and a cadre of staff prior to obtaining an interview with each woman, as all of these women were high status and had many demands on their time. However, once we did interview them, they were all gracious, open, and very receptive to helping us to connect with other women. We were most successful at increasing our sample by using the snowball technique (Babbie 1986; Sias and Jablin 1995). With this technique, we asked each inter-viewee to recommend us to a colleague, usually at a different company, who met our criteria but had a different story to tell. This method led us to the majority of our interviewees. Although all of our participants gave us permis-sion to share their stories, we refer to them by a pseudonym to protect their privacy.

FIFTEEN CAREER STORIES

Semi-structured interviews were conducted over a six-month period. The interviews were approximately one hour in length and were tape-recorded and transcribed, garnering a typical response length of 15–20 single-spaced pages. Sixteen open-ended questions focusing on career history, career plans and strategies, mentoring relationships, and networking were asked. Sample interview questions included items such as: What drew you to the entertain-ment business originally? Describe your defining moment in your career. What career strategies do you use that are most helpful to you in your career? Describe any unwanted learning experiences and how did you recover? Tell me about the role of networking and mentoring in your career. What advice would you offer someone trying to break into the field? Probes related to each question were asked as appropriate.

Additional information about these women was collected from their bio-graphies obtained by their staff and through information from newspapers and trade journals. Throughout each interview, the women appeared to provide candid answers to all our questions.

ANALYTIC STRATEGY

The purpose of the data analysis was to answer two major questions. First, what career patterns emerge for these women? For example, what techniques did they use to navigate different stages of their career? Secondly, what com-petencies do they bring to these careers that are especially well suited for success? For instance, how did they approach setbacks and challenges in their career? In order to answer these questions, we used a qualitative data analysis technique suggested by Taylor and Bogdan (1998). In this technique, they argue that qualitative analysis should combine the purposes of identifying themes and finding new insights while also considering how these data fit within existing theories. The first approach most closely resembles techniques used in grounded theory (Glaser and Strauss 1967), described as 'discovering theories, concepts, hypotheses, and propositions directly from data rather than from a priori assumptions, other research, or existing theoretical frameworks', (Taylor and Bogdan 1998: 137). The second approach we used to understand the interview data can most closely be defined as analytic induction, or what Katz (1983) refers to as analytic research. Within this approach, the purpose is to fit data to existing explanations of social phenomena. One advantage of combining these two approaches is that it allows the researcher both to refine and to refute existing theory (Taylor and Bogdan, 1998).

In addition, we also followed Taylor and Bogdan's advice (1998) that the process of data analysis should be iterative and, therefore, begin with the first interview. In order to satisfy this goal, we spent time discussing which questions were working and which were not after the first five interviews. We decided to discontinue some lines of questioning, while looking to explore others in more depth. Once all the interviews were completed, the final data-analysis efforts involved rereading the transcript of each interview at least two times in its entirety. Three independent coders also read each transcript to categorize similarities and dissimilarities among the group of women with respect to careers, individual characteristics, and career advice. The coders' analyses were used to identify the final content categories to summarize the research findings.

The data from the content analysis was interpreted within existing career theory and used to identify those themes that appeared to explain unique aspects of these women's careers. We chose to use Jones' typology (1996) related to the interaction of boundaryless careers and project networks as a foundation for the development of our own conceptual model, as Jones' model was based on interviews with project workers in the entertainment business. Our conceptual model maps the progress of women's careers and incorporates their future plans (Fig. 12.1). In addition, we uncovered a number of important competencies that appeared instrumental in helping these women progress in their careers.

CAREER MOVEMENTS

One oft-repeated comment shared by the participants was their frustration in not having any 'maps or guides to tell them how to progress from points A to B'. Career researchers have echoed this frustration as well. As Sullivan (1999)

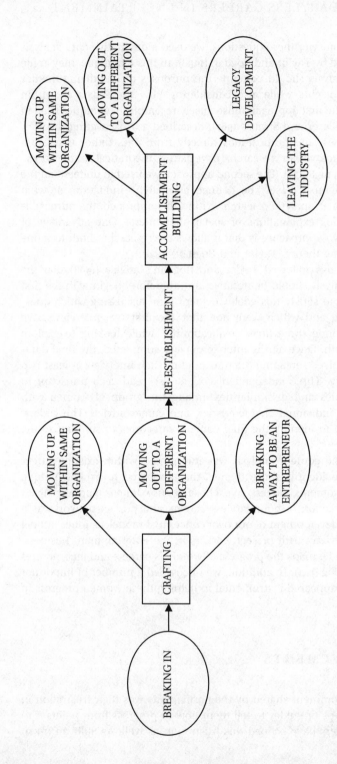

Fig. 12.1. Career movement map.

pointed out, there is a dearth of contemporary career stage models that reflect the complexity of today's career environment. In a notable exception, Jones (1996) used archival data and interviews with five men and women from various areas of the entertainment industry (casting coordinator, cinemato-grapher, grip/electrician) to create a four-phase model of careers in project networks. While this work provides an excellent starting point, it does not capture the unique experiences of high-status executive women in the enter-tainment industry. The model that we suggest is distinct from Jones' model of project workers in the entertainment industry in two important ways. First, nearly all had experienced at least a brief foray as an entrepreneur, usually fairly early in their careers. Secondly, nearly all of our women fast-tracked rather quickly and had to undergo periods of re-establishment and accom-plishment building.

Breaking in

Consistent with the observations by Jones (1996), the women in this sample demonstrated an extraordinary amount of persistence and drive in gaining entry to the entertainment industry. In addition, these women belied the myth prevalent in the entertainment industry that it is nearly impossible to break in without important connections. Indeed, every one of these women began her career with virtually no powerful connections. They used tried and true methods such as participating in internships, informational interviews, volun-teering their time and talents, and taking entry-level positions, such as pages (tour guides), secretaries, and assistants, to break into the industry. Most had little knowledge, and few skills or abilities beyond a college degree. They all had a fervent desire to work in the entertainment industry. An example of one participant's story is as follows:

When I got to LA I got a job as a restaurant hostess and didn't know a soul in the entertainment business. So, I volunteered to work on a Hispanic telethon. The day of the show the Associate Producer quit and the producer told me to do cue cards. So for 12 hours, not knowing Spanish, I did cue cards. I never knew where one word ended and the next word began. After 12 hours, I figured it out. After that experience, the producer offered me a job as a production assistant and I was so happy to be getting donuts and building sets.   (Kim, freelance producer)

Crafting

Our evidence concurs with Jones's observations (1996) that this initial career stage is important as it is the phase in which our participants learned about the industry norms as well as the unique culture of their organizations in their first, entry-level positions. In addition, in this phase these women began to develop a network, in some cases through formal mechanisms and professional organizations. They also began to develop formal professional relationships, create a reputation, and began informal networking activities. (See also Poehnell and Amundson, this volume.) In this stage, many of these women set goals for themselves. One participant revealed that:

I was an assistant at CAA [Creative Artists Agency] and it was a year of hell, I have to say. But you learn so much and the resources available to you are so broad that you can really educate yourself very quickly. The contacts you make are lifelong. My goal was not to get tracked as an assistant. The goal is to get yourself so good, so fast that you get out. I was up-front with my boss about my goals and she told me that if I stayed for a year, she would help me find my next (and better) position.   (Susie, vice-president of development)

Moving on

Most of our interviewees (86 percent) stayed in their initial positions for almost two years. Then the women's career paths seemed to diverge. All of the women in this sample found higher-status positions either by moving up in the same organization, by moving out to a different organization, or by breaking away to become an entrepreneur. Kate's experience was representative of many of our participants in the moving out category. 'I moved over from CAA and got my first executive job at Disney, which was a big jump to go from being an assistant to having an assistant (after three years of two entry-level assistant jobs)' (Kate, vice-president, production company).

A smaller percentage obtained promotions within their same organizations (30 percent). Mary, who was promoted seven times in a ten-year period while working for the same organization, is an example of the moving-up category and she shared her experience: 'I got a job as a college sophomore as an intern doing live Monday–Friday shows like Regis and Kathy Lee. Pre-production meetings started in the morning and I showed up early to meetings—it really made a positive impression' (Mary, cable news executive).

Interestingly, many of the women (80 percent) eschewed the relative security of being an employee and broke away to pursue entrepreneurial ventures, if not immediately following their first position in the entertainment business, then usually just shortly thereafter. Their reasons for pursuing entrepreneurial ventures seem to fall into two categories. The women left either to pursue higher-level work or to seek their 'big break'.'My problem was that I was too good as a secretary and couldn't seem to move up. So, I partnered up with another woman that I met at a networking event to form our own production company. Within five weeks, we had sold five movie ideas! Unfortunately, they never got made. After that I joined the executive ranks at Disney through being recommended by an old friend' (Linda, senior vice-president).

Alternatively, some of the women left to have more flexibility for their family. 'I started my own company from scratch and was so proud of myself because

I got a client right away. I did it to get more flexibility (in balancing work and family). I found out though that I am not really an entrepreneurial person and it was hard for me to do that' (Susie, vice-president of development).

After several years, most found that the entrepreneurial lifestyle was not for them, met with limited success, or were wooed back into an organization by an exciting opportunity. Several, however, found that the entrepreneurial lifestyle was conducive to their needs or allowed them the opportunity to realize a vision or provided a match to their values. As one production company owner indicated: 'I wanted to work in a place that was respectful, family-oriented, and allowed people to grow. People who work for me seem to feel the same way. I started the company with three people three years ago. Now we have seventy people who work for us and are producing six cable TV shows' (Terry, president, independent production company).

During this phase, these women learned many new skills that they carried with them into future phases of their careers. In this stage, many learned resilience, how to market themselves, and the importance of embracing growth opportunities. In sum, the two major reasons for pursuing entrepreneurial ventures cited by these entertainment executives—leaving to gain better career opportunities and leaving to find a better work–family balance—are representative of reasons given by many other female entrepreneurs in other industries as well (Moore and Buttner 1997; Winsor and Ensher 2000).

Re-establishment

After either moving up within an organizational setting or moving out to pursue entrepreneurial ventures, either temporarily or permanently, most of the women had a period of re-establishment. In this phase, the women had to re-establish themselves as professionals in their new setting. For example, if they moved up within the same organization, then they faced the challenge of gaining respect and sometimes managing former peers. For those women who moved out to different organizations, they needed to learn new players and organizational norms, and socialize themselves not just to a new position but to a new corporate culture as well. The women who broke away to become entrepreneurs found themselves faced with the terrifying and exhilarating prospect of seeking out new business, wooing former colleagues, and managing the vagaries of freelance work. In this stage, many honed their managerial skills and tried innovative ways of managing and connecting with others.

I sat down with the offer to start a cable division and cable network. The thing I had never done was start from scratch. And I thought, 'Can I do it? Can I build a team, can I get distribution?' You know there were a lot of things that I would have in that new job that I had never done before. And I liked being challenged—almost like being an entrepreneur but with someone else's checkbook. When I got to my company I wanted to create a place with no titles. I wanted a world where people didn't become obsessed with becoming a VP or Senior or whatever. I could not make it fly. But ultimately I used the team-management approach. Here we have a buddy system (i.e. legal and distribution hooked up) and by and large, it works.   (Amy, president, major cable network)

In this stage, many of the women found it critical to rely on their network. The participants were unanimous in agreeing that they tended to rely heavily on informal networks consisting of friends of both genders, rather than on membership in professional formal organizations. Many found that much of their social life or downtime was shared with colleagues in the entertainment business. One participant shared her story about being fired and how key individuals and her network helped her to recover.

The day after Thanksgiving they walked into my office and fired me. That night there was a big——party. I said to myself, 'I bought that show and I put the party together—I am not going to miss it.' So I went to the party and told everybody I was fired. It was in the Trades for two days. I wasn't going to hide. I have to say I was touched by the amount of support and help I got. People returned phone calls and made calls for me and I was calling Presidents of companies. Brandon Tartikoff was one of the first people to call me after I was fired and he guided me into getting into the network. Ultimately, it worked out as I got this job.   (Laurie, vice-president, network)

In sum, based on the experiences of women in this phase, it seems likely that women relied primarily on informal friendship networks for support, rather than on formal support groups. In addition, women were more likely to have diverse constellations of mentors and role models, which included powerful men and women in various positions and levels, rather than relying on a monogamous mentoring relationship.

Accomplishment building

The majority of the women in this phase were extremely satisfied in their careers. In this stage, many of the women indicated the importance of giving back to their network in a variety of ways. As one participant shared: 'I am serving as a mentor for others. I have two kids right now that have given me scripts. I've gotten many people their first agent. Sometimes I have a problem [in that I give] more time to other people than to myself' (Ann, writer and former production executive).

Some mentioned the importance of sharing stories, helping other women, or serving as mentors. In this area, many women cited significant accomplishments, such as winning an Emmy, being recognized by their professional community (that is, being named by *Hollywood Reporters* as one of the top fifty most powerful women in Hollywood), or making a difference by being responsible for high-quality shows.

Moving up, moving out, legacy development, or leaving the industry

What is next for this group of extraordinary women? When these women were asked where they saw themselves in the next five years, we received a variety of responses, which fell into one of four categories: moving up within the same organization, moving out to a different organization, legacy development, or leaving the industry altogether.

Developing a legacy was a concern of the highest-status women in our sample, who were already in the top positions in their organizations. These women were not as concerned with obtaining the next position as they were with leading their companies forward and making their mark. For example, one of our participants shared that: 'I really love what I am doing now because it is so full of possibilities. The next step is going to be losing that label of cable and thinking of ourselves as broadband. You have to think that in the future our content is going to be delivered nine million different ways. The question is are we creating content that is exciting enough, relevant enough?' (Amy, president, major cable network).

Only one or two of the participants seemed somewhat disenchanted and saw themselves perhaps leaving the industry in the near future. 'My main complaint is the lack of guidance and that I don't have a mentor. I am not sure if I will stay in this industry or not. I have yet to see a woman in this business in their forties or fifties who seems really happy' (Kate, vice-president, production company).

In this section, we have provided an overall map of career movement and mobility. In the next section we address specific strategies used by the women to navigate their own personal journeys.

CAREER-ENHANCING STRATEGIES

Through our interviews with these women we gained insight into career-enhancing strategies. Many women outlined specific techniques they used to advance their careers, while we inferred some strategies from the many stories they chose to share with us. We grouped these strategies into those used in connecting with others, such as networking, mentoring, and managing, and those strategies that promote and maintain self-reliance, such as self-management, and including the management of emotions or what is popularly known as 'emotional intelligence'. Rather than viewing these factors as a separate list of competencies or strategies, we chose to place them within the Connective Leadership Model (Lipman-Blumen 1996). According to Lipman-Blumen, networking and empowering management behavior are instrumental behaviors that specifically help maximize interactions with others. Self-management and the management of emotions are behaviors that map both to the direct style necessary to accomplish one's own tasks and to those instrumental activities required to develop good personal relationships with others. Finally, seeking out mentors assists in career development directly, in as much as it contributes to task accomplishment and to the development of relationships with others.

Connections with others

Networking. Research suggests that networking activities are an important connection with others that help in career advancement (Tichy 1981). Some preliminary work claims, however, that the way in which women network is in fact different from what is known about the networking patterns of men (Ibarra 1993). Within our current sample of women, one of the keys to networking appeared to be a person's professional reputation. Some women reported utilizing formal networking opportunities early in their career but relying on informal networks later in their career. As one vice-president said, networking really boils down to 'doing good work and not being too difficult'. Another said, 'I am just a very social person. I attend a lot of social events—a lot of dinners and parties. I talk on the phone a lot. I know so many people I don't really need to network' (Laurie, vice-president, network).

All the women appeared to recognize the vast importance of maintaining relationships in their industry. We often heard the women refer to the 'small-town' nature of either network or cable TV. They also talked about not using their personal relationships without giving something back. For example, Kate, a production company vice-president, said, 'I prioritize relationships and don't just call people when I need something.'

Mentoring. Mentoring relationships are often cited as one of the most important strategies for enhancing one's career (e.g. Kram 1985; Baugh *et al.* 1996; Ensher and Murphy 1997; Murphy and Ensher 1997; Ragins and Cotton 1999). We began the research process interested in determining the prevalence and type of mentoring relationships that existed for the women in our study. All interviewees were asked about the role mentors had played in their careers. A large percentage (close to 90 percent) reported having some form of mentoring relationship throughout their career. Somewhat surprising, however, was the form of the mentoring relationship. While approximately 50 percent reported traditional mentoring relationships with those a few career levels ahead, many reported relying on their peers for career support. For example, Bonnie, a woman who owned her own production company, said she looked for advice almost exclusively from women in her industry whom she would either consider peers or as role models because they were running their own shows. The

younger women, and entrepreneurial women, were somewhat less likely to
have had influential mentors.

From our discussions we heard over and over again that the type of support
received differed by type of mentor. Support appeared to fall within the categories offered by previous research (Noe 1988; Scandura 1992; Ensher *et al.*
2001). Those with male or female traditional mentors reported that these
mentors provided more in the way of instrumental support and they looked to
them for role modeling. Basically they provided insights into accomplishing
their jobs. Bonnie, a freelance producer, said, 'You need a male for the power
deal.' These women recognized that to open other doors the mentor needed a
power base. The women also, though, looked to peers for support. Most of
them reported relying on close friends for the type of psychosocial support.
Interestingly, about five women, who were in more entrepreneurial settings,
expressed pride about doing it relatively all on their own.

In sum, for these women mentoring appeared important, but only two of
them really identified a person who took them under his or her wing and
actually helped them with many aspects of their careers. It is interesting to
note that one of the few participants who indicated that she might leave the
entertainment business pointed to a lack of mentoring as being a compelling
aspect of her decision, which is consistent with previous research related to
organizational commitment and turnover (Ensher *et al.* 2000*a*). Many of our
women took mentoring where they could get it. Many sought out the advice of
others whenever and wherever they could. Despite the fact that few of the
women had senior-level mentors, those with more tenure in the industry talked
about the joy they associated with mentoring and coaching others and those
with less tenure mentioned the fact that they wanted to provide career guidance to others in the future.

Management/leadership style. We were curious whether operating as managers
and supervisors in the entertainment business required management styles that
differ from styles found in other organizations. As mentioned previously, some
of these women reported trying out new management strategies involving
teams and empowerment. Many also felt dissatisfied with some of the typical
male models of leadership that were autocratic, or with women who used these
autocratic styles. For example, one woman quit her job when, as she explains:

She was a screamer; she was just a terrible person to work for. And she did something
really shocking and it was so disappointing because it was a woman who was in charge.
She would love to call you in and tell you how awful you were. There was a mistake that
I had made and the way she handled it was to call me into her office and in front of
three other managers tell me that everything that I had ever done for the show was
awful.   (Kim, freelance producer)

Another woman, Terry, said that she did not like the volatile behavior she
witnessed in the entertainment industry and wanted to do something about it

by starting her own company. This woman prided herself on the way she managed and mentored others in her organization. She felt that nurturing behavior was scarce in the industry and she provided more to her employees than is typical.

Not all women, however, reported using these empowering types of management styles. For example, a handful of women who owned their own production companies were very excited by the control they could exert in the complete production of a project—from the concept, the writing, the filming, and the editing. But some women reported a need for balance between power and nurturing, as shown here: 'I think when I originally started that I was very worried about being pushy. Like if I were forthright with someone I would worry I would offend them. And then I realized how valuable that is. People need to be pushed. And also it is important to know when to pull back and not to be a pit bull...I think its personal for each woman. You have to find your style' (Susie, vice-president, network).

The women in this study understood and utilized connections with others in their industries. The importance of the type of connections appeared to differ by their current organizational setting. Those running their own production companies connected with colleagues outside their organizations and worked hard to provide an environment that encouraged the best from their people. Those who worked internally with an organization talked exclusively about their team members and the importance of providing learning opportunities. If these women had moved around from company to company, they also understood the importance of maintaining a network of friends and colleagues in the industry.

Self-reliance

The interview process gave our participants a chance to demonstrate many of the personality characteristics that one would suspect contributed to their current career success. Career development requires the use of many self-regulatory processes in order to engage in specific, useful career-enhancing behaviors. Manz and Sims (1984) identify self-problem assessment, self-goal setting, self-rehearsal, self-observation and evaluation, and self-reinforcement and/or punishment as important behaviors.

Collectively these skills are called self-management and refer to an individual taking responsibility for the managerial aspects of his or her job (Manz and Sims 1980). Direct application of self-management in organizational functioning has been examined in the context of self-management strategies for reducing absenteeism (Frayne and Latham 1987; Latham and Frayne 1989); as a method for socializing newcomers to organizations (Saks and Ashforth 1996); as an effective leader behavior strategy (Manz and Sims 1989); and as a method that contributes to team effectiveness (Cohen *et al.* 1997; Uhl-Bien and Graen 1998).

Furthermore, self-management has been suggested as a strategy for obtaining career objectives (Wexley and Latham 1980), used as a supplement to mentoring (Murphy and Ensher 2001) and can be particularly useful for entrepreneurial women (Ensher *et al.* 2000*b*). An additional component of self-management is the use of positive cognition. This class of cognitive strategies includes self-talk, mental imagery, and a focus on positive beliefs and assumptions to engage in constructive thought patterns. These strategies have often been used in sports psychology (see e.g. Kendall *et al.* 1990) and have more recently been investigated in the context of self-leadership (Manz and Neck 1991; Neck and Manz 1992). Neck and Manz (1996: 445) found that individuals who were trained in the use of positive cognition 'experienced increased mental performance, positive affect, job satisfaction, and decreased negative affect relative to those who did not receive the training'.

We found that many women in our study in fact used many of these techniques, although a lesser number mentioned them spontaneously. Amy, a cable network president, reported a number of behaviors that fall within those related to self-management. In particular one woman said, 'she felt very uncomfortable being comfortable...she was always seeking challenges that pushed the envelope'. She spoke about always asking 'what's next'. She attributed this preference to her place in the family. 'I'm the firstborn...You know I had to be the family pioneer. I was the older one: I went to school first; I kept going into one new environment after another after another' (Amy, president, major cable network).

It also appeared that the entertainment industry required a great deal of self-motivation and an ability to deal with uncertainty. This is in line with what Jones and DeFillippi (1996) found as indicative of the boundaryless careers in the entertainment field. As one woman in our study put it, 'I think you really have to be not afraid of taking risks. And I think you really have to not be looking for security. Because it's the most insecure business...I think you really have to have this fundamental belief in yourself that you can make it happen' (Judy, independent production company owner).

One woman suggested that you need to 'Have a goal and plan' while another said, 'you must have a vision'. But there were also a number of women who appeared more opportunistic, guided by an overwhelming passion just to do good work, to tell a story, or to interact/commune with people. These sentiments were especially strong among the women writers and program and segment producers.

In the popular management literature the concept of emotional intelligence has been touted as an important competency or characteristic that predicts a whole host of life and career successes (Goleman 1998). Emotional intelligence was originally defined as a person's ability to manage his or her emotions successfully and also to understand emotions of others (Salovey and Mayer 1990). The specific components include the ability to recognize one's own emotions or feelings as they happen; the ability to handle these emotions; the ability to engage in self-control to motivate oneself; the ability to recognize the emotions of others, and the ability to handle relationships. Within the context of leadership and career management, these skills are very important for working in close relationships with others as well as maintaining professional motivation throughout one's career (Goleman 1998; Murphy 2001; Riggio and Murphy 2000).

The women in this study exhibited high emotional intelligence, including the ability to manage their emotions and to understand and read the emotions of others. These same women pointed to a number of places where they exhibited a great deal of self-awareness. Phrases such as 'Making adjustments and working on the fly' and 'dealing with changes as they arise because TV is organic and parameters change' were typical of the women we spoke to.

A cable network president mentioned how the skill of reading others was very helpful in negotiations. In fact a very prominent person in the industry once told her the following:

'You know you always want the women on your team to negotiate.' When I asked him why, he said, 'Because a woman never walks into this room the same way twice.' He said, 'With a man, you know exactly how that guy negotiates. That guy's a tough one, that guy skips on this, that guy [********] 'cause they repeat their behaviors over and over and over.' He said, 'With a woman he never knows what the next day is going to bring, 'cause they're able to keep the other side slightly off balance and it's a great strength for a business.' (Amy, president, major cable network)

Emotional/social skills appeared to be more characteristic of the more tenured women. Many from this group were able to articulate many of their strengths and weaknesses when it came to understanding themselves and others. Also, when asked to reflect on the type of mistakes they had made, many of the higher-level women related incidents about when they learned important lessons in recovering from mistakes and improving their future actions. 'I remember learning early on not to panic. I had to learn that the hard way. I panicked over a deadline and I went and grabbed a tape off someone's shelf. Unfortunately, I grabbed the wrong one. But I did recover in the end by taking responsibility and admitting my mistake' (Beth, vice-president, cable network).

Those skills that involve careful management of emotions transcend situations and appear to contribute in other areas relating to connections with others. One network producer, Stacie, put it this way: 'there is nothing wrong with thoughtful politics.' Another woman, Nancy, a vice-president, offered the following: 'There is a market for people who are conscientious about their work and low maintenance. ... I've cleared a path for myself because of that. I don't bring drama. I don't go into the situation and create drama. I figured out a long time ago people are hiring me not to make me the boss, but so that I can make them look better' (Nancy, cable industry vice-president, programming and development).

In sum, research suggests that individuals need strong self-management skills and high emotional intelligence for career success. These qualities may be especially important in boundaryless environments, like the entertainment industry, that require strong self-motivation and the ability to manage inter-connected relationships in order to accomplish objectives.

CONCLUSION

The purpose of this study was to talk to women executives in the entertainment industry to learn how they creatively shaped their careers and brought changes to this creative industry. (See also Peterson and Anand, Chapter 13, on how careers shape fields.) Not surprisingly, the women we studied shared many of the same characteristics and goals of the other creative individuals discussed in other chapters of this book. First, like the managers and professionals seeking alternative workload arrangements studied by Buck, Lee, and MacDermid (Chapter 5), some of the women we interviewed broke from male-dominated organizations in order creatively to balance their work and life demands. These women started firms to gain flexibility and offered jobs to others also seeking a more family-oriented work environment. Both our study and the work of Buck and associates illustrate the impact of non-work forces on career decisions and the lessening of boundaries between the work and non-work domains. Secondly, much like Spanish film director Pedro Almodóvar (Alvarez and Svejenova, Chapter 10), some of the executive women we studied became entrepreneurs in order to follow their own passions. By gaining control over work design and structures, both Almodóvar and the women in our study were able to release their creativity from the boundaries of organizational rules and procedures and focus on projects that they found personally meaningful. Thirdly, the women we interviewed used their *knowing-how, knowing-why* and *knowing-whom* competencies to weave career paths different from the traditi-onal careers and to develop projects different from the projects typically found in the male-based entertainment industry. Their careers were strengthened by the connections and networks they built as they moved from project to project and firm to firm. As described by Jones (Chapter 11), the women developed reputations, expertise, and connections and learned to signal these compe-tencies to others in the business. For example, many of the women began their careers as assistants, secretaries, or in other entry-level positions so that they could learn the basic rules of the game of the entertainment industry—that is, the context in which signals were interpreted. Many of the women emphasized developing good collaborative relationships and avoided being tagged as 'drama queens' so they would gain reputations as solid professionals.

While this chapter adds significantly to our knowledge regarding creative careers, there are several methodological limitations that must be addressed.

First, this study relies on a small sample of extraordinarily successful women from primarily the television industry, many of whom have gained distinction in the cable industry. Cable television became a significant competitive force only during the 1990s and thus perhaps has presented a more open playing field for women. A future study comparing women in TV with their counterparts in the motion picture industry might present a very different picture. Also, the women in this sample were all quite advanced in their careers and had the benefit of hindsight and an existing network of relationships. Future research that provides a more comprehensive perspective of women in the creative industry by interviewing women at the beginning of their careers would be very enlightening and might lead to very different conclusions.

Another limitation of this study is in the homogeneity of the sample with respect to ethnicity, as all of our study participants were white. In recent years, Hollywood, and in particular the TV industry, has been severely criticized by the African-American and Latino communities for the lack of representation behind and in front of the camera (Braxton 1999). Indeed, the *Hollywood Reporter*'s most recent published list of the 100 most powerful women in Hollywood (Grosz 2001) revealed a glaring lack of non-white female power-brokers. Listening to the stories of women of color might reveal an entirely new set of strategies and challenges. In addition, although we celebrate the successes of these women, as noted earlier our exuberance is tempered by the fact that parity for women in other key positions in the entertainment business has not been achieved (Lauzen 1999). As more women gain power in executive positions, they will likely enable women in other key positions, such as directors, directors of photography, and actors, to make significant strides as well. In sum, while this study is an important first step in contributing to our understanding of the mobility of executive women in the TV industry, we must continue to increase our knowledge of women's creative careers in other aspects of the entertainment business, including the film industry and for those in both- above and below-the-line positions.[1]

This study makes three distinct contributions to the understanding of the boundaryless career concept and the careers of women. First, although recently there has been an increase in conceptualizations about boundaryless careers (Arthur and Rousseau 1996; Hall 1996; Sullivan *et al.* 1998), there have been relatively few studies that have examined these newer career types or the experiences of women in non-traditional career settings (Sullivan 1999). The entertainment industry is ideal for studying the boundaryless career, because it does not support traditional organizational forms or careers (Sonnenfeld and

---

[1] In the entertainment business, for TV and motion picture budgets a distinction is made between expenditures for personnel who are seen as fixed costs (i.e. grips, extras, day players, line producers, etc.) and those whose values and thus salaries can fluctuate wildly (i.e. actors, directors, and producers). Those who are seen as fixed costs are referred to as 'below the line'. Those whose salaries vary dramatically are often referred to as 'above the line' personnel or 'talent' and are perceived as making a distinct creative contribution to the project.

Peiperl 1988; Miles and Snow 1994). Our study illustrates how the careers of these women executives exhibit the hallmarks of the boundaryless career, especially on-the-job action learning, the development of multiple peer learning relationships, and self-management. By examining the fluid structures of the careers and organizations in this industry, we may be able to develop a framework of how other organizations are evolving in response to rapid technological change and increased global competition. The entertainment industry may be indicative of the future of many other industries as we move away from traditional organizational structures.

Secondly, this study provides important insights into the career development of executive women. Relatively little research has been conducted on the career experiences of women (Gallos 1989; Powell and Mainiero 1992, 1993). The traditional career stage models, which have dominated much of career research, were developed to explain the careers of men, were tested primarily with male samples, and fail to apply to the majority of women (Roberts and Newton 1987; Ornstein and Isabella 1990; Smart and Peterson 1994). Although a separate theory of career development for women has been called for (Gallos 1989; Tharenou et al. 1994; Sullivan 1999), no such theory has been developed. The career map of executive women proposed in this chapter may provide a starting point for the development of such a theory. By examining women's careers not as a linear progression from one promotion to another, but as a process of creative growth and development, the map suggests that women may re-evaluate and redefine their career choices at key points in their careers. For example, while some women in our study continued in the same firm, others left the relative safety of an organization to develop entrepreneurial ventures. Moreover, our study found that these women rose relatively rapidly in a traditionally male-dominated industry. It has been suggested that the boundaryless career era may be more effective at leveling the career playing field than previous attempts, including discrimination laws and affirmative action (Sullivan and Mainiero 2000). Women may be more successful than men in working in newer organizational forms where empowerment, relationships, and team skills are emphasized over competition (Cooper et al. 1993; Fletcher 1996; Hall 1996; Hall and Mirvis 1996). The abilities most associated with being effective in boundaryless careers (for example, focus on process over outcomes, cooperation, and greater sensitivity to employees' needs), are typically defined in US culture as feminine traits (Gallos 1989; Fondas 1996). Future research needs to extend this study and investigate whether women are better suited to boundaryless careers and advance more quickly in newer organizational structures.

Thirdly, this study provides important insights into careers in creative industries. Surprisingly, the management literature is relatively bereft of studies related to the entertainment business, even though it is one of the most profitable and, arguably, influential industries in the United States. Furthermore, there have been few books or articles written about women's unique experiences in creative industries. For example, although Phillips (1991), Obst (1996), and Hamsher (1997) provide first-hand accounts of the challenges, opportunities, and pitfalls of being powerful women in the entertainment business, they offer few specific strategies for women entering male-dominated fields or for enhancing the success of the boundaryless careerist. Jobs in industrialized nations are becoming increasingly knowledge and creative focused, while manual and clerical jobs are being replaced by technology. By understanding the careers of these women, we may gain a greater understanding of how most jobs will be enacted in the future.

In sum, this study has: (1) expanded our knowledge of new career patterns, especially of those who moved away from the boundaries of the traditional organization and explored entrepreneurial activities; (2) expanded our understanding of the career experiences and strategies of women who have successfully navigated in a male-dominated industry and offer suggestions to women seeking such executive positions, and (3) re-examined the importance of traditional mentoring and further explored the use of peer learning to support and maintain a boundaryless career. Sullivan's recent review (1999) of the career literature indicates that, although the number of studies on the newer career forms is increasing, relatively few have provided an in-depth analysis of boundaryless careers, and even fewer have examined the boundaryless career experiences of women. Thus, while the popular press proclaims 'The End of the Job' (Bridges 1994) and a 'Free Agent Nation' (Pink 1997–8), and while more organizations are implementing new career management systems (Hall 1996), academic research continues to lag behind the development of this important new career phenomenon. It is hoped that this study will encourage future research into boundaryless careers.

REFERENCES

Arthur, M. B., and Rousseau, D. M. (1996), 'The Boundaryless Career as a New Employment Principle', in M. B. Arthur and D. M. Rousseau (eds.), *The Boundaryless Career: A New Employment Principle for a New Organizational Era* (New York: Oxford University Press), 3–20.

Ayres-Williams, R., and Brotherton, P. (1999), 'Five Hot Business Fields for Women', *Black Enterprise*, 30/2: 107–14.

Babbie, E. (1986), *The Practice of Social Research* (Belmont, Calif.: Wadsworth Publishing Company).

Balio, T. (1985), *The American Film Industry*, 2nd edn. (Madison: University of Wisconsin Press).

Baugh, S. G., Lankau, M. J., and Scandura, T. A. (1996), 'An Investigation of the Effects of Protégé Gender on Responses to Mentoring', *Journal of Vocational Behavior*, 49: 309–23.

Bowen, D. D., and Hisrich, R. D. (1986), 'The Female Entrepreneur: A Career Development Perspective', *Academy of Management Review*, 11: 393–407.

Braxton, G. (1999), 'The Guild Joins Push for Diversity', *Los Angeles Times*, 27 Oct., F1.

Bridges, W. (1994), 'The End of the Job', *Fortune*, 19 Sept., 62–74.

Brush, C. G. (1992), 'Research on Women Business Owners: Past Trends, A New Perspective and Future Directions', *Entrepreneurship Theory and Practice*, 5–30.

California Trade and Commerce Agency (2000), *California: An Economic Profile* (Sacramento, Calif.: California Trade and Commerce Agency, Jan.), http://commerce. ca.gov.economy.

Cohen, S. G., Chang, L., and Ledford, G. E. (1997), 'A Hierarchical Construct of Self-Management Leadership and its Relationship to Quality of Work Life and Perceived Work Group Effectiveness', *Personnel Psychology*, 50: 275–309.

Coolidge, S. D. (1999), 'Hollywood's New Heroines: Entrepreneurial Women Claim More of an Industry's Key Roles', *Christian Science Monitor*, 13 Sept., 15–18.

Cooper, W. H., Graham, W. J., and Dyke, S. (1993), 'Tournament Players', in G. R. Ferris (ed.), *Research in Personnel and Human Resource Management* (Greenwich, Conn.: JAI Press), 83–132.

DeFillippi, R. J., and Arthur, M. B. (1996), 'Boundaryless Contexts and Careers: A Competency-Based Perspective', in M. B. Arthur and D. M. Rousseau (eds.), *The Boundaryless Career: A New Employment Principle for a New Organizational Era* (New York: Oxford University Press), 116–31.

Dickerson, M. (1997), 'Ready, Ms. De Mille: Women Shaking up Hollywood with Start-Ups', *Los Angeles Times*, 3 Sept., D1–2.

Dogar, R., and Diamond, J. (1997), 'Who's Who in Hollywood', *Working Woman*, 22/11: 36–9.

Durant, R. (2000), 'Open to the Source: Synchronicity and Creativity in Organizations', working paper.

Eagly, A. H., and Johnson, B. T. (1990) 'Gender and Leadership Style: A Meta-Analytic Study', *Psychological Bulletin*, 108: 233–56.

Ensher, E. A., and Murphy, S. E. (1997), 'Effect of Race, Gender, Perceived Similarity, and Contact on Mentor Relationships', *Journal of Vocational Behavior*, 50: 460–81.

——Donaldson, S. I., and Grant-Vallone, E. (2000*a*), 'Longitudinal Examination of Mentoring Relationships on Organizational Commitment and Citizenship Behavior', *Journal of Career Development*, 26/4: 233–47.

——Murphy, S. E., and Vance, C. M. (2000*b*), 'Mentoring and Self-Management Career Strategies for Entrepreneurs', *International Journal of Entrepreneurship*, 1/2: 99–108.

——Thomas, C., and Murphy, S. E. (2001), 'Comparison of Traditional, Step-Ahead, and Peer Mentoring on Protégés' Support, Satisfaction, and Perceptions of Career Success: A Social Exchange Perspective', *Journal of Business and Psychology*, 15: 419–38.

Fletcher, J. K. (1996), 'A Relational Approach to the Protean Career', in D. T. Hall (ed.), *The Career is Dead: Long Live the Career* (San Francisco: Jossey-Bass), 105–31.

Fondas, N. (1996), 'Feminization at Work: Career Implications', in M. B. Arthur and D. M. Rousseau (eds.), *The Boundaryless Career: A New Employment Principle for a New Organizational Era* (New York: Oxford University Press), 282–93.

Frayne, C., and Latham, G. (1987), 'Application of Social Learning Theory to Employee Self-Management of Attendance', *Journal of Applied Psychology*, 72: 387–92.

Gallos, J. V. (1989), 'Exploring Women's Development: Implications for Career Theory, Practice, and Research', in M. B. Arthur, D. T. Hall, and B. S. Lawrence (eds.), *Handbook of Career Theory* (New York: Cambridge University Press), 110–32.

Gansberg, A. L. (1999), 'Chronology: Notable Moments for Women in the Entertainment History', *Hollywood Reporter* (Dec.), 56.

Gardner, H. (1993), *Creating Minds* (New York: Basic Books).

Glaser, B. G., and Strauss, A. (1967), *The Discovery of Grounded Theory: Strategies for Qualitative Research* (Chicago: Aldine).

Goleman, D. (1998), *Working with Emotional Intelligence* (New York: Bantam Books).

Grosz, C. (2001), 'Women in Entertainment: The Power 100', *Hollywood Reporter*, 321/9: 9–63.

Hall, D. T. (1996), 'Long Live the Career', in D. T. Hall and Associates, *The Career is Dead: Long Live the Career* (San Francisco: Jossey-Bass), 1–12.

—— and Mirvis, P. H. (1996), 'Careers as Life-Long Learning', in A. Howard (ed.), *The Changing Nature of Work* (San Francisco: Jossey-Bass), 323–61.

Hamsher, J. (1997), *Killer Instincts* (New York: Broadway Books).

Helgesen, S. (1990), *The Female Advantage: Women's Ways of Leadership* (New York: Doubleday Currency).

Ibarra, H. (1993), 'Personal Networks of Women and Minorities in Management: A Conceptual Framework', *Academy of Management Review*, 18/1: 56–87.

Jones, C. (1996), 'Careers in Project Networks: The Case of the Film Industry', in M. B. Arthur and D. M. Rousseau (eds.), *The Boundaryless Career: A New Employment Principle for a New Organizational Era* (New York: Oxford University Press), 58–75.

—— and DeFillippi, R. J. (1996), 'Back to the Future in Film: Combining Industry and Self-Knowledge to Meet the Career Challenges of the 21st Century', *Academy of Management Executive*, 10/4: 89–103.

Katz, J. (1983), 'A Theory of Qualitative Methodology: The Social Science System of Analytic Fieldwork', in R. M. Emerson (ed.), *Contemporary Field Research* (Boston: Little, Brown), 127–48.

Kendall, G., Hrycaiko, D., Martin, G. L., and Kendall, T. (1990), 'The Effects of an Imagery Rehearsal, Relaxation, and Self-Talk Package on Basketball Game Performance', *Journal of Counseling Psychology*, 32: 263–71.

Kram, K. E. (1985), *Mentoring at Work: Developmental Relationships in Organizational Life* (Glenview, Ill.: Scott Foresman).

Krebs, B. (1999), 'Entertainment Industry Leading Manufacturing Sector', *Newsbytes News Network*, 16 Dec.

Latham, G. P., and Frayne, C. A. (1989), 'Self-Management Training for Increasing Job Attendance: A Follow-up and Replication', *Journal of Applied Psychology*, 74: 411–16.

Lauzen, M. (1999), 'By the Numbers', *Hollywood Reporter* (Dec.), 72.

Leonard, D., and Swap, W. C. (1999), *When Sparks Fly: Igniting Creativity in Groups* (Boston: Harvard Business School Press).

Lesher, D. (1996), 'Wall Street Firm Upgrades State's Credit Rating', *Los Angeles Times*, 27 Feb., A1.

Lipman-Blumen, J. (1996), *The Connective Edge: Leading in an Interdependent World* (San Francisco: Jossey-Bass).

Manz, C. C., and Neck, C. P. (1991), 'Inner Leadership: Creating Productive Thought Patterns', *Academy of Management Executive*, 5: 87–95.

—— and Sims, H. P., Jr. (1980), 'Self-Management as a Substitute for Leadership: A Social Learning Theory Perspective', *Academy of Management Review*, 5: 361–7.

—— —— (1984), 'Searching for the Unleader: Organizational Member Views of Leading Self-Managed Groups', *Human Relations*, 37: 409–24.

—— —— (1989), *Superleadership: Leading Others to Lead Themselves* (New York: Prentice-Hall).

Miles, R. E., and Snow, C. C. (1986), 'Organizations: New Concepts for New Forms', *California Management Review*, 28/3: 62–73.

—— —— (1994), *Organization Strategy, Structure and Process* (New York: McGraw Hill).

Moore, D. P., and Buttner, E. H. (1997), *Women Entrepreneurs : Moving beyond the Glass Ceiling* (Thousand Oaks, Calif.: Sage).

Murphy, S. E. (2001), 'Leader Self-Regulation: The Role of Self-Efficacy and "Multiple Intelligences"', in R. Riggio, S. Murphy, and F. Pirozzolo (eds.), *Multiple Intelligences and Leadership* (Mahwah, N.J: Lawrence Erlbaum Associates), 163–86.

—— and Ensher, E. A. (1997), 'The Effects of Culture on Mentoring Relationships: A Developmental Model', in S. Oskamp and C. S. Granrose (eds.), *Cross-Cultural Work Groups* (Thousand Oaks, Calif.: Sage).

—— —— (2001), 'The Role of Mentoring Support and Self-Management Strategies on Reported Career Outcomes', *Journal of Career Development*, 27/4: 229–46.

Neck, C. P., and Manz, C. C. (1992), 'Thought Self-Leadership: The Impact of Self-Talk and Mental Imagery on Performance', *Journal of Organizational Behavior*, 12: 681–99.

—— —— (1996), 'Thought Self-Leadership: The Impact of Mental Strategies Training on Employee Cognition, Behavior, and Affect', *Journal of Organizational Behavior*, 17/5: 445–67.

Noe, R. A. (1988), 'Women and Mentoring: A Review and Research Agenda', *Academy of Management Review*, 13: 65–78.

Obst, L. (1996), *Hello, He Lied* (New York: Broadway Books).

Ornstein, S., and Isabella, L. (1990), 'Age versus Stage Models of Career Attitudes of Women: A Partial Replication and Extension', *Journal of Vocational Behavior*, 36: 1–9.

—— Cron, W. L., and Slocum, J. W. (1989), 'Life Stages versus Career Stage: A Comparative Test of the Theories of Levinson and Super', *Journal of Organizational Behavior*, 10: 117–33.

Parisi, P. (1999), 'Open-Door Policy', *Hollywood Reporter* (Dec.), 5.

Phillips, J. (1991), *You'll Never Eat Lunch in this Town Again* (New York: Random House).

Pink, D. H. (1997–8), 'Free Agent Nation', *Fast Company* (Dec.–Jan.), 131–47.

Post, T. (1999), 'The Convergence Gamble', *Forbes*, 163/4: 112–17.

Powell, G. N., and Mainiero, L. A. (1992), 'Cross-Currents in the River of Time: Conceptualizing the Complexities of Women's Careers', *Journal of Management*, 18: 215–37.

—— —— (1993), 'Getting Ahead—in Career and Life', in G. N. Powell (ed)., *Women and Men in Management* (Newbury Park, Calif.: Sage), 86–224.

Ragins, B. R., and Cotton, J. (1999), 'Mentor Functions and Outcomes: A Comparison of Men and Women in Formal and Informal Mentoring Relationships', *Journal of Applied Psychology*, 84: 529–50.

Riggio, R., Murphy, S. E., and Pirozzolo, F. (2001), *Multiple Intelligences and Leadership* (Mahwah, N.J: Lawrence Erlbaum Associates).

Roberts, P., and Newton, P. (1987), 'Levinsonian Studies of Women's Adult Development', *Psychology and Aging*, 2/2: 154–63.

Saks, A. M., and Ashforth, B. E. (1996), 'Proactive Socialization and Behavioral Self-Management', *Journal of Vocational Behavior*, 48: 301–23.

Salovey, P., and Mayer, J. D. (1990), 'Emotional Intelligence', *Imagination, Cognition and Personality*, 9/3: 185–211.

Scandura, T. A. (1992), 'Mentorship and Career Mobility: An Empirical Investigation', *Journal of Organizational Behavior*, 13: 169–74.

Sellers, P. (1998), 'The 50 Most Powerful Women in American Business, *Fortune*, 138/7: 76–98.

Sias, P. M., and Jablin, F. M. (1995), 'Differential Superior–Subordinate Relations, Perceptions of Fairness, and Coworker Communication', *Human Communication Research*, 22: 5–38.

Smart, R., and Peterson, C. (1994), 'Stability versus Transition in Women's Career Development: A Test of Levinson's Theory', *Journal of Vocational Behavior*, 45: 241–60.

Sonnenfeld, J. A., and Peiperl, M. A. (1988), 'Staffing Policy as a Strategic Response: A Typology of Career Systems', *Academy of Management Review*, 13/4: 588–600.

Sullivan, S. E. (1999), 'The Changing Nature of Work: A Review and Research Agenda', *Journal of Management*, 25: 457–84.

——and Mainiero, L. A. (2000), 'Women's Careers: Directions and Strategies for a New Age', paper presented at the National Academy of Management Meetings, Toronto.

——Carden, W., and Martin, D. (1998), 'Careers in the Next Millennium: A Reconceptualization of Career Theory', *Human Resource Management Review*, 165–85.

Swanson, J. L. (1992), 'Vocational Behavior, 1989–1991: Life Span Career Development and Reciprocal Interaction of Work and Nonwork', *Journal of Vocational Behavior*, 41: 101–61.

Taylor, S. J., and Bogdan, R. (1998), *Introduction to Qualitative Research Methods: A Guidebook and Resource*, 3rd edn. (New York: John Wiley).

Tharenou, P., Latimer, S., and Conroy, D. (1994), 'How do you Make it to the Top? An Examination of Influence on Women's and Men's Managerial Advancement', *Academy of Management Journal*, 37: 899–931.

Tichy, N. (1981), 'Networks in Organizations', in P. C. Nystrom and W. H. Starbuck (eds.), *Handbook of Organization Design*, 2 vols. (New York: Oxford University Press), ii. 225–48.

Uhl-Bien, M., and Graen, G. B. (1998), 'Individual Self-Management: Analysis of Professionals' Self Managing Activities in Functional and Cross-Functional Work Teams', *Academy of Management Journal*, 41/3: 340–50.

Watkins, C. E., and Subich, L. M. (1995), 'Annual Review, 1992–1994: Career Development, Reciprocal Work/Nonwork Interaction, and Women's Workforce Participation', *Journal of Vocational Behavior*, 47: 109–63.

Wexley, K. N., and Latham, G. P. (1980), *Developing and Training Human Resources in an Organization* (Pacific Palisades, Calif.: Goodyear).

Wiatrowski, W. J. (1994), 'Small Business and their Employees', *Monthly Labor Review* (Oct.), 29–35.

Winsor, R. D., and Ensher, E. A. (2000), 'Choices Made in Balancing Work and Family: Following Two Women on a Seventeen-Year Journey', *Journal of Management Inquiry*, 9/2: 218–31.

IV

CAREERS CREATING INDUSTRIES

The general theme of this section is the idea that individual careers can serve to structure whole industries. Although the notion that individual careers and collective social structures are reciprocally constructed is now well accepted, the various authors in this section note that career theory has predominantly developed in one direction. Put simply, that development has been to examine the way host arenas shape individual careers. By taking a contrary direction, and leaping beyond the conventional arenas of organizations and occupations, the authors challenge usual thinking. The three chapters in this section develop theoretical propositions about how careers shape industries *instead* of industries shaping careers. Moreover, all three chapters provide specific examples to support their claims. This part serves to extend and emphasize the dual meaning of career creativity explored in this book. Career creativity can refer to careers in themselves, but it can also apply to the economic institutions—in this case industries—through which societies function.

The opening chapter by Richard 'Pete' Peterson and N. Anand continues the discussion of careers in creative industries begun in Part III. The authors contend that there are two types of fields, normative and competitive. Normative fields are those that are structured top down through regulative forces of the state or of professional groups, and have been the subject of exhaustive study by institutional theorists. The authors argue that competitive fields that are market based tend to be structured bottom up and are ideal locations for studying the manner in which careers shape fields. The logic of competition within such fields allows for entrepreneurial deviation from existing practices, typically through changes in regulation, technology, or markets. Deviations from existing practices are enacted through unconventional career moves of a few individuals (like Hank Williams) who structure new possibilities and serve as role models for those who follow in their wake. Peterson and Anand argue that, in this fashion, the unstructured careers of pivotal individuals lead to structured fields.

In the following chapter, Monica Higgins shows that new fields emerge from a few central organizations in existing industries. Higgins argues that past career histories of the individuals leading nascent firms serve as important signals to investors, prospective employees, and other field participants (see the chapter by Jones in Part III on the importance of career signaling). In a sample of 246 firms in the emerging US biotechnology industry that made an initial public offering (IPO) in the stock market between 1979 and 1996, she finds that most new firms were led by top management teams with significant experience in established firms in the pharmaceutical and health-care industry. In 23 percent of these new biotech firms, there was at least one individual in the top team with a previous career history at Baxter, the prestigious health-care organization. Higgins contends that Baxter's risk-taking and entrepreneurial culture, its decentralized organization design, and its supportive social networks provided the right structural context for individuals to break free and contribute to the emergence of a new industry.

In the section's final chapter, Robert DeFillippi and Michael Arthur further explore the links between individual careers, occupational communities, individual companies, and entire industries. The authors start with the assumption that certain individuals' careers are so exceptionally creative that they alter the very context that originally nurtured their creative practices. Using the example of the development of the Linux operating system, the authors show that a small community of dedicated software programmers initially nurtured the career of creator Linus Torvalds. As the community grew exponentially, so did its influence. Its members came to be recruited into new or existing firms involved with the commercialization of the Linux system. Such firms are now at the heart of an emerging sub-field that challenges existing norms and practices within the software industry. DeFillipi and Arthur argue that what Torvalds began provides an alternative model of industry formation, one that starts with a pivotal role for creative and unconventional careers.

Taken together, by stressing the importance of individual careers in the structuring of whole industries, the chapters in this section signal an important turn for career theory. Peterson and Anand provide a general framework describing how careers can come to structure fields. Higgins presents details of career patterns within certain germinal firms that create the context for the emergence of new industries. DeFillippi and Arthur develop an alternative model of industry formation, one that begins with a creative career that is linked to nurturing communities that provide social and economic capital to found new firms. By painting a novel—though necessarily incomplete—picture of how careers create industries, they provide a starting point in an important conversation, one that we urge others to join and to continue.

13

How Chaotic Careers Create Orderly Fields

RICHARD A. PETERSON AND N. ANAND

The concept of 'field' has become increasingly popular with students of organization theory. DiMaggio and Powell (1983: 148) formally defined an organizational field as 'those organizations that, in the aggregate, constitute a recognized area of institutional life: key suppliers, resource and product consumers, regulatory agencies, and other organizations that produce similar services or products'. The concept is central to an institutional view of organizations, and theorists have used the term to denote formations of organizations that are similar, have common practices, or share a certain focus of attention such as a market (Scott 1995). The popularity of the notion of field may partly be because it transcends earlier dualistically related concepts such as 'organization' and 'environment' or 'firm' and 'industry' that deny the embeddedness of the one in the other and also because it slips across levels of analysis, allowing for a more naturalistic explanation of organizational phenomena.

While organization theorists increasingly deploy the concept of field, it remains relatively under-theorized. For example, a number of scholars have used the idea of field in trying to explain the origin, development, and diffusion of particular models of careers such as those of physicians (Starr 1982), college athletes (Stern 1979), and women priests (Chaves 1996), to name but three. The general proposition that we take from these studies is that fields, more than individual organizations, shape careers. In other words, careers are particular institutional forms nested within and wrought by field-level, rather than purely organization-level, dynamics. Career theory has taken a similar turn. For example, articles in the influential volume on boundaryless careers edited by

We thank Michael Arthur, Suellen Littleton, Claire Peterson, and Pat Thornton for their helpful comments.

Arthur and Rousseau (1996) clearly illustrate the unraveling of organizations as internal labor markets and tightly shut containers of careers. Instead they show contemporary careers as lines that are etched between organizations and within organizational fields.

Barley (1989) observed that individual careers and institutions are reflexively related, yet a dearth of research is focused on how careers are instrumental in shaping organization fields. Sociologists, for example, generally focus on how fields structure careers. They are largely concerned with social mobility, describing the movement of individual or occupational careers within an organizational field (Maranda and Comeau 2000). In so doing, they have largely overlooked the reciprocal influence of careers in constituting organizational fields. The same is true in the study of individual career lines. Nystrom and McArthur (1989), for example, note that researchers have traditionally focused on the ways organizations shape careers and not vice versa.

TWO MODELS OF FIELD FORMATION

Long-established fields, such as the auto industry and the public-school system of a nation, come to take on such a sense of inevitability that it is not easy to see how they are very differently structured from each other. The structuring mechanisms are most clearly evident when fields are forming or reforming. So we will focus first on field formation. We identify two different models of field formation that are being deployed by institutional theorists. To highlight their differences, we term the two models 'normative' and 'competitive' following Anand (2000). They provide divergent accounts of the contexts and processes of field formation as well as of the structuring of mature fields. Moreover, and as important for our current discussion, they suggest the appropriateness of quite different career strategies.

NORMATIVE FIELDS

The normative model of field formation can be synthesized from the case studies of Paul DiMaggio, in particular his work on the creation of the US art museums field (DiMaggio 1991). He shows that the museums field was constructed in the period 1920–40 through the implementation of John Cotton Dana's vision of a museum as an accessible, interactive, and interpretative space devoted to the best of art and shaped by academically trained curators. The extensive financial support of the Carnegie Corporation of New York (a philanthropic foundation) and the consolidation of a new class of academically trained and accredited professional art curators were galvanized to translate Dana's vision into reality.

DiMaggio's description of the institutionalization of the art museum illustrates *normative* rather than market-based *competitive* institutional forces for three linked reasons. First, it was largely protected from market forces by private philanthropy. Secondly, its development was largely governed by the occupational norms and values of a dominant occupational group whose legitimacy relies heavily on a mix of government and professional self-regulation. Thirdly, in the early days it had a strong central cultural entrepreneur, John Dana, who had both the schema (or vision) for structuring the emerging field and the resources to mobilize the normative institutional forces that enabled the field to form (see Sewell 1992). DiMaggio's account of the institutionalization of theater, opera, and dance fields in the USA during the period 1900–40 (DiMaggio 1982*a*,*b*) further exemplifies this model. In all three performing art fields, cultural entrepreneurs induced a break from market forces and established strong linkages to occupational groups located primarily in seats of higher education.

Peterson (1981) and Beisel (1990) further specify the motives and skills required for individuals, organizations, or coalitions to act in an entrepreneurial fashion in order to enable their institutional moves. Ferguson (1998) provides a recent example of the workings of the normative model in her description of the formation and institutionalization of the field of gastronomy in Paris. An evolving nexus in socially turbulent nineteenth-century France among an elite class of food writers (comprising journalists, novelists, and social commentators) and a rising nascent occupational class of chefs and restaurateurs, sponsored by a politically well-connected clientele, helped create gastronomy as a cultural field. Ferguson sees the social forces that contributed to the demise of the monarchist model of government and the rise of republicanism as being primarily responsible for providing the prototypes for modern-day French chefs.

The model of a normative field stresses 'top-down' processes (Scott 1995: 140) in field structuration. In this view, regulative forces existing at upper societal levels exert a strong influence on the structure of institutional patterns at a lower level. Thus, the macro-dynamics of field-level forces are seen as the primary shaper of organization-level career patterns. An illustration of this view can be seen in Baron, Dobbin, and Jennings' sociological history (1986) of the evolution of modern personnel administration. They largely emphasize the federal government's large-scale manipulation of labor markets, union activities, and personnel practices during the Depression and the Second World War in creating institutionalized career paths for personnel administrators. This normative account supports the conventional view that normative field forces shape predictable bureaucratic careers.

COMPETITIVE FIELDS

Leblebici and associates' account of the formation of the US radio broadcasting field exemplifies the alternative, competitive model of field formation

(Leblebici *et al.* 1991). They show that the enduring structures of the US radio field were initiated in the 1930s by 'shady traders, small independent stations, renegade record producers, weaker networks, [and] enterprising advertising agencies' at the margin of the nascent broadcasting industry (Leblebici *et al.* 1991: 358). The authors assert that the now-conventional institutional practice of sponsored commercial radio broadcasts began with 'Doctor' J. R. Brinkley's efforts to hawk quack therapy that was difficult to advertise in the more legitimate mass media. Brinkley exploited the newly emerging medium of radio by setting up the high-wattage station KFKB in Milford, Kansas, to attract a wide-ranging clientele. The initial success of his venture facilitated the form-ation of a competitive commercial radio field in the USA that was markedly different from the state-sponsored normative model established in the UK by the BBC. The competitive model in the USA led to the formation of networks of radio stations to assemble the programming necessary to induce major national advertisers to use the new medium of radio.

Leblebici *et al.*'s account suggests an alternative model of field formation in which the micro-dynamics of unconventional careers at an organizational level structures higher-level field practices. In this 'bottom-up' view of field struc-turation (Scott 1995: 142), radical and disruptive institutional changes are most likely to be introduced by social agents with unconventional careers coming from the fringes of a field. These individuals innovate and subvert the existing scheme of things in order to adapt and flourish, and their success in turn alters institutional patterns at the level of the field.

This competitive model best fits a field that is shaped largely by market forces. Competitive marked-based fields typically come to have a few large oligopolistic firms in the center and a large number of more specialized firms in the periphery (Carroll 1985). Organizations at the center tend to be large and inertial, and, as a result, conservative and hierarchically organized. Organiza-tions on the margin, on the other hand, tend to be small and led by agentive entrepreneurs who are not constrained by the dead weight of bureaucratic 'wisdom', and they have the flexibility of being able to experiment with alternatives in changing circumstances. The unstable market characteristic of creative industries means that fields are periodically open to being reformed along new lines by entrepreneurial agents who have experience in the field but are frustrated by the restrictions of conventional ways of doing things in changing circumstances. The agency of such entrepreneurs, which generally involves making unconventional career moves, results in the creation of new schemas and resources, leading to the restructuring of the field at large so that their opportunistic careers shape structured fields. In the following section we describe the sources of entrepreneurial agency within competi-tive fields.

Ralph Peer's unconventional and entrepreneurial role in shaping the com-mercial country music field of the 1920s provides an excellent case in point (Peterson 1997). Peer had been successful working for OKeh Records in the nascent field of commercial country music, where he was making the then princely sum of $16,000 a year. He wanted to move to the dominant record company of the era, RCA-Victor, but they offered him a flat $5,000. When he objected to this cut in pay, they replied that the Treasurer of the company was making only $8,000, so he withdrew to dabble in several inventive ventures including song publishing. In a year he went back to RCA with a new proposal. He offered to produce records for one dollar a year on condition that he keep the publication rights for all the new songs he recorded. A dollar a year sounded whimsical to the RCA executives because at that time music publishing meant creating sheet music for sale in a retail market, and profits came from the large number of people who played music in the home. The RCA executives knew that few country music fans read music or even owned pianos, so with no prospects of sheet music sales, RCA agreed to Peer's offer. But Peer was not interested in sales of sheet music; he realized that, with the recently revised copyright law, copyright holders were required to receive a fixed fee for every copy of each recording of their song.

Peer's rambling and untidy career, so different from the ordered career path of RCA bureaucrats of his time, flourished by taking advantage of the opportunities provided by changing the structural contexts with the field. His entrepreneurial exploitation of innovative aspects, in turn, helped to create a new order within the commercial music field, an order built around the creation, licencing, and distribution of recorded music. Peer became wealthy from the song royalties generated by Jimmie Rodgers, the Carter family, and the other country music and blues writer-performers he discovered. Over the course of time country and blues writers such as Hank Williams and Chuck Berry, nurtured in the music field created by Peer, evolved into rock music, which by the mid-1950s successfully challenged the New York-based Tin Pan Alley system of song writing, thus again changing the music field (Peterson 1990; Ennis 1992).

Sometimes entrepreneurs bring their new ideas from a quite different field, as can be seen in another recent case drawn from the commercial music field. For decades *Billboard* magazine retained its position as the premier trade magazine in the music industry by producing the most reliable weekly charts of record sales. Charts were based on information from a sample of retail record outlets. In 1990, two marketing consultants, Mike Shallet and Mike Fine, brought their wide experience in electronic inventory control gained in the retail food and pharmaceutical fields to the music field. By electronically linking every modern record store cash register in the country to a central computer they could instantly generate a world of market information of great interest to record companies and, as a by-product, generate a weekly chart far more accurate than *Billboard*'s. They formed a service called 'SoundScan', and, by the time that *Billboard* realized that the rival system was becoming a reality, it found that SoundScan had already contracted the rights to the electronic sales figures of the major record retailers, leaving *Billboard* out in the cold. Not wanting to lose its place as the most reliable source of industry performance information, *Billboard* magazine negotiated with SoundScan to publish its chart in *Billboard*. The new chart revealed the booming country and rap music sales of the early 1990s, which, in turn, led to much greater investment in those segments of the market (Anand and Peterson 2000). As in the case of Peer's innovations, SoundScan had field-altering consequences unanticipated by the original change agents.

Up to now we have been talking about field formation. From this point on, we will leave aside the dynamics of normative fields and concentrate on the dynamics of competitive fields. Having just seen the vital role of several entrepreneurs in restructuring fields, we turn now to considering more directly the conditions that facilitate entrepreneurship.

CONTEXTS OF ENTREPRENEURIAL ACTIVITY

Joseph Schumpeter articulated the distinctive properties of entrepreneurship in 1934. In contradistinction to 'ownership' and 'invention', for him entrepreneurship involves the unique recombination of pre-existing elements of production. Henry Ford thus provides a paradigmatic example of the entrepreneur because he did not invent any of the processes and practices with which his name is identified. Instead he successfully brought them together in a way that was unique and, at the time, contrary to business practice, and in the process he reshaped the automobile industry.

While researchers sometimes identify entrepreneurship with the ownership of the means of production, and such a usage is appropriate in research on the founding of firms, many acts that involve a creative recombination of the factors of production are made by women and men who *manage* firms, or divisions within firms, without having significant ownership interest in the firm (Peterson and Berger 1971). Such entrepreneurs have sufficient *control* over some of the elements of production and use their control to recombine elements in novel ways. Thus entrepreneurship is the antithesis to, and an antidote for, the bureaucratic forms of organization as characterized a century ago by Max Weber and characteristic of twentieth-century corporations.

In the decades since Schumpeter first wrote on the subject, the terms 'entrepreneur' and 'entrepreneurship' have come to be used in several quite different ways, and often more than one is used in a given discussion, causing confusion and misunderstandings. So it is useful to make explicit our use of the concept here. In the first place, the meanings of the term can be divided into supply-side and demand-side usages (Thornton 1999). The supply-side perspective focuses on the traits that motivate individuals to entrepreneurial activity. This view is most useful for those wanting to locate born entrepreneurs or to teach people how to act in an entrepreneurial way (Robinson and

Hayes 1991). The demand-side perspective focuses on the structural conditions both in organizations and in organizational fields that make entrepreneurial activity more or less likely. This view is most useful to people interested in reducing the many organizational, legislative, and economic factors that inhibit entrepreneurship and in creating environments conducive to the flowering of entrepreneurial activity (Peterson 1981).

In practice, entrepreneurial activity blossoms when the structural conditions inhibiting its development are removed, even when the formal values of a society or an organization are hostile to its expression. Oberschall's study (1973) of small business people in Zambia clearly shows that a class of persons said to be temperamentally unfit for entrepreneurial activities by their cultural tradition can rapidly move into the entrepreneurial business sector when the opportunity presents itself. During the colonial period of what was then called Northern Rhodesia, business activities were in the hands of English and Asian immigrants. Native Africans were presumed to be unmotivated to enter business because of their collectivist cultural values. With Zambian independence and economic reform, the discrimination they had faced in custom, law, and administrative practice was eliminated, and Africans rapidly and successfully moved into the small-scale business sector of the economy. It is particularly notable that these 'instant' entrepreneurs were not drawn from a cadre that had been trained in colonial times; they did not come from an ethnic group marginal to Zambian society; they were not drawn disproportionately from one ethnic group; and they were not driven by their distinctive values to seek achievement for its own sake. In fact, as Oberschall shows, they were different from their fellow Zambians only in the range of their own personal experiences that had given them skills and models of behavior on which to draw. Peterson (1981) provides numerous further examples of this rapid shift to entrepreneurial activity when the legal and customary barriers to entry are eliminated.

As Thornton (1999: 19) notes, 'until recently the supply-side perspective...has been the dominant school of research'. Consequently we give prime attention to the conditions fostering the expression of entrepreneurship. In doing so, we focus on the process or activity of 'entrepreneurship', not on the person or formal status of 'entrepreneur' (Schumpeter 1934; Thornton 1999). We take both supply-side and demand-side uses of the term to be vitally important in career building, but, as we want to link agency to organizational field and career, we focus on the demand-side here. These points will be developed and exemplified in the next section.

COMPETITIVE FIELD DYNAMICS

Robert Michels (1915) identified an 'iron law of oligarchy' operating in political fields. According to this law, organizations that are democratic in intent come to be more nearly oligarchal in their form over time. Numerous scholars have found evidence of this law in practice (Fligstein 1990). If there is an iron law of oligarchy operating in democratically organized fields, there is, we argue, a cognate 'iron law of oligopoly' at work in fields organized around markets. Early in their lives, market-driven fields characteristically exhibit competition between many firms, but over time most of the competitors fail or are absorbed, while an ever smaller number becomes huge and together they come effectively to control the market field. The degree of oligopoly of a field is called the level of concentration and is usually measured as the proportion of the market controlled by the largest firms. Characteristically in the free market and mixed economies, the end state of maturity, monopoly, is not reached because of government regulative protection.

This evolution from competition to oligopoly characterizes the railroad, steel, oil, and automobile fields and most of the other industries formed in the years between 1870 and 1920 (Dobbin and Dowd 2000). This iron law of oligopoly has controlled the new consumer products and services industries of the nineteenth century as well. Examples range from groceries and motel chains to fast-food stores and the film industry. They all show steadily increasing levels of concentration. Economists lauded the evolution from competition to oligopoly as the 'maturation' of a field, arguing that only oligopolists have sufficient resources to engage in significant research and new product testing (Schumpeter 1934). But this trend to oligopolistic control of a field seems to be contradicted by the changes now taking place in such diverse fields as entertainment, for example filmmaking (Jones 1996) and in high technology such as software (Saxenian 1996).

In order to show the role of creative individuals and the environments they engender in creating the new form of competitive field dynamics, we focus on the field of commercial music because over the last half century it has steadily evolved toward the open field model. It is useful to develop the case at some length, because the changes involved in creating the new world of competitive fields are not the result of a single act of entrepreneurial innovation or change in the environment of the field; rather they result from the iterative impacts of dozens of such actions and the changing field they engender. (See, for example, the chapter by Alvarez and Svejenova in this volume on the structural conditions that helped the creativity of the Almodóvar brothers to flourish.)

Introducing the music industry case

The level of concentration in the US recorded music industry has followed a quite different trajectory from that predicted by the textbook free-market model.[1] Born out of the pooling of patents by a few firms at the turn of the

---

[1] Parts of this section not otherwise referenced are taken substantially from Peterson (1990).

twentieth century, the levels of concentration in the music business were initially very high, but they dropped in the years following, until the Great Depression of the 1930s effectively destroyed all of the smaller fledgling independent firms and left only the well-capitalized majors, RCA and Columbia records (Sanjek 1988). The levels of concentration remained very high up through the decade following the Second World War, with the four top firms controlling 81 percent of all hit recordings in 1948. However, the level of concentration has been on a roller coaster in the decades since. By 1955 the concentration ratio had gone down to 74 percent, then in the four years between 1956 and 1959 it plummeted to an unprecedented low of 34 percent, as independent companies including Motown, Atlantic, Dot, and the like began to compete successfully in the field. By 1962, the nadir of control by the majors, the four leading firms controlled just 25 percent of the market (Peterson and Berger 1975). In the forty years since, the proportion controlled by the leading firms has risen gradually, to reach levels comparable to those of the late 1940s, so that four multinational corporations control over 80 percent of the total world market for popular music (see Lopes 1992; Negus 1999).

Examining this remarkable volatility throws light on the factors that made it possible for entrepreneurs in the field to follow creative careers that in turn reshaped the commercial music field's structure. In drawing on the wealth of examples of entrepreneurship, we will focus on the reasons behind changes that took place in the popular music industry between 1948 and 1958.

The middle of the 'middle-of-the-road' years of the Eisenhower presidency, 1955, hardly seemed like the time for a major aesthetic revolution. Yet it was in the brief span between 1954 and 1956 that the rock aesthetic displaced the jazz-based aesthetic in American popular music. Frank Sinatra, Patti Page, Perry Como, Johnnie Ray, and Doris Day gave way on the popular music charts to the likes of Elvis Presley, Chuck Berry, the Platters, Buddy Holly, Little Richard, Carl Perkins, and the growing legion of rockers. If rock and roll did not emerge spontaneously out of a new *Zeitgeist* of the mid-1950s, then what did give rise to rock and why did it emerge so abruptly in this brief period? Singly or in combination, three influences have most often been cited. These include supply-side factors, notably the arrival of Elvis Presley, and demand-side factors, notably the unusually large baby boomer cohort born after the Second World War and the transformation of the commercial music industry.

It is tempting to characterize eras in terms of the leaders of the time. In this vein, it is possible to point to specific individuals like Chuck Berry, Little Richard, Elvis Presley, and Jerry Lee Lewis and say that rock emerged in the late 1950s because, like other creative circles of artists, they began their creative efforts at this specific moment. In bringing into question this 'supply-side' explanation, we do not for a moment belittle their accomplishments. But, as we have suggested above, in any era there are many more would-be creative individuals than are ever able to reach notoriety, and, if a greater number become successful in a specific period, it is because of a favorable opportunity structure. Thus Presley and the rest did not cause the rock revolution, but simply took advantage of the opportunities that became available to them, and in the process they created new institutional patterns within existing fields.

What of the 'demand-side' explanation of the emergence of rock music? The remarkably large cohort of newly affluent young people, the vanguard of the 'baby boom', could not relate to the jazz-based sensuous slow dance music created for 20 year olds approaching the age of first marriage. Although it can be argued that the uniquely large baby-boom cohort was important to changes taking place in popular music in the mid-1960s, it did not cause the emergence of rock in the mid-1950s. In fact, it could not have been the cause. After all, in 1954 the oldest of the baby-boomers were only 9 years old, and half had not even been born yet. Consumer tastes are vitally important in driving all consumer product industries, and the newly affluent teens and pre-teens comprised the heart of the market exploited in the rise of rock music. But market demand in the USA did not just change suddenly between 1954 and 1956. Rather it had been changing gradually for over a decade and remained largely unsatiated because the decision-makers in the culture industry simply did not recognize it was there (Peterson and Berger 1975; Ennis 1992).

It is indeed ironic that the commercial culture industry, which is dedicated to making money by providing the mass of people with the kinds of entertainment that they want, was systematically blind to the unstated demand for cultural products that spoke more directly to the condition of young people. Ironically it was the structure of arrangements, habits, and assumptions of the commercial culture industry itself that caused the blindness, and as importantly it was the systematic change in these factors that created the opportunity for rock to emerge. We will briefly identify factors relating to law, technology, markets, and organization field structure. Each stimulated or frustrated acts of entrepreneurial innovation large and small. No one of these was sufficient to making the change, but they all had to align for the rapid change in the industry to take place.

Law and regulation

Even though the emphasis in market-based fields is on free competition, laws and government regulatory agency rulings are absolutely essential to the formation of stable market-based fields. Moreover, they generally have consequences unintended by their formulators. In the present instance, copyright law and federal government regulation of radio station broadcasting licenses were important in making possible the advent of rock music, though in ways that were completely unintended and unanticipated.

Copyright Law. From the 1930s US Copyright Law was used by the American Society of Composers, Authors, and Publishers (ASCAP), a private membership company, effectively to control access to exposing new music to the public (Sanjek 1988), and by 1950 an oligopoly of just eighteen New York publishers determined which songs could reach the public ear (Ryan 1985: 104). These oligopolists shared an aesthetic accenting well-crafted conventional love themes, strong melodies, and danceable jazz rhythms. The work of black musicians in the blues, jazz, rhythm-and-blues, and what later came to be called soul genres was systematically excluded, along with songs in the developing Latin and country music traditions. Ryan (1985) shows this with numerous specific examples. The effect was that these forms could not reach a wide audience via movies and radio. In a 1939 contract dispute with ASCAP the radio networks formed a rival licensing agency, Broadcast Music International (BMI), which signed publishers and writers that had been excluded from membership in ASCAP. The advent of BMI inadvertently made it possible for large numbers of writers and publishers in these genres from which rock developed to profit from their work.

Thus, for example, with direct encouragement from BMI, in 1942 two Nashville-based country music entrepreneurs, Roy Acuff and Fred Rose, formed a publishing company. In 1946 they signed the fledgling country music entertainer Hank Williams to a writing contact. In 1951 several of his songs became national pop hits after Rose persuaded pop music producer Mitch Miller to record rising pop idol Tony Bennett singing Hank Williams' 'Cold, Cold Heart'. The song stayed at number one on the *Billboard* Pop music charts for six weeks. The next year Williams' songs recorded by Bennet, Patti Page, Jo Stafford, and Frankie Lane were also pop hits (Escott 1994). The message did not escape the pop music producers, and soon there were many good songs being created by writers and controlled by publishers working outside the New York Tin Pan Alley formula.

FCC regulation. A number of local, state, and federal government regulatory agencies arguably influenced the advent of rock, but the Federal Communications Commission (FCC) that regulates the number and allocation of broadcasting stations through the USA played a vital role. Throughout the 1930s when interest in radio was growing rapidly the FCC restricted the number of stations licensed to each market to three to six. This meant that each of the established networks, NBC (with its Red and Blue Networks), CBS, and Mutual, had an outlet, and there might be one independent station or two. A large number of applications for new stations were submitted, but these were denied or deferred 'in the public interest' because the networks lobbied successfully to maintain this small number of stations. The networks relied on music provided by the major New York publishers and played live by orchestras. All this changed in 1947 when the FCC began to approve most of the backlog of applications, and, in a matter of just four years, the number of radio stations authorized to most markets doubled in number (Sterling and Haight 1978).

Most of the new licenses went to poorly capitalized independent stations that could ill afford to hire live musicians. Their entrepreneurial radio programmers relied heavily on phonograph records supplied *gratis* to them by fledgling regional record companies who were experimenting with local artists and eager to use radio airplay to promote their new recordings. Thus, in a mutually beneficial exchange, the flood of new local stations gave a ready outlet to music of dozens of fledgling entrepreneurial music producers working outside the Tin Pan Alley mold. The successful companies formed in this way include Sun (Memphis), Chess (Chicago), Atlantic (New York), King (Cincinnati), Dot (Nashville), and Motown (Detroit). Each brought a distinctively different sound to popular music.

Technology

As noted above, innovations in technology, such as the advent of digital music recording and distribution, often have a destabilizing effect on the structure of fields, thus providing the scope for entrepreneurial innovators. Here we will show the importance of the advent of two new technologies: the transistor radio receiver and the 45 r.p.m. record.

The transistor radio. Until the mid-1950s, radio receivers used a set of large, power-consuming, heat-generating, and fragile vacuum tubes. Their use dictated that sets would be large, heavy, and expensive pieces of furniture. While most American homes had a radio, few had more than two, and radio broadcasters catered to this 'family context' pattern of listening. Auto radios were the exception, and portable radios were not common. These so-called portables were relatively large, fragile, and, because of the large batteries required, quite heavy, but all this changed in the mid-1950s when transistors became available. American radio manufacturers intended to introduce transistors as a prestige item in their top-of-the-line radio, TV, and phonograph consoles. According to their plan, transistors would be introduced into cheaper radios only gradually in succeeding years.

Japanese manufacturers such as Sony upset this strategy by shipping to the US hundreds of thousands of cheap, lightweight, compact transistor radios that operated on small flashlight batteries. Quickly young Americans learned to take these extremely inexpensive sets to school, to the beach, to parties, to work—everywhere they went. No longer restricted to programming for 'family entertainment tastes', innovative independent radio station 'personality' disk jockeys, the likes of Alan Freed and Wolfman Jack, became very popular playing music aimed directly at the interest of teenagers. Their success depended not only on choosing teen-oriented songs but also on bantering with their listeners about rock music and other topics of interest to teens. The older Tin

Pan Alley pop songs that depended on well-crafted but abstract lyrics, and the singers who sang them from Bing Crosby and Doris Day to Dinah Shore and Frank Sinatra, quickly went out of favor.

The 45 r.p.m. record. From the inception of the industry before the turn of the twentieth century, the major phonograph record companies battled over alternative music recording and reproducing technologies in the hopes of garnering the lion's share of the consumer market. By the mid-1920s the major companies agreed to pool patents, and the 10-inch 78 r.p.m. shellac disk had become the standard. Following the Second World War an enterprising group of engineers at Columbia Records began intensive experimentation to develop a long-playing high-fidelity record. A newly developed vinyl material was used for the disks because it held the musical fidelity better than the older shellac, and in 1948 Columbia was ready to release its 12-inch, $33\frac{1}{3}$ r.p.m. LP. General Sarnoff, long-time head of RCA, was appalled that the much smaller firm had trumped his vaunted research department. He ordered his engineers quickly to bring to market an alternative system. Their response was to produce the 7-inch vinyl 45 r.p.m. record.

The 45 single record was important to the advent of rock because it was (virtually) unbreakable. One of the greatest expenses of 78s was the extreme care that had to be taken in handling and shipping them, and each of the major record companies developed a national distribution system that was geared to handling its own delicate 78s. Since the small record companies could not afford the costs of the national distribution of 78s, it was virtually impossible in 1948 for them to have a national hit record. The smaller, lighter, virtually indestructible 45s made it much cheaper to ship records in bulk, making feasible the development of independent national distribution companies. As importantly for the promotion of new songs, it also made it practical for small record companies to use the mail service to send promotional copies to radio stations, thereby fostering the development of rock and roll as a genre.

Market

The word 'market' corresponds loosely with audience, consumers, and the like. More precisely it refers to the audience as it is conceptualized by the industry. As we will see, the advent of rock was marked by a dramatic transformation in the conception of the market.

The homogenous market of 1948. In 1948 just four radio networks competed with each other. In effect, they saw the radio audience as one vast homogenous market. Together they worked to maintain their collective dominance, and, at the same time, they competed fiercely with each other to increase their own 'slice' of the homogenous market 'pie'. Much as in the Hollywood film industry of the time, they created variants of previously successful formulas and designated new programs with the broadest possible appeal that would offend as few as possible. This radio oligopolist's strategy conforms to Peterson and Berger's proposition (1975) that the fewer the number of competitors in a market, the more homogenous will be their products and the lower will be the rate of innovation.

The situation was quite similar in the record business. As noted above, the four largest firms accounted for 81 percent of all the hit records in 1948. As in the case of radio industry programming, the big four record companies competed with each other to increase their own slice of what was seen as a homogenous national market for recorded popular music. Again the oligopolists' marketing strategy put an accent on 'sameness'. The practice of producing 'cover records' provides an excellent case in point. When a company, large or small, had a hit record on a song, the other oligopolists would immediately 'cover' it by putting out their own recording of the same song by one of their own singers or orchestras. The practice of covering hits also helped to keep independent companies from successfully competing in the market.

An example will help to show the process. When in 1947 Bullet Records of Nashville released 'Near You' by the Francis Craig orchestra, it gained considerable record sales in the region because the Craig orchestra was a regular performer on WSM, a powerful radio station broadcasting from Nashville. Within weeks of the success of the Bullet recording, each of the four major record companies had released its own version, and all of these reached hit status in the weeks that followed, completely eclipsing sales of the original version by the independent record company.

The heterogenous market of 1958. When the radio network programs were transferred to television in the late 1940s, an increasing amount of radio airtime was filled with recorded music. Initially radio programmers played a wide range of records in the belief that the audience would become bored and turn to another station if they did not present a variety of sounds. In early 1950 the enterprising music director at the independent KWOH radio station in Omaha, Nebraska, made a significant observation. Eating lunch at a diner with one of his disk jockeys, he and his colleague became extremely annoyed with a waitress who kept putting money into the jukebox to play the same two songs over and over and over again. Then it dawned on him that she was voluntarily spending her own money for this extremely narrow range of music, so this must be what she, and perhaps thousands like her, wanted to hear. Since his station was not doing well in the ratings, he decided to experiment. He began a policy of playing, throughout the entire day, nothing but what the trade magazine charts showed were the top forty hit records, changing this mix of records weekly when the new hit charts were released. Within weeks his station became the most listened-to station in Omaha, and within months almost every major radio station in the USA had copied this new formatting principle, which had come to be called 'Top 40' (Morthland 1992).

One might assume that introduction of the Top-40 format reduced the aesthetic range of music heard on the air. In most cases, however, it did not have this effect in 1954. This is because virtually all of the songs that had been heard on the air fit the big-band crooner aesthetic, while, because the charts were based not only on radio airplay but also on jukebox play and record sales, many rhythm and blues records as well as some country music records were charted. Thus, for the first time, these sorts of records began to receive wide exposure via the radio (Gillett 1983). Once the idea of turning a radio station into something like a jukebox with forty selections had been established, there was rapid experimentation with the idea.

By 1958 industry executives had come to view the radio market as a set of distinct 'segments' (teen-oriented Top 40 as well as soul music, country music, classical music, jazz, religious music, middle of the road, and so on), each with jukebox-like radio stations catering to its distinct music preferences. Thus the view of a single homogeneous pie with four oligopolistic networks contending for a larger *slice* was passé. Now the market was viewed as a mosaic of distinct *segments*, each with its own aesthetic. Rather than seeking the sound that would offend no one, now the innovative programmers sought out music that might offend, shock, or bore many people but would rivet the attention of the targeted segment of the audience. These changes in the way the radio market was defined had immediate consequences for the record industry. Beginning in late 1954, and increasing rapidly for the next several years, there was a greatly increasing demand for an ever-widening aesthetic range of records. The major companies were slow to react, and, as we have already noted, a large number of small companies filled the new demand for the distinct markets defined by the new radio formats.

Updating the music field case

It is easy to talk of abstract forces such as law and regulation, technology, and market-shaping competitive fields, but, as the examples of enterprising innovation presented in this section of the chapter illustrate, it is the cumulative result of numerous entrepreneurial career moves and the accompanying new possibilities created by their actions that lead to the reshaping of fields. As we have seen, given the right field conditions, the micro-dynamics of individual careers can shape the structure of competitive fields. We began by showing how music industry expert Ralph Peer's decision to follow an unconventional path created by the newly enacted Copyright Law not only allowed for other publisher-entrepreneurs who followed in his footsteps, but also influenced the styles of music that were subsequently heard over the airwaves, bought in record shops, and recorded in studios. The circumstances surrounding the advent of the SoundScan system of creating music charts illustrated the changes that can be introduced by innovators coming from outside a field. In this section we have seen how a linked set of entrepreneurial actions and field dynamics progressively created an open field conducive to still further changes in the short span of years between 1948 and 1958. By hundreds of innovative actions enacted by individuals, the highly dynamic commercial music field reacted to the new reality created by the changes in law, technology, and market just described (Peterson and Berger 1971; Hirsch 1972).

This process was not complete by 1958. As of that year the commercial music field consisted of a few large inflexible vertically integrated multinational firms and hundreds of independent record companies with even more specialty firms performing just one function in the total creative process. But by the 1990s the structure of the field had evolved still further. The oligopolistic firms pushed to retain commercial control in the volatile field by focusing on the marketing and distribution of music while externalizing creative risks. They outsourced a greater proportion of their creative functions, such as artist development and record production, in order to reduce costs and to react more rapidly to changes in taste. At the same time they aggressively purchased smaller record companies and formed autonomous divisions representing the full array of narrow markets from children's records and jazz to heavy metal and rap. In the process the once tightly coupled vertically integrated oligopolists became hollow shells focused on the distribution and marketing of music in a loosely coupled field, and, in the process, encouraging a more open system of creative production (Lopes 1992; Negus 1999).

By the early years of the twenty-first century the commercial music field consisted of four multinational corporations (Warner, Sony, BMG, and EMI) each with numerous more-or-less autonomous single-market niche-oriented labels. Their structure conforms to the 'finance' conception of control (Fligstein 1990), where the firm is viewed as a collection of assets that need to be managed efficiently (Robbins 1993). All of the mid-size corporations in the commercial music field had been absorbed by that time, but there was a large number of small independent companies, most of which operated in a single market niche, many specialty firms that provide one or another specific service, and an even larger number of individuals providing their services on a project-by-project basis. The innumerable small companies and contract arrangements make for highly unstable careers. However, the multinationals continually form, buy, reorganize, and divest themselves of units, so even they do not provide job security and predictable careers. Because of this, the loosely coupled commercial music field gives wide scope for creative careers. For virtually all those involved, the locus of the career is now the field and not the current employer, and, as in contemporary team sports, players work very hard for their employer not so much out of long-term loyalty to the team but to ensure and enhance their own career prospects in the field at large.

INNOVATIVE CAREERS IN THE STRUCTURING OF COMPETITIVE FIELDS

Normative fields tend to have fixed paths that reproduce existing status hierarchies. A clear case is provided by the royal-era French art painting world that was rationalized by the Royal Academy and made for a highly formal style of art (White and White 1993). This case suggests to us that in normative fields, governed largely by field-wide regulations and occupational norms, patterns of individual conformity to the rules and the norms help reproduce stasis in field structure.

In contrast to normative fields, competitive fields are largely open to the vagaries and uncertainties of the market. The key dynamic structuring a competitive field is the continual interaction between markets and careers (Faulkner and Anderson 1987). Since the strategy of even the largest firms is to spread a large investment over a number of small projects, managers in the large oligopolistic firms have constantly to decide how to allocate resources. A firm can choose to back new and risky ventures or relatively safer projects relying on tried-and-tested resources; often firms have a portfolio of units representing both types of choices (Negus 1999). We have shown above that the former course of sponsoring untried and innovative projects involves the willingness on the part of individuals to bet their careers on opportunities created by change in field-level forces such as regulation, technology, and markets. As White and White (1993) clearly show, this pattern characterized the French fine art world after 1850 and, beginning with the 'impressionist' style, made for rapid stylistic innovation in art.

The music industry once seemed to be exceptional, but now many industries are moving toward much the same structure. An important consequence is that labor markets that were once internal to the firm become field-wide labor markets. The resulting migration of personnel within the field is a critical mechanism influencing the balance of stasis and change within a field. Studies drawn from a number of fields show the importance of such careers in shaping fields.

Pfeffer and Leblebici (1973) argue that executive migration is a key mechanism for reducing marked-based uncertainty. Their study reveals that, the higher the levels of uncertainty in a field, the more rapid are the rate of personnel flows between organizations. Industries with huge spurts of innovation are characterized by dense migration of people moving within and between organizations. These unruly trade routes, which imply discontinuous and untidy career paths, constitute the very locus of innovative activity within competitive fields, as observers of the software (Saxenian 1996) and biotechnology industries (Powell *et al.* 1996) demonstrate. If these migration patterns did not exist, we argue, competitive fields would become increasingly static, and organizations with greater market power would become increasingly dominant, making for a vertically integrated and more nearly monopolistic field structure rather than the loosely coupled oligopolistic structure that is seen in industries like commercial music and film. The mobile careers of personnel within a field help induce a homogenizing force through the more even distribution of market knowledge across the entire field.

Boeker (1997) refined the proposition set forth by Pfeffer and Leblebici (1973). He demonstrated that, when executives and key personnel move, they not only carry knowledge from one company to another, but also actively act on their knowledge. In a sample of semi-conductor firms, Boeker (1997: 216) found that 'if a manager moves from Firm 1 which competes in product markets A, B, and C, to Firm 2, which competes in C, D, and E, there is an increased likelihood that Firm 2 will enter product markets A or B'.

Several other studies support the contention that in uncertain environments market knowledge is spread through migration, and we note but three here. First, Peterson (1978) shows that the movement of rock and roll disk jockeys in the 1970s to the country radio field resulted in a 'new country radio' that resembled pop and rock music in its format and content rather than the music programmed by country radio disc jockeys who came up in the country music field. Secondly, the work by Thornton and Ocasio (1999) suggests that the increasing 'market-orientation' strategy among higher education publishers in the USA has largely been achieved through executive succession. In the 1950s, the field was split between two conceptions of control, one traditionally valuing the scholarship and erudition of the publisher, and the other valuing the publisher's marketing ability. The increasing movement of marketer-publishers into the field has resulted in a decrease in the prominence of traditional, scholarly publishing houses. Third, Kraatz and Moore (2002) find that in the field of higher education the migration of administrators from professional schools to traditional liberal arts colleges is leading to the increased offering of professional programs within the latter. Taken together, these studies suggest that the migration of executives and expert personnel helps keep the balance between stasis and change, leading us to propose that the 'opportunism' of personnel migration patterns leads to 'structured' or increasingly isomorphic fields.

The success of firms in all the creative industries depends on the efforts of key creative personnel. Being in high demand, they can make successful careers by moving from one firm to another (Faulkner and Anderson 1987). As Weick (1996) observes, the boundarylessness of producers' careers induces in turn a field that seems boundaryless. This type of field structure, fully formed in the music and film industries by the early 1990s, with a few oligopolistic firms creating a market for a number of outsourced producer-managed projects, serves as model not only for a number of modern industries such as software and high technology, but also for older industries seeking to adapt to new market conditions (Robbins 1993). One career model that results is that of the freelance producer working as a corporate subcontractor for specific creative projects (Peterson and White 1979; Jones 1996).

In fields characterized by a high rate of entrepreneurial innovation, many actors from firms to individuals use the tactic of imitating those who are currently the most successful market performers. One tactic discovered by the Bielbys in the television industry is to imitate the products that have been 'hits' in the marketplace (Bielby and Bielby 1994). In the case of the commercial music field, music charts such as those compiled by *Billboard* magazine rapidly disseminate market performance on a weekly basis. Market information in the form of performance charts, bestseller lists, and box-office numbers provides cues about people, products, and performances that are used in resource allocation decisions, and these resources, in turn, lengthen the careers of those invested in, thereby providing continuity within the field (Anand and Peterson 2000). The presence of project-brokers, such as talent agencies, facilitates the process of assembling a team with the goal of imitating the most successful 'hits' (Bielby and Bielby 1999). And, as argued by Anand and Peterson (2000), such market information, whether it is accurate or not, importantly shapes these fields.

SUMMARY

Although careers and fields are reflexively linked, the manner in which careers shape fields is under-theorized. In this chapter, we have made a beginning by noting that there are in fact two ways of structuring fields, the one normative and the other competitive. Competitive fields, we suggest, are more open to being shaped by careers than are normative fields. Using primarily examples from the music industry, we argue that shifting structural contexts (such as changes in laws, technology, or markets) create opportunities for entrepreneurial agency that are manifest in the form of unconventional career moves.

In the aggregate, such moves make for both 'chaotic careers' and 'orderly competitive fields'. By 'orderly competitive fields' we mean the balance of innovation and imitation, and of stasis and change, that results when organizations are continually restructured in the process of trying to stay abreast of the rapidly consumer tastes that will sustain them. By 'chaotic careers', we mean a series of jobs that do not have a fixed or predictable progression; rather such careers are opportunistic and chaotic evolving, collage-like, with a pastiche of experience on various projects. Individuals with chaotic careers move from one organized activity to another, they jump from one pool of talent to another, and they move from one location to another. Taken together, these actions alter the structure and functioning of competitive fields. We conclude by showing how such chaotic careers create fields that are orderly.

REFERENCES

Anand, N. (2000), 'Defocalizing the Organization: The Sociology of Richard A. Peterson', *Poetics*, 28: 173–84.

—— and Peterson, R. A. (2000), 'When Market Information Constitutes Fields: Sense-making of Markets in the Commercial Music Industry', *Organization Science*, 11: 270–84.

Arthur, M. B., and Rousseau, D. M. (1996), 'The Boundaryless Career as a New Employment Principle', in M. B. Arthur and D. M. Rousseau (eds.), *The Boundaryless Career: A New Employment Principle for a New Organizational Era* (Oxford: Oxford University Press), 3–20.

Baker, W. E., and Faulkner, R. R. (1991), 'Role as Resource in the Hollywood Film Industry', *American Journal of Sociology*, 97/2: 279–309.

Barley, S. R. (1989), 'Careers, Identities, and Institutions: The Legacy of the Chicago School of Sociology', in M. B. Arthur, D. T. Hall, and B. S. Lawrence (eds.), *Handbook of Career Theory* (Cambridge: Cambridge University Press), 41–65.

Baron, J. N., Dobbin, F. R., and Jennings, P. D. (1986), 'War and Peace: The Evolution of Modern Personnel Administration in the US Industry', *American Journal of Sociology*, 92: 350–83.

Baty, G. B., Evan, W. B., and Rothermel, T. W. (1971), 'Personnel Flows as Inter-organizational Relations', *Administrative Science Quarterly*, 16: 430–43.

Beisel, N. (1990), 'Class, Culture, and Campaigns against Vice in Three American Cities, 1872–1892', *American Sociological Review*, 44: 44–62.

Bielby, W. T., and Bielby, D. D. (1994), ' "All Hits are Flukes": Institutionalized Decision-Making and the Rhetoric of Network Prime-Time Program Development', *American Journal of Sociology*, 99: 1287–313.

—— —— (1999), 'Organizational Mediation of Project-Based Labor Markets: Talent Agencies and the Careers of Screenwriters', *American Sociological Review*, 64/1: 64–85.

Boeker, W. (1997), 'Executive Migration and Strategic Change: The Effect of Top Manager Movement on Product-Market Entry', *Administrative Science Quarterly*, 42: 213–36.

Carroll, G. R. (1985), 'Concentration and Specialization: Dynamics of Niche Width in Populations of Organizations', *American Journal of Sociology*, 90: 1262–83.

Caves, R. E. (2000), *Creative Industries: Contracts between Art and Commerce* (Cambridge, Mass.: Harvard University Press).

Chaves, M. (1996), 'Ordaining Women: The Diffusion of an Organizational Innovation', *American Journal of Sociology*, 101: 840–73.

DiMaggio, P. J. (1982a), 'Cultural Entrepreneurship in Nineteenth-Century Boston, Part I: The Creation of an Organizational Base for High Culture in America', *Media, Culture and Society*, 4: 33–50.

—— (1982b), 'Cultural Entrepreneurship in Nineteenth-Century Boston, Part II: The Classification and Framing of American Art', *Media, Culture and Society*, 4: 303–22.

—— (1991), 'Constructing an Organizational Field as a Professional Project: US Art Museums, 1920–1940', in W. W. Powell and P. J. DiMaggio (eds.), *The New Institutionalism in Organizational Analysis* (Chicago: University of Chicago Press), 267–92.

—— and Powell, W. W. (1983), 'The Iron Cage Revisited: Institutional Isomorphism and Collective Rationality in Organizational Fields', *American Sociological Review*, 48: 147–60.

Dobbin, F., and Dowd, T. (2000), 'The Market that Antitrust Built: Public Policy, Private Coercion, and Railroad Acquisitions, 1825–1922', *American Sociological Review*, 65: 635–57.

Ennis, P. H. (1992), *The Seventh Stream: The Emergence of Rocknroll in American Popular Music* (Hanover, NH: Wesleyan University Press).

Escott, C. (1994), *Hank Williams: The Biography* (New York: Little Brown).

Faulkner, R. R., and Anderson, A. B. (1987), 'Short-Term Projects and Emergent Careers: Evidence from Hollywood', *American Journal of Sociology*, 92: 879–909.

Ferguson, P. P. (1998), 'A Cultural Field in the Making: Gastronomy in Nineteenth Century France', *American Journal of Sociology*, 104: 597–641.

Fligstein, N. (1990), *The Transformation of Corporate Control* (Cambridge, Mass.: Harvard University Press).

Gillett, C. (1983), *The Sound of the City: The Rise of Rock'n'Roll* (New York: Pantheon).

Hirsch, P. M. (1972), 'Processing Fads and Fashions: An Organization-Set Analysis of Cultural Industry Systems', *American Journal of Sociology*, 77: 639–59.

Jones, C. (1996), 'Careers in Project Networks: The Case of the Film Industry', in M. B. Arthur and D. M. Rousseau (eds.), *The Boundaryless Career: A New Employment Principle for a New Organizational Era* (New York: Oxford University Press), 58–75.

Kraatz, M., and Moore, J. (2002), 'Executive Migration and Institutional Change', *Academy of Management Journal*, 45: 120–143.

Leblebici, H., Salancik, G. R., Copay, A., and King, T. (1991), 'Institutional Change and the Transformation of Interorganizational Fields: An Organizational History of the US Radio Broadcasting Industry', *Administrative Science Quarterly*, 36: 333–63.

Lopes, P. D. (1992), 'Innovation and Diversity in the Popular Music Industry', *American Sociological Review*, 57: 57–71.

Maranda, M.-F., and Comeau, Y. (2000), 'Some Contributions of Sociology to the Understanding of Career', in A. Collin and R. A. Young (eds.), *The Future of Career* (Cambridge: Cambridge University Press), 37–52.

Menger, P.-M. (1999), 'Artistic Labor Markets and Careers', *Annual Review of Sociology*, 25: 541–74.

Michels, R. (1915), *Political Parties: A Sociological Study of the Oligarchical Tendencies of Modern Democracies*, trans. E. Paul and C. Paul (New York: Hearst's International Library).

Morthland, J. (1992), 'The Rise of Top 40 AM', in Anthony DeCurtis, James Henke, and Holly George-Warren (eds.), *The Rolling Stone Illustrated History of Rock and Roll* (New York: Random House), 102–6.

Negus, Keith (1999), *Music Genres and Corporate Cultures* (London: Routledge).

Nystrom, P. C., and McArthur, A. W. (1989), 'Propositions Linking Careers and Organizations', in M. B. Arthur, D. T. Hall, and B. S. Lawrence (eds.), *Handbook of Career Theory* (Cambridge: Cambridge University Press), 490–505.

Oberschall, A. (1973), 'African Traders and Small Businessmen in Lusak', *African Social Research*, 16: 274–502.

Peterson, R. A. (1978), 'The Production of Cultural Change: The Case of Contemporary Country Music', *Social Forces*, 45: 292–314.

Peterson, R. A. (1981), 'Entrepreneurship and Organization', in P. C. Nystrom and W. H. Starbuck (eds.), *Handbook of Organizational Design* (Oxford: Oxford University Press), 65–83.

——(1990), 'Why 1955? Explaining the Advent of Rock Music', *Popular Music*, 9: 97–116.

——(1997), *Creating Country Music: Fabricating Authenticity* (Chicago: University of Chicago Press).

——and Berger, D. G. (1971), 'Entrepreneurship in Organizations: Evidence from the Popular Music Industry', *Administrative Science Quarterly*, 16: 97–107.

—— ——(1975), 'Cycles in Symbol Production: The Case of Popular Music', *American Sociological Review*, 40: 158–73.

——and White, H. (1979), 'The Simplex Located in Art Worlds', *Urban Life*, 7: 411–39.

Pfeffer, J., and Leblebici, H. (1973), 'Executive Recruitment and the Development of Interfirm Organizations', *Administrative Science Quarterly*, 18: 449–61.

Powell, W. W., Koput, K. W., and Smith-Doerr, L. (1996), 'Interorganizational Collaboration and the Locus of Innovation: Networks of Learning in Biotechnology', *Administrative Science Quarterly*, 41: 116–45.

Robbins, J. A. (1993), 'Organization as Strategy: Restructuring Production in the Film Industry', *Strategic Management Journal*, 14: 103–18.

Robinson, P., and Hayes, M. (1991), 'Entrepreneurial Education in America's Major Universities', *Entrepreneurship Theory and Practice*, 15/3: 41–52.

Ryan, J. (1985), *The Production of Culture in the Music Industry: The ASCAP–BMI Controversy* (Lanham, Md.: University Press of America).

Sanjek, R. (1988), *American Popular Music and its Business: From 1900 to 1984* (New York: Oxford University Press).

Saxenian, A. L. (1996), 'Beyond Boundaries: Open Labor Markets and Learning in Silicon Valley', in M. B. Arthur and D. Rousseau (eds.), *The Boundaryless Career: A New Employment Principle for a New Organizational Era* (Oxford: Oxford University Press), 23–39.

Schumpeter, J. A. (1934), *Theory of Economic Development* (Cambridge, Mass.: Harvard University Press).

Scott, W. R. (1995), *Institutions and Organizations* (Thousand Oaks, Calif.: Sage).

Sewell, W. H. (1992), 'A Theory of Structure: Duality, Agency, and Transformation', *American Journal of Sociology*, 98: 1–29.

Starr, P. (1982), *The Social Transformation of American Medicine* (New York: Basic Books).

Stern, R. N. (1979), 'The Development of an Interorganizational Control Network: The Case of Intercollegiate Athletics', *Administrative Science Quarterly*, 22: 242–66.

Sterling, C. H., and Haight, H. R. (1978), *The Mass Media: Guide to Music Industry Trends* (New York: Aspen Institute).

Thornton, P. H. (1999), 'The Sociology of Entrepreneurship', *Annual Review of Sociology*, 25: 19–46.

Thornton, P. H. and Ocasio, W. (1999), 'Institutional Logics and the Historical Contingency of Power in Organizations: Executive Succession in the Higher Education Publishing Industry, 1958–1990', *American Journal of Sociology*, 105: 801–843.

Weick, K. E. (1996), 'Enactment and the Boundaryless Career: Organizing as we Work', in M. B. Arthur and D. M. Rousseau (eds.), *The Boundaryless Career: A New*

Employment Principle for a New Organizational Era (Oxford: Oxford University Press), 40–57.

White, H. C., and White, C. A. (1993), *Canvases and Careers: Institutional Change in the French Paining World*, rev. edn. (Chicago: University of Chicago Press).

Wilensky, H. (1961), 'Orderly Careers and Social Participation', *American Sociological Review*, 70: 137–58.

14

Careers Creating Industries: Some Early Evidence from the Biotechnology Industry

MONICA C. HIGGINS

In general, the literature on careers has focused on understanding the deter-minants of individual-level career outcomes such as professional advance-ment, work satisfaction, and career choice and change (e.g. Kilduff and Day 1994; Malos and Campion 2000). Such research has led to a host of interesting findings regarding the psychological, sociological, and organizational factors that affect individuals' career trajectories. Rarely, however, have researchers studied how individuals' career trajectories or sequences of work experiences affect outcomes that extend beyond the individual—to the organization or industry levels. This missing link, from the micro-level of individuals' careers to the macro-level of the development of organizations in an industry, is the focus of the present chapter. Both the quantitative and qualitative data I introduce here suggest that the careers of executives in the biotechnology industry—and, especially, two central employment affiliations—played a major role in the industry's development.

Organizations are made on the backs of individuals' careers; leaders and managers of organizations affect the fate of organizations and, in turn, the devel-opment of industries. Individuals' career histories shape who those individuals are, how they lead and manage, and outsiders' perceptions of the same, affecting organization-level outcomes. However, this micro–macro link—from individuals' careers to organizational outcomes or, more boldly, to the evolution of industries—has rarely been studied. When organizational scholars study the comings and goings of companies in an industry, they often adopt a popula-tion ecology perspective on the phenomenon, focusing on the ebbs and flows of clusters of companies—of environmental niches—as they exist in the busi-ness environment (e.g. Hannan and Freeman 1977; Lomi 1995). The backgrounds of individual leaders and managers—and the ebbs and flows of their careers—often remain unexplored.

To investigate how careers create industries, I investigate early evidence from one industry—biotechnology. I focus in particular on one aspect of the evolution of the biotechnology industry: the initial public offerings (IPOs) of the firms that comprise the industry. The IPO is one of the most important events in the lifetime of a young firm. With the transformation from private to public ownership, young US firms become subject to intense scrutiny from shareholders, the investment banking community, the Securities and Exchange Commission (SEC), and thousands of potential investors. With a significant number of IPOs, what was previously simply a group of young organizations engaged in similar business emerges as a recognizable collective—an industry. As more firms go public, an industry is 'put on the map'; analysts begin to track these groups of firms and to compare their values, developing a marketplace for investors that, in turn, spurs the growth of the firms. Thus, the IPOs of young firms are essential events in the emergence of an industry.

The IPO transaction is complex, expensive, and time-consuming (for a full discussion of the process, see Bochner and Priest 1993). Information asymmetries abound between the firm and its potential investment community, creating a role for the reputation effects and signaling that have been studied by finance scholars for decades. In industries such as biotechnology, product development cycles are extremely long (seven to ten years) and the needs for cash are in the hundreds of millions of dollars (Burrill and Lee 1993), further exacerbating the effects of the uncertainty surrounding the IPO transaction. Moreover, the quality of the technology on which biotechnology companies are founded is also complex and highly uncertain. While some have argued that the better the technological quality of a young firm, the easier it is for the firm to attract the attention of the investment community and so have a successful IPO (e.g. Deeds *et al.* 1997), observing direct evidence of firm quality is problematic. Even seemingly obvious indicators, such as the number of patents held by a firm, have received mixed reviews in recent studies of their effects on investors' perceptions (DeCarolis and Deeds 1999). Thus, while the technological advancement of a firm's product is important, it may not be a sufficient indicator of firm quality.

In such a context, a young firm's senior executives' ability to signal the firm's quality to the investment community is paramount. The leaders of young firms have many different ways to highlight their firms' value. For example, top executives can showcase the firm's strategic alliances and venture capital partnerships to signal the endorsements the firm has received from powerful third parties. In a similar fashion, licensing agreements the company has for any of its proprietary products or technologies, either with other biotechnology companies or major pharmaceuticals, might send positive signals regarding both the firm's endorsements and its technology. Beyond the firm's partnerships, investors may also consider the timing of the IPO—that is, how hot or cold the marketplace is when the firm is trying to go public (e.g. Lerner 1994).

Yet what else, beyond these firm- and market-level factors, influences perceptions and expectations regarding young firms, and, so, the making of an industry? One important signal of firm quality that a firm's top managers can utilize in selling the young firm to the investment community is the career histories of those leading the firm through the IPO process. The better the capabilities and connections of the firm's top executives, the more confidence outsiders should have in the firm's ability to generate a viable product, to manage internal resources effectively, and to bring products to market. Favorable signals of the quality of a firm, its top management team, and the team's social and human capital should attract the attention of the investment community—in a manner similar to the process described by Jones (this volume) in which individual players in creative industries can signal identity, competency, and relationships to the industry as a whole. Here, I examine the effects of signals associated with individuals' careers on the success of a firm's IPO and, as a collective of firms going public, on the evolution of an industry.

CAREER HISTORIES AND THE IPO

When a company files its S-1, the legal document required by the SEC for transition to public status in the USA, it is required to list the five-year career histories of the managing officers and board members in a section called 'Company Information'. This information is made available to interested investment banks prior to the S-1 filing and, later, during the firm's 'road show' to potential investors, as it tries to attract investors to endorse the firm. Thus, along with other characteristics of a new venture, the career histories of those leading and managing the firm may provide valuable signals to the investment community regarding the firm's potential.

From a theoretical perspective, organizational scholars often conceptualize a 'career' as an individual's sequence of work experiences (e.g. Arthur *et al.* 1989; Cochran 1994). There are a variety of important aspects of an individual's prior work experiences that constitute his or her career. First, one can consider the nature of the work or the specific job-related activities that an individual engaged in (for example, expanding operations into a specific region or country, or executing an organizational change initiative). Secondly, one can consider the specific role or job functions fulfilled (for example, working in a marketing or finance function). And, thirdly, one can consider the types of organizations or employers for which an individual worked. Each of these three aspects— here, with respect to the careers of biotechnology executives—will be considered separately and examined with respect to the signals it might convey to the investment community.

The CEO's career

First, I consider the career of the individual whose prior work experience probably signals the most in the uncertain context of an IPO—the Chief Executive Officer (CEO). The better the background of the CEO, the more confidence the investment community will probably have in the firm's ability to get off to a good start in the industry—in the short run, the ability to go public, and, in the long run, the ability to generate returns for investors. Considering the aforementioned dimensions of task-specific work experience, job function, and prior employment, we can put ourselves in the shoes of potential investors and ask the following questions: (1) will the CEO's prior task-specific work experience benefit the firm in its quest to go public—to be specific, has the CEO had prior IPO experience in the industry; (2) does the CEO's prior job function suggest that he or she will be able successfully to set the direction of the firm—to be specific, has the CEO had prior experience as a CEO (or rough equivalent, such as a president); and (3) does the CEO's affiliation with a previous employer suggest that he or she acquired capabilities and connections that could benefit the young firm?

Regarding the last question, (3), both the prestige and the type of employer(s) for whom the CEO has worked are relevant aspects of the CEO's career history. Prior research has suggested that individuals' ties to prestigious others indicate that they may have access to valuable resources, affecting career outcomes such as obtaining a high-status job (Lin *et al.* 1981). Extending this line of thinking to the level of the firm, I propose that ties to prestigious organizations—specifically, top executives' previous employers—may signal to the investment community the availability of valuable resources, affecting the firm's quest for financial capital. Such resources could be in the form of scientific information and contacts, which one might have by virtue of having worked for a pre-eminent research institution such as the National Institutes of Health (NIH). Or, these resources could be in the form of industry-specific information and contacts, which one might have by virtue of having worked for a prestigious biotechnology firm. Or, these resources might be in the form of information and contacts that could help the young firm bring a product to market, which one might have by virtue of having worked for a prestigious pharmaceutical or health-care company. Therefore, with respect to a biotechnology CEO's prior employment, it would be valuable to know if he or she had worked for a prestigious research institution, biotechnology firm, or pharmaceutical/health-care firm in the past.

Figure 14.1 presents data on the careers of CEOs of biotechnology companies that went public in the USA between 1979 and 1996. The sample consists of executives working at 296 biotechnology firms that went public; the firms were founded between 1961 and 1994. Approximately 86 per cent of the firms specialized in the development of therapeutics and/or human diagnostics; the

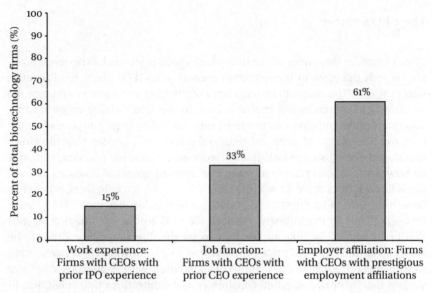

Fig. 14.1. CEO career histories.

Note: $n = 296$ public biotechnology firms.

majority of the remaining firms specialized in agriculture and/or other bio-logical products, generally with the expressed intention of engaging in thera-peutic applications in the future. The average age of the companies at the time of their IPOs was 4.87 years. The career history information for the firm's senior executives was gathered from the final IPO prospectuses of the 296 firms and then coded to create a database of career histories of over 3,200 biotechnology executives.[1]

Figure 14.1 shows that 15 percent of the firms that went public had CEOs with prior IPO experience in the industry, 33 percent of the CEOs had immediately prior experience as CEOs, and 61 percent had an employment affiliation with a prestigious research organization, biotechnology firm, and/or pharmaceutical/ health-care company. If we consider each type of employment affiliation separ-ately, the CEO's employment with a prestigious pharmaceutical/health-care company is the most frequent. Specifically, 40 percent of the public biotech-nology firms had a CEO who had worked for a prestigious pharmaceutical/ health-care organization, compared with only 13 percent and 14 percent who had worked for prestigious research and biotechnology organizations, respectively.

[1] For more information on the construction of the database and coding of career histories, please see Higgins and Gulati (2001).

Although these data do not consider private firms nor is the analysis predictive, this descriptive information does suggest that there may be relationships between the CEO's career history and his or her firm's ability to go public that are worthy of future research. In particular, the data suggest that the investment community may attend to the employment-based affiliations of the leaders of these young firms even more than the specific tasks or job functions they held in their careers. In the past, organizational scholars have suggested that firms benefit from having prestigious organization-level affiliations such as alliances (e.g. Podolny 1993; Stuart *et al.* 1999). The present data point to the possibility that firms may also benefit from prestigious affiliations derived from their CEOs' career histories.

The IPO team's career histories

During the IPO process, future partners and investors from the investment community are likely to be in direct contact not just with the CEO, but with other members of the firm's management and upper echelon. For example, investment bankers often meet the Chief Financial Officer (CFO) to understand the firm's financial situation and forecasts. They also often meet the head(s) of research, such as the Chief Scientific Officer (CSO) or equivalent, to understand better the firm's technology, products, and pipeline. The signaling value of the career histories of those who lead and manage the firm, therefore, is likely to extend beyond the CEO.

First, I will consider the career histories of the core management team—that is, the CEO, CFO, and CSO (or equivalent)—rather than just the CEO. This core management team is a subset of the entire IPO team, defined here to include both the managing officers and members of the firm's board of directors. Figure 14.2 shows the percentage of firms that went public that had at least one core management team member with prior IPO experience, with relevant prior experience in specific job functions/roles, and with at least one person who worked for a prestigious research organization, biotechnology company, and/ or pharmaceutical/health-care company.

As depicted in Fig. 14.2, the ratios for the core management team increase by at least one-third in each category, relative to the percentages with respect to the CEO alone. Twenty-one percent of the public firms had at least one person with prior IPO experience, 73 percent had at least one core IPO team member with relevant functional experience in his or her prior position, and 80 percent had at least one core IPO team member with a prestigious employment affiliation. Separating out this latter category, of the firms that went public, approximately 51 percent of them had an individual on their core IPO team who had worked for a prestigious pharmaceutical/health-care company, compared to 36 percent and 24 percent of firms with core management team

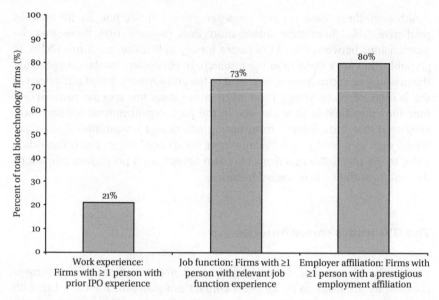

Fig. 14.2. Core management team career histories.

Notes: core management team = CEO, CFO, CSO (or equivalent); $n = 296$ public biotechnology firms.

members who had employment affiliations with prestigious research or biotechnology organizations, respectively.

Next I consider the career histories of the members of the entire IPO team—that is, both the managing officers and the board members of the firm. These descriptive data are represented in Fig. 14.3. The average size of an IPO team in the sample was eleven people. Almost 70 percent of the firms had at least one individual on their IPO teams with prior IPO experience. Since it would be extraordinarily difficult reasonably to classify the relevance of previous job functions for all of the members of the IPO team, the job function/role category is not shown in Fig. 14.3. Looking at the prior employers of the top executives, nearly all of the firms (96 percent) had one or more IPO team members with a prestigious research, biotechnology, or pharmaceutical/health-care employment affiliation. Remarkably, the pharmaceutical/health-care employment-based affiliation accounted for 89 percent of the firms; research institution and biotechnology company affiliations accounted for 70 percent and 58 percent of the firms, respectively.

What does this signify? At the most general level, these descriptive data point to the likelihood that the career histories of a young firm's IPO team carry with them important messages that are relevant to the external community regarding the firm's ability to get off to a good start and, possibly, to survive in the industry. The fact that nearly 70 percent of the firms that were able to go

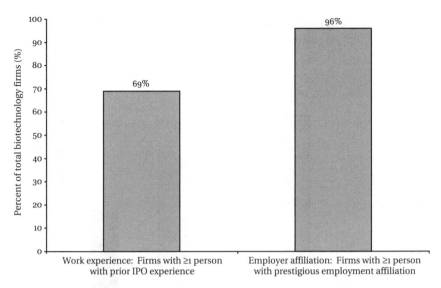

Fig. 14.3. IPO teams career histories.

Notes: IPO team = all managing officers and board members at the time of the IPO; $n = 296$ public biotechnology firms.

public had someone on their IPO team with previous biotechnology IPO experience suggests that the career experiences of these leaders may be instrumental, or at least perceived as instrumental, in the young firm's short-term goal of going public. Secondly, the number of companies with core IPO team members who had relevant functional or role-specific experience was also about 70 percent, suggesting that the capabilities obtained earlier in these leaders' careers may be transferred or perceived to be transferred, which can benefit the young firms' search for financial resources. Thirdly, the most striking connection appears to be the relevance of the employment-based affiliations of the IPO team members. Nearly all of the firms that were able to go public had at least one IPO team member who had worked for a prestigious research, biotechnology, or pharmaceutical/health-care organization prior to joining the start-up. Further, for nearly all of the firms, the type of employment affiliation that was the most prevalent on their teams was an affiliation with a prestigious pharmaceutical/health-care organization.

Figure 14.4 summarizes the percentage of biotechnology companies that had prestigious employer affiliations by type—pharmaceutical/health-care, bio-technology, or research organization—for the entire IPO team, the core team, and just the CEO. As discussed, for each level of analysis, the most prevalent type of affiliation was with prestigious pharmaceutical/health-care organizations.

Why might this one aspect of senior executives' careers, their employment-based affiliations with major pharmaceutical/health-care organizations, be

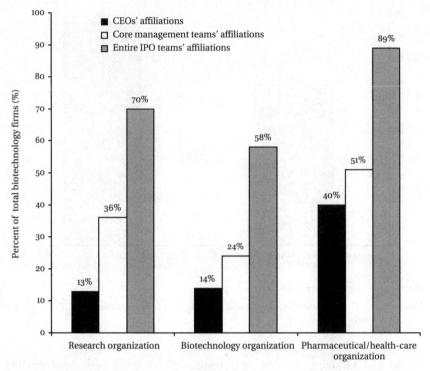

Fig. 14.4. Prestigious employer affiliations, by type.

Note: $n = 296$ public biotechnology firms.

particularly important to young biotechnology firms going public? Stepping back to understand the life cycle of a biotechnology product may be helpful. The typical biotechnology product goes through the following stages on its way to market: discovery stage, research, pre-clinical development, phases I through III clinical trials, new drug approval (NDA) filing/FDA approval pending, final market approval, and revenue generation. Generally, when biotechnology firms go public, their lead products are in early clinical stages of development and, hence, years away from generating revenue. Investors who are evaluating the firms' potential during these early stages look for indications that the firm has the ability to bring a product all the way through the time- and effort-consuming clinical trials and to the marketplace. Pharmaceutical/health-care organizations are engaged in exactly this sort of 'downstream' activity—bringing drugs and health-care products to market. The fact that members of a young biotechnology firm's IPO team have prior experience at a prestigious downstream organization may thus signal to the investment community that the firm has valuable capabilities and connections that can assist the firm in successfully reaching the revenue-generation stage. Further, the simple fact that these executives chose to leave large, established pharmaceutical/health-care companies to join young biotechnology firms may also signal the firms' quality. Such executives should be viewed as especially good judges of the firms' potential and, so, likely to associate themselves and their careers with companies they deem to be 'good bets.'

As one biotechnology executive I interviewed described,

The external community has limited bases for assessment. It's really about perceived quality; you don't *really* know. There is no sure way to judge a young biotech[nology] firm. So, you judge the firm based upon the management team's ability to bring in part of the puzzle. The idea was to get someone from a high-profile institution—an institution with some sort of intellectual property position to plan for development—and then to go out and hire a small management team and raise some money! But finding the right people is tough. A lot of senior execs from major pharma[ceutical]s...help tell the story. I don't know, but I expect some showed up, helped the company go public but didn't last long. It's hard to go from managing a cast of thousands with a big salary to a small start-up—it's a pretty good selection process, though. I guess it all goes to the mix of the team—finding the right balance.

EMPLOYMENT-BASED AFFILIATIONS AND THE IPO: A SECOND LOOK

Thus far, preliminary descriptive evidence from the biotechnology industry suggests that the careers of the individuals who lead firms through the IPO process may be related to organization-level outcomes such as the ability to go public. As a collective, then, executives' career histories—particularly their employment-based affiliations—may be valuable signals to critical third parties, such as investors, who can affect the growth of new ventures and, in turn, an industry. While prior research has investigated how organizational factors affect individuals' career trajectories (e.g. Gunz 1989), it appears that the reverse may also be true: that individuals' career trajectories affect the growth of organizations and the industries of which they are a part. In particular, this preliminary evidence from the biotechnology industry suggests that a particular type of employment-based affiliation matters—affiliations with prominent pharmaceutical/health-care organizations, organizations that engage in downstream activities relative to biotechnology firms.

Now, let us take a closer look at these data on the pharmaceutical/health-care employment affiliations of these biotechnology executives. In the data set I constructed, there are fifty pharmaceutical/health-care organizations that were classified as 'prominent' over the time period of the study. This coding scheme was based upon revenue rankings per year and included both US-based as well as international firms. An individual on the IPO team was coded as having worked for a prominent pharmaceutical/health-care organization if he or she had either worked for or sat on the board of such a firm. The majority of the affiliations in my data set were based upon prior management positions, as opposed to board seats. Since all fifty firms were considered 'prominent', any number of these employment affiliations could be related to the likelihood that a young biotechnology firm goes public. Indeed, we would expect there to be relatively equal distribution across the fifty prestigious pharmaceutical/ health-care employers since they were all of a similar type and size. Yet, if we take a closer look at the data, this does not appear to be the case.

According to the CEO data, twenty-one of the biotechnology companies in my data set went public with a CEO who had worked for one specific health-care organization, Baxter International (formerly Baxter-Travenol). The next most represented pharmaceutical/health-care company was Johnson & Johnson, with eleven CEOs in the data set. When looking at the three-person core management team, we find the same pharmaceutical/health-care organization dominating the field: twenty-seven firms had core management teams with at least one person from Baxter, while the next most common prestigious employment affiliation was SmithKline, which accounted for twenty of the biotechnology firms. The most striking fact, however, comes from the career histories of the entire IPO team: sixty-seven companies, or 23 percent of the entire database of biotechnology firms that went public between 1979 and 1996, had at least one person on their IPO team who had worked for Baxter. The next highest pharmaceutical/health-care organization was Johnson & Johnson, which had employment affiliations with members of fifty-five companies (18 percent of the database). Further, if we simply look at the total number of occurrences of people in the database—that is, the number of times IPO team members sat on firms that went public (i.e. one person who was on two IPO teams would count twice)—the Baxter affiliation again appears the most frequently, ninety-one times. The next highest occurrence is SmithKline, which occurs seventy-six times. Finally, if we look at the number of unique people in the database with prestigious pharmaceutical/health-care affiliations, Baxter comes out on top again. Baxter had eighty-three unique people in the data set, as compared with SmithKline, Bristol Myers Squibb, Johnson & Johnson, and Abbott Labs, which all had between fifty-six and sixty people represented.

According to recent estimates by Recombinant Capital, Baxter's involvement in the industry is not unique to the IPOs of the biotechnology industry. This research suggests that the majority of biotechnology firms were founded by individuals who came from specific major pharmaceutical and health-care organizations: 'the vast majority of biotech's first-generation leaders got their training either at Abbott, Baxter, or American Hospital Supply' (Van Brunt 2000: 8). In sum, it appears that some career histories mattered more than others in helping to get the biotechnology firms founded and to move from private to public status. As my data indicate, especially with regard to the latter, Baxter is the single most represented company in the career histories of those individuals who were instrumental in the development of the biotechnology industry.

The next obvious question to ask is, why? Saxenian's account (1994) of the making of Silicon Valley similarly suggests that there were significant contributions of specific firms to the making of this high-technology region. Although she was not studying an industry in and of itself, her investigation into the origins of that region reveal the predominance of certain players. Saxenian suggests that specific institutions, such as Stanford, Fairchild Semiconductors, Hewlett-Packard, and, later, Lockheed, spawned much of the growth and development in this region in California—development, she argues, that could not have occurred elsewhere. That, perhaps, is also a story about the significance of careers in building a collective of firms. However, research by Kenney (2000) and colleagues suggest that the emergence of that region was due to a host of factors that led to the development of a self-perpetuating ecological system. In their work, they acknowledge the importance of other forms of institutions such as venture capital firms, law firms, the military, and the political environment—factors that extend well beyond the career histories of individual players.

The growth of the biotechnology industry has some differences from that of Silicon Valley that are worth mentioning. Here, I merely offer some speculation, as these are preliminary data worth much more research and attention. First, this is not a simple story about regional advantage. While the biotechnology industry is bifurcated in terms of geography, with two major centers of activity in the Cambridge/Boston and San Francisco areas, one clear difference is the location of Baxter vis-à-vis the start-up biotechnology firms versus the location of organizations that Saxenian suggested played a role in the development of Silicon Valley. Baxter's headquarters were in Deerfield, Illinois (near Chicago), and yet most biotechnology firms were founded on either the east or west coasts. Therefore, the ecosystem that Kenney and colleagues describe, consisting of a variety of institutions that served various functions necessary for the growth of the industry and were concentrated in one geographical area, was not present for the biotechnology industry in the same way that it was for Silicon Valley. While it is true that scientists and, later, executives of biotechnology firms did work in concentrated geographic areas such as Cambridge/Boston and San Francisco, the business side of these enterprises resulted from an influx of people from outside these academic regions.

The second major difference appears to be the structure of the founding teams of firms in biotechnology versus those established in Silicon Valley. Biotechnology firms generally had more than one founder—a scientific founder and a business founder. The scientist was often someone working in a major scientific laboratory such as the Whitehead Institute or the Dana Farber Cancer Institute. As discussed, the business founders often came from major pharmaceutical/health-care organizations in other areas of the USA. These initial conditions differ from those high-technology firms in Silicon Valley in which there was less division of labor among the founders; indeed, many of the early founders in the Silicon Valley firms were engineers and, so, the expertise necessary for a successful business resided in a single individual (or group of individuals who shared common knowledge). In the biotechnology industry, in order for individuals from major pharmaceutical/health-care organizations to join up with scientists and launch these young biotechnology firms, they had to stretch beyond their own career experience and join a new venture that was, to them, both uncertain and ambiguous. This difference in the nature of the founding teams meant that this was a particularly strong situation in which people from organizations such as Baxter made decisions to change careers. In sum, I would speculate that this was, in many respects, a higher-risk career decision than it was for those individuals who left well-established firms in the San Mateo area to launch firms in Silicon Valley. As one of the early founders described, in the early years of the industry, 'you [had] to force yourself to make decisions based on imperfect information...early on [in the history of the biotech industry], we truly felt it was a great experiment' (Van Brunt 2000: 8).

Why, then, would individuals leave a well-established pharmaceutical/ health-care organization such as Baxter, to become involved in new bio-technology firms in a high-risk, uncertain, and entirely new industry on the east coast? Further, why were executives from this one firm, Baxter, significantly more involved than those from other major pharmaceutical/health-care organizations in the development of the industry? Having provided preliminary evidence that affiliations with particular firms can have an effect on the growth and development of young firms and, as a collective of firms, on the growth of an industry, I now offer suggestions for future research to explore the questions just posed.

SPECULATIONS AND DIRECTIONS FOR FUTURE RESEARCH

Stepping back from the comparison with Silicon Valley, I offer three specula-tions as to why Baxter careers mattered in the growth and development of the biotechnology industry: (1) Baxter's entrepreneurial culture, (2) Baxter's organ-izational design, (3) Baxter's social network.

George Rathmann, founder of the major biotechnology firm Amgen, described how both Baxter and Abbott Labs had different, more entrepren-eurial cultures than most other pharmaceutical/health-care organizations when the biotechnology industry began:

Abbott and Baxter put a lot of people...into biotech....It wasn't an accident that so many people came from those companies. People were receptive about moving into biotech in the first place because the companies had an entrepreneurial mindset. [Abbott and Baxter are] in a different class [from Lilly, Merck, Schering-Plough, Pfizer and American Home Products]....The pharmas in general tend to be ingrown and passive.

They don't necessarily see any reason to change the status quo and they aren't really interested in 'shaky' ventures. Especially in the early days of biotech's history, I don't think the average pharmaceutical executive was interested in or would have been suitable to head a biotech company.   (Van Brunt 2000: 14)

Baxter was well known for its entrepreneurial culture. In general, Baxter adopted what they called the 'Wee Willie Keeler' strategy of 'hit 'em where they ain't' (a reference to a Hall of Fame baseball player from the early part of the twentieth century) in which the company targeted niche opportunities that had been neglected by other companies. This has been described as a 'high-risk' corporate strategy, when compared with other hospital or medical product companies (Cody 1994). Further, the company was one of the earliest to institute a profit-sharing plan, in 1945, that aligned its employees around the company's entrepreneurial and risk-taking strategy. As Gabe Schmergel, founder of Genetics Institute, and one of the first executives to leave Baxter to be involved in the biotechnology industry, described: 'The atmosphere [at Baxter] was electric.... If you did your job, you were left alone and given more responsibility. Interesting, isn't it? The reward for outstanding performance was to get less management attention!' (Cody 1994: 10–11).

As another early founder and former Baxter manager described to me, 'we were like a band of brothers and some sisters. So it was an incredible period of growth and entrepreneurial atmosphere. It's amazing... how entrepreneurial Baxter was... how non-bureaucratic it was.' Perhaps, as a result of the organizational culture, the individuals who worked in this company had a lower threshold for leaving a well-established firm to venture out and start a new company in an industry that did not even yet exist.

In general, as discussed, the perceived risks associated with making a career transition from a pharmaceutical/health-care firm to a young biotechnology firm were probably great during the late 1970s and early 1980s: there was technological risk associated with the long time horizons required to bring a biotechnology product to market; there was financial risk associated with the need to raise hundreds of millions of dollars of cash to run these small firms; and there were career-related risk factors such as partnering with a scientific founder with expertise different from one's own. Yet, it is conceivable that working for an entrepreneurial company such as Baxter would lower these perceived risks and perhaps even entice a pharmaceutical/healthcare executive to venture out and experiment in a related, and yet unknown and undefined, business.

Secondly, the organizational design of Baxter supported this entrepreneurial culture. Information gathered from my own interviews with executives in the industry suggest that Baxter was a highly decentralized and flat organization, unlike the other pharmaceutical/health-care organizations. Baxter employees were promoted up and out to lead and manage divisions, as part of their own career development. Since these divisions were run rather autonomously, division heads felt as though they were, as one former Baxter manager described it, 'running [their] own companies'. As another ex-Baxter manager explained to me, 'Baxter was quite decentralized. ... I don't know, we must have had forty country managers. ... then these young people very quickly gained tremendous general management experience.' In short, not only did the company culture encourage entrepreneurial behavior such as risk taking and innovative thinking on the job; the design of the organization also enabled people to take on increasing levels of responsibility, which was serendipitously preparing them for running new ventures.

This type of organizational design created both excitement and fear simultaneously, as young executives took on such huge responsibilities. As one former Baxter manager described, 'it [was] a common experience of pressure, fun, fear, because there was incredible fear of failure in Baxter. You failed, you were out and there were no excuses, there was no nothing. You screwed up, you were gone. [These were] tremendously exciting times for young people; Baxter gave to the very young tremendous responsibility on a sink-or-swim basis.' This general management experience may also have been recognized by outsiders, such as venture capitalists, who were interested in funding new companies, making Baxter a superb target or breeding ground for CEOs of the future.

Thirdly, one of the motivating factors for Baxter managers to create and lead young biotechnology firms may have been the existence of a powerful social network. Although this sink-or-swim atmosphere at Baxter did create competition among colleagues, it was also an intense environment in which individuals developed tremendous respect for one another as they tried to take on such enormous responsibility. As one former Baxter manager described:

[At] Baxter, they had a lot of meetings. ... So you got to learn from other people and they got to learn a bit about your business. I don't know very much about the artificial organs business or the parenteral products business. I know enough just for interaction with those people. So it was really dynamic and ... we had a lot of fun. And it was a sink-or-swim operation too. I mean the guys that I'm talking about that all became my friends were all guys that kind of bubbled up to the top. And I had friends, people who didn't [interact in similar ways], who weren't bubbling up to the top.

So, despite the sink-or-swim environment, there was an atmosphere of camaraderie that enabled the Baxter managers to form a solid network—one that was established enough by the early 1980s for individuals to call on each other for help, as they began their new ventures. In fact, I would speculate that, while both Baxter and Abbott were similar entrepreneurial institutions from which people launched their careers into biotechnology, the reason that we find Baxter much more involved later in the evolution of these firms is due to the networks developed at Baxter. Put differently, although the perceived threshold for entry into an entrepreneurial venture could have been about the same for Baxter people as it was for Abbott, what allowed for the diffusion of individuals during the later growth stages of the industry could have been the types of relationships that were formed at Baxter. As one executive described,

'[X, a Baxter colleague,] left in 1980. We kept in contact when he came out here. [X] had been asking me when I would come out. I said, "No, I can't do this yet." And so anyway, in 1983, I finally made it out. I spoke with [him] and I said okay, you win. So then I came out.'

While this sort of recruiting behavior may not be characteristic of all the firms started by Baxter employees, one possible reason why Baxter remained involved beyond the founding of the companies to their IPOs is the ongoing instrumental support of the networks the employees had developed while at Baxter. Indeed, my own interviews suggest that ex-Baxter employees developed their own formal alumni group and held annual events to reconnect with each other. Beyond this, it appears that several of the early founders of the bio-technology industry from Baxter developed informal mechanisms for staying in touch, such as parties and vacations together—gatherings that were conducive to help-giving and help-receiving that may have been critical to the people launching young firms in the new industry. I would speculate that, while Abbott and Baxter may both have had entrepreneurial cultures and decen-tralized organizational structures, it is possible that the social networks developed at Baxter were simply better, enabling the companies founded by Baxter and the involvement of these individuals to have a more lasting effect on the growth of the biotechnology industry.

These speculations as to the relevance of the career histories of executives in the biotechnology industry suggest several next steps for research. The first is to compare the career histories of individuals in both Abbott and Baxter to understand the similarities and differences between what appears to have been a cohort of individuals who left major pharmaceutical/health-care organ-izations to start the biotechnology industry in the late 1970s and early 1980s. Secondly, I would recommend engaging in qualitative research to understand the extent to which the subjective aspects of these individuals' careers differed. For example, was there truly less perceived risk by the individuals who decided to join the early founders after the first wave of people left the pharmaceutical/ health-care organizations? Or, put another way, did the process of diffusion in the biotechnology industry differ from pharmaceutical/health-care firm to pharmaceutical/health-care firm and why? Further, were there differences in the helping behavior or networks of the two groups that facilitated one group having a more lasting impact than the other? These are only a few questions that could be pursued in future research on the way that careers were instrumental in creating the biotechnology industry.

CONCLUDING THOUGHTS

In this chapter, I have focused on one industry in particular, presenting only preliminary evidence to suggest that there are associations between individuals' careers and the making of an industry, associations that are worthy of future research. I note that organizational scholars who study populations of organizations have also turned their attention to the relationships between individual career moves and industry dynamics (e.g. Haveman 1995). Much of this work has focused primarily on the effects of industry-level phenomena such as the founding, merger, and dissolution of companies, on opportunity structures, and, so, on individuals' jobs and careers. Thus, macro-level organizational research has begun to integrate micro-level events associated with individuals' careers into industry studies. The research proposed here runs in the opposite direction, extrapolating from careers and relationships up to the level of organizational outcomes. I hope that engaging in research that addresses how careers create industries will inform this macro-level research in at least two respects. First, this research will focus on interpersonal relationships and networks, placing career moves such as the founding of firms into an important relational context. Secondly, the approach suggested will be qualitative, rather than entirely quantitative, providing in-depth understanding of how individuals' career experiences and relationships affect the early stages of entrepreneurial firms and young industries. Further, it is hoped that this work will expand the inquiry of careers research, which has, traditionally, focused on individual-level outcomes, to understand more macro-level questions such as the impact of individuals' careers on the making of industries. This approach marks a departure from prior careers research and, yet, as this preliminary evidence suggests, may be an area of inquiry well worth investigating.

REFERENCES

Arthur, M. B., and Rousseau, D. M. (1996) (eds.), *The Boundaryless Career: A New Employment Principle for a New Organizational Era* (New York: Oxford University Press).
—— Hall, D. T., and Lawrence, B. S. (1989) (eds.), *Handbook of Career Theory* (Cambridge: Cambridge University Press).
Bochner, S. E., and Priest, G. M. (1993), *Guide to the Initial Public Offering*, 2nd edn. (New York: Merrill Corporation).
Burrill, G. S., and Lee, K. (1993), *Biotech 94* (San Francisco: Ernst & Young).
Cochran, L. (1994), 'What is a Career Problem?', *Career Development Quarterly*, 42: 204–15.
Cody, T. G. (1994), *Innovating for Health: The Story of Baxter International* (Deerfield, Ill.: Baxter International).
DeCarolis, D. M., and Deeds, D. L. (1999), 'The Impact of Stocks and Flows of Organizational Knowledge on Firm Performance: An Empirical Investigation of the Biotechnology Industry', *Strategic Management Journal*, 20: 953–68.
Deeds, D. L., DeCarolis, D., and Coombs, J. E. (1997), 'The Impact of Firm-Specific Capabilities on the Amount of Capital Raised in an Initial Public Offering: Evidence from the Biotechnology Industry', *Journal of Business Venturing*, 12: 31–46.

Gunz, H. P. (1989), 'The Dual Meaning of Managerial Careers: Organizational and Individual Levels of Analysis', *Journal of Management Studies*, 26: 225–50.

Hannan, M. T., and Freeman, J. (1977), 'The Population Ecology of Organizations', *American Journal of Sociology*, 82: 929–64.

Haveman, H. A. (1995), 'The Demographic Metabolism of Organizations: Industry Dynamics, Turnover, and Tenure Distributions', *Administrative Science Quarterly*, 40: 586–92.

Higgins, M. C., and Gulati, R. (2001), 'Getting off to a Good Start: The Effects of Upper Echelon Affiliations on Interorganizational Endorsements and IPO Success', working paper, Harvard Business School, Boston.

Kenney, M. (2000) (ed.), *Understanding Silicon Valley: The Anatomy of an Entrepreneurial Region* (Stanford, Calif.: Stanford University Press).

Kilduff, M., and Day, D. V. (1994), 'Do Chameleons Get Ahead? The Effects of Self-Monitoring on Managerial Careers', *Academy of Management Journal*, 37: 1047–60.

Lerner, J. (1994), 'Venture Capitalists and the Decision to Go Public', *Journal of Financial Economics*, 35: 293–316.

Lin, N., Ensel, W. M., and Vaughn, J. C. (1981), 'Social Resources and Strength of Ties: Structural Factors in Occupational Status Attainment', *American Sociological Review*, 46: 393–405.

Lomi, A. (1995), 'The Population Ecology of Organizational Founding: Location Dependence and Unobserved Heterogeneity', *Administrative Science Quarterly*, 40: 111–44.

Malos, S. B., and Campion, M. A. (2000), 'Human Resource Strategy and Career Mobility in Professional Service Firms: A Test of an Options-Based Model', *Academy of Management Journal*, 43: 749–60.

Podolny, J. M. (1993), 'A Status-Based Model of Market Competition', *American Journal of Sociology*, 98: 829–72.

Saxenian, A. L. (1994), *Regional Advantage: Culture and Competition in Silicon Valley and Route 128* (Cambridge, Mass.: Harvard University Press).

Stuart, T. E., Hoang, H., and Hybels, R. C. (1999), 'Interorganizational Endorsements and the Performance of Entrepreneurial Ventures', *Administrative Science Quarterly*, 44: 315–49.

Van Brunt, J. (2000), 'Biotech's Impeccable Lineage', *Signals: The Online Magazine of Biotechnology Industry Analysis*, 22 Mar.; www.signalsmag.com.

15

Career Creativity to Industry Influence: A Blueprint for the Knowledge Economy?

ROBERT J. DEFILLIPPI AND MICHAEL B. ARTHUR

Developments in the theory of creativity have begun to converge with contemporary ideas in career theory, and in particular about the impact of careers upon larger creative contexts, such as companies, industries, and host economies. Specifically, Csikszentmihalyi's systems view (1999: 314–15) sees creativity not simply as an individual act, but as '*interaction* between producer and audience'. He also sees a creative act as introducing larger social change 'that will be transmitted through *time*' (emphases added). We take inspiration from Csikszentmihalyi in our conception of career creativity, which we define as a series of creative acts over time, which in turn influence the surrounding context over time. The context, as we will address it here, includes the influence of career creativity on subsequent community, company, and industry evolution. This influence will be illustrated through the remarkable story of the 'Linux' open source software community and its originator, Linux Torvalds.

Our career creativity perspective takes three assumptions from Csikszentmihalyi's work (1996, 1999). First, individual creativity is viewed as arising from a dialectical or interactive process, in response to a set of rules and practices transmitted from an existing domain. To cite Csikszentmihalyi (1999: 315), 'One can be a creative carpenter, cook, composer, chemist or clergyman because the domains of woodworking, gastronomy, music, chemistry and religion exist.' Subsequently, the novelty, such as a new gastronomic recipe or chemical compound, is selected for inclusion in the domain. This is similar to the evolutionary variation–selection–retention framework associated in career theory with work by Miner and Robinson (1994) and Weick (1996). In this chapter we demonstrate a comparable process in the evolution of the Linux community.

A second assumption we take from Csikszentmihalyi is that creative individuals introduce change, in our case specifically through their job performance. In evolutionary terms, this involves an individual 'producing a variation which is selected by the environment' (Csikszentmihalyi 1999: 316) through job (and in turn career) behavior. This concurs with recent observations about 'idiosyncratic jobs' (Miner 1990), which in turn influence other jobs and careers in the same domain. We examine how Linus Torvalds created the Linux operating system project and also created the role of the Linux community organizer. The success of his project and role as community organizer results in a Linux domain that supported first half a dozen, then hundreds, then thousands of people worldwide in jobs and careers (some voluntary and non-profit and others quite profitable) that became embedded in the Linux community project.

A third assumption we draw from Csikszentmihalyi is that creative people and their creative careers fundamentally change the context or domain that originally nurtured their creative practices. The change is effected through 'gate-keepers'—for example, 'the teachers, critics, journal editors, museum creators, agency directors and foundation officers' (Csikszentmihalyi 1999: 315) through whom change is introduced. We illustrate how the open software movement that predated Linus Torvalds was impacted by his Linux operating system project (Wayner 2000). In the space of a few years, the system appears to have fundamentally transformed established practice in the open software domain. This transformation has brought about new commercial software activities to mediate between the emergent Linux community and the information technology marketplace.

We proceed by briefly proposing a model of the links from career to community to company to industry change. After that we offer our principal example. We use this example to illustrate some of the nuances of the model and the methods through which the proposed links occur. We suggest from the picture of Torvalds' career, and of the careers of the army of computer 'hackers' who supported his work, that the model may have broad application in the contemporary economy. It is a model that emphasizes how careers shape employment contexts, rather than how the companies that provide employment shape careers.

FROM INDUSTRY TO CAREER: THE WAY WE USED TO SEE THINGS

It used to be that the 'industrial state' view of economic life dominated the way we envisioned work and careers. In one direction, the large corporation was supposed to control its industry by 'reach[ing] forward to the markets that it [was] presumed to serve and, beyond, to bend the customer to its needs' (Galbraith 1967: 6). In another direction the corporation and its techno structure were supposed to control the communities or groups within it, through people's identification with 'the preferable [goals] of the organization' and consequent adaptation 'in the hope of influencing [those] goals' (Galbraith 1967: 157–8). Thus, 'for all but the pathologically romantic, this [was] not the age of the small [sic] man' (Galbraith 1967: 32). Worse, from the standpoint of this volume, was the dim view taken on the entrepreneurial qualities of 'imagination, capacity for decision and courage in risking money' that may be associated with creative behavior. It was felt that 'none of these qualifications [was] especially important for organizing intelligence or effectively competing with it' (Galbraith 1967: 58).

It may be argued we have come a long way since Galbraith's work appeared. However, it may also be argued that the great majority of management and organizational research still falls within the model that he described. Few research papers openly confront the neat picture of corporations and their internal groups and careers that Galbraith painted. One influential book took issue with claims about the loss of large corporate power, suggesting that 'the high road to economic growth and development' was for 'the bigger firms to help upgrade the technical capabilities of their generally smaller suppliers' (Harrison 1994: 245). The road would, in turn, conserve 'our shared understanding of what constitutes a working "career"' (Harrison 1994: 34). A later article argued forcefully that American 'welfare capitalism', the provider of 'everything from "fringe" benefits to Social Security to career employment' (Jacoby 1999: 124–35), was far from dead. Rather, the notion that corporations and 'career jobs' are 'the keystone of economic security in American society' has persevered and remains 'on trajectory' (Jacoby 1999: 139).

In sum, there remains a view among some commentators that large corporations control their industries, in one direction, and the communities and careers through which work gets done, in another direction. Let us now turn to an alternative picture.

FROM CAREER TO COMMUNITY TO COMPANY TO INDUSTRY

We have developed the model in Fig. 15.1 as a vehicle for exploring the links connecting individual career learning to emergent industry learning. The model is consistent with ideas about the career as a 'repository of knowledge' (Bird 1996). However, we extend those and related ideas by asserting that the process leading to knowledge accumulation—that is, knowing—involves more than the direct absorption of new skills and expertise.

First, in the case of the individual *career*, we see a person's learning aspirations driven by what we call *knowing-why*—that is, by his or her emergent motivation and identity (and incorporating related ideas about interests, personality, and lifestyle) as he or she engages with the world of work (Mirvis

Career

People develop their careers through three 'ways of knowing'. *Knowing-why* reflects a person's motivation and identity, *knowing-how* reflects a person's skills and expertise, and *knowing-whom* reflects a person's contacts and reputation. The process of individual learning involves interaction among all three ways of knowing.

Industry

People's career investments in companies are simultaneous investments in host industries. Accruals to company learning diffuse through career mobility and networking into larger patterns of industry learning. Companies participate in industry learning through new project sponsorship and related company learning endeavors.

Community

People's community attachments reflect *overlapping (knowing-why) identities, persistent (knowing-whom) social engagement,* and *shared (knowing-how) learning* agendas. Project communities reflect multiple, shifting personal career situations. Project participants invest their past learning in anticipation of new learning opportunities.

Company

Companies develop 'core competencies' through the accumulation of *cultural capital, human capital, and social capital.* Companies learn through the interplay of these three forms of capital. Project sponsorship provides for new company learning opportunities, which unfold alongside project performance.

Fig. 15.1. The links among career, community, company, and industry learning.

and Hall 1996). Secondly, we see learning as also influenced by what we call *knowing-whom*—that is, by the contacts and reputation (including professional attachments, mentors, and sources of information) on which a person draws in his or her work (Raider and Burt 1996). Thirdly, we see both *knowing-why* and *knowing-whom* combining to stimulate what we call *knowing-how*—namely, a person's accumulation of skills and expertise (including what are commonly referred to as formal and informal, and explicit and tacit knowledge) (Nonaka and Takeuchi 1995).

Secondly, we see people's unfolding career investments influencing the *community* attachments that they make. Various recent writers have suggested that people voluntarily attach themselves to 'communities of practice', which involve closely overlapping (*knowing-why*) member identities, affirmed by persistent (*knowing-whom*) social interaction and leading to shared (*knowing-how*) agendas about the practice of work (Brown and Duguid 1991;

Wenger 1998). Mirvis (1997) makes a similar case for communities to include 'the [*knowing-why*] emotive experience of feeling close together' and of 'living at least some of your [*knowing-whom*] life with others' in the pursuit of shared (*knowing-how*) obligations and commitments. In their career behavior people associate themselves with various 'pure types' of community, including those centered in a particular industry, occupation, project activity, ideological purpose or company objective to which the project community members subscribe (Parker and Arthur 2000).

Thirdly, it has been suggested that a *company* learns through three unfolding arenas of non-financial capital (Hall 1992), which we label here as company-based cultural capital, human capital, and social capital respectively (Arthur *et al.* 1999). A company's cultural capital reflects the shared (*knowing-why*) beliefs and values of its members and their related investment in its mission (Barney 1986). A company's human capital draws on the body of both tacit and explicit (*knowing-how*) skills and expertise available to the company (Reed and DeFillippi 1990). A company's social capital reflects the set of supplier, alliance partner, and customer contacts with which the company's members have (*knowing-whom*) relationships, and which provide complementary capabilities or information (Burt 1992). Companies frequently host the kinds of communities of practice described above, but in doing so draw on diverse sources, 'often crossing the restrictive boundaries of the organization to incorporate people from outside' (Brown and Duguid 1991: 49).

Finally, companies typically participate with one another through their host *industry*, and in doing so engage in 'population level learning' with one another (Miner and Mezias 1996; Robinson and Miner 1996). This occurs through 'an embedded logic of exchange' involving the interplay of cultural, human, and social capital whereby companies contribute to and draw learning from one another (Uzzi 1996). People who are 'at the periphery' of their companies have a particular opportunity to engage in inter-company—and therefore industry—learning endeavors (Richter 1998). Industry learning also occurs through career mobility as a participant company absorbs the knowledge of its newest members (March 1991). It is increasingly recognized that such mobility, and the self-interested career behavior underlying it, can be vital to the health of industries at large (Powell 1998), and that learning can accrue to the industry while participant firms come and go (DeFillippi and Arthur 1998).

SOME PRELIMINARY EVIDENCE

Figure 15.1 is an oversimplification, although in our view a necessary one to confront commonplace company-centric ideas about industry development. The systems of social evolution are more interdependent than the figure allows. Nevertheless, the figure provides a model to explore Csikszentmihalyi's underlying notion (1999) of the interaction between a creative individual and his or her audience. It also breaks down Csikszentmihalyi's notion of a creative domain into incremental steps—community, then company, then industry—that suggest the adaptation of career creativity by progressively larger audiences. The figure also reflects something of Giddens's ideas on structuration, as redrawn by Barley (1989)—that is, of people's careers first shaping and then being shaped by the institutions they help create. It also captures a central theme in Weick's work on the enactment of careers—namely, that 'restructuring originates from the bottom up' through 'assertion of personality and collective improvisation [that] first strengthens situations and then redraws organizational boundaries' (Weick 1996: 44).

In recent work we have illustrated the applicability of Fig. 15.1 by reference to the independent filmmaking industry (which has persistently outperformed the old studio-centric alternative), the Silicon Valley high-technology industry (which appears to rely on enduring community but temporary company attachments), and the New Zealand boat-building industry (a highly adaptive industry cluster that earned successive America's Cup victories from a relatively tiny host population and economy) (Arthur *et al.* 2001). All three industries reflect high levels of innovation, and thereby suggest relatively high opportunities for career creativity. All three have an underlying project-based approach to industry development, which, as Weick (1996) suggests, may allow for the kind of experimentation through which career creativity can make its mark.

A further feature of contemporary, innovation-centered industrial life is the emergence of the World Wide Web. The Web now has a pervasive effect on all industries, not just the high-technology industry that first spawned it. Some claim that the Web and its ability to host virtual connections across disparate buyers, sellers, and other stakeholders have become the primary mechanism for the accumulation of knowledge-based capital (Tapscott *et al.* 2000). In what follows, we will further test the cycle represented in Fig. 15.1 by reference to a Web-specific example—namely, Linux.

PICKING UP THE STORY: THE OPEN SOFTWARE MOVEMENT

The open source software movement began in the early 1970s, when software specialists from the leading university centers for computer science, including Massachusetts Institute of Technology (MIT), as well as precocious enthusiasts still in high school, were discovering a shared passion for programming.[1] Their joint enthusiasm extended to their sharing of programming solutions or 'hacks', as they came to be called. The programmers, calling each other 'hackers'

---

[1] This section draws heavily from the detailed history of hacker culture by Eric Raymond (1999). Although other sources complementing Raymond's account are duly noted in the reference citations, we would be remiss not to acknowledge our deep indebtedness to the colorful and detailed history by Eric Raymond.

as a term of respect, shared their work both in physical space through hobbyist clubs and in virtual space through electronic bulletin boards. There quickly evolved a culture that valued efficient and unique programming code, as well as its members' investment in voluntary 'side projects' that did not have commercial value (Raymond 1998). Furthermore, the programmers sometimes used their non-standard hacks to complete projects for their employers (Logue 2000).

Richard Stallman, an 18-year-old Harvard student working at MIT's Artificial Intelligence Lab in 1971, has reflected that the early open software days were 'a bit like the Garden of Eden. It hadn't occurred to us not to cooperate' (McHugh 1998: 6). However, a 'fall from grace' (Raymond 1999) occurred in the 1980s, when most of the members of the artificial intelligence group at MIT were hired away by a private corporation and ceased sharing their software solutions with their former collaborators. Trade secrecy and licensing replaced freely available software and collaborative sharing of software challenges. Instead of people sharing in the further development of Linux code, corporations began to develop their own incompatible variations.

In the PC world, a similar Rubicon had been crossed six years earlier when former software hobbyist and Harvard student Bill Gates wrote 'An Open Letter to Hobbyists'. In his open letter, Gates wrote: 'Most of you steal your software... One thing you do is prevent good software from being written. Who can afford to do professional work for nothing?' (McHugh 1998: 7). The battle lines were now drawn between Gates' Microsoft and other major corporations and the apparently disorganized group of university computer programmers, who had long enjoyed the camaraderie of their shared passion for solving and sharing software challenges.

In 1985, Stallman, by now one of the leading figures at the MIT artificial intelligence unit, reluctant to join his former colleagues in the commercial software world of trade secrecy and tightly controlled proprietary software, founded the Free Software Foundation (FSF) to promote free software projects. This shared mission would be grounded in a specific open source project, code named GNU, to develop an operating system that could be freely shared among all interested hackers. For the next decade Stallman attempted to develop such an operating system. However, a 19-year-old Finnish graduate student would ultimately realize Stallman's vision.

BEGINNING A NEW CYCLE: LINUS TORVALD'S CAREER

Linus Torvalds might well have become a journalist.[2] His father, Nils, was a journalist for Finnish TV, and his mother, Anna, was a graphic artist at the

---

[2] Much biographical detail on Linus Torvalds is derived from an article first appearing in the *San Jose Mercury* (31 Aug. 1999). However, several additional sources were consulted to

Finnish News Agency. Torvald's paternal grandfather was also a journalist. But it was his maternal grandfather, Leo Tornqvist, a professor of statistics at University of Helsinki, who exerted the most profound influence on Torvalds. In 1980 grandfather Leo bought his first personal computer and invited his grandson to join him in exploring this new technology. The 10-year-old Torvalds was an avid student and, after his grandfather died, young Torvalds took the computer home and was soon writing computer programs.

Computing became Torvalds' total passion. His only other hobby was—and he alleges still is—reading science fiction and horror books. By the time Torvalds enrolled at the University of Helsinki, he described himself thus: 'I was very self-assured when it came to programming and not very self-assured when it came to anything else' (*San Jose Mercury* 1999). This self-description is almost a caricature of the hacker, and over the years Torvalds consistently projected this persona in countless interviews with computer industry analysts and journalists. In many respects he became the poster boy for hacker culture and the open source software movement in the 1990s.

By 1991, Microsoft was the dominant supplier of operating systems for personal computers through its ubiquitous DOS (disk operating system) and more recent Windows operating system. However, Torvalds shared the view common to the open source software hackers of the time that Microsoft's operating systems were 'kludges': inelegant, messy compilations of patchwork fixes to inherently flawed source code that was proprietary to Microsoft and thus not accessible to frustrated users (Jaffee 1999).

The 19-year-old Linus Torvalds decided to create his own operating system as a personal vehicle for learning about how operating systems work. This project evolved into his doctoral dissertation at the University of Helsinki (Jaffee 1999). He began this project by building upon the work begun a decade earlier by Stallman's FSF and its GNU operating system project. Over a six-month period in 1991 Torvalds worked on his personal operating system at his mother's apartment. After completing his operating system, he talked to some fellow students who had access to the largest file transfer protocol (FTP) sites in Finland and they arranged for Torvalds to put his new operating system on electronic file. He named the system Linux as a combination of his own first name and the Unix operating system that had inspired him. Torvalds reports that he also spoke to five other people and invited them to look at his operating system on electronic file and to download it for their personal use.

THE LINKS TO A VIRTUAL COMMUNITY

Ultimately, ten people downloaded Torvalds' publicly available first operating system and five of them sent back 'bug' fixes, code improvements, and new

corroborate the factual claims of this article, and these additional sources are referenced throughout the chapter.

features. By December of 1991 more than 100 people worldwide had joined in Linux newsgroup and mailing lists. By 1992 the number of Linux users was 1,000, which grew to 20,000 in 1993, 100,000 in 1994, 500,000 in 1995, 1,500,000 in 1996, 3,500,000 in 1997, and over 7,500,000 by the end of 1998 (McHugh 1998).

These user numbers themselves are less remarkable than the fact that every single user is provided direct access to the source code for the Linux kernel (the core of the operating system). All users are encouraged to play with the operating system and to do with it as they wish. The only copyright restriction is the requirement that every user make all his or her changes in the kernel (their patches) available to everybody else. This is the exact opposite of the more usual practice of copyrights to restrict user access and imitation. Linus Torvalds invited the world to use his creation and make it better, and he did not charge anyone a licensing fee to do so. He also did not prohibit them from replicating his operating system for their use as they saw fit.

In response, the worldwide 'virtual community' of Linux hackers has evolved into one in which hundreds of thousands of hours of time have been freely given to make Linux better, without any direct compensation to the volunteer patch providers. Torvalds is both the inspirational leader and nexus of a virtual community of users who contribute a steady stream of patches (bug fixes, code improvements, and new features) to each new version of Linux. Torvalds consults with a handful of trusted computer science colleagues on which patches to incorporate in the next version of the Linux kernel (source code) core, which is then released worldwide for renewed scrutiny by an ever-expanding legion of Linux enthusiasts. Whereas five users in 1991 contributed patches to the first Linux release, by 1998 more than 10,000 voluntary pro-grammers worldwide were involved in Linux testing and code improvements (McHugh 1998).

Over the past decade Torvalds has remained the linchpin of the Linux operating system and its never-ending project of rapid releases and improve-ments. However, other technical programmers who have contributed to the improvement of Linux have earned informal recognition and roles within the Linux community. The two most important roles within this community are the *credited developer* and the *maintainer*. *Credited developers* are those people whose contributions to any particular version of a Linux software release are acknowledged in the credit files, which have accompanied each system release since 1994. By July 2000, approximately 350 contributors from over thirty countries had been acknowledged as credited developers (Moon and Sproull 2000).

Maintainers are those Linux participants responsible for particular modules of the Linux kernel. Maintainers review mailing list submissions (bug reports, fixes, and improvements) relevant to their modules and build them into larger patches, which they submit back to the Linux community and to Torvalds directly. A recent assessment of Linux patch contributions identified 147 maintainers of Linux modules (Moon and Sproull 2000). Torvalds has indicated that he gives preferential attention to patches submitted by recognized maintainers of modules and by his inner circle of programming consultants, such as Alan Cox, who is widely acknowledged as the second most central person within the community and the likely successor to Torvalds as community organizer (Wayner 2000).

LINKING COMPANY AND COMMUNITY LEARNING

Linux community members have argued with some impressive evidence that their open source development process produces more stable operating systems (that is, systems less prone to inexplicable crashes). The functionality and reliability of the Linux product have over the years spawned an ever-growing number of companies to market, distribute, and provide tools for Linux applications. These market-driven companies are not constrained by the Linux copyright from selling their services, but they are constrained from becoming monopoly suppliers of any proprietary version of Linux. All Linux derivative software must have its source code freely shared on the World Wide Web. As a result, these companies must compete on the quality of their service, and on their ingenuity in finding new applications for a non-proprietary, universally available (free) Linux operating system.

Despite these constraints, there is a growing number of young companies providing Linux-based tools and services, among them several who have attracted the attention of Wall Street. The most publicized has been Red Hat Software, a distributor of shrink-wrapped versions of Linux and a publisher of Linux books, open source tools, and technical support. Red Hat's initial public offering (IPO) achieved in less than two months a market capitalization of slightly more than $7 billion (Raynovich 1999). One observer estimates that Linux IPOs in 1999 alone raised more than $100.6 billion, with the average deal worth about $191 million (Paulson 2000). These observations predate the subsequent downslide in market valuations of Red Hat and other 'dot-coms'. However, the overall evidence remains impressive that increasing numbers of established and start-up companies are using Linux applications (*The Economist* 2001).

Linux insiders report that the major Linux-based commercial businesses have offered pre-IPO access to long-time members of the Linux developer and commercial user communities. Registered Red Hat, VA Linux, and Andover.Net customers as well as Linux code developers allegedly receive notification of pending IPOs and an opportunity to participate early in the public offerings for Linux-based distribution companies (Logue 2000). This practice is a prime example of the open source Linux community's commitment to their members.

Participants to the Linux development community are regularly recruited to software start-ups and in many cases the most celebrated and seasoned contributors to Linux development are part of the start-up founding team (Vizard 1998). Torvalds himself has been recruited to a series of highly attractive daytime jobs. As this work goes to press he is employed at Transmeta, a microprocessor development company in Silicon Valley, where Torvalds now lives with his wife and children. Although the company is not involved in Linux-related technology development, one condition of Torvalds' employment is that he is allowed to use 50 percent of his work time on Linux-related activities (Hibbard 2000).

Other Linux community members have also leveraged their enhanced career capital into more remunerative jobs and more challenging programming project assignments. Thus, the Linux project has become a valuable test bed for aspiring hackers to prove their mettle and to earn and then leverage professional community recognition. Some Linux companies directly fund Linux development work. For example, Red Hat funds development work by Linux maintainer and 'inner circle' member Alan Cox, who does not work directly for Red Hat. This form of Linux development funding is viewed as an invaluable mechanism for Linux commercial companies to support the continuation of the Linux community phenomenon. According to Red Hat's Chief Operating Officer, Tim Buckley:

> The last thing we want to do is start getting isolated from the (Linux) community, which we are accused of a bit, but only because we are getting bigger and have a reputation... [It] makes us want to double our efforts. We...give everything back to the community. [We] have three or four of the top [Linux] kernel developers on our payroll and they're not developing Red Hat stuff—that's just another sign that we're trying to make sure the community and the kernel development remains solid.   (MacCormack and Herman 1999: 11).

THE FURTHER EVOLUTION OF THE SOFTWARE INDUSTRY

As companies like Red Hat are showered with publicity in such traditional business media outlets as *Fortune* and the *Wall Street Journal*, the awareness of the Linux brand is expanding from its original base in the university software community to the server community that routes messages between nodes on the World Wide Web. It is here that the superior reliability of the Linux operating system is highly valued for repetitive computer network operations, such as managing printers, e-mail services, or Internet connections (Shinal 1999). Thus, it appears that the very Internet and World Wide Web infrastructure that made possible the community of Linux developers is the first commercial market beneficiary of the tools and applications created by this community.

Established corporations in the information industry have begun to take notice. IBM, for example, has now become a major contributor to a Linux-based web page program called Apache (Harmon 1999). Furthermore, IBM has committed $1 billion for 2001 to make its entire product line, from PCs to mainframe, Linux compatible (*The Economist* 2001). Finally, the Linux community appears to be creating a growing number of 'infomediary' electronic commerce companies to facilitate more productive linkages between Linux developers and potential Linux users. For example, SourceXchange is such a web site for bringing together corporations and engineers to complete specific projects. The site helps organize open source Linux developers for corporate clients who will then pay for services provided on a project-by-project basis (Raynovich 1999).

In summary, let us refer back to the model we introduced earlier in this chapter (Fig. 15.1). The emergence of the Linux operating system traces back to Linus Torvalds' (*knowing-why*) career motivation, the (*knowing-how*) skills in software programming he developed, and the (*knowing-whom*) community he attracted to his UNIX-based software development efforts. An emerging community of hackers who shared his enthusiasm for the Linux project and complemented his talents further developed Torvalds' work. That community in turn gave rise—and as we write this continues to give rise—to a range of entrepreneurial companies offering enhancements to the underlying Linux standard. The collective efforts of that growing range of companies are having an ever-greater influence over the software industry.

STORY OR BLUEPRINT: WHAT CAN WE LEARN FROM THE LINUX EXAMPLE?

The history of Linus Torvalds and his associates is not an isolated example of creative careers becoming magnets for the development of creative communities, and these in turn fostering creative companies and new industries and industry segments. The history of high technology is full of examples of creative individuals inspiring shared (*knowing-why*) visions and collaborative (*knowing-whom*) social interactions leading to the development of new (*knowing-how*) capabilities and groundbreaking new architectures. One example of many is that of Carver Mead and his California Institute of Technology collaborators who gave rise to a succession of Silicon Valley semiconductor companies throughout the 1970s and 1980s (Gilder 1989). The spin-off software and semiconductor companies resulting from Torvalds' and Mead's initiatives offer examples of what has been called the 'Silicon Valley Way' (Saxenian 1994), involving people pursuing their own creativity, attracting a small community of followers, founding a company, and taking a turn at changing the industry. The innovation resulting from creative communities is arguably the same for the geographically defined creative communities of Silicon Valley as it is for the global and virtual communities of Linux (Tuomi 2001).

Do we stop, however, at applying the lessons of the Torvalds example to a limited high-technology world remote from the occupations and industries in which most careers unfold? Or do we draw lessons for other project-based industries, such as the film industry, which we see as a crucible of creative careers (DeFillippi and Arthur 1999), but which others argue still conforms to traditional thinking about corporate dominance (Phelan and Lewin 1999)? Do we emphasize the observations of contemporary writers on 'communities of practice' that 'we all belong to many' such communities (Wenger 1998: 158) and that these 'often [cross] the restrictive boundaries of the organization to include people from the outside' (Brown and Duguid 1991: 49)? Or do we succumb to the suggestion that we restrict our thinking to communities sub-sumed by a single corporation (Liedtka 1999), and risk drifting back to the assumptions of the industrial state?

Looking more directly at industries, do we accept strategic management guru Michael Porter's emphasis (1998: 77) that 'increasingly local things' drive industry evolution, and that these things involve 'knowledge, relationships and motivation' (and connect closely to the *knowing-why*, *knowing-whom*, and *knowing-how* framework for thinking about careers)? Do we also accept his claims that 'there is no such thing as a low-tech industry' (Porter 1998: 89), and that personal relationships and community ties foster the flow of information in industries everywhere? Do we further accept his argument that individual experiences through 'positive feedback loops' (Porter 1998: 88) drive new business formation and in turn the way industries unfold? By extension, do we rely on the notion of corporate welfare mentioned at the beginning of this chapter, or do we look for something different—some kind of 'career welfare' that places greater faith in the creativity of the individual but provides these creative workers with portable health-care and pension benefits that are not company controlled (DeFillippi and Arthur 1994)?

Is, then, the story of Linus Torvalds a story of one 'great person', as popular business and entrepreneurial literatures would have us believe? Or is it the story of many more 'great people', all of whom wanted to help develop the Linux system? Is that story in turn an allegory for a larger group—namely, the creative, enthusiastic, and responsible workforce who make a habit of doing more than any job description asks? Is the Torvalds story one to which the reader can relate, as we can, to people he or she knows well? In sum, is there much more potential for career creativity distributed throughout the workforce than the notion of the industrial state and its inheritors would allow? Have the 'deep potentials of the human spirit' (Csikszentmihalyi 1996: 20) yet to be realized in the knowledge economy?

We have argued here that career creativity involves community attachments, which not only influence individual career trajectories, but also give rise to the creation of companies and collaborations that transform the host industry. We anticipate that the new economy will increasingly be characterized by the types of linkages we have outlined, and which the story of the Linux operating system illustrates.

REFERENCES

Arthur, M. B., Inkson, K., and Pringle, J. K. (1999), *The New Careers: Individual Action and Economic Change* (London: Sage).

——DeFillippi, R., and Lindsay, V. (2001), 'Careers, Communities, and Industry Evolution: Links to Complexity Theory', *International Journal of Innovation Management*, 5/2: 239–56.

Barley, S. R. (1989), 'Careers, Identities and Institutions: The Legacy of the Chicago School of Sociology', in M. B. Arthur, D. T. Hall, and B. S. Lawrence (eds.), *Handbook of Career Theory* (New York: Cambridge University Press), 41–65.

Barney, J. (1986), 'Organizational Culture: Can it be a Source of Competitive Advantage?', *Academy of Management Review*, 11: 656–65.

Bird, A. (1996), 'Careers as Repositories of Knowledge: Considerations for Boundaryless Careers', in M. B. Arthur and D. M. Rousseau (eds.), *The Boundaryless Career* (New York: Oxford University Press), 150–68.

Brown, J. S., and Duguid, P. (1991), 'Organizational Learning and Communities of Practice: Toward a Unified View of Work, Learning and Innovation', *Organization Science*, 2/1: 40–57.

Burt, R. S. (1992), *Structural Holes* (Cambridge, Mass.: Harvard University Press).

Csikszentmihalyi, M. (1996), *Creativity: Flow and the Psychology of Discovery and Invention* (New York: HarperCollins).

——(1999), 'Implications of a Systems Perspective for the Study of Creativity', in R. J. Sternberg (ed.), *Handbook of Creativity* (Cambridge: Cambridge University Press), 313–35.

DeFillippi, R. J., and Arthur, M. B. (1994), 'The Boundaryless Career: A Competency-Based Perspective', *Journal of Organizational Behavior*, 15/4: 307–24.

————(1998), 'Paradox in Project-Based Enterprise: The Case of Film-Making', *California Management Review*, 40/2: 125–39.

————(1999), 'Paradox Revisited: A Reply to Phelan and Lewis', *California Management Review*, 42/1: 186–91.

DiMaggio, P. J., and Powell, W. W. (1983), 'The Iron Cage Revisited: Institutional Isomorphism and Collective Rationality in Organizational Fields', *American Sociological Review*, 48: 147–60.

The Economist (2001), 'The Penguin gets Serious', Economist.com Sunday, 11 February; http://Economist.com/displayStory.cfm?ID = 486918.

Galbraith, J. K. (1967), *The New Industrial State* (Boston: Houghton Mifflin).

Gilder, G. (1989), *Microcosm* (New York: Touchstone/Simon & Schuster).

Hall, R. (1992), 'The Strategic Analysis of Intangible Resources', *Strategic Management Journal*, 13: 135–44.

Harmon, A. (1999), 'A Surge in Popularity of Software that Unlocks the Code', *New York Times on the Web*, 4 Jan., 1–3; www.nytimes.com/library/financial/010499outlook-techweb.html.

Harrison, B. (1994), *Lean and Mean: The Changing Landscape of Corporate Power in the Age of Flexibility* (New York: Basic Books).

Hibbard, J. (2000), 'Transmeta's Big Gamble', *Red Herring*, 76 (Mar.), 113–26.

Jacoby, S. M. (1999), 'Are Career Jobs Headed for Extinction?', *California Management Review*, 42/1: 123–45.

Jaffee, S. (1999), 'Linux Takes Off—But Where is it Really Going?', *BW Online Daily Briefing*, 27 Apr., 1–6; www.businessweek.com/bwdaily/dnflash/apr1999/nf90427a.htm.

Levy, S. (1984), *Hackers* (Cambridge, Mass.: MIT Press).

Liebman, L. (1999), 'The "Lintel" Value Proposition', *PlanetIT*, 12 Nov., 1–4; www.planetit.com/techecenters/docs/linux/technology/PIT19991109S0045?printDoc = 1.

Liedtka, J. (1999), 'Linking Competitive Advantage with Communities of Practice', *Journal of Management Inquiry*, 8/1: 5–16.

Logue, B. (2000), Personal Communication, 18 Feb., Boston.

MacCormack, A., and Herman, K. (1999), 'Red Hat and the Linux Revolution', Harvard Business School Case 9-600-009.

McHugh, J. (1998), 'For the Love of Hacking', *Forbes*, 10 Aug., 1–12; www.forbes.com/forbes/98/0810/6203094a.htm.

March, J. G. (1991), 'Exploration and Exploitation in Organizational Learning', *Organization Science*, 2/1: 71–87.

Miner, A. (1990), 'Structural Evolution through Idiosyncratic Jobs: The Potential for Unplanned Learning', *Organization Science*, 1/2: 195–210.

——and Mezias, S. J. (1996), 'Ugly Duckling no More—Pasts and Futures of Organizational Learning Research', *Organizational Science*, 7/1: 88–99.

——and Robinson, F. (1994), 'Organizational and Population Level Learning as Engines for Career Transition', *Journal of Organizational Behavior*, 15: 345–65.

Mirvis, P. (1997), ' "Soul Work" in Organizations', *Organization Science*, 8/2: 193–206.

——and Hall, D. T. (1996), 'Psychological Success and the Boundaryless Career', in M. B. Arthur and D. M. Rousseau (eds.), *The Boundaryless Career: A New Employment Principle for a New Organizational Era* (New York: Oxford University Press), 237–55.

Moon, J. Y., and Sproull, L. (2000), 'The Case of the Linux Kernel', *First Monday*, 5/11; http://firstmonday.org/issues/issue5_11/moon/index.html.

Nicolini, D., and Meznar, M. B. (1995), 'The Social Construction of Organizational Learning: Conceptual and Practical Issues in the Field', *Human Relations*, 48/7: 727–46.

Nonaka, I., and Takeuchi, H. (1995), *The Knowledge Creating Company* (New York: Oxford University Press).

Parker, P., and Arthur, M. B. (2000), 'Careers, Organizing and Community', in M. A. Peiperl, M. B. Arthur, R. Goffee, and T. Morris (eds.), *Career Frontiers: New Conceptions of Working Lives* (Oxford: Oxford University Press), 99–121.

Paulson, L. D. (2000), 'Linux Millionaires', *PlanetIT*, 2 Feb., 1–4; www.Planetit.com/docs/PIT20000208S0072.

Phelan, S. E., and Lewin, P. (1999), 'Paradox in Project-Based Enterprise: What Paradox?', *California Management Review*, 42/1: 180–6.

Porter, M. E. (1998), 'Clusters and the New Economics of Competition', *Harvard Business Review*, 76: 77–90.

Powell, W. W. (1998), 'Learning from Collaboration: Knowledge and Networks in the Biotechnology and Pharmaceutical Industries', *California Management Review*, 40/3: 228–40.

Raider, H. J., and Burt, R. S. (1996), 'Boundaryless Careers and Social Capital', in M. B. Arthur and D. M. Rousseau (eds.), *The Boundaryless Career: A New*

Employment Principle for a New Organizational Era (New York: Oxford University Press), 187–200.

Radosevich, L., and Zerega, B. (1998), 'Free Money Model: Open Source Software can Make Business Sense', *World.com*, 8 June, 1–5; www.infoworld.com/cgi-bin/displayStory.pl?/features/980608free.htm.

Raymond, E. S. (1996), *The New Hacker's Dictionary*, 3rd edn. (Cambridge, Mass.: MIT Press).

—— (1998), 'The Cathedral and the Bazaar', www.tuxedo.org./~esr/writings/cathedral-bazaar/cathedral-bazaar-1.html.

—— (1999), 'A Brief History of Hackerdom', www.tuxedo.org/~esr/writings/hacker-history?hacker-history.html.

Raynovich, R. S. (1999), 'Wall Street Likes that Linux Spirit', *RedHerring.com*, 9 Sept., 1–4; http://redherring.com/insider/1999/0909/news-linux.html.

Reed, R., and DeFillippi, R. J. (1990), 'Causal Ambiguity, Barriers to Imitation and Sustainable Competitive Advantage', *Academy of Management Review*, 15: 88–102.

Richter, I. (1998), 'Individual and Organizational Learning at the Executive Level', *Management Learning*, 29/3: 299–316.

Robinson, D. F., and Miner, A. S. (1996), 'Careers Change as Organizations Learn', in M. B. Arthur and D. M. Rousseau (eds.), *The Boundaryless Career: A New Employment Principle for a New Organizational Era* (New York: Oxford University Press), 76–94.

Rosenbaum, J. E., and Miller, S. R. (1996), 'Moving in, up or out: Tournaments and Other Institutional Signals of Career Attainment', in M. B. Arthur and D. M. Rousseau (eds.), *The Boundaryless Career: A New Employment Principle for a New Organizational Era* (New York: Oxford University Press), 350–69.

San Jose Mercury (1999), 'Linus the Liberator', *SiliconValley.com*, 31 Aug., 1–6; www.mercurynews.com/svtech/news/special/linus/story.htm.

Saxenian, A. L. (1994), *Regional Advantage: Culture and Competition in Silicon Valley and Route* 128 (Cambridge, Mass.: Harvard University Press).

Shinal, J. (1999), 'Cashing in on a Revolution', *Forbes*, 5 Aug., 1–3; www.forbes.com/tool/html/99/aug/0805/feat.htm.

Tapscott, D., Ticoll, D., and Lowy, A. (2000), *Digital Capital: Harnessing the Power of Business Webs* (Boston: Harvard Business School Press).

Tuomi, I. (2001), 'Internet, Innovation and Open Source: Actors in the Network', *First Monday*, 6/1; http://firstmonday.org/issues/issue6_1/tuomi/index.html.

Uzzi, B. (1996), 'Close Encounters of the Sociological Kind: Organizational Fields as Markets', *Advances in Strategic Management*, 13: 419–30.

Vizard, M. (1998), 'Open Source Guru: Linux Creator and Freeware Visionary Linux Torvalds won't mix Marketing with Developing', *Infoworld*.com, 8 June, 1–4; www.infoworld.com/cgi-bin/displayStory.pl?/interviews/980608torvalds.htm.

Von Hippel, E. H. (1987), 'Cooperation between Rivals: Informal Know-How Trading', *Research Policy*, 16: 291–302.

Wayner, P. (2000), *Free for All: How Linux and the Free Software Movement Undercut the High Tech Titans* (New York: HarperCollins).

Weick, K. E. (1996), 'Enactment and the Boundaryless Career', in M. B. Arthur and D. M. Rousseau (eds.), *The Boundaryless Career* (New York: Oxford University Press), 40–57.

Wenger, E. (1998), *Communities of Practice: Learning, Meaning, and Identity* (New York: Oxford University Press).

16

Staying Creative about Careers

MICHAEL B. ARTHUR, MAURY A. PEIPERL, AND N. ANAND

It has been evident throughout this book that career creativity has two meanings. One refers to creativity in the shaping of individual careers. The other refers to creativity in work arrangements and their consequences that careers bring about. This duality of meaning is useful, as it allows us to appreciate the recursive influences of individual careers and broader work arrangements upon one another.

A range of ideas from previous chapters suggest that both careers and creativity engage with a variety of 'fields' that lend meaning to a person's behavior from both the person's own and more collective societal perspectives. Here, we refine and combine previous uses of the term 'field' to connect both of the principal concerns of this book—that is, careers and creativity. We then explore a range of alternative fields indicated in the preceding chapters through which careers unfold and creativity is stimulated. We emphasize that the range of fields, and thereby the significance of career creativity, extend far beyond the traditional arenas of organizations and occupations through which careers have traditionally been studied.

In the second part of this chapter we explore the question of the relevance of the contributions here to the world of practice. We do so by adopting a 'benchmark', a set of recent books directed to the world of senior managers, who may in turn be seen as prospective gatekeepers for the kind of messages that this book conveys. For each of the fields explored, we ask how much the contributions in this book appear to overlap with or go beyond ideas to which senior managers are being exposed.

We conclude by asserting the importance of career creativity in both meanings of the term. The importance stems from the way our topic takes us

We are indebted to Tim Hall and Kerr Inkson for their helpful feedback on an earlier draft of this chapter.

beyond the traditional fields through which careers have been studied, and engages with further fields through which career creativity occurs. We submit that it behooves a variety of gatekeepers—academics, managers, policy-makers, and not least career actors themselves—to keep the interplay among these multiple fields in mind if the prospective social and economic consequences of career creativity are to be realized.

THE FIELDS OF CAREER ENGAGEMENT

The study of careers has traditionally been linked to either the world of occupations or the world of organizations. The link to occupations comes from the disciplines of education and psychology and their interest in so-called vocational choice and subsequent satisfaction with that choice. The link to organizations comes from the disciplines of sociology and management and their interest in how careers unfold through employment arrangements. However, the traditional links have been breaking down. One set of disciplines sees emergent discontinuity as 'challeng[ing] the fundamental principles and standards on which career theory, research and practice have stood' (Collin and Young 2000: 8). The other set sees traditional organizational perspectives 'neglect[ing] the role of career mobility' in the knowledge-based economy (Peiperl *et al.* 2000). The comfortable reliance on occupations or organizations as adequate and separate arenas of inquiry is now gone.

Let us reflect briefly on the meanings applied to the term 'field' in this book and related works. As conceived in Lewin's view of group dynamics, a field consists of the 'totality of coexisting social entities, such as groups, subgroups, members, barriers, channels of communication, etc.' (Lewin 1951: 200). In turn, Lewin invoked the physical science metaphor of magnetic field forces to consider a group's readiness for change. Although not using the term 'field' directly, Becker (1974) developed the related notion of the 'artworld'—a consensually defined understanding, taken for granted by participants, that makes possible the production and consumption of works of art. This relates closely to Gardner's more selective view (1993: xiii) of a field for creativity as a 'group of knowledgeable individuals...who judge the quality of...new work', and of Csikszentmihalyi's related view (1999: 315) of a field consisting of 'gatekeepers', who decide what does and does not gain acceptance in a particular domain of activity. In all these meanings, fields are socially defined contexts for individual behavior.

We add two caveats to the above views. First, fields are interdependent. This is especially so in career behavior, where people's career investments are simultaneously made in more than one arena, and where creativity in one arena (such as a new sales technique in one company) can be transferred to another arena (by taking the technique to other companies in the industry)

(Arthur *et al.* 1999). The second caveat is that fields are frequently contested. This is the case in Bourdieau's sense (1968, 1993) that members compete through the positions and relationships that surround a focal activity, and in the related sense of organization theorists about how fields frame industry competitiveness (DiMaggio and Powell 1983; Scott 1995). With these points in mind, in this last chapter we view a field as 'any institutional context that people use as a reference point in their career behavior'.

In keeping with the above, the preceding chapters suggest six principal kinds of field through which career creativity occurs. They may be called company, family, occupational, industry, cultural, and self-designing fields respectively. The sections below define and elaborate on each of these themes in turn.

Company fields

One traditionally popular field for understanding careers is the company field (where by company we mean any institution, whether public or private, for-profit or not-for-profit, that provides paid work). The company, in this sense, is prominently seen as the provider of 'organizational careers' (Van Maanen 1977), where the guiding assumption is that a person's career is likely to continue to unfold within the same company setting. The assumption still underlies a range of ideas about company strategy, human-resource management (HRM) and the provision of ancillary employment benefits such as job security, pension, health insurance, and so on (Perrow 1996).

Traditional company constraints. One prominent theme in the preceding chapters covers a well-aired complaint—namely, that the very purpose and underlying design of companies mitigates against the prospects for creativity to occur. Accordingly, Poehnell and Amundson (Chapter 6) alert us to the popular conception of 'management', most commonly associated with notions of planning, control, regulation, structure, and power in the public mind, in contrast to notions inviting greater employee creativity. Similarly, Inkson reminds us of the prominence with which we associate careers with what he calls Type 3 paths—namely those prescribed according to Weberian (bureaucratic) principles, and claiming 'to provide all the expertise a company might need from within' (Inkson, Chapter 2, p. 26).

An extension of the complaint about Type 3 careers bemoans the apparent bias toward bureaucracy over creativity at the same time as creativity is becoming seen as an 'essential business skill' (Poehnell and Amundson, Chapter 6, p. 105). Moreover, the company's propensity to reinforce Type 3 careers brings with it a systemic bias toward explicit knowledge rather than tacit knowledge, even though the latter is the more likely spur toward creativity. Thus, company management systems tend to 'reward the master, not the learner, and the exploitation, rather than the exploration' (Södergren, Chapter 3,

p. 35). If companies want more creativity, they must address the root problem of the kind of careers that they reinforce.

Opening up company structures. A prominent answer to the above constraint, and one that retains a focus on the company as the client for career creativity, is to change the context in which careers unfold. Several chapters join Weick (1996) in pressing companies to celebrate the 'weakening' in traditionally strong (and therefore constraining) internal company structures, since weak structures can bring in greater creativity. They argue for 'backwards' movement to Type 1 career paths (Inkson, Chapter 2), for the provision of 'glasscutters' or 'passports' for career passage across previously impermeable internal career boundaries (Gunz, Evans, and Jalland, Chapter 4), and for a greater emphasis on project-based teams as a basis for more flexible career opportunities (Södergren, Chapter 3). The return of international assignees provides a particular example where company openness to alternative career possibilities might benefit both company and employee (Hall, Zhu, and Yan, Chapter 9).

Promoting creative processes. A related set of messages focuses on the role of company *processes*, rather than underlying company structure. Thus, the cultivation of tacit knowledge (Södergren, Chapter 3), or the promotion of 'careercraft' (Poehnell and Amundson, Chapter 6), calls for company cultures and leadership that encourage creativity rather than conformity. A greater respect for the importance of time in people's lives (rather than a traditional fear of time wasting) may bring more creative solutions to work/family conflict as well as other conflicts between work time and private time (Buck, Lee, and MacDermid, Chapter 5). Companies can also engage in creative 'matchmaking' between leased executives and regular employees to facilitate the effective transfer of the executives' expertise (Parker, Chapter 7). A persistent emphasis on stronger relational ties can result in companies being 'nuclei of trust and affection' through which creativity is encouraged to flow (Hall, Zhu, and Yan, Chapter 9).

Keeping creativity around. The question of how to promote creative processes raises a related one of how those processes might be sustained. A suggestion coming from several of our chapters is for companies to promote the kind of individual and collaborative internal opportunities that will continue to attract creative contributors. A related suggestion is that sustaining creative career behavior calls for persistent attention to the balance between a company's managerial and creative tasks (Alvarez and Svejenova, Chapter 10). Companies may not only model this balance through their leaders—as do the Almodóvar brothers filmmaking duo—but also encourage a similar pattern of 'symbiotic careers' among others. Moreover, these links need not be exclusively with other company members. Taking the idea further, companies can make it a point to tap into creative career behaviors sustained by extra-company fields, as illustrated in the employment of Linux operating system experts (DeFillippi and Arthur, Chapter 15).

A need for caution regarding human resource management. It will be instinctive for many readers to suggest that the above issues fall under the rubric of 'human resource management' (HRM) and thereby look for action to the department assigned to specialize in that function. However, the very use of the term signals problems. As Inkson (Chapter 2, p. 28) cautions, the 'resource' metaphor implies that 'individuals are assumed not to *have* resources under their own control but to *be* resources under the control of the organization'. He adds (Chapter 2, p. 29) that 'the resource metaphor reinforces the view that careers are created by companies as an incidental by-product of their resource-developing activities'. This caution on the potentially stultifying effect of the HRM function is echoed in Buck, Lee, and MacDermid's view (Chapter 5) of HRM as the 'gatekeeper' function standing in the way of more creative reduced-load work arrangements, and in Hall, Zhu, and Yan's conclusion (Chapter 9) that companies are 'homeostatic systems' fundamentally resistant to people's creative career adaptation.

How companies spawn new (and more creative) companies. A contrasting suggestion to those previously offered is to appreciate the conditions that encourage new companies to form. One set of conditions results from 'Fitzgerald's curse', whereby the (US) social assumption that there are 'no second acts' drives fallen leaders to recommit their talents in a new setting (Sonnenfeld, Chapter 8). Another set of conditions underlies Ensher, Murphy, and Sullivan's evidence (Chapter 12, p. 229) from the entertainment industry, where people's (in this case women's) more proactive career behavior led to their creating 'organizations that encouraged new ways of thinking'. Similarly, Higgins' evidence (Chapter 14, p. 280) from biotechnology points to new companies 'made on the backs of individuals' careers', and frequently with the help of old company connections. Larger arguments point to the interplay of large firm (control-based) and small firm (creativity-driven) influences in competitive markets (Alvarez and Svejenova, Chapter 10), and of knowledge diffusion across firms being a natural by-product of people's career behavior. The common factor here is not so much of advice *to* companies, but of advice *about* companies, and the predictable parts that they play as larger patterns of career creativity unfold.

Family fields

We use the term 'family' here both in its original meaning as the members of the same household or as kinfolk, and in its derivative meaning as a group of people united by common features or ties. This leads to two principal links to family fields, as follows.

Family as kinfolk. Regarding the original meaning of family, there is a message that people bring established family ties to their careers. Accordingly, they may be observed in 'creatively redesigning the balance of their work and non-work lives' on their families' behalves (Buck, Lee, and MacDermid, Chapter 5, p. 77). A special case of this occurs with leased executives, who find that temporary, project-based career assignments allow the freedom and flexibility to pay more attention to family investments (Parker, Chapter 7). People's career creativity may also be directly supported by family members, as of course happens in many family business arrangements. A particular form of family support is exemplified in the case of the Almodóvar brothers, where Augustín's deep faith in his brother's creative capacities gave rise to a company whose success and emergent culture mirror the brothers' attachments to one another (Alvarez and Svejenova, Chapter 10).

Family as a united group. In its second meaning, family is not what we inherit through birth, but rather the enduring support system we develop around our careers. In this looser sense, a loyal family of believers who continue to have faith in a person's talents can be critical for that person's 'creative resilience' (Sonnenfeld, Chapter 8), and families of industry peers can be critical to the creative successes of people pursuing careers in media (Ensher, Murphy and Sullivan, Chapter 12). Two relatively new kinds of family are also suggested. One is the kind sustained through past 'employment-based affiliations' (Higgins, Chapter 14, p. 280), and whereby, for example, a family of Baxter International alumni had a profound influence over subsequent creativity in their industry. Another relatively new kind of family is one based on virtual attachments, such as those cultivated by the Linux operating system developers (DeFillippi and Arthur, Chapter 15). In all these cases, the communal support creative career actors found in each other influenced the evolution of both companies and industries.

Occupational fields

A further traditionally popular field for studying careers is the occupation, which also features prominently in the lessons offered throughout this book. However, traditional approaches to individual-occupation matching have presumed occupations remain largely unchanged, whereas a focus on career creativity directly challenges that assumption.

Occupation as a host to creativity. One particular message ties occupation back to the traditional idea of craft, where creativity, alongside skill, is seen as an essential component of craft-based behavior (Poehnell and Amundson, Chapter 6, p. 105). Craft allows us to respond broadly to Csikszentmihalyi's observation that most creative people 'don't follow a career laid out for them, but invent their jobs as they go along.' (quoted in Poehnell and Amundson, Chapter 6, p. 105). Occupations—including professional occupations with codified bodies of knowledge—provide meeting grounds for the exchange and further development of tacit knowledge among high-technology workers (Södergren, Chapter 3), leased executives (Parker, Chapter 7), filmmakers (Alvarez and Svejenova, Chapter 10), and software writers (Defillippi and Arthur, Chapter 15).

Occupational processes. Occupational fields, like company fields, invite consideration about how career creativity processes might be stimulated. Again, the concept of craft appears prominent, involving 'self-customizing construction rather than production to a pre-specified blueprint' (Inkson, Chapter 2, p. 29). It is notable that craft has a metaphorical aspect to it that can invite creative career behavior in response (Poehnell and Amundson, Chapter 6, p. 105). Jazz and street theater are related metaphors (Inkson, Chapter 2, pp. 29–30) and ones that extend an invitation for creativity to collaborative teams, around a shared product that transcends members' individual contributions. What may be important here is the 'propulsive' influence of any metaphor on the occupational processes that host it (Inkson, Chapter 2, p. 32). To put it in question form, how much does the metaphor promote new (creative) versus traditional (bureaucratic) occupational career behavior? A related question is what kind of appeal may be made to a person's identity to encourage the pursuit of fresh occupational challenges (Hall, Zhu, and Yan, Chapter 9)?

Interplay of occupational and employment arrangements. An important aspect of creativity within occupational fields concerns the way these fields interconnect with the company fields in which much employment takes place, and by way of which career creativity reaches the market for goods and services. People commonly make overlapping 'career capital' investments, whereby a main attraction of company employment is the chance it provides for people to continue to be creative in their occupation (Inkson, Chapter 2). Both Parker's (leased executive (Chapter 7)) and DeFillippi and Arthur's (Linux software (Chapter 15)) 'career communities' are variants on the idea of 'occupational communities' that explicitly transcend the boundaries of any single company. Hall, Zhu, and Yan's evidence (Chapter 9) is that committed career actors—in their case returning overseas expatriates—would rather leave for a new employer than have their emergent occupational talents go neglected.

Helping occupationally based creativity along. The observation of occupationally based creativity invites a question of how it might be stimulated. One suggestion is to provide more 'glasscutters' or 'passports' to break through the divisions between related occupations to allow the freer flow of people and ideas (Gunz, Evans, and Jalland, Chapter 4). Another suggestion is to better understand the signaling behavior of occupational specialists and in turn to nurture the kind of contexts that allow such signaling to occur (Jones, Chapter 11). The direct argument on behalf of occupational creativity can be linked to a larger one about the constraints of regulation, and the benefits of political freedom (Hall, Zhu, and Yan, Chapter 9). Moreover, the promotion of open contexts can encourage specialists from different occupations to connect with and contribute creativity to each other. This can be seen in the example of the Almodóvar brothers, and in the broader interplay of business and artistic functions that filmmaking and other creative industries promote (Alvarez and Svejenova, Chapter 10).

Industry fields

We turn next to industry fields, which substantially reflect traditional, broadly recognized distinctions according to industry. However, as with occupational fields, we need to look beyond constraining assumptions about the permanence of any industry, or about demarcations between industries.

Modeling from creative industries. One key concern of this book has been about what might be drawn from the so-called creative industries, and profitably transferred to other industry settings. The underlying logic is seductive. Creative industries function largely through project-based initiatives, such as the making of a film. Each project provides an opportunity for creativity. However, this is tempered by funding and marketplace realities. Thus, creative industries reflect a persistent dialog between creative and business agendas (Caves 2000). They further provide a high degree of flexibility, allowing new ideas to emerge and old ideas to fade as projects come and go (Alvarez and Svejenova, Chapter 10; Jones, Chapter 11). They also provide a context for new learning, as well as for the (creative) transfer of that learning as people move between projects (Peterson and Anand, Chapter 13). The so-called creative industries appear to have much to offer other industries where creativity is now seen to be in higher demand.

Career processes in creative industries. A prominent argument from the preceding chapters concerns people's direct investment in their adopted industries, rather than relying on organizations or occupations as intermediaries. DeFillippi and Arthur's argument that industries can be the beneficiaries of people's (*knowing-why*) identities, as well as of their (*knowing-how*) expertise and (*knowing-whom*) network investments is supported by a range of other authors. Moreover, all three 'ways of knowing' can contribute to the signaling that takes place among industry members and in turn to the evolution of market niches within the industry (Jones, Chapter 11). Industry identification appears as an important platform of trust among industry collaborators in, for example, filmmaking (Jones, Chapter 11), biotechnology (Higgins, Chapter 14), and software writing (DeFillippi and Arthur, Chapter 15), and can prevail beyond shared project or employment experiences. The 'symbiotic careers' of the Almodóvar brothers suggest a model for other industry collaborators, both within and beyond company boundaries, to join creative endeavors (Alvarez and Svejenova, Chapter 10).

Creative industry outcomes. Much of the evidence in this book points beyond creative industry processes toward their outcomes. Women professionals in entertainment serve as a counterpoint to 'powerful men', introducing creativity in the form of different, more feminized industry practices (Ensher, Murphy, and Sullivan, Chapter 12). Frustrated returnees from expatriate assignment (Hall, Zhu, and Yan, Chapter 9), or fallen executives (Sonnenfeld, Chapter 8), are both described as transferring their creative energies toward industry rather than company outcomes. Leased executives gather industry experience in one setting and then transfer it to another setting, leaving other workers to sustain the new systems that the executives introduced (Parker, Chapter 7). Career actors, these days linked by virtual connections across geographic and national boundaries, appear to underlie creative successes across the high-technology industry (Gunz, Evans, and Jalland, Chapter 4) and its cousin the software industry (DeFillippi and Arthur, Chapter 15).

Industry cycles. Embedded in the evidence from several chapters is the suggestion of persistent and cyclical interplay between people's careers and the host industry. This is directly illustrated in DeFillippi and Arthur's 'blueprint' (Chapter 15) for industry evolution illustrated through the Linux operating system. It is also indicated in Ensher, Murphy, and Sullivan's observation (Chapter 12) that career 'accomplishment building' translates into industry change, and in Higgins' identification (Chapter 14) of the 'missing link' between the micro-world of careers and the macro-world of industries. Thus, the initial public offering joins the completed film or software project, or the transfer of the frustrated executives' energies, as a significant industry event in the perpetual cycling between people's career behaviors and their host industries.

Creatively modified clusters. One trend in boundaryless career theory has been to explore careers sustained in the kind of industry clusters popularized by Porter (1990, 1998) and characterized by Silicon Valley careers (Saxenian 1996). The chapters here suggest two important modifications to that evidence, and suggest the 'cluster' may increasingly refer to *social* space rather than physical space. Former Chicago-based employees of Baxter International were instrumental through their subsequent behavior in transferring their expertise to the geographically remote Boston area, through the networks they had developed (Higgins, Chapter 14). Linux software developers present an early example of international collaboration spanning the boundaries of any one geographic cluster (but perhaps drawing on multiple geographically local networks as well) (DeFillippi and Arthur, Chapter 15). Career creativity and its social support can modify—and in the future may more frequently modify— the underlying industry arrangements that host it.

Cultural fields

Cultural fields may be seen to reflect the principal cultural influences that affect careers. These include not only national, regional and organizational cultures, but also international cultural influences in the sense of, for example, being a European, or a member of a company or occupation with a culture that spans international borders, or being party to a certain political affiliation.

Stimulating novelty. According to Csikszentmihalyi (1996), cultural fields can influence career creativity in at least two ways. First, cultural fields can be reactive or proactive in stimulating novelty. The chapter by Södergren presents contrasting pictures of company cultures that promote rather than (as they are frequently described to do) discourage career creativity. However, the influence of cultural fields is not restricted to company cultures. The industry culture of the commercial music field prior to the 1950s was largely reactive, whereas after the mid-1950s, following changes in law, technology, and market, it became more proactive toward novel styles in music (Peterson and Anand, Chapter 13). The same authors further suggest that a proactive culture, compared to a reactive one, is likely to foster a number of alternative career choices. A similar conclusion may be drawn from work suggesting that successful geographically concentrated industry clusters of firms are more innovative than more isolated firms (Porter 1998).

Filtering innovations. Csikszentmihalyi's other way for cultural fields to influence career creativity is through the kinds of narrow or broad filters they bring upon creative endeavors. Pedro Almodóvar was able to make his films only after the political regime in Spain changed from a narrow to a broad filter to allow more liberal funding of art projects (Alvarez and Svejenova, Chapter 10). As a consequence of a broader filter, new career structures (such as the symbiotic form) flourished. One can also observe that the culture of the upstart biotechnology industry was more conducive to creativity than its relatively established counterpart of pharmaceuticals (Higgins, Chapter 14), or that the cultures of certain kinds of software company are more likely to accelerate creativity (DeFillippi and Arthur, Chapter 15).

Linking to the social system. Cultural fields also vary in the extent to which they provide support for local innovations through their connections to the rest of the social system. Various companies have been described to stimulate innovation through their employees and yet to be relatively unsuccessful in promoting that innovation in the customer marketplace. A contrasting case is the one where the players from such company cultures stayed connected and forged successful links into the alternative world of biotechnology (Higgins, Chapter 14). The Open Software Foundation may be seen as an example of professional association promoting a culture that provided links to new career opportunities for both members and non-members (DeFillippi and Arthur, Chapter 15). In turn, the Foundation might stimulate people away from Type 3 career paths (laid down by others) toward Type 1 paths involving more individual trail blazing (Inkson, Chapter 2).

Culture-based disconformity. A notable alternative argument in these pages is that culture promotes career creativity through people's *dis*conformity. Thus, fallen executives' response to 'Fitzgerald's curse' in US culture was to be creative despite being written off by that culture (Sonnenfeld, Chapter 8). People returning from successful expatriate assignments, and exposed to new stimuli, appear reluctant to settle back into the company cultures they knew before (Hall, Zhu, and Yan, Chapter 9). Another example, this time regarding industry culture, is that of women collaborating to promote a more feminized entertainment industry culture than they faced when establishing their own careers (Ensher, Murphy, and Sullivan, Chapter 12).

Self-designing fields

In this final category, we revisit and extend previous observations and bring them back to the individual career. Specifically, we ask how the effects on the various fields for career creativity, as well as on the interplay between fields, can be traced back to the career behavior of their participants. The term 'self-designing fields' is chosen to emphasize that we are describing career behavior that is volitional, even idiosyncratic, but may have larger systemic effects.

Introducing variety. An important effect of career behavior stemming from self-driven rather than institutionally driven forces is the introduction of variety that many now see as necessary for economic progress. The 'career craft' argument brings with it Michalko's notion (1998) of people thinking 'productively' rather than 'reproductively' (Poehnell and Amundson, Chapter 6). Similarly, leased executives are seen as engaging in Bateson's 'creative acts' (1994) through their perpetual willingness to see challenge in getting to a problem, achievement in solving the problem, and choice in moving on to new problems (Parker, Chapter 7).

These sentiments are further echoed in other chapters—for example, in Södergren's report (Chapter 3) of professional workers seeking persistent 'role-redefinition' and Alvarez and Svejenova's observation (Chapter 10) that creativity involves a person's resistance to compromise. All of these examples may be broadly characterized as part of the 'supply side' of entrepreneurship (Peterson and Anand, Chapter 13)—that is, of career creativity leaving its mark on the fields with which it engages.

Building identity. Another important observation is how career creativity builds individual identity. We are not speaking here, as many (Chicago School) writers have spoken before, of identity adaptation in response to outside institutional forces. Rather we are talking about the opportunity for personal development, and therefore the development of a more 'complicated' (Weick and Berlinger 1989) or evolved identity that creative career behavior can bring. Perhaps most graphic among our examples is the story of Linus Torvalds' growth from curious student to industry phenomenon (DeFillippi and Arthur, Chapter 15). However, the capacity for the kind of identity development that Torvalds went through appears broadly distributed, as suggested in the imagery of 'unleashing the genie from the bottle' through international assignments (Hall, Zhu, and Yan, Chapter 9). The same authors further emphasize what several other chapters infer—namely, that identity development needs to be understood as stemming from a person's career history, and the versatility reflected in that history.

Promoting participation. Putnam (2000) has recently made a compelling argument that promoting participation among actors within and between fields leads to increased social capital, which in turn unlocks knowledge and resources that create new possibilities. Contexts that promote participation help develop relational knowledge and connect unattached resources. Evidence from chapters in this volume affirms that people see knowledge as relational— that is, occurring *between* individuals rather than as an abstract product. The relational, partly tacit, aspect of knowledge building is described as anticipating the explicit codification of that knowledge—in a company's product announcement, a new movie, or a new software release—later on. Further evidence here suggests that people are quite willing to cross field boundaries to seek out new knowledge, as did professional workers through their use of extra-company networks (Södergren, Chapter 3). Other chapters suggest that migrating executives take with them ideas and connections to a new location in order to spur innovative activity by creating new sets of resources (Peterson and Anand, Chapter 13; Higgins, Chapter 14).

Creating career communities. In many cases, the relationships through which career creativity and knowledge generation occur may be understood as much more than personal networks. They emerge as what have been called 'career communities'—namely, member-defined communities from which people derive career support (Parker and Arthur 2000). Sometimes, career communities involve close friends and family, and evolve to provide the support and continuity that a project-based career may otherwise be lacking. A vivid example is that of a self-designed career community among women in entertainment—a community that not only supported the women's careers but also brought change to the host industry (Ensher, Murphy, and Sullivan, Chapter 12). The emergence of the Linux operating system shows the potential significance of 'virtual communities' in the era ahead (DeFillippi and Arthur, Chapter 15). Mutual support among leased executives, in conjunction with career support from enduring friends and family, provide the continuity that makes project-based careers successful (Parker, Chapter 7). A sense of community can transcend both companies and projects and in doing so contribute to enduring creativity in filmmaking (Alvarez and Svejenova, Chapter 10).

Creating inter-field connections. Finally, our chapters provide evidence that not only do careers link between fields; they further create the unfolding connections among fields. One vivid example is the portrayal of the links among artist, the artworld, and the artistic labor market evidenced in the filmmaking industry (Alvarez and Svejenova, Chapter 10). More generally, entrepreneurial careers in filmmaking and other so-called creative industries are seen as the threads that create the tapestry of institutions through which those industries take shape. One chapter provocatively cites Weick (1996) in claiming that the logic of a career as a knowledge creation process is still 'waiting to be constructed' (Södergren, Chapter 3, p. 54). Perhaps that logic is now becoming clearer. However, by definition, the outcomes of that knowledge creation can never be known in advance. In other words, the logic calls for a fundamental faith in the creative capacity of career behavior before its outcomes become visible.

BENCHMARKING CAREER CREATIVITY

How creative is a book on career creativity? What, if anything, is fresh in the pages that have gone before? How might the ideas from those pages engage with the larger 'domains' (Csikszentmihalyi 1999: 314) of employment arrangements through which careers play out? How can we calibrate the ideas against the world of practice, or against other ideas competing to be adopted into practice? Even if there is much that is fresh, what is the risk of the contributors to this book and their supporters having a cozy conversation among themselves but no substantial impact on the world of practice? If this were to happen, our efforts would fall short of the hopes we expressed at the outset. Those hopes reflected the influential views of both Gardner (1993) and Csikszentmihalyi (1996, 1999) that creativity comes to life when it is recognized beyond its originators—that is, by the larger society to which it speaks.

As Csikszentmihalyi (1999: 315) notes, the adoption of ideas is controlled by 'gatekeepers' responsible for the spread of those ideas. One prominent group of gatekeepers are those management consultants and professors who write directly for senior managers. The reader-managers may be seen to have risen to influential social positions from which to embrace the kinds of career creativity chronicled here. We will therefore attempt in this last section to benchmark the ideas from this book against four popular books directed at management and employment practice. Our selection is somewhat random, and biased toward mainstream English-speaking ideas. However, all of the authors have gained a wide reputation for influencing management thinking over recent years. They also exhibit what we see as some healthy disagreement over where to begin and what is most important. In our assessment, the four books appear to be a useful set of reference points to see if the ideas chronicled 'in here' (in this book) are already being touted 'out there' (in the world where careers play out).

A further feature of the benchmark we adopt is that the books all appear to have both creativity and careers at the heart of their message. Two of the books come from academic sources, and two come from senior management consultants. Two focus principally on the link from company strategy to employment practice; two focus more on the link from employment practice to company strategy. The academic books are Kanter's *Evolve!* (2001) and O'Reilly and Pfeffer's *Hidden Value* (2000). The consultants' books are Hamel's *Leading the Revolution* (2000) and Katzenbach's *Peak Performance* (2000). One might argue that our selection is biased toward one kind of field, what we have called company fields. However, we would suggest that the role of management is to be sensitive to all the fields of career creativity, and to recruit that creativity— wherever it originates—to the company's advantage. It seems a valid question to ask whether managers are being alerted to the fields of creativity that this collection identifies.

The benchmark books' main messages about career creativity are summarized below. So, too, is the respective coverage that each book gives to each of the fields for career creativity identified. The consultants' books are covered first, followed by the academic books, in publication date order.

Leading the Revolution (Hamel 2000) speaks of the need to innovate, 'in the sense of radical new business models' and is presented as 'a book for those who believe that the future is something you create, not something that happens to you' (p. xii). It envisions a shift to an 'age of revolution' (p. 4) where 'never has it been a better time to be a rebellious newcomer' (p. 10). Accordingly, individuals must 'wriggle free from the strictures of a linear world' and collectives must reverse a 'massive failure of collective imagination'. Both individuals and collectives need to 'learn to dream' (p. 11) if they are to participate in the new business models envisioned.

Hamel's appeal to the individual 'revolutionaries' is concerned principally with their influencing company fields. 'Will you', he asks the reader, 'embrace the new innovation agenda', and 'do you care enough...to take responsibility for making your company revolution-ready?' (p. 29). Family and occupational fields get no attention, but industry fields are embraced in the attention paid to California's Silicon Valley, where the book describes 'thousands of novel business ideas' competing in 'an open market for business concept innovation' (p. 27). There is also substantial coverage on how companies can form effective partnerships with one another in industry space (pp. 88–100). However, the principal use of Silicon Valley is as a metaphor to return the focus to the company, charged to 'bring Silicon Valley inside' (p. 263) by promoting an internal market for talent and ideas. Both cultural fields and self-designing fields are implicated, but in ways that once more return to company fields: through the contrast between 'old' and 'new' business models (p. 16) that runs throughout the book, and where companies tied to the old models are the targets for the revolutionaries' efforts.

Peak Performance (Katzenbach 2000) focuses on employment practice, and argues that it is 'energized workforces [that] deliver higher [peak] performance' (p. ix) for their companies. The book is inclusive in the range of careers it implicates, defining the workforce as 'all employees across the baseline of the organization who either make the products, design the services, or deliver value to customers' (p. xii). Companies, it is argued, need to 'believe strongly in each employee', harness their employees' 'emotional energy', and pursue 'enterprise performance and worker fulfillment with equal rigor' (pp. 11–12). Those that do stand to gain the 'peak performance' that the book's title proclaims.

The emphasis here is clearly on the company field, and of career creativity being properly 'channeled' so that it does not 'divert the organization from its purposes and goals' (p. 17). Family-type fields are also implicated in the proposals for the company to promote a sense of belonging through 'the camaraderie of co-workers' (p. 23), and to generate 'collective energy' involving 'broad-based teamwork, multiple real teams [and] widespread mutual support and assistance' (p. 202). The notions of the career actor being engaged in either occupational or industry fields get no attention, except in the limited sense of these being embedded within the employment arrangements of the company. The same limitation applies to cultural fields, addressed in a directive to attend to 'internal [company] cultural imperatives' (p. 242). The message on self-designing fields is also constrained, proposing an 'employee value proposition' that is claimed to be in alignment with Cappelli's 'new deal' (1999) of managing the market-driven workforce (pp. 244–5). However, the book offers what seem familiar exhortations, rather than any further elaboration of what the market is or how it functions.

Hidden Value (O'Reilly and Pfeffer 2000) also focuses on employment practice, and in doing so challenges the recent emphasis placed by McKinsey and other management consultants on the so-called war for talent. The book challenges companies to 'build an organization that helps make it possible for regular folks to perform as if they were in the top 10%' (p. 2). The companies that succeed, it is argued, will do so 'by engaging the knowledge, experience, skills and energy of their people' (p. 3). In turn, the companies will derive the 'hidden value' that 'resides in the intellectual and emotional capital of the firm and is in the power of the minds and hearts of its people' (p. 8).

This book emphasizes an overlay between company fields and family fields, opening with a reference to Tolstoy's aphorism 'Happy families are all alike' (p. x) and going on to suggest that the 'right' organization offers its employees 'a sense of community, security, and mutual trust and respect' (p. 8). An extension of the same thinking considers cultural fields from the standpoint of company culture, seen as a principal 'management' task for a company's leaders (p. 15). The book includes a mix of company examples, including some in high-technology arenas where there is intense competition for technical and managerial talent. Accordingly, industry fields and occupational fields are implicated in what we might call recruiting fields in which companies search for talent. However, that search is characterized in a one-way view—'Hire and retain!'—of the recruiting field's usefulness. The world portrayed is one in which companies are asked to care deeply for their employees, but not for the parallel extra-company fields that may give careers and career creativity (and in the long term the companies themselves) much of their vitality.

Evolve! (Kanter 2001) centers on the emerging Internet-based 'digital world' described to thrive on 'imagination and visualization' (p. 40). Career actors are viewed as participants in 'improvisational theater' where they must 'be willing to take on unfamiliar roles, think on their feet, pay attention to several things at once, walk into situations for which they are not prepared, and ad lib' (p. 111). The contemporary workforce is seen to seek 'the opportunity to think creatively' (p. 199) and to eschew blind loyalty in favor of 'the opportunity to grow and stretch' (p. 226). In turn, 'assets carried by people' are those increasingly 'most critical to success' (p. 221).

This book once more emphasizes company fields, as both the focus of its research and the principal targets for its conclusions. Family fields are represented through the observation that 'American employers can no longer act as though they do not exist' (p. 213) and in a concluding worry about whether 'the lonely crowd or the connected community' (p. 301) will become the dominant image of the future. On occupational fields, the book acknowledges 'knowledge nomads' who 'like members of medieval craft guilds take their craft from place to place and bring their friends with them' (p. 221). However, there is no further elaboration about the hypothesized guilds as fields for creativity in their own right. Industry fields are not covered. Cultural fields are covered through extensive advice on how companies might develop and maintain 'e-cultures' of their own. Self-designing fields are clearly indicated, not least in the view of the Internet age reality that 'everyone is potentially connected to everyone else' (p. 16). The dominant message, though, is about companies 'winning the talent wars' by 'retaining people a little longer than their peers' (p. 203) rather than tapping into self-designing fields in any more original way.

In sum, the four books firmly support the prospects for company fields to serve as hosts to career creativity. However, the acknowledgment of alternative fields for creativity is limited. Where those alternatives are addressed, such as in the industry field of California's Silicon Valley (Hamel 2000), the family field of the innovative team (Katzenbach 2000), or the occupational field of knowledge nomads (Kanter 2001) the intention is often to have the reader-manager apply the idea within his or her own company, rather than celebrate the existence of the field as an entity in itself. The image presented by the authors in this book, of people investing through their careers in a variety of fields for creativity, and of companies and host economies as beneficiaries of those investments, is largely missing.

CONCLUSION

We began this chapter by observing that the study of careers has principally focused on occupational or organizational (company) fields respectively. However, the synthesis of ideas presented here suggests there are at least five kinds of field—company, family, occupational, industry, and cultural fields—through which career creativity occurs. There is also a sixth kind of field—what we have called 'self-designing fields'—which seems critical for people to introduce variety, and to build both identity and community, through which greater career creativity can occur. Self-designing fields do not so much define existing institutional ground as suggest how new institutions get introduced. The emergent picture across the six kinds of fields is not of people making career investments in one field or another, but rather of multiple career investments with a cumulative effect.

Our 'benchmark' exercise concluded that only a subset of the ideas presented in this book are so far being promoted by one group of gatekeepers for career creativity—influential writers of books for senior managers—that we sought to sample. We applaud those books for the positive messages that they bring about career creativity. At the same time, it seems constraining that the message appears to be that the manager's role is about facilitating the career creativity of others rather than acting creatively on his or her own; and that career creativity is to be confined everlastingly by the exigencies of the corporation. Hamel's revolutionaries may rebel only to the extent that they do not actually walk out. Katzenbach's peak performers are literally 'harnessed' in a company yoke. The 'hidden value' of O'Reilly and Pfeffer in the end adds value only to the shareholders of the enlightened firm. Kanter's evolving careerists find their creative adaptations used as cannon fodder in larger 'talent wars'.

Our essential human potential and dignity make us worth more than this. Managers should recognize that the ability of fledgling career actors to rebel, to peak, to stretch their wings, and to evolve drives them to act across multiple fields. This is because in the end every definition of corporate purpose, however broad, is more exclusive than any definition of an individual's potential.

The greater the diversity of fields of opportunity, the more the creative spirit will flourish, in the interests of all.

This is why the contributors to this book have so much to add to the conversation. They begin not with the formal credo or strategic direction of any company, but rather with a sense for the pulsating energy, natural curiosity, and lateral vision of the creative individual. Their accounts do not recommend that we subordinate these individuals to collective objectives, but that we trust people to find their own ways and intersections on the journey to creative outcomes. The voices of these contributors, and of the millions of creative people on whose behalf they speak, need to be heard.

If creativity occurs across the range of fields identified, and if the benefits and connections across those fields are gained through the kinds of career behavior described, the next step is to get the message out. We urge our authors and our readers—if you agree with us—to help us in the task.

REFERENCES

Arthur, M. B., and Rousseau, D. M. (1996) (eds.), *The Boundaryless Career: A New Employment Principle for a New Organizational Era* (New York: Oxford University Press).

——Inkson, K., and Pringle, J. K. (1999), *The New Careers: Individual Action and Economic Change* (London: Sage).

Bateson, M. C. (1994), *Peripheral Visions* (New York: HarperCollins).

Becker, H. S. (1974), 'Art as Collective Action', *American Sociological Review*, 39: 767–76.

Bourdieu, P. (1968), 'Intellectual Field and Creative Project, *Social Science Information*, 8/2: 89–119.

——(1993), *The Field of Cultural Production* (New York: Columbia University Press).

Cappelli, P. (1999), *The New Deal at Work: Managing the Market-Driven Workforce* (Boston: Harvard Business School Press).

Caves, R. E. (2000), *Creative Industries: Contracts between Art and Commerce* (Cambridge, Mass.: Harvard University Press).

Collin, A., and Young, R. A. (2000) (eds.), *The Future of Career* (Cambridge: Cambridge University Press).

Csikszentmihalyi, M. (1996), *Creativity: Flow and the Psychology of Discovery and Invention* (New York: HarperCollins).

——(1997), *Finding Flow in Everyday Life* (New York: Basic Books).

——(1999), 'Implications of a Systems Perspective for the Study of Creativity', in R. J. Sternberg (ed.), *Handbook of Creativity* (Cambridge: Cambridge University Press), 313–35.

DiMaggio, P. J., and Powell, W. W. (1983), 'The Iron Cage Revisited: Institutional Isomorphism and Collective Rationality in Organizational Fields', *American Sociological Review*, 48: 147–60.

Gardner, H. (1993), *Creating Minds* (New York: Basic Books).

Hamel, G. (2000), *Leading the Revolution* (Boston: Harvard Business School Press).

Kanter, R. M. (2001), *Evolve! Succeeding in the Digital Culture of Tomorrow* (Boston: Harvard Business School Press).

Katzenbach, J. R. (2000), *Peak Performance: Aligning the Hearts and Minds of Your Employees* (Boston: Harvard Business School Press).

Lewin, K. (1951), *Field Theory in Social Science* (New York: Harper).

Michalko, M. (1998), *Cracking Creativity: The Secrets of Creative Genius* (Berkeley, Calif.: Ten Speed Press).

O'Reilly, C. A., III, and Pfeffer, J. (2000), *Hidden Value: How Great Companies Achieve Extraordinary Results with Ordinary People* (Boston: Harvard Business School Press).

Parker, P., and Arthur, M. B. (2000), 'Careers, Organizing and Community', in M. A. Peiperl, M. B. Arthur, R. Goffee, and T. Morris (eds.) *Career Frontiers: New Conceptions of Working Lives* (Oxford: Oxford University Press), 99–121.

Peiperl, M. A., Arthur, M. B., Goffee, R., and Morris, T. (2000) (eds.), *Career Frontiers: New Conceptions of Working Lives* (Oxford: Oxford University Press).

Perrow, C. (1996), 'The Bounded Career and the Demise of the Civil Society', in M. B. Arthur and D. M. Rousseau (eds.), *The Boundaryless Career: A New Employment Principle for a New Organizational Era* (New York: Oxford University Press), 297–313.

Porter, M. E. (1990), *The Competitive Advantage of Nations* (New York: Free Press).

—— (1998), 'Clusters and the New Economics of Competition', *Harvard Business Review*, 76: 77–90.

Putnam, R. D. (2000), *Bowling Alone: The Collapse and Revival of American Community* (New York: Simon & Schuster).

Saxenian, A. L. (1996), 'Beyond Boundaries: Open Labor Markets and Learning in Silicon Valley', in M. B. Arthur and D. M. Rousseau (eds.), *The Boundaryless Career: A New Employment Principle for a New Organizational Era* (New York: Oxford University Press), 23–39.

Scott, W. R. (1995), *Institutions and Organizations* (Thousand Oaks, Calif.: Sage).

Van Maanen, J. (1977) (ed.), *Organizational Careers: Some New Perspectives* (New York: Wiley).

Weick, K. E. (1996), 'Enactment and the Boundaryless Career: Organizing as we Work', in M. B. Arthur and D. M. Rousseau (eds.), *The Boundaryless Career: A New Employment Principle for a New Organizational Era* (New York: Oxford University Press), 40–57.

—— and Berlinger, L. R. (1989), 'Career Improvisation in Self-Designing Organizations', in M. B. Arthur, D. T. Hall, and B. S. Lawrence (eds.), *Handbook of Career Theory* (New York: Cambridge University Press), 313–28.

NAME INDEX

SUBJECT INDEX